A TRAIN NEAR MAGDEBURG

A TEACHER'S JOURNEY INTO THE HOLOCAUST

Matthew A. Rozell

WOODCHUCK HOLLOW PRESS

Hartford · New York

Copyright © 2016, 2026 by Matthew A. Rozell. Rev. 2.10.2026 LARGE PRINT. All rights reserved. No original part of this publication may be reproduced, distributed, or transmitted in any form or by any means without the prior written permission of the publisher. Grateful acknowledgement is made to the following authors for the use of edited excerpts of previously published material: Aliza Vitis-Shomron, Leslie Meisels, Fred Spiegel, and Peter Lantos. Please see author notes.

The conclusions reached in this work are solely those of the author and should not be attributed to any of the institutions mentioned in this book.

Information at matthew@ matthewrozellbooks.com
Maps by Susan Winchell.

Front cover credit: Major Clarence L. Benjamin, 743rd Tank Battalion.
Back cover photo credits: Twilight Studios; Kris Dressen, SUNY Geneseo.

A Train Near Magdeburg: A Teacher's Journey into the Holocaust/ Matthew A. Rozell. –– 1st ed.

Publisher's Cataloging-in-Publication Data

Names: Rozell, Matthew A., 1961-
Title: A train near Magdeburg: a teacher's journey into the Holocaust, and the reuniting of the survivors and liberators, 70 years on / Matthew A. Rozell.
Description: Hartford, NY: Woodchuck Hollow Press, 2016. | Includes bibliographical references.
Identifiers: LCCN 2016912597 | ISBN 978-1-948155-50-2 large print pbk. | ISBN 978-0-9964800-2-4 (paperback) | ISBN 978-1-948155-09-0 (hardback) | ISBN 978-0-9964800-3-1 (ebook)
Subjects: LCSH: Holocaust survivors--Biography. | Holocaust, Jewish (1939-1945)--Germany--Biography. | Holocaust, Jewish (1939-1945)--Germany--Personal narratives. | World War, 1939-1945--Jews--Rescue--Germany. | World War, 1939-1945--Historiography. | BISAC: HISTORY / Holocaust. | HISTORY / Military / World War II.
Classification: LCC DS134.4 .R76 2016 (print) | LCC DS134.4 (ebook) | DDC 940.53/18092--dc23.

matthewrozellbooks.com

Printed in the United States of Americ

A TRAIN NEAR MAGDEBURG

*George C. Gross and Carrol 'Red' Walsh.
Somewhere in Europe, 1945. Credit: George Gross.*

[COMPANION AUDIOBOOK AVAILABLE AT MATTHEWROZELLBOOKS.COM.]

Battle-hardened veterans learn to contain their emotions, but it was difficult then, and I cry now to think about it. What stamina and regenerative spirit those brave people showed!
— GEORGE C. GROSS, US ARMY LIBERATOR

Never in our training were we taught to be humanitarians. We were taught to be soldiers.
— FRANK W. TOWERS, LIBERATOR

[After I got home] I cried a lot. My parents couldn't understand why I couldn't sleep at times.
— WALTER 'BABE' GANTZ, US ARMY MEDIC

I cannot believe, today, that the world almost ignored those people and what was happening. How could we have all stood by and have let that happen? They do not owe us anything. We owe them, for what we allowed to happen to them.
— CARROL S. WALSH, LIBERATOR

I grew up and spent all my years being angry. This means I don't have to be angry anymore.
— PAUL ARATO, HOLOCAUST SURVIVOR, ADDRESSING HIS LIBERATORS FOR THE FIRST TIME

It's not for my sake, it's for the sake of humanity, that you will remember.
— STEPHEN B. BARRY, HOLOCAUST SURVIVOR

A TRAIN NEAR MAGDEBURG
TABLE OF CONTENTS

Author's Note 13

BOOK ONE 23
Hell on Earth 25
The Last Transport 91
Darkness Descends 107
Lost in Germany 125
The Ash Yards of Poland 157
A Child in Holland 249
'Hungary is Judenrein' 283

BOOK TWO 351
Coming Home 353
A Date with the Cosmos 371

A Time to Die 381

The Bulge and Beyond 421

BOOK THREE 445

What the Soldiers Saw 451

'The Americans Are Here' 475

'I'll never forget today.' 529

BOOK FOUR 551

'The Indomitable Spirit' 553

'Now I know what I fought for.' 583

'For the Sake of Humanity' 589

The Medics 609

The Orphan 637

Denial 641

The Mystery 649

'What do you want the world to be?' 671

EPILOGUE 679

About this Book/Acknowledgements 713

List of Reunions 733

NOTES 735

June 6, 1944
Amsterdam

'This is D-Day,' the BBC announced at 12 o'clock. This is the day. The invasion has begun!

Is this really the beginning of the long-awaited liberation? The liberation we've all talked so much about, which still seems too good, too much of a fairy tale ever to come true?...

The best part of the invasion is that I have the feeling that friends are on the way. Those terrible Germans have oppressed and threatened us for so long that the thought of friends and salvation means everything to us!

— ANNE FRANK, DIARY ENTRY,
SIX DAYS BEFORE HER 15ᵀᴴ BIRTHDAY

April 15, 1945
Somewhere in Germany

Dear Mr. Huppert,

You will probably be wondering who I am and what business I have, writing to you.- I am one of the millions of soldiers of the United States Army, who is fighting for all the oppressed peoples of the world and hopes to have reestablished decency and honor to all mankind, with the defeat of Hitlerism.
Two days ago, it was the privilege of our unit to be able to liberate a trainload full of people of all nations imaginable, who were being transferred from a concentration camp near Hannover to some other place. Our advances were so swift that the SS guards left this particular train where it was and took off.
That is how I became acquainted with your wife, Mrs. Hilde Huppert, who

asked me to drop you this note saying that both she and your son Tommy are both healthy and well, and now being well taken care of by our military governmental authorities. In actual fact, your wife wrote a message for you on a piece of paper in pencil, which she asked me to convey to you. Unfortunately, however, the penciled lines faded in my pocket, and I can no longer read what was written on it. The contents of the message, though, were to let you know that your wife and son are both safe and sound.

I am sure that your wife will soon be able to get into contact with you directly through the Red Cross, and I hope that in a none too distant future, your family will once more be peacefully united.

Sincerely yours,
Cpl. Frank Gartner
743rd Tank Battalion

Farsleben train, moment of liberation, Friday, April 13, 1945. Two American tank commanders and their major liberate the train, deep in the heart of Nazi Germany. Stunned survivors come to the realization that they are saved. Major Benjamin snaps the photo.
Credit: Major Clarence L. Benjamin, 743rd Tank Battalion.

Author's Note

A photograph taken by an Army major seventy years ago flickers to life on the screen. In it, a profound drama unfolds before the eye. The caption on the museum website reads:

A female survivor and her child run up a hill after escaping from a train near Magdeburg and their liberation by American soldiers from the 743 rd Tank Battalion and 30th Infantry Division.

Record Type: Photograph
Date: 1945 April 13
Locale: Farsleben, [Prussian Saxony] Germany
Photographer: Clarence Benjamin
Photo Designation: LIBERATION – Germany: General
Train to Magdeburg/Farsleben

Keyword:
CHILDREN (0–3 YEARS)
CHILDREN/YOUTH
SURVIVORS
TRAINS
WOMEN

The picture defies expectations. When the terms 'Holocaust' and 'trains' are paired in an online image search, the most common result is that of people being transported to killing centers—but this incredible photograph shows exactly the opposite. And there are many things about this story that will defy expectations. Fifteen years after I brought this haunting image to the light of day, it has been called one of the most powerful photographs of the 20th century. It has been used by museums and memorials across the world, in exhibitions, films, mission appeals, and photo essays. Schoolchildren download it for reports; filmmakers ask to use it in Holocaust documentaries. Yad Vashem, the Israeli Holocaust Martyrs' and Heroes' Remembrance Authority, even employed it as the backdrop for Israel's state ceremonies in the presence of survivors, their president, prime minister, the entire government, top army brass, and the chief rabbi in a national broadcast on the 70th anniversary of the liberation and aftermath of the Holocaust. I know, because they reached out to me for it—me, an ordinary public school teacher, six thousand miles away.

For over half a century, a copy of this photograph and others were hidden away in a shoebox in the back of an old soldier's closet. By spending time with this soldier, I was able to set in motion an extraordinary confluence of events that unfolded organically in the second half of my career as a history teacher. Many of the children who suffered on that train found me, and I was able to link them forever with the men who I had come to know and love, the American GIs who saved them that beautiful April morning. A moment in history is captured on film, and we have reunited the actors, the persecuted, and their liberators, two generations on.

*

It is a cool spring morning. In the background, down the hill, are two cattle cars. If we look closely, we can see a figure sitting on the edge of the opening of a boxcar, perhaps too weak to climb out yet soaking up some energy from the warming April sun. In front of him, a wisp of smoke seems to rise from a small makeshift fire that others have gathered around. The sound of gunfire is echoing nearby; a metallic clanking sound is growing louder at the top of the hill.

This is an appropriate backdrop for the marvel unfolding in the foreground. Now only a few steps away, a woman and perhaps her young daughter are trudging up the hill toward the photographer. The woman has her hair wrapped in a scarf and is clutching the hand of the girl with her right hand. Her left arm is extended outward as if in greeting; her face is turning into a half smile in a mixture of astonishment and enveloping joy, as if she is on the cusp of accepting the belief that she and her daughter have just been saved.

In contrast, the little girl is shooting a sideways glance away from the camera. Her expression is one of distress—she looks terrified. So what is really happening, and what are the amazing stories behind the picture?

On this morning in Germany in 1945, she may very well be responding to the two Sherman tanks that are now clattering up to the train behind the photographer, who is in the Jeep with the white star.

Following the mother and daughter up the hill towards the soldiers are two other women. One welcomes the tanks with outstretched arms and a wide grin as she moves up the hill. The other follows behind her. She appears to be crying.

It is Friday, the 13th of April, 1945. Led by their major scouting in a Jeep, Tanks 12 and 13 of 'D' Company, 743rd Tank Battalion, US Army, have just liberated a train transport with thousands of sick and emaciated victims of the Holocaust. In an instant, Major Clarence L. Benjamin snaps a photograph so fresh and raw that if one did not know better, one might think it was from a modern cellphone, although it will be soon buried into his official report back to headquarters.

But what have they stumbled upon? Where have these people come from?

And what do the soldiers do now?

*

In this never-before-told narrative, you will learn of the tragedies and the triumphs behind the photograph firsthand from the people who lived it. You will enter the abyss of the Holocaust with me, which the United States Holocaust Memorial Museum defines as *'the systematic, bureaucratic, state-sponsored persecution and murder of six million Jews by the Nazi regime and its collaborators.'* You will meet the survivors of that train as they immerse you in their worlds as civilization collapsed around them, and the soldiers who fought their way across war-torn Europe, some wondering what their true purpose was before stumbling upon the Holocaust. You and I will visit the camps and authentic sites together, and we be present with the Americans who found themselves confronted with industrial-scale genocide. And I will lead you safely out of the chasm as we witness the aftermath—the miracles of liberation and the re-unification of the victims and their saviors, first, second and third generations, in my own classroom and all over the world seven decades later.

In many respects, this story should still be buried, because there is no logical way to explain my role in the climactic aftermath. I was born sixteen years after the killing stopped, a continent away from the horrors and comfortably unaware of the events of the Holocaust and World War II for much of my life. I was raised in the sanctuary of a nurturing community and an intact family. I am not Jewish and had never even been inside a synagogue until my forties. I'm not observantly religious, but I am convinced that I was chosen to affirm and attest to what I have experienced. In this book I rewind the tape to reconstruct how indeed it all came to be—the horrors of the experiences of the Holocaust survivors, the ordeals and sacrifices of the American soldiers, and the miracles of liberation and reunification.

As the curtain descends on a career spanning four decades, consider this also one teacher's testament—a memoir of sorts, but more a story of being caught up as an integral part of something much bigger than myself, driven by some invisible force which has conquered the barriers of time and space. I too became a witness, and this is what I saw.

Matthew Rozell
Hudson Falls, New York
September 2016

Western Europe and major concentration camps mentioned in this chapter, late in the war. Credit: Susan Winchell.

BOOK ONE

THE HOLOCAUST

Our group marched in the middle of the road, with a few stone houses to our left, curious eyes staring at us from the windows. I felt deep humiliation, but the people who should have felt the shame were those staring at us from the houses. We were innocent, defenseless people; they were partners in the annihilation of millions of innocent souls.

–Irene Bleier, age 17

Bergen-Belsen Memorial, Summer 2013. Source: Author

CHAPTER ONE

Hell on Earth

Bergen-Belsen Memorial, 2013

Out of the corner of my eye, I catch the silent movement of an animal drifting cautiously out of the German woodland, moving slowly out to graze on the grass in the field. The deer looks up, and for a moment her gaze meets mine. The animal is sleek and beautiful, and in this moment we are both transfixed, in the place of horror. Growing up in the foothills of the Adirondack Mountains of upstate New York, I've seen plenty of deer before, but here there is an almost telepathic current between us.

She:
What are you doing here?
You can't be here.

Me:
What are YOU doing here?
You can't be HERE.

But there she stands, and here we are. She is peace, and she is life.

I blink my eyes, and like the ghosts of the past, she has vanished. But she is not gone.

*

To the casual observer, there is nothing out of the ordinary here. Nature is reclaiming her domain—white birch and fir trees, green ferns and meadows, mowed fields with traces of walkways—but I look closely. Scattered bricks and bits of ceramic shards, cracked cement and twisted rusted metal fragments, broken window glass shimmering up from the dirt. I've been in the woods exploring abandoned farmsteads lots of times, and as an avocational archeologist I have done my fair share of uncovering historical ruins before, but here there is a difference. Lingering just below the surface of the present are the remnants of the evil of the past. And there are no casual observers at a place called Bergen-Belsen.

A concrete gutter channel runs into the woods. A looming obelisk beckons in the foreground, drawing me past overgrown mounds embedded with their baleful inscriptions:

HIER RUHEN 800 TOTE APRIL 1945
HIER RUHEN 1000 TOTE APRIL 1945
HIER RUHEN 2500 TOTE APRIL 1945

Here rest eight hundred dead. A thousand dead. Twenty-five hundred, dead. April, 1945.

*

If you have a hard time placing the horrors of Bergen-Belsen in your mind, bring back the image of the British soldier with the white bandana over his mouth and nose maneuvering a small bulldozer to tumble hundreds of naked corpses like ragdolls into an open pit. Picture again the film footage of captured SS guards, heaving emaciated bodies over their shoulders like potato sacks, stepping haphazardly into the mass grave, or the SS women guards dragging the deceased by the feet, the dead animated only by the macabre bobbing of heads on the earth. This is Bergen-Belsen, where the most unsettling and sinister becomes matter-of-fact, the archetype of the evil that Allied soldiers were just beginning to encounter that spring of 1945. The mighty Third Reich, conceived with haughty promises to rule the world for a thousand years, convulsed inwardly as hammering blows thundered from all sides, even while thousands of the persecuted were still arriving at their final destination in the railyard just beyond the camp, as the birds sang and the cannons roared.

*

In early April, the British Army was pushing relentlessly into northwest Germany in the Allied drive for Berlin. On Thursday, April 12, German officers appeared under a white flag at the British lines to make an unusual request. They proposed a local truce around the camp called Bergen-Belsen, fearful that a raging typhus epidemic might sweep the countryside if the camp was overrun in a warzone and the inmates not contained.

After some negotiations, advance elements of the British Army were finally able to enter the camp three days later on Sunday, April 15, 1945. Here they met the camp commandant Josef Kramer and his contingent of SS and Hungarian guards. Kramer told the British that it would be unwise for them to disarm his men—for not only would they likely be torn limb from limb by vengeful prisoners, but the threat of not being able to contain the epidemic was apparent.

Utter chaos and scenes of horror greeted the British and Canadian soldiers who walked into the hell that was Bergen-Belsen. Soldiers were now face-to-face with 60,000 prisoners who were in various states of starvation and illness—many of whom, surrounded by thousands of corpses, were in the final throes of death themselves[1]. Eight hundred died on the day of liberation, and 14,000 more would die in the weeks to follow, the camp deliberately burned to the ground by the British to combat the spread of disease.

Today, we assume that we know all about the World War II concentration camp system devised by the Nazis in their quest to eliminate their enemies and kill the Jews. In reality, they had existed long before the war broke out, the first ones opening in Germany (namely Dachau and others) at the beginning of the Nazi regime in 1933. The SS, Hitler's early 'protection squadron' selected for unquestioning obedience, fanatical loyalty, and commitment to racial purity, evolved into a complex organization with many branches and was specifically charged with the administration of the camps. Political dissidents, 'criminals,' and 'asocials' were among the first to be incarcerated, but as time went on, the number of camps grew, and their purposes were sinisterly modified. By 1943 the plan to eliminate the Jews was operating at full swing—in tandem with an unprecedented scale of slave labor as prisoners were worked to death as a matter of state policy—although, in point of fact, the total annihilation of the Jews would take precedence, to the irrational extent of committing economic resources to the task as the war was being lost.

Heinrich Himmler, Reichsführer of the SS, was the man most responsible for carrying out the policy of the elimination of the Jews. On Hitler's behalf he commanded the orchestration of the 'Final Solution' from Berlin, overseeing the deployment of mass murder shooting squads on the eastern frontier, the construction of the concentration camps, and the 'resettlement' of the deported. As time went on and the war progressed, the new masters of Europe imposed their will and retooled the system to suit their twisted agenda. According to the British commentators after the Belsen Trials, concentration camp objectives fell into several categories: Extermination, Slave Labor, Sick, Experimental, and Training.[12] In the East, the names of Auschwitz-Birkenau, Belzec, Sobibor, and Treblinka would become synonymous with mass murder on an industrial scale. Ravensbrück was a women's camp providing slave labor to the nearby Siemens Company plants, and it was also a training center for female SS guards. The vast Auschwitz complex included three main camps and facilities for mass murder, a major slave labor complex, and horrible pseudo-scientific experiments on human guinea pigs.

Belsen, on the other hand, was somewhat different both in its origins and its evolution in the framework of abomination. In its span as a prisoner-of-war and later a concentration camp, up to 120,000 men, women, and children had been

---

[1] *Extermination*- The term 'extermination,' when used in the context of industrial-scale mass murder, is common, but it is problematic for the author, for reasons to be developed.

imprisoned here; most of them today remain anonymous, as the SS destroyed the records as the Allies closed in. Following the German invasion of the Soviet Union, captured Russian soldiers began arriving here, (then known as Stalag XI C); in the winter of 1941–1942, 14,000 Soviet prisoners of war, allowed nothing more than holes dug into the frozen ground for shelter, died of starvation and exposure to the elements.

As fortunes in the East began to turn with the reversals of the German offensives at Stalingrad and elsewhere, Himmler was not above considering alternative methods of survival for the Nazi regime, to buy time, as it were, until Germany could get on its feet again and continue full throttle with its policy of eliminating the Jews. Perhaps on a purely economic level, the exchange of some Jews deemed valuable could give the Reich 'breathing space' for this purpose.[3] In April 1943, an exchange camp under SS administration was opened at Bergen-Belsen, holding Jews from occupied Europe who held certificates or papers that may have made them useful for exchanging for Germans interned abroad, or for hard currency, or for reserve bargaining purposes. While these prisoners, many of them families (or more accurately, fragments of families), were not compelled to undertake forced labor or wear prison uniforms, miserable conditions and rations deteriorated rapidly with the transfer of brutal SS administrative staff from Auschwitz to Belsen in the beginning of 1945. In addition to the exchange camp, in March of 1944 Belsen had also been designated as a sick or 'recovery' hospital camp for inmates from other slave labor facilities who were not deemed quite ready to be worked to death as labor pools throughout the Reich shrank. It was a fact that most of these prisoners would never recover.

In late November, a new commandant was assigned to the camp. Ever since his arrival from Auschwitz on December 1, 1944, Josef Kramer affected a depraved indifference, encouraging his kapos to mete out vicious beatings and carry out endless roll calls, forcing weak prisoners to stand for hours at a time in the most extreme weather conditions.[2]

---

[2] *Kapos*-camp police. They were prisoners selected by the SS as volunteers to supervise their fellow prisoners in exchange for privileges.

Kramer brought with him to Bergen-Belsen many of the leadership characteristics that marked his development as a career SS man in the concentration camp system. Dubbed 'The Beast of Belsen' and portrayed as a hulking gorilla-like animal at his trial by the British press, the reality was probably much more unimaginative, even banal. He joined the SS in 1932 not because of any diehard fanatical Nazi conviction, but because he needed a job. He rose through the ranks by carrying out orders without the slightest moral or ethical qualm. At the Auschwitz killing center, he had no problem carrying out his orders. At his trial, he admitted forcing some of the victims into the gas chambers himself. At the time, it was stated of him,

> 'His type was that of the perfectly obedient underling with no scruples of any kind. If 500 men were ordered for execution at 0900 hours, they would be there to the minute and to the man, not a man too few nor a minute late. But this efficiency and the acts to which it led him sprang from his desire to keep a

safe, comfortable job, rather than from any deep-rooted Nazi conviction. In the dock, at least, his appearance was not that of a brute though his features were coarse and his figure short and broad; and he seemed to derive considerable amusement both from the gorilla caricatures and from some of the more imaginative stories about him which appeared in the newspapers at the time of the trial. It was incongruous to observe such evidences of human emotion in a man guilty of crimes as inhuman as his.'[4]

At Belsen, he was generally given free rein from Berlin. Survivors consistently remember the roll call counts, or 'appell.' Reveille was generally very early in the morning, and no one was exempt—even the very ill were dragged out and forced to stand, sometimes for hours, in the cold and dark. If one moved, or collapsed, one suffered the consequences.

Hadassah Bimko Rosensaft, a Jewish dental surgeon from Poland, had observed Kramer's SS underlings at work in Auschwitz before being selected to work in the hospital at Bergen-Belsen. At the Belsen Trial conducted by British authorities in the fall of 1945, which ran for 54 days, 'Ada' was one of the principal witnesses, and confronted her tormentors with her testimony.[3]

Ada Bimko

The treatment was so that it is hard to describe, blows were raining down and then at roll call we had to stand about for hours and hours in snow, in rain, in heat, or in cold. On its own, the standing about exhausted us entirely. If anybody moved during roll call, then the whole block to which we belonged had to stand for hours and sometimes kneel down, even with their arms raised high. If somebody came too late to roll call, the whole camp had to stand on parade for many hours and he, the culprit, was beaten so badly that he sometimes died from it. In the hospital I saw a number of people with wounds on their hands and legs, but particularly frequently on their heads, coming from blows. I left Auschwitz and arrived in Belsen

---

[3] *confronted her tormentors with her testimony*-the four survivors in this chapter who testified at the Belsen Trial (Bimko, Sophia Litwinska, Fritz Leo, and Harold Osmond Le Druillenec) were NOT liberated on the 'Train near Magdeburg.' Every other survivor quoted in this book (30 of them) was on that transport. See 'Epilogue.'

on November 23, 1944, and Kramer arrived in the first days of December 1944.

Eleven-year-old Sara Gottdiener, from Hungary, could not forget.

Sara Gottdiener Atzmon

At the end of November it was very cold in Europe. Finally I was given some rags and one black ladies' shoe with a high heel and one red girls' shoe. Imagine the agony of a young girl having to walk unevenly like that for half a year.

In those shoes I marched into Bergen-Belsen concentration camp on December 2, 1944. In those shoes my legs froze while I was enduring roll calls, which lasted between two to five hours.

Some of the SS staff that accompanied Kramer from Auschwitz also stood trial with him.[4] One of those who testified was Dr. Hadassah 'Ada' Bimko, a Jewish prisoner who was spared the gas chamber at Auschwitz to working in the hospital there and at Bergen-Belsen. A

---

[4] *also stood trial with him*-Forty-four other accused individuals were tried with him. Kramer and seven other men, and three women, were executed by hanging on Dec. 13, 1945. Nineteen others were also found guilty and received varying sentences.

skilled dental surgeon, she saved thousands of children and other prisoners, although her own parents, husband and young son were murdered almost immediately upon arrival at Auschwitz.

The prosecutors continued.

Ada Bimko

Interviewer: What were the conditions at Belsen when you first arrived?—The conditions were bad, but the internees there were not beaten and there were no roll calls. In the morning there was either coffee or soup, for midday meal about half a pint of soup, and in the evening one-sixth of a loaf of bread, three times a week. The other three times, instead of bread, soup again. This ration does not kill instantly, but if you lived on these rations for a long period under those conditions, you must inevitably die. At the end of January and in February other SS men and women arrived from Auschwitz.

Was there any change after Kramer and the others arrived?—Yes. We had suddenly the feeling that Belsen was going to become a second Auschwitz. For instance, they started with roll calls, appell, and those SS men who previously did not hit the prisoners started now to do so. I remember when

Russian prisoners were working in the women's camp erecting a hut. Four of them were so weak that when they carried a wall, the side of this hut, they had to bend down very low to be able to do so. Kramer came and started shouting at them, 'Quicker, quicker,' but these people were unable to work quicker. Then he went to the Russians and kicked them. I worked in the hospital at Belsen and many prisoners were admitted suffering from beating. Some of them could be attended to at once and their wounds bandaged, but some of them were in such a state that they had to remain in the hospital.

What was the medical supply situation?—We received very small quantities. We had 2,200 patients in the hospital, and apart from that, 15,000 sick women in camp. For a whole week we received only 300 aspirin tablets.

One of the accused you recognized this morning was the man at the far end of the front row of the dock [Karl Franzioh]. What can you tell us about that man?—He was in charge of the kitchen in the women's camp. Near the kitchen there was a room where potatoes were peeled, and there a young woman internee was bending down to take a few peelings of these potatoes which were lying about when suddenly this man jumped out of the kitchen with his gun in his hand and shot her twice. I was only a few yards away from the spot, and approached the wounded woman, and very soon, I had to state that she was dead.[5]

Another prisoner, twenty-nine-year-old Sophia Litwinska of Poland, testified.

Sophia Litwinska

I left Auschwitz in the autumn of 1944, and, after being at other camps, reached Belsen approximately three months before the liberation by British troops. [They] put me to work in Kitchen No. 2 in the men's camp for a few days, after which I was transferred to Kitchen No. 1 where there were two SS men, one Aufseherin, a supervisor, and a Jewish kapo with the Christian name Hilde.[5]

[On one occasion shortly before liberation] the man in charge of the kitchen told us he was going

---

[5] *Aufseherin*-female guard

to lock up for an hour or two. All the SS men had a meeting, and we waited in front of the kitchen. Near the kitchen there were remains of vegetables, and one or another of the prisoners tried to get a potato or two. At that moment the SS men returned and started shooting, and many of the prisoners were killed.

Ilse Forster was in charge of Kitchen No. 1. A girl took a potato and she saw it and took her into the kitchen. There she started beating her so severely that the poor girl could not help herself and defecated. I could not look longer and ran out of the kitchen. She dragged the girl out of the kitchen and continued to beat her until her very death. She beat her until she was dead, and when she died, she still kicked her with her feet. Then, she returned to the kitchen and laughed hysterically. We went out later and saw the girl, and two men came and dragged her away, whether to the crematorium or to be buried elsewhere, I do not know. I saw shooting at Belsen every day.

Dr. Fritz Leo was a German doctor who had been imprisoned since 1935. He arrived at Bergen-Belsen on February 7, 1945, and described what he saw.

Fritz Leo

We had a number of patients with bullet wounds, every week three or four at least. Only the smaller wounds could be treated. There were people who tried out of despair to go through the barbed wire and were shot at, and also those who approached the kitchens and tried to get a potato or a turnip. I have seen a great number of people who were shot dead or wounded by the guards.

With the coming of February 1945, events careened out of control. As the Third Reich reeled from the pressure of the advancing Allies in the East and West, tens of thousands of camp prisoners were on the move, with many of them destined for Bergen-Belsen. Bergen-Belsen was, as one author has put it, 'the terminus, the last station of the Holocaust.'[6] Prisoner access to water became extremely limited. Typhus, typhoid fever, and tuberculosis were now rampant, and the crematorium broke down.
The doctor continued his testimony.

Fritz Leo

Interviewer: What was the position with regard to typhus?—Typhus was rampant in Men's

Compound No. 1 early in January and in No. 2 early in February. It was spreading very strongly through lice, and against lice we had absolutely nothing, neither water, clean clothes, bathing facilities, or delousing powder, so from the end of February, typhus was spreading like fire through the whole camp and consequently nearly everybody in our camp got it.

Throughout history, typhus has stalked humanity in the wake of wars, famine, and natural disasters. The bacterium is transmitted from one infected human to another by the louse; one scratches the bitten area and rubs the bacterium into the open wound. Symptoms include severe headache and muscle aches, sustained high fever and chills, rashes and coughs, stupor, sensitivity to light, delirium, and in many cases, death.

Interviewer: What was the position with regard to water supplies in the camp?—We could get water from some tanks sometimes for two or three hours a day, but then, for whole days, no water at all was available. In No. 2 compound, there were no facilities at all for bathing. Some of the doctors and nurses had the possibility of having a bath. Our compound got no fresh clothing or underclothing at all, although supplies were available in the stores.

What was the position with regard to latrines in the camp?—The situation was a real catastrophe. We had a few latrines which were soon blocked, and, in spite of all our efforts, we could not get them cleared. The people were too weak to build new ones. These weak and dying people simply defecated wherever they stood or wherever they lay about. They were too weak to move and so the whole camp became very soon almost a latrine itself.

What happened to people who died in the camp?—The first week, they lay about for days and slowly were dragged away and put in the crematorium where they were burned, but soon the crematorium was not big enough to cope with them, and then, they started to put up bonfires. They put the corpses into high piles to burn them wherever they were. Later, wood became so scarce that those high piles could not be dealt with in that way, as we heard that the Administration of Forestry prohibited the use of wood for that purpose, and consequently the bodies simply lay where they were. As every day the number of people who died was over a thousand, the result was that every day several thousand bodies were lying about in the camp in a terrific state, green and swollen through the heat, some of them stinking. Later, they were put in a stone block, and only before the liberation by the British troops did the SS start digging big graves for these people.

What was the food in the camp like?—About half a liter of turnip soup per man per day in the beginning; about 300 grams of bread were issued; later, however, less, and in the last few weeks no bread at all.

Under no circumstances were those rations sufficient to preserve life. Even those who came in in a fit and healthy state lost their strength after a few weeks, and those who came in a weakened state died in a few days or weeks.

Jean Weinstock had arrived in Bergen-Belsen with a Polish group in the summer of 1943, the first group of 'exchange' Jews.

Jean Weinstock Lazinger

We went to Bergen-Belsen in July 1943. And we were the first civilians in that camp. We used to get a slice of bread and coffee in the morning. And we used to get this turnip soup. Sometimes we used to get spinach soup with white worms on top. And there were a couple doctors there, they said, 'You better eat it, because it's protein.' But I was unable to do that.

They separated the men from the women, but we were able to see each other through the day. After 5:00 the men had to be in their barracks and the women had to be in the women's barracks. We had bunk beds… but, as they were bringing other people from different [places], our camp got smaller and smaller. We were divided by the wires and we were able to speak to the people on the other side, and I remember exactly when the train came from Holland. There was hunger, there was cold, then they brought the Hungarian Jewish people… it was right in the next barrack from us, we had a hard time because they spoke a different language than us, but some people spoke German, so we were able to communicate a little bit.

Istvan Berenyi, who later anglicized his name to Stephen Barry, arrived at Belsen single and without family in early December 1944 from Hungary, destined for the Hungarian camp recently vacated by a transport of exchange Jews going to Switzerland.[7] In a 2009 interview, he related the horror of Belsen, especially the infamous nearby Block 10.

Steve Barry

I have exact dates [of my arrival at the camp] and I will tell you why. I spent my twentieth birthday on a train going to Bergen-Belsen, and it was December 7, 1944. So I know exactly the dates.

[My friends and I] were totally, totally green. We really did not understand what was happening to the Jews, what was happening in Poland. It was 'an enigma wrapped in a mystery,' if I may use Mr. Churchill, because we knew that things were bad, but we did not realize that we were going to be systematically murdered!

We never came in contact with any of the SS. We came in contact with what was called the kapos. They were the camp police. The camp police consisted of prisoners who kind of ruled over the other inmates. And to show how totally silly we were, we asked them if there was a commissary in the camp and could we use money to buy something there! [*Laughs*] This is how totally removed from reality we were.

Of course, then we walked from the train station to our camp, and walking through the camp, believe me, it was an eyeful. To begin with, some people could not walk, and they were shot on the way, walking to the camp. We saw the barbed wire; we saw the emaciated people. So all of a sudden reality sank in, and we knew, or we started to understand, what we were faced with.

Then we went to a shower. They took everything—you had to drop everything you carried, and you got undressed, and then took a shower, not realizing at that point that this could have been the end of us, not knowing anything about the showers in Auschwitz and so on. So when we showered and put our clothes back on, we lost all our baggage. Whatever little we carried with us, it was gone. So the only thing we owned was the clothes that were on our bodies.

Interviewer: When you think back to the months that you spent at Bergen-Belsen, what would you say is the clearest memory of your time?

[*Pauses*] I saw human flesh being eaten in the camp next to us. And I had no idea who they were. They took the cadavers and obviously they must have had some medical people there, because they knew exactly how to get to the liver with a simple incision; the liver is a very edible part of a human being. [*Hesitates; sighs*] I hate to say this, but it is the truth. I would think that that was probably as far as one can sink. I saw people being beaten; I saw people dying from hunger, which is an extremely painful death. I guess it is just not known—and hopefully never will be—that you do not just keel over from hunger. It is a very painful way of dying. And I witnessed some of that, and of course every morning I saw the dead bodies stacked up like wood and taken to a crematorium. They had to get rid of the bodies somehow, so that the disease did not keep spreading. [*Swallows*] And unfortunately later on the crematorium was no longer operating, and they were just digging huge holes and they were putting the bodies in there.

*Mass grave at Bergen-Belsen, July 2013.
Source: Author*

Eighteen thousand people perished in March 1945 alone. Harold Osmond Le Druillenec was a British national living in the occupied Channel Island of Jersey when on June 5, 1944—the day before D-Day—he was arrested for helping a Russian prisoner to escape some time before, and also for possessing an illegal wireless radio set. After spending time in various concentration camps, he arrived at Bergen-Belsen on April 5, only ten days before the liberation of the camp. In his graphic testimony on the fourth day of the Belsen Trial the following September, he described the frantic conditions as the Germans began to deal with the mounting corpses.

Harold Osmond Le Druillenec

Interviewer: Were you allowed out of the hut at all during the [first] night?—No. It was humanly impossible to get out since the whole floor was just one mass of humanity—it would have meant walking across people in order to get out—in any case, the door was shut. People were lying against it, and I think that it was locked as well.

What was the atmosphere inside that hut like?—Well, it is rather difficult to put into words. I do not think it is humanly possible to describe that—it was vile. I think I have told you sufficient to make you realize that the smell was abominable; in fact, it was the worst feature of Belsen Camp. A night in those huts was something maybe a man like Dante might describe, but I simply cannot put into words.

Will you now tell the Court about the first day you began work?—In the beginning the work was rather interesting because we were herded as a block, some six or seven hundred maybe, into the mortuary yard by means of blows, the language we understood pretty well by then; we were made to understand that we had to drag these dead bodies a certain route to what we were to find to be large burial pits. The procedure was to take some strands of blanket from a heap where the effects and clothing of the dead had been put, tie these strips of blanket or clothing to the ankles and wrists of the corpses, and then proceed to walk to the pits. We started work at sunrise and were up quite a long time before that. We got no food before we started and worked till about 8 o'clock in the evening. In those five days or so I spent on this burial work neither a spot of food nor a drop of water passed my lips.

Will you describe one of these days?—After the usual terrible night, we started the appell first. After about two hours of that, we would be herded in the usual manner to this yard. We tied the strips of blankets to the wrists and ankles of the dead bodies, which we picked out most carefully. Firstly, we found the shortest corpse possible; they were all emaciated and thinner than anything I had imagined before, so by getting the shortest we were bound to get the lightest. Secondly, we chose one that was not too black. Our first task in the morning was to bury the fresh dead that had been brought from the various huts in my portion of the camp to the mortuary yard, not those which were in the hut. Despite the fact that there must have been over 2,000 all told occupied in this work, it used to take us nearly the whole morning to empty that yard prior to going into the rooms to start burying the old dead. We then left the northernmost gate of the yard with the body dragging behind, usually allowing maybe two meters between the foremost people dragging and the body in front. If you allowed more than that, a hit on the head made you hurry up to reduce the distance. We made our way along the central road towards the burial pits. Along this road, stationed at intervals, were orderlies to see that the flow of dead to the pits carried on smoothly; they were particularly numerous near the kitchen and the reservoir water.

One of the most cruel things in this particular work was the fact that we passed this water regularly on every trip, and although we were dying of thirst, we were not allowed to touch it or get anywhere near, nor were we allowed to get to the heap of swede [rutabaga] peelings near the kitchen. A few of those would have made us a very fine meal indeed in the state we were in.

Nearing the pits, I found out that the pits themselves were being dug by so-called 'free' foreign workers. I cannot very well explain my feelings when I first saw one of those pits which already contained many dead and had to throw my particular corpse on top of those others already there.

During the dragging process, I noticed on many occasions a very strange wound at the back of the thigh of many of these dead. First I dismissed it as a gunshot wound at close quarters, but after seeing a few more I asked a friend and he told me that many prisoners were cutting chunks out of these bodies to eat. On my very next visit to the mortuary I actually saw a prisoner whip out a knife, cut a portion out of the leg of a dead body, and put it quickly into his mouth, naturally frightened of being seen in the act of doing so. I leave it to your imagination to realize to what state the prisoners were reduced for men to chance eating these bits of flesh taken out of black corpses.

What was the attitude of the SS and of the orderlies you have mentioned while all this was going on?—To get on with the job as quickly as possible. My own idea is that it was to make a good impression on the advancing British Army. We knew it was coming. We could hear the guns and I think the whole idea was to clear the camp of as many dead as possible before they arrived. I would like you to picture what this endless chain of dead going to the pits must have looked like for about five days from sunrise to sunset. How many were buried I have no idea. It must have been vast numbers—certainly five figures.

What happened to a prisoner who fell out on this parade?—You didn't dare to fall out, but many collapsed on the way—just lay dead by the roadside, or died. They in turn were lifted by a team of four and taken to the pits. People died like flies on the way to these pits. They did not have the necessary energy to drag even those very light bodies. A man who faltered was usually hit on the head, but many people were cunning, and if no orderlies were around, they used to leave their corpses stranded by the roadside and go back to the mortuary for another, because they would pass the kitchen or reservoir, and they still had hopes that they would reach some food or water.

Were you struck at all yourself during this period?—
Oh, many times. You were bound to get hit in the normal course of the day. You were bound to get hit on the head in the morning getting out of the hut, whether you were out first or last. You were bound to be hit in getting to the mortuary and all along the way to the pits. They were just odd blows here and there, given, I suppose, for the fun of the thing. One ceases to question in a concentration camp why things happen. One is taught from the very beginning just to accept things as they are.[6]

On April 22, 1945, a Canadian Royal Air Force food and hunger expert and eyewitness noted, 'There apparently is little concern and no marked line between the living and the dead, for those who are alive today may be dead tomorrow. In fact, during the critical stage of the food [shortage] in this camp, some of the inmates

---

[6] 'One is taught from the very beginning just to accept things as they are.' In composing this chapter, the author has made reference to graphic encounters with cannibalism, which many readers will find disturbing. My intent is not shock value, but rather to portray the conditions in this section of the camp on the eve of liberation. Would humanity be better served if the troublesome details were omitted? Is the entire chapter not troublesome? Such is the instructor's quandary in the teaching of the Holocaust. Indeed, such material should be employed judiciously, but always with the guiding question of, 'Why am I presenting such material?' The author acknowledges this dilemma and has chosen not to avoid the topic in the larger context of this book.

have turned to cannibalism and thereby the dead helped to sustain life for the living until food was made available after liberation.[8]

Irene Bleier was a seventeen-year-old girl from Hungary who entered the exchange camp in late 1944.

Irene Bleier Muskal

I met someone who had been in Bergen-Belsen for some time, and asked him what sort of work we would be doing here. He looked at me flabbergasted and coldly answered that no one comes to work at Bergen-Belsen—everybody comes here to die. I never saw this person again, his blunt answer only intensifying my already overflowing desperation. Unceasing tears rolled down my face for days.

After several more exhausting hours standing outside, we were at last allowed to move inside the barracks of Block 10. Our building was next to the gate. A high barbed-wire fence separated us from a group of Jews from Holland in a different block. Inside the barracks, over 200 people took up their abode on three-tiered bunk beds.

The suffering of body and soul further numbed our brains. We turned into objects to the will of others, like robots, the living dead. We choked in pain. This condition penetrated my soul for years to come, impeding my feelings.

Kurt Bronner was taken from Budapest, Hungary, and imprisoned with his father in Bergen-Belsen. There, he lost his parents.

Kurt Bronner

Two weeks after we arrived, my dad started to cough. One morning, I heard men reciting prayers, and someone said to me, 'I'm sorry. Your father is dead.' Eighteen years old, I didn't know; I never faced death before. Then in the morning they took the bodies out; I tried to follow my dad's cart, being taken to the so-called cemetery—[but I could not find him, there were so many bodies]. And a week later, I saw my mother through the barbed wire; we started talking, she wanted to know how dad is, and I lied and I said, 'He's fine, he's sleeping'—I didn't want to burden her with the bad news. [*Pause*] And then a German woman guard started to beat my mother. [*Pause*] You are on this side of the fence, and on the other side is your mother, and there is nothing you can do. And that is the last time that I saw my mother; I don't know what happened to her; I tried to find out, and all they could tell me was, fifteen thousand women died without any names.

Eleven-year-old Sara also had vivid memories.

Sara Gottdiener Atzmon

At Bergen-Belsen I graduated from the University of Death. For me it was always cold—there was continuous frost. We were almost without clothes. I slept on a narrow-tiered bed bunk together with my sister Matti and her 2½ year old son. He was coughing all the time and I thought that he would not make it.

Later in life, I began painting. My second work about the Holocaust was 'Tiers of Death' because every morning there would be some dead bodies on the bunks. Death always came as a surprise to us; we thought that nice man over there looked strong and that he would make it. But no, some simply did not have the strength to endure any more hunger and suffering. Now people finally understood what I was trying to say, through my painting.

When the mounds of dead bodies started to pile up nearby in a frightening manner, we, the children, made bets between us as to who would die tomorrow and who would die the day after. Every one of them had his signs. I had become an old woman already, eleven and a half years old. Still, in my childish naiveté, I gave my sister Shoshana one-half of my daily bread ration, for her 13th birthday.

Even if I'll paint all my life, I will not be able to describe the suffering that was going on in that camp, and especially the stench. Maybe some people are more expert than me in describing the small details. But I only tried to touch on the most painful things: fear, hunger, filth, hopelessness, and despair.

The despair was the most dangerous. But we children always tried to repress the despair and joke about things, even though our bodies were infested with lice and covered with itchy sores, because for half a year we did not wash. This was something impossible to get used to. Mother said that she did not want to be put naked on the cart that carries away the dead, because it's cold there—she will walk on foot to the crematory.

A man walks through a wooded area near Bergen-Belsen with rows of corpses of prisoners who perished there. April 1945.
Credit: USHMM, courtesy of Dr. Clifford Teich

During the breaks between roll calls, if it wasn't too cold, I would stand by the fence and look at the naked dead bodies with their gaping mouths. I used to wonder what it was that they still wanted to shout out loud and couldn't. I tried to determine who were men, and who were women. But they were only skin and bones. I tried to imagine how I could dress these dead bodies in clothes for dinner; their pale skin color did not always match the clothes.

In those days, when everyone fought desperately for one more minute to live, for one more crumb of food, our mother would stand where they dispensed the soup, which consisted of potato peel and cattle turnips, and implore people to give only one spoonful of their ration to us children. This is how she succeeded in saving the lives of some who were already dying, whose death on the next day would have been certain.

The main street of Bergen-Belsen. July 2013. Source: Author

Uri Orlev was a young teenager from Warsaw. His mother had died in the Warsaw Ghetto; with his younger brother and aunt he was sent to Bergen-Belsen.

Uri Orlev

I invented a story that this war, this ghetto, the Germans, the camp, all this never existed. What really happened was that I was the son of the Emperor of China. My royal father had put me on a bed, and had ordered it to be placed on a large, high podium. Twenty Chinese mandarins were called to my bedside, instructed to put me to sleep and make me dream of war, so that when I inherit the throne, I would never make war again, knowing how bad wars are.

*

Camp commandant Kramer filed a report to Berlin on March 1, 1945, explaining the dire circumstances as transports from all over the Reich continued to arrive. He noted supply problems and overcrowding, and that of the 42,000 inmates in his camp, 250–300 died each day from typhus. In it he also noted the exchange camp and the Jews there, and how it would be of great consequence to be rid of them.

Josef Kramer

```
Bergen-Belsen, 1st March, 1945.

Gruppenführer, it has been my inten-
tion for a long time past to seek an
interview with you in order to de-
scribe the present conditions here. As
service conditions make this impossi-
ble, I should like to submit a written
report on the impossible state of af-
fairs and ask for your support…
```

State of Health

The incidence of disease is very high here in proportion to the number of detainees. When you interviewed me on 1st December, 1944, at Oranienburg, you told me that Bergen-Belsen was to serve as a sick camp for all concentration camps in North Germany.[7] The number of sick has greatly increased, particularly on account of the transports of detainees, which have arrived from the East in recent times-these transports have sometimes spent eight to fourteen days in open trucks. An improvement in their condition, and particularly a return of these detainees to work, is under present conditions quite out of the question. The sick here gradually pine away till they die of weakness of the heart and general debility. As already stated,

---

[7] *Oranienburg*-Chief SS administrative headquarters and training center, outside of Berlin.

the average daily mortality is between 250 and 300. One can best gain an idea of the conditions of incoming transports when I state that on one occasion, out of a transport of 1,900 detainees over 500 arrived dead. The fight against spotted fever [typhus] is made extremely difficult by the lack of means of disinfection…

On the question of putting the internees to work, I have contacted the employment authorities. There is a chance of being able to make use, in the near future, of woman labor. There is no availability here of making use of male labor. In addition to the concentration camp prisoners, there are here still about 7,500 internees ('Exchange Jews'). SS Hauptsturmführer Modes from RHSA. IV. A. 4b was here last week and informed me that these Jews would be removed in the near future.⁸ It would be much appreciated if this could be done as soon as possible, for in this way accommodation could then be found for at least 10,000 concentration camp prisoners. Because of the spotted fever danger, SS Hauptsturmführer Moes is not willing to take these Jews away at the present time. These Jews are to go partly to Theresienstadt and partly to a new camp in Württemburg. The removal of these internees is particularly urgent for the reason that several concentration camp Jews have discovered among the camp internees their nearest relations-some their parents, some their brothers and sisters. <u>Also for purely political reasons- I mention in this connection the high death figure in this camp at present- it is essential that these Jews disappear from</u>

---

⁸ *RHSA*—SS Reich Main Security Office. The organization's stated duty was to fight all 'enemies of the Reich' in and out of the borders of Nazi Germany.

here as soon as possible [*author's emphasis*].

With that I wish to close my present report. In this connection, Gruppenführer, I want to assure you once again that on my part everything will definitely be done to bridge over this difficult situation. I know that you have even greater difficulties to overcome and appreciate that you must send to this camp all internees discharged from that area; on the other hand, I implore your help in overcoming this situation.

Heil Hitler, yours truly,
J. Kramer., SS Hauptsturmführer

On March 19, one of Himmler's main deputies, SS ObergruppenFührer Oswald Pohl, visited Bergen-Belsen on an inspection tour.

Josef Kramer

I went through the camp with him and showed him the worst parts... He saw the whole camp and told me that what he had seen that day in Belsen he had never seen anywhere before. I told him that if they sent me nothing but sick people I would not be able to show him anything better. We returned to the office and had a conversation to try and find means to improve the situation. My proposals were to cease all new transports and to transfer all so-called exchange Jews with their families... [He] decided there and then to send a telegram, and to comply with my request...[9]

Fully aware that the noose was closing around his boss Himmler, Pohl arranged for the evacuation of nearly seven thousand in the exchange camp to the camp Theresienstadt in Czechoslovakia, perhaps in the hopes that these Jews might prove useful in negotiations with the Allies even as more transports arrived.[9] [10] Between April 6 and 10, 1945, 6,700 men, women, and

---

[9] *Jews might prove useful in negotiations with the Allies even as more transports arrived-* By this time, Himmler was clearly assessing his options, and would be about to attempt to enter into separate peace negotiations with the western Allies through an intermediary, without Hitler's knowledge.

children from the exchange camp passed through the camp gates and marched several kilometers to the railhead that many had arrived at months or years earlier. But they were not told the objective and had no way of knowing whether they were being led out to be shot in a ditch or moved on to be gassed elsewhere; Belsen had no gas chambers. Some would be murdered before reaching the train platform.[11]

Aliza Melamed was a teenage survivor of the Warsaw Ghetto.

Aliza Melamed Vitis-Shomron

Allied planes fly above us making a dull sound and there is nothing to stop them. A few days ago, there was an air battle between English and German planes, right above the camp. I hid with the others under the bunks, not that I was afraid, but a shrewd thought was on my mind: Now, just before liberation and the end of the war, I could be killed by an Allied bullet or bomb…

I am sure there is no God—only chance rules my life. There is no one to pray to, no one to beg—maybe my lucky star that has protected me until now will continue to do so… Will I manage to survive? A sweet feeling of revenge fills me as I realize that our murderers are also suffering and being killed!

My strength has waned; my feet are swollen from hunger. I have become apathetic to my surroundings.

Irene Bleier Muskal

In accord with my daily routine, I was just loafing about by the barbed wire fence inside the courtyard of Block 36. My gaze was directed toward two important locations over the fence—the kitchen and the cattle feed pile.

Suddenly, a band of SS officers appeared on the scene. A tall officer bawled out, 'Where is the dog?' Soon, Mr. Fisher [the block leader] presented himself. This strange occurrence keenly aroused my interest. Does this signal good tidings as to our destiny? For better or worse, we find out in a few short minutes.

Orders from higher Nazi authorities called for a group of two thousand tormented Jewish souls—Hungarian, Polish, Dutch, Spanish, and Greek—to leave Bergen-Belsen for good.[10] The instruction singled out large families, but those who preferred to stay and be liberated in this camp were allowed to do so, while those singles who wished were allowed to join with this, the first transport to leave. At this time, I could think of no greater desire than to walk out alive through the big open gates of the Bergen-Belsen concentration camp on my own two feet. Together with my mom, my sister Jolan, and my two brothers, I felt this was a great privilege, an immeasurable reward from the Almighty.

In less than ten minutes, two thousand 'living dead' stood in lines of five, as was the order of the SS Nazi leader named Kramer. Adults aged over twenty-one were given four cigarettes. As we stood in rows, my acquaintance F.F. came to my side to wish me speedy liberation from Nazi reign. In turn, I wished him the same good tidings.

With our meager belongings on our backs, we thus began marching out of Bergen-Belsen after

---

[10] *Spanish and Greek*-The Jewish population of the Greek city of Salonika was devastated between March and August of 1943. Out of 46,000 people, only 73 Greek Jews and 367 Jews of Sephardic Spanish descent and nationality made it to Belsen. The rest were whisked to Auschwitz and murdered. Shepard, Ben. *After Daybreak: The Liberation of Bergen–Belsen, 1945.* New York: Schocken Books, 2005. p214.

unbearable suffering of many months. At our sides were armed Nazi guards, but now I could not care less; I just disregarded their presence. With an elevated feeling, I walked on the camp's main road, leading us toward our long-yearned-for freedom.

As we approached Block 10, the unfolding spectacle encompassed me. I saw a colossal hill made of skeleton cadavers while yet living skeleton-like creatures sat cross-legged on the bare earth or wallowed in their own filth. I dared ask the Nazi guard who walked by what would happen to the pitiful creatures in Block 10. He answered that all those creatures would shortly perish.

Aliza Melamed Vitis-Shomron

On April 6, an unexpected order came to prepare for evacuation. We heard the thunder of cannons in the distance; they said that the city of Hannover was in the hands of the Allied armies. And they are approaching the little town of Celle.

Evacuation? To where? To the gas chambers?

There was a terrible smell in the air. I was hardened, cynical, and no longer capable of feeling anything. After the terrible murders in Block 10, adjacent to us, nothing could move me. But I remembered I had to survive to tell the world about my friends who were killed in the Warsaw Ghetto Uprising. I hugged my mother and sister. They mustn't separate us!

Mother consults Uncle Leon Melamed. Aunt Irena, practical as usual, is already packing the most important things. 'There is nothing we can do,' she says with typical decisiveness. 'We have no choice. There is no point in staying in a camp that is no longer getting supplies of food. We'll starve before they come to liberate us.' We agree with her. We get into a long line, men, women, and the children who are with us, hundreds of Jews from various blocks.

The people's faces mainly express uncertainty and acceptance of the situation. We again pass by the piles of skeletons, new ones every day. In the huge camp on the other side of the road, we see shadowy figures moving.

Mother and I take the few remaining clothes, the notes I have written in the camp and on the

Aryan side, and a passport photo of father.[11] We have no personal documents, nothing reminiscent of our previous life. Mother has only a silver fruit knife that she took with us when we went to the 'selektzia' in Warsaw.[12]

Irene Bleier Muskal

At the time, our bodies were completely weakened, and we stood at the edge of the grave. Finally, we reached the huge open gate, where the armed Nazi guards at each side of the sentry box no longer frightened me. Proudly, with a sense of relief, I walked through the gate, leaving the Bergen-Belsen death factory behind me.

Agnes Fleischer was a ten-year-old girl from Hungary.

Agnes Fleischer Baker

I remember Bergen-Belsen well—the stack of dead, the stack of skeletons. My father was dead by

---

[11] *the notes I have written in the camp and on the Aryan side* -Vitis–Shomron kept a diary on scrap during her persecution. Here she refers to her time in hiding outside the Warsaw Ghetto, on the 'Aryan side.'

[12] *'selektzia'*– selection for work or for death

that time. I had my tenth birthday in Bergen-Belsen, only by that time we didn't know the dates. The months before we left, I remember being cold.

Days before we were to leave, someone who could differentiate artillery fire from air bombardment said he heard artillery fire, so somebody is close. Then came that April day, the sixth, and my mother told us that the kapo said we are moving out in five minutes. We had nothing to do there, so five minutes was more than enough time for us to [get ready to] go anywhere. I was standing with my sister and my mother said to me, 'You know, we should not go. For a piece of bread, I can arrange to stay here.' I said, 'No, we should go.'

It was seven kilometers from the camp Bergen-Belsen to the rail station, and it goes through a forest. We had to walk and we were close to three thousand people. It was a hilly kind of road and if you were in the middle like my mother, sister, and I were, you could see the first people in the group, the first walkers. And I kept asking my mother, 'Are they shooting yet?' I thought that that was where they were going to shoot us, in the woods, you know. I was sure, there were so many trees and going through the forest, that they're going to get rid of us there. At that point I don't remember being scared; it was just a matter of fact.

Ariela Lowenthal was an only child of six when the war came to Poland. Her parents had already been murdered by the time she and her aunt and uncle arrived in Bergen-Belsen; her uncle then died there.

Ariela Lowenthal Mayer Rojek

I was born in 1933 in Poland, where I spent time in a ghetto and a prison. I then spent two years in Bergen-Belsen.

When told to prepare ourselves for the departure on the train, I was already very weak and sick. Two weeks prior I had a very high fever. I was in Bergen-Belsen with my aunt, my father's sister, as by then I had lost my entire family.

The Germans let us know that all those who could not walk would have to stay behind. My aunt wanted to stay because she knew that I was already very weak; however, I insisted on going. I said to my aunt, 'You know that they kill the weak and the sick. We will go with the healthy people.'

Although I was only 11½ years old, my aunt listened to me. I probably had a very strong will to live.

Before we left, they gave each of us a raw potato, and somehow we managed to bake them over a wood fire. My aunt then said to me, 'You know that now is the Passover holiday'—we barely remembered what day of the week it was, let alone the date. On Passover, according to the story, our forefather Moses took us out of Egypt. Maybe G-d is bringing us to freedom, and maybe we will live?

You know, the whole camp was divided into small camps, and every [sub]camp had a wire fence. We had to walk to the train station and when we went out from our camp, we went on the main road. On both sides of us—[it was like we were] walking in the middle of a tunnel—on both sides were white mountains of corpses. They could not get rid of the corpses, so it was terrible, and you had to walk in the middle. I remember my aunt, to this day, saying, 'Don't look! Don't look!'

We walked a few kilometers to the train, and out of weakness we dropped most of the things that we still had with us.

Seventeen-year-old Laszlo 'Leslie' Meisels of Hungary weighed just 75 pounds as he and his family shuffled along the seven kilometers towards the railhead.

Leslie Meisels

When I entered Bergen-Belsen, I was a strong, robust, marching 175-pound 17-year-old. Four months and three days later, I was a shuffling skeleton, 75 pounds, barely able to move.

[When we started out, we were] in the third row of the column, and we were going so slow that we ended up almost at the very end. Had we started out at the center or in the second half of the column, we would have been shot like others who were not able to keep up. Those people told the guards they had to sit down for a moment to rest, but they didn't have a chance to stand up because a bullet to the head ended it.

Fritz 'Fred' Spiegel was nearly thirteen and incarcerated with his young sister, with no parents to look after them in Bergen-Belsen.

Fred 'Fritz' Spiegel

We were a ragged group with tattered clothes, damaged even more when we pulled off the Jewish star that we had worn all those years.

The Germans did not want the local population to know who we were. Many people were almost barefoot as we no longer had decent shoes. We walked unnoticed through the town of Bergen; the inhabitants in the houses on both sides of the road had their shutters closed. Some people in our column fell and were left by the wayside. Then, suddenly a small girl fell, and a German guard hurriedly picked her up and helped her to move on. I noticed the guard was crying. I had never before noticed any German guard having sympathy for the children in the camp, even though many children were starving to death or dying of typhus. So why was this German guard crying? Did he suddenly take pity on this young girl? Or was he upset when he realized it was all over and Germany was going to lose the war?

Aliza Melamed Vitis-Shomron

My legs won't carry me. The road seems endless; the body is weak and not used to moving. Every step calls for an inhuman effort. We crawl along slowly.

[A girl] is carrying her 5-year-old brother on her back. Her face is red with the effort. The child has no strength left, he is apathetic. Their mother walks beside them and slaps him gently on his face. Her legs are also swollen from hunger. I walk on. I can't help them—I have no strength left.

Suddenly, a man walks up to me. I recognize him: It is my neighbor from the next bunk. Without a word, he puts his arms under my armpits and drags me along. I lean on him with all the weight of my body. I didn't get to know him although we 'lived next door,' and now he is helping me!

Who can understand the depths of good and evil in the hearts of men? This small deed, the hand held out in support at a critical moment, imbued me with hope and strength to continue on my own.

People begin to drop their belongings. We also stop every fifteen minutes and sadly throw down a few things. At the end of the march my backpack only holds a little food and two or three items of underclothes.

Fred 'Fritz' Spiegel

After a long and difficult walk, we finally reached the train station where a train consisting of many cattle wagons was waiting for us. The floors were covered with straw and it was difficult for most of us, especially the children, to climb into the wagons. Each wagon was overcrowded, and we had only a slice of bread each, taken from the camp.

Leslie Meisels

When we arrived at the rail yard and were ordered to climb up into the cattle wagon, I had seen an open railcar loaded with red beets a few train cars away. Even though we knew that the punishment would be terrible, some people went there and got a few pieces. A piece of red beet, even raw, was enough to sustain four people—me, my mother, and my two brothers—for a day. I asked my mother to empty the pillowcase, which was our main carrying case, and give it to me. I shuffled there, put in a half-dozen or so beets, and carried it back.

When I arrived at the track next to our freight car, an SS guard with his back to me was aiming and shooting to death a 10 or 11-year-old little boy who had two red beets, one in each hand. He committed such a horrible crime that immediate execution was the right punishment, according to this hatefully minded SS guard. While he was shooting that little boy to death, I was able to hand my bundle to someone who gave it to my mother. When he turned around, he just barked at me to get up. Had he turned around 10 or 15 seconds earlier, I wouldn't be here speaking to you now.

Irene Bleier Muskal

We march to the railway station of Bergen–Celle. We are again herded inside empty cattle trucks filled to their capacity—we can only sit. There is not enough room to stretch our numbed legs. As is our habit, no sleep will come to our eyes; hunger and thirst prevents this. As the sun rises after a sleepless night, I get up to see what is happening outside the cattle trucks.[13] I slowly walk out and discover a business exchange just opposite our transport. A group of Ukrainians guarded an open rail car of red beets and exchanged one red beet for each cigarette.

I turn to my mother with a thrilling sense and ask her to give me four cigarettes to exchange for beets. She gave me the cigarettes, but as I step off the cattle truck, I am terribly disappointed. The Swabian SS guards are now beating my fellow Jews with their heavy rifles as punishment for the exchange.[14] They were striking my people on the head, face, and back without any compassion. I felt distressed and benumbed and was now rooted to the spot. I just leaned against the side of the cattle truck. Within a few minutes, the exchange area was clear of Jews. Sure enough, the Ukrainian exchangers are not assaulted, even though they exchanged things that belonged to the Nazi

---

[13] *As the sun rises after a sleepless night-* this first transport to leave Belsen did not leave until additional cars were attached on April 7.
[14] *Swabian-*ethnic German people who are native to or have ancestral roots in the cultural and linguistic region of Swabia, in southwest Germany.

authorities while we Jews exchanged our own property.

The Ukrainians stayed close by with only the German SS guards now patrolling the grounds. The instinct of hunger does not comprehend fear and guides my legs toward one of the armed SS guards. Still numb and speechless, I show him the four cigarettes with an imploring look, indicating my plea to this murderous enemy of mine. He immediately understood and advised me to make a quick run before his commanding officer reappeared on the scene. I had hardly finished this exchange when the area once again filled up with my fellow suffering companions. The exchange goes on until the SS guards again strike out with their rifles. My mom evenly divides the four beets between the five of us, and we eat with relish.

Aliza Melamed Vitis-Shomron

Suddenly, we see railway carriages. Surprisingly, they are normal 'Pullmans,' not freight cars.[15] The exhausted people lie down on the platform. At the

---

[15] *they are normal 'Pullmans,' not freight cars*-The train consisted of perhaps 50 mixed passenger and freight cars. Some survivors recall heavy weapons towards the rear, perhaps an additional car with anti–aircraft artillery guns.

station we are given a little food and water. The journey has begun.

Irene Bleier Muskal

Saturday, April 7, 1945. Our transport is stranded at the Bergen–Celle railway station. Our irresponsible captors no longer provide us with food. After suffering from constant starvation for six long months at the death factory of Bergen-Belsen, the German SS leaves us now in total hunger and total thirst. We are too exhausted, dizzy, and weak to grasp how grave our situation is.

What do the Nazis have in mind?

*

July 5, 2013/ Bergen-Belsen Memorial

I scuffle along the pathways, lost in thought. On a summer tour of the authentic sites of the Holocaust with fellow teachers from all over the United States, Bergen-Belsen is the first major camp we visit. How fitting.

I am only here for a day, but it is like I have been here before. Of course, I haven't; instead, I have been studying the Holocaust and communicating with the Bergen-Belsen Memorial administrators for years—there is even an exhibit here in the new interpretive center based in part on the work I have done as a high school teacher. I have come to know many friends who were imprisoned here, whose parents still lie here, somewhere. And some of them lived here for years after their liberation, reconstructing their lives in the displaced persons camp for the opportunity to begin a new life from the ashes of stolen childhood. And on this very day back home, a tank commander is being laid to rest in the foothills of the Adirondack Mountains.

My friend. Their angel.

The group moves on to the House of Silence. As we will do at every site we visit, we pause and reflect. Pauline, with tears, leads the small service. Elaine, our tour leader, asks me to recite the Mourner's Kaddish as candles are lit.

Mourners leave notes here. In this small room of reflection and remembrance, the Queen of England herself paid her first and only visit to a concentration camp, seventy years after the liberation. Here she found a handwritten lament:

If I could live my life again, I would find you sooner.

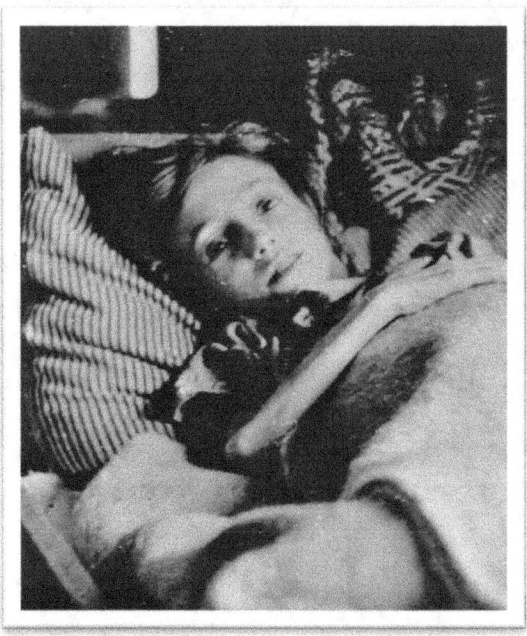

A twelve-year-old Jewish girl lies in bed after her liberation in Bergen-Belsen. Helena Rabbie was born in Amsterdam on September 8, 1933, and died in Bergen-Belsen on April 24, 1945, eleven days after the liberation.
Credit: USHMM, courtesy of Maurice Raynor.

Outside, a single stone marks that Anne Frank and her sister Margot lie here somewhere, their youthful promise snuffed out in those terrible weeks just before the liberation. But where they rest, no one will ever really be sure.

Today, I feel the presence of the dead as I take this all in, moving slowly through the heath and barrows of Bergen-Belsen, steps in a long journey back into the past and reuniting American soldiers with the people whom they saved from the edge of the abyss. This journey will carry me from my small hometown to the halls of power at the New York State Capitol and the U.S. Capitol Rotunda in Washington, D.C.; to the cities of the American South and to Canada; to horrors and wonders in Germany, the Czech Republic, and Poland; and to Jerusalem and the Holy Land, a passage that in many respects should have never happened to a small-town American boy and teacher like me.

But it did.

CHAPTER TWO

The Last Transport

*I will give them an everlasting name,
That shall not be cut off.*

— Isaiah 56:5

Our teacher group at the Bergen-Belsen Memorial has lunch in the cafeteria and Bernd Horstmann asks us if we would like to see the exhibit on the evacuation transports. This is not our first meeting; Bernd has been working with survivors and their families for many years at the memorial site and all over the world. As the Custodian of the Book of Names, it is his responsibility to help reconstruct the data destroyed by the SS as the British forces moved in. To date, out of the 120,000 who passed through the gates, less than half that number have been identified. The preface to the two-volume edition of the *Book of Remembrance*, which lists the name, birthdate, place of birth, and date of arrival for the victims at Bergen-Belsen, as well as the place and date of death—or of liberation—reads as follows:

> *Dedicated*
> *To the children, women, and men*
> *Who were humiliated, tormented and murdered in*
> *Bergen-Belsen.*
> *I will give them an everlasting name,*
> *That shall not be cut off.*
> *(Isaiah 56:5)*

Bernd shows us to the gallery where the new exhibits reside. There, we discuss the circumstances of the evacuation of the camp and the creation of the new exhibit; his colleague Christian Wolpers had stumbled upon the photographs that the liberators had taken, which I had written about and placed online in 2002. As the afternoon winds down, we board the bus for Hannover, where we will pick up the train for Berlin.

*

After each of these confrontations with evil, we teachers must come to grips with what we have experienced, trying to formulate our pedagogical points of view. Tour leader Steve remarks that for him, Bergen-Belsen is sacred ground. One teacher is upset and even angry at the absence of structures in the camp, finding it impersonal and cold. Some agree that our first visit to an authentic site of a concentration camp leaves many of the 1945 horrors to be imagined. I chime in and say that while it is important to know all of the history that we learned here, it is frankly overwhelming, and at the end of the day it is maybe not enough to say you understand it. But it is also important to try to make sense of the history that came after liberation. The barracks had to be put to the torch. The former prisoners, themselves, residing here for up to five difficult years after the war waiting for permission to move on and rebuild their lives, put up the first signage and memorials to the dead.

Bernd Horstmann and author, Bergen-Belsen Memorial, Evacuation Transports exhibit. Credit: Jerrilynn Miller.

It's a heavy day. At Hannover on a Friday evening, we dine at the train station in small groups. In the crush to board the proper rail cars, we almost lose some of our group. I can't find a seat, but a German man, seeing my trouble, motions for me to take his place. I settle in, thanking him. The train picks up speed and glides silently and comfortably through the picturesque countryside. I look up at the monitor and see that the next stop is Brunswick (Braunschweig), on the way to Magdeburg, before heading to Berlin. Then it dawns on me. I am following roughly the same route as the transport from that April in 1945; what takes us less than an hour will take the Bergen-Belsen evacuees nearly a week.

Peter Lantos, from Hungary, was just six years old, and accompanied by his mother. His father had died in Bergen-Belsen.

Peter Lantos

In the distance there was the sound of muffled explosions, and excitement ran through the train at the possibility that the Allies might arrive to capture the station before the train could depart. But the muffled noise was only the echoes of far-away raids, and after long hours of waiting through the night, the train finally pulled out of Bergen station the next morning.

It was a long journey. The train travelled slowly, rarely gathering pace. Frequently it came to a halt, often on the open tracks, occasionally at small stations. Our food, however carefully rationed by my mother, did not last long—we were hungry and thirsty. The compartments were full, and there was not the remotest chance of stretching out. Nevertheless, the train was more comfortable than those that had delivered us to Bergen-Belsen. We were travelling with the aimlessness of a child's toy train, meandering round the same track again and again. The train changed directions several times, and we recognized places we had passed earlier. But if at first we were bored by the slow progress and monotonous rhythm of the train, we soon found excitement.

The guards accompanying us had anti-aircraft guns. These they fired at low-flying Allied aircraft which zoomed menacingly close to the train. We were terrified thinking that they were going to bomb us, mistaking our train for a transport carrying German soldiers. Suddenly, we heard explosions.

Panic broke out. Everyone scrambled to leave and find safety under the trees, away from the track. We were no exception. Under the shelter of the trees, my mother again took me through a macabre but sensible procedure. She had already rehearsed me several times on what I should do and say in case I survived and she did not. I had to repeat my name and my parents' names and our address at home as identification information I already knew. As a further safety measure, she introduced me to other women who would look after me should she die—a reciprocal arrangement made by a couple of mothers who agreed to become guardians of each other's children. But we survived the air raids, which ceased after a short while; the pilots must have realized the nature of the train's cargo.

Fred 'Fritz' Spiegel

Very soon the doors were closed, and it became quite dark as there were no windows, merely a small opening near the top. Then the train began moving, traveling slowly eastward, or so some of the people with us seemed to think when they looked out the opening at the top.

This journey continued for about six days. The train stopped many times to let other trains pass, and we were even bombed by the Allies a couple of times. Luckily the bombs missed us, but I remember one particularly heavy bombardment near the town of Stendal.

Unfortunately, the bombs were not the only danger. Many people died on the way, either of typhus or starvation.

Ariela Lowenthal Mayer Rojek

In one of the stations, we saw a cargo train carrying beets. A good friend of mine convinced me to go steal the beets, and with my last strength, I went. The beets tasted like the Garden of Eden, and my aunt said they tasted like melon. Of course, I didn't remember how melon tasted.

The train continued to some place and stopped—on one side there was a forest and on the other side the Elbe River. I remember the place exactly as it looks in Dr. Gross's photograph.[16] American planes flew low above us and apparently took pictures that showed people and children. The German guards that were still there to watch over us started to shoot with machine guns at the planes. Our people asked them to stop shooting, but they refused. We got off the train and hid under the wheels.

---

[16] *Dr. Gross's*- Liberator George C. Gross

My aunt sat with me under the wheels and took out a little notebook that contained the names and addresses of our relatives in America. She told me to learn all of this by heart because you never know who the bullet will hit, and when the war would end, I should contact these relatives and ask them to take me in. I listened to her and learned everything by heart. Even today, I remember some of these names and addresses.

Leslie Meisels

Those red beets were the only food in the six days while we were on the train, to stay alive. The clothing, the stench, was indescribable. When you needed to go, [by the time you got to] that five-gallon pail, which was already overflowing, it was too late, and the other pail with our water was already empty. It was horrible—screaming, crying, and all the noise—and the stench—indescribable.

Agnes Fleischer Baker

You get used to this kind of awful thing. At first, when we were out of a comfortable existence, you couldn't get to the 'bathroom,' and you had to pee your pants, then, at first, you thought, that's kind of normal. It's a pee. I can't elaborate on that. See, I didn't see myself as stinking and as disgusting, [but] I had a hunch that I was stinking and disgusting. When I think back on the smell, it was really, really terrible.

Aliza Melamed Vitis-Shomron

We traveled by train for six days. The train moved little, it remained standing a great deal. The frontline was everywhere and chaos all around us. German families fled with their belongings in all directions in carts and on foot. Have they been encircled? What a cheerful thought! Our leaders and various oracles, experts in solving riddles and interpreting rumors, say that the Germans want to use us as hostages. Besides our group, hundreds of Dutch, Greek, and Hungarian Jews are with us on the train, all supposed to be exchanged, from the special camps in Bergen-Belsen. In the meantime, the most important thing is to get a hold of food.

During one of the stops, I saw people jumping from the train and rolling down. I also wanted to do so, but my sister was quicker and out already. I joined her. We rolled down the high embankment to a wonderful pile of animal feed, yellow turnips. I filled up my dress feverishly, grabbing as much as I could carry, and climbed back. But at the moment when all the children and youth began climbing up, guards on the roof of the train opened fire on us. The Germans were apparently surprised and reacted late. I ran and lost my sister. I didn't see a thing, but I was determined to get the turnips into the carriage. The bullets whistled around us, but I didn't drop the turnips. I didn't even look back to see who fell and who survived. Only on reaching the top, under cover, did I look back in great fear, in search of my sister Mirka. She stood up next to me, trembling but smiling. We had food for the rest of the journey.

Leslie Meisels

On the sixth day of our journey, April 12, a Thursday afternoon, we were about fifteen kilometers from Magdeburg, a city on the Elbe River about halfway between Berlin and Hannover. The train stopped on a curve near a bridge over the river, which wasn't unusual, since a red light frequently stopped the train for a short period. This time, however, there wasn't any movement. We later found out that the Nazis had devised a new plan—they wanted to position the train on the bridge and blow it up so that they could both kill us and stop the Allied advance. Somehow, though, the engineer and his assistant had gotten wind of the plan. They, too, must have heard the rumbling explosions from the front line and realized that the end of the war was imminent. Not wanting to die, they just ran off while the train was stopped at the red light, leaving the train and its cargo behind.

Steve Barry

Since I was not locked into a cattle car, I could open the door of the third-class passenger car where we were. So, I see the SS changing into civilian clothes and disappearing toward the town that was nearby somewhere; we didn't see the town. So, they disappeared, they changed. We saw them changing into civilian clothes because they disappeared in civilian clothes.

I could have gotten off the train, but we were still in the middle of Germany. At that moment, we were extremely weak; I know because just getting on and off the train, or just walking, or making normal moves, was quite an effort because by that time, I weighed ninety pounds, so obviously I lost a great deal of weight, and I lost a great deal of muscle and everything else that goes with it. Fortunately, I was twenty. Had I been younger or much older, I probably wouldn't have made it, I would guess. And the way we looked, I don't think we could have gotten too far. An escape was really just not possible, because they could shoot you on sight anyway. So we hadn't even thought of going too far from the train. What we were thinking of was trying to get some food. We knew that there were a couple of passenger cars where the SS guards were staying. My two friends and I, the first chance we had, got out of the car and walked over to these two railroad cars, hoping to find something to eat. Well, unfortunately, we didn't. What we did find were rifles, ammunition, overcoats, German uniforms; no food.

Through their weariness, Barry and his friends saw that the Germans had returned.

Mounted SS troops came around, rode by the train, and started to yell, '*Raus, Raus, get out of the train! Get out of the cars!* And we saw them putting up machine gun nests. So obviously, even at that last moment, they were still trying to murder us.

Leslie Meisels

After a while, the guards opened all the doors, and the commandant ordered all males above the age of twelve to get out of the wagons and go over to a little embankment across from the train. Then, while we were facing our respective cattle wagons that contained our family members, a machine gun was set up in front of each wagon.

Irene Bleier Muskal

April 12, 1945. We now reached the most crucial hour of our life during World War II under German Nazi rule. From each and every truck, a Jewish leader was asked to appear before a high-ranking SS officer, who issued a disastrous order that we immediately carried out. All men between the ages of sixteen and sixty were to line up in columns of five in front of the cattle trucks, with the angels of death fluttering around.

A paralyzing darkness seized me. They were going to gun down the men with machine guns in front of the cattle cars, and then blow up the rest of us—babies, small children, women, and the elderly—in the cattle cars. That was the decree that the Nazi beast devised when its hour of doom came—our SS captors decided to annihilate us all.

CHAPTER THREE

Darkness Descends

I heard somebody smashing down the door, and the noise of breaking glass.
— FRED 'FRITZ' SPIEGEL, GERMAN JEW, KRISTALLNACHT

A world away on the East Coast of the United States, a breaking news bulletin interrupted radio programming around dinnertime on Thursday, April 12. Americans were stunned to learn of the sudden death of the president of the United States as he sat at a table at his private retreat in Warms Springs, Georgia, earlier that afternoon. How could this be? The only president that many had ever known was now dead at age 62, just as Allied troops were poised to stab at the heart of the Reich.

In the early morning hours of Friday, April 13, 1945, Minister of Propaganda Joseph Goebbels reported the news to Hitler. Deep in the Führerbunker as Soviet forces prepared to assault the city, Hitler heard Goebbels assure him that a turning point was at hand, that this was 'written in the stars,' just as previous astrological readings had also foretold the start of the war and previous victories.[12] To his Minister of Armaments, Albert Speer, Hitler proclaimed, *'Here we have the great miracle that I have always foretold! The war is not lost! Read it! Roosevelt is dead!'*

His jubilation was short-lived. Later that same day, news would reach him that Vienna had fallen to the Soviets as the Red Army completed its preparations for the final siege on the capital. In desperation, Hitler announced to besieged Berliners that Soviet troops would be met with 'mighty artillery waiting to greet the enemy.'

Imperial Germania lay in shambles. The Reich that would last a thousand years was in its final death throes. And millions of Germans and their collaborators were lost in astonished, terrible wonderment at the height from which they had fallen so precipitously. It was not supposed to be like this! Hitler had promised greatness and the vanquishing of their enemies. And there were no bigger enemies of the Germanic peoples than the Jews and their infection.

There were no secrets. Hitler laid out his plans all along as he developed the party platform—simple answers to complex problems. But while the insidiousness of the invective struck fear in the hearts of the fractional minority of Germans who were Jews, no one could predict just how far this madness would go. No one could believe that in a short six years, two-thirds of European Jewry would be murdered by the Nazis and their willing accomplices.

How could this happen? Like many infections, the terror incubated slowly and innocuously from the dregs of society; from the back alleys of Munich rose up a movement that proclaimed glory and greatness, revenge and revolution. Setbacks would occur, but struggle is the father of all things, after all. From the pain and the suffering, a new race of mankind would emerge. The weak would give way to the strong, and from the blood of the martyrs of the movement Germany would be purified and reconciled on its destined plane of glory. Sieg Heil; All hail, victory.

January 30, 1933. Adolf Hitler, with the win of his Nazi party in the Reichstag election of November 1932, comes to power in the depths of the Great Depression. Like his future adversary Franklin Roosevelt, he promises a platform of change and gives hope to myopic millions. Fearing 'Red Revolution,' they reward him with dictatorial powers following the torching of the Reichstag. With the death of the aged president Von Hindenburg, the office of president and chancellor is combined. Der Führer, the Leader, is cultivated as a god.

The new government moves swiftly to restrict the civil liberties of Germany's half million Jews, who make up less than one percent of the population but who nevertheless are prominently represented in urban settings, in professional fields, in academia. Many of these families have German roots going back centuries, and in fact identify more closely with their German heritage than their Jewish identity.

Legislation unfolds incrementally at first. A one-day boycott of Jewish business is proclaimed. Non-Aryan civil servants are forcibly retired. Kosher butchering is forbidden by law.[17] Non-Aryan children find it harder to be admitted to schools and universities. Jewish newspapers can no longer be sold in the streets.

At prestigious universities, Jewish professors are fired and students gather raucously before bonfires of books. Torchlight parades and jackboots on cobblestones herald the time of terror. The huge party rallies in Nuremberg rivet the nation; at the party gathering in 1935, race laws for the purity of German blood are formally institutionalized. Now it is a punishable crime for a Jew and an Aryan to be in love. And even those with

---

[17] *Aryan*-The Nazis were obsessed with an ideology based on the myth of racial purity. All of human history was based on racial struggle, Hitler said, and the Nazis classified Jews as an inferior, corrupted 'race' slated for destruction, lest the German nation perish as the result of racial mixing. See USHMM article, 'Victims of the Nazi Era: Nazi Racial Ideology'.

Jewish grandparents who had converted to Christianity were now defined as Jews, even if their families had not practiced Judaism for generations. Disenfranchisement followed as those now legally defined as Jews were unceremoniously stripped of their citizenship rights. Identity documents were stamped with a red letter 'J'. 'Jews Not Welcome' signs appear in shop windows, though in deference to foreign visitors, the Führer orders them removed from public view during the Summer Olympic Games in Berlin in 1936 to cloak the increasing atmosphere of persecution. The window for escape is also rapidly shrinking; Jews find it difficult to obtain passports for travel abroad. But the discrimination is incremental, so the question begged is, should they leave? After all, this is their rightful home, Germany. Surely, the injustice will be righted when the world steps in or a new government comes to power. *Who could possibly imagine the slave labor factories, the killing fields and forests, the industrialized mass murder, and the complicity of the ordinary man—even the neighbors—in the horrors to come?*

Increasingly, Jews were also being impoverished by the state. Jews were now required to register their property, and non-Aryan businesses were taken over by other Germans, the pitiful compensation set by the state. Jewish doctors could not treat non-Jews, and Jewish lawyers lost their occupation. *Who could afford to leave?* Discounting the rampant antisemitism of the day, most nations had extremely rigid immigration policies, and at the international Evian Conference held at the French resort in 1938, almost every nation involved turned its back and refused to reconsider their immigration policies in the wake of an obviously humanitarian crisis.[13] *Where would they go?*

*

A turning point came on the night of November 9-10, 1938. In Paris, a German embassy official was shot by a desperate Jewish teenager. When he died from the wounds, Party officials meeting in Nuremberg decided to use the assassination as a pretext to launch state-sponsored pogroms aimed at German communities throughout Germany, Austria, and occupied Czechoslovakia. Propaganda Minister Joseph Goebbels announced that 'the Führer has decided that ... demonstrations should not be prepared or organized by the Party, but insofar as they erupt spontaneously, they are not to be hampered.'[14] The Night of Broken Glass raged on in the Reich as thousands of shop windows were smashed, Jewish businesses were plundered, and hundreds of synagogues were set afire as firemen stood idly by to ensure the flames did not damage neighboring buildings. Thirty thousand Jewish men were arrested, many of them to be incarcerated at the first camp to be used for this purpose: Dachau. Many would never return to their families. In the wake of the violence and extensive property damage, German officials levied the cost of the cleanup on the Jewish population. The German Jewish community was fined a billion marks (nearly 400 million dollars in 1938) to compensate German insurers for their payouts, and many were now utterly ruined economically.[15] In a measure designed to exacerbate the destruction of Jewish life in Germany, severe punishments and restrictions immediately followed. Remaining Jewish schoolchildren were expelled from public schools and universities. Plays, movies, concerts, and other forms of public entertainment were off limits. Jews could no longer drive. They were forced to hand over their securities and even jewelry. By the following year, radios would be turned in to the German police. The noose was closing.

At this moment, Fred 'Fritz' Spiegel was a German boy of six.

Fred 'Fritz' Spiegel

I was born in Dinslaken, Germany, on April 21, 1932, a small town at that time of about 20,000 inhabitants, to a German Jewish family. My family had been living in this general area for hundreds of years. My father, Sigmund Spiegel, loved to play football, and I have a picture of him together with his teammates on the 1913 Dinslaken soccer team. He had been a sergeant in the German army in World War I and was badly wounded in the Battle of Verdun. He had received many decorations for valor in battle, including the Iron Cross. My uncles and grandfather had also served in the German army. My father died in December 1933, when I was one year old, so I do not really remember him except from stories my mother and other people told me.

After my father's death, my grandfather, Louis Spiegel, came to live with us. One of my earliest memories is of my grandfather playing skat, a German card game, in the evenings at our house with his friends and neighbors. My grandfather was well known and friends with nearly everybody in town. Behind our house there was a nice park, and Grandfather used to take me there for walks and so that I could play with the neighborhood children. He would sit on one of the park benches and talk to his friends, while keeping a watchful eye on me.

Around 1936, when I was four or five years old, things started to change and my park was not so nice anymore. Older kids started to pick on me, tried to beat me up, threw stones and dirt on me, and called me 'dirty Jew.' Then my grandfather's friends also started to curse him, and he decided it was time to get out of the park. When I went home, I asked my mother, 'How come those kids call me 'dirty Jew'? Am I dirty? I took a bath this morning.'

After a few more incidents, we did not go to the park anymore, even though it was almost our back yard. After that my grandfather started to take me to the Jewish orphanage to play. The orphanage had been established many years earlier for the whole area called the Rhineland. It was much safer there in the huge house with the large fenced-in yard. The older kids kept an eye on me while I played with the other little kids in the orphanage. It was really fun and I soon knew a lot of the kids. However, I longed to play in the park, the beautiful park by our backyard, with its big lawns, lake, and tall trees. But this had become too dangerous for a Jewish child. I never played there again.

*

November 9, 1938. That day and the next few days, I will never forget for the rest of my life. I was six and a half years old, still living in Dinslaken. I was living with my mother, my older sister Edith, and my grandfather. I had started going to school a few months before. As Jews were not allowed to go to the local schools anymore, we went to the Jewish school which had been established many years earlier. I remember Mr. Weinberg, the teacher, because he rented a room in our house.

There was just this one teacher, plus a few teacher's aides. My Aunt Klara was visiting us that day, November 9. It became dark early, and that evening, I went to visit the elderly couple, Mr. and Mrs. Brockhausen, who rented a third-floor apartment from my mother in our house. I had become very friendly with them and even though non-Jews were not supposed to rent from Jews anymore, they had refused to leave. They invited me to come the next morning and join them for breakfast, something I had often done in the past.

I woke up early the next morning, November 10. Looking out the window, I noticed a lot of smoke coming from the direction of the synagogue. Also groups of men were running around armed with pickaxes and all sorts of other tools. I had no idea what they were doing and what was happening, but it looked scary and threatening. I asked my mother, but she also did not know what was going on. Then I decided to go upstairs; maybe they knew something. After all, Mr. Brockhausen was a retired policeman, surely he would know. When I arrived upstairs they were up and waiting for me. They did not know what was happening;

at least, that was what they said. However, when I asked them about the smoke, they said the synagogue was on fire, but the fire engines were there. 'Not to worry, Fritz. The fire will surely be put out soon.'

Burning synagogue in Ober-Ramstadt, Hesse; Darmstadt, Germany,
November 10, 1938. Credit: USHMM, courtesy of Trudy Isenberg

Mrs. Brockhausen was preparing the breakfast when suddenly I heard a deafening noise downstairs coming from the direction of our apartment. Then I heard somebody smashing down the door and the noise of breaking glass. My mother and sister started to scream. I wanted to run downstairs, but Mr. Brockhausen held me back. I could clearly hear things being smashed downstairs and being thrown out of the window on to the street below. Finally I went downstairs. The entrance door to our apartment, which was partially glass, had been smashed. Upon entering, I found that many things had been totally destroyed, the windows broken, and much of our furniture and crystal was on the pavement below. My mother, sister, and Aunt Klara were standing on the balcony crying. My grandfather had been arrested and taken away by two policemen. Mr. Brockhausen came in and tried to calm everybody. Soon the two policemen returned. We were told we could not stay in our apartment and had to go with them. On the way out, we passed by the downstairs apartment that was empty because the Abosch family, a Jewish family who had rented it from my mother, had been expelled to Poland a few weeks earlier. Their apartment was totally destroyed. People were standing in the street and watching as the Jewish families left their houses, and some of them spit at us and threw stones and sand. We passed by the synagogue, still burning. The policemen brought us to the Jewish school where we were told that we had to stay overnight. Apparently after we left our apartment, some of the Nazis came back. They tried to set the house on fire. Mr. Brockhausen stopped them, claiming the house belonged to him.

In the middle of the night, my mother woke me up. She wanted me to say goodbye to my babysitter from the orphanage. As I found out years later, the children still living in the orphanage were terribly abused during Kristallnacht. The Jewish community had then decided to take the thirty children from the orphanage to Cologne, Germany, from where they were sent afterwards to Belgium and Holland to try to keep them out of harm's way. That night was the last time I ever saw my babysitter.

Most of the about thirty children living in the orphanage at the time of Kristallnacht did not survive the Holocaust. According to the diary kept by Yitzhak Sophoni Herz, the director of the orphanage at that time,

The police ordered us to get ready for a march through the center of Dinslaken. I was to be responsible for preparing this march. The news that there would be a 'Judenparade' spread like wildfire.[18] The people of Dinslaken stood three and four deep along the sidewalk to await the Judenparade. Most people cursed and taunted us but on the faces of a few there was disgust at the proceedings.

In front of the parade were two policemen, flanked by uniformed Nazis. The little children of the orphanage were forced to climb into a hay wagon and four older boys were forced to pull this wagon.

The Jewish cemetery, where my father and grandmother were buried, was not spared either. It was completely vandalized; headstones were smashed and overturned.

A few days after Kristallnacht, we left our house in Dinslaken. My mother sent Edith and me to live with relatives in Holland. The border into Holland

---

[18] *Judenparade*-a 'parade' of Jews through the town

had been closed for refugees leaving Germany; however, after the Kristallnacht pogrom, the Dutch authorities relented and allowed children who had relatives living in Holland to come into their country.

Fred and his sister received a fortuitous reprieve from the terror. Unfortunately, it would not last long.

CHAPTER FOUR

Lost in Germany

The preeminent scholars of the Holocaust tell us that the Holocaust began on January 30, 1933, the day that Hitler came to power. They will also agree that the word 'holocaust,' from the Greek referring to a burnt offering to the gods at the temple, is now considered an inadequate name, and perhaps on some levels inappropriate.[16] Saul Friedländer sees it as an event that is impossible to put into normal language. Raul Hilberg, in his groundbreaking work at the beginning of the 1960s, called it the 'Jewish Catastrophe' or destruction; in Hebrew,

'HaShoah.' Yehuda Bauer, who first classified it as the watershed event that it is, still struggles with the label 'Holocaust' and falls back on the 'genocide of the Jewish people,' which he tells us is unprecedented in the history of mankind. The language escapes us.

In Germany, Kristallnacht was not the beginning, but marked a major turning point for Germany's Jews. Six years after the elections which had brought the Nazi ideology to the forefront, it marked the moment when the political, social, and economic persecution of Germany's Jews became much more sinister, with mass incarcerations, open murders on the streets, and hugely ramped up physical destruction of property. Our exploration of the authentic sites of the Holocaust should rightly begin here, in the cradle of the place where democracy failed, with catastrophic consequences for the Jews of Europe, and for the world.

July 4, 2013/Hadamar, Germany

It's Independence Day back home in the States, and this morning I am on a bus with our group of American teachers in the heart of Hesse country in Germany on our way to the Hadamar Memorial site, where the secret T–4 euthanasia program got underway. On my unplanned music playlist, the heavy and foreboding opening chords of Soundgarden's "Fourth of July" is the first sound to set the mood as we glide through the farms and fields of the picturesque German countryside. It's followed on the playdeck by "Lost in Germany" by the band King's X, describing a bewildering bus tour here in this country—it's probably not a coincidence, and an apt metaphor for what I will experience here this week.

We turn off the highway and make our way to the town of Hadamar. It is small and almost quaint, the streets winding us up to the big building on the hill. The bus driver negotiates the tight turns like an expert, and we are at the hospital. The town lies below us.

We step off the bus. A nurse guides a patient in a wheelchair; Hadamar is still a functioning psychiatric center. But it is also a historical memorial site, and certainly related to the topic at hand—the Holocaust.

Somehow our appointment here has been crossed up and not quite anticipated. It seems that a group of German schoolkids have the tour booked at the moment and we cannot enter into the bowels of the institution, where one can still see the basement rooms that functioned as the early experimental gassing chambers. And today maybe that is what was meant to be.

So instead we are inside of the bus garage, a simple wooden barn with a plain dirt floor, so horribly, terribly ordinary. Haunting portraits of murdered children look at us. This is the face of 'Aktion T–4,' dreamt up and administered from 'TiergartenStrasse 4' in Berlin. School buses with blacked-out windows carried the selected children through the picturesque town and up the hill to the hospital garage, where boys and girls could be discharged out of sight—no one had to know, but everyone did; the program was an open secret. At Hadamar, local children even taunted those arriving on the buses, 'as children will.'

My notes tell me that doctors and nurses did the killing—starving, injecting, and later gassing; there were no cases of doctors or nurses who refused. So much for that Hippocratic Oath.

The hospital garage at Hadamar. July 2013. Source: Author

It was Nazi Germany's first foray into government-sponsored mass murder, predating the mass murder of the Jews by a couple of years. But it was here that the tools of mass murder, from gas chambers to deceiving the victims, were refined. Before long, five such centers would be operating throughout Germany and one in Austria.

As the clouds of war gathered over Europe in the summer of 1939, Reich doctors and midwives were mandated to report any child with any disability or developmental issues from birth to age three; five thousand infants and toddlers were murdered under this system. Later, the program would be expanded to include all children up to age 17, and eventually, to adults. In October 1939, doctors and public health officials were instructed by Hitler himself to encourage parents to give up their children to these state-run clinics.

With the decree of the Führer, there was huge 'peer pressure' for families to have their disabled children institutionalized, to commit government resources instead on the healthy. You would have seen 'Useless Eater' posters with disabled children featured, and other 'life unworthy of life' propaganda. Although in reality the machinations for the program had begun before the outbreak of war, later documents were altered to make the euthanasia program seem as if it were part of wartime measures. Records were falsified to indicate that the deceased had died a natural death, when in fact lethal injection, starvation, and neglect, and later gassing by carbon monoxide, was the norm.

By definition, the T–4 euthanasia program is not the Holocaust, but it is concurrent and intersects. Here we have the first evidence of gassing of human beings. How else do you figure out how to build efficient gas chambers? Trial and error, of course. Engineers who go on to build Treblinka, Sobibor, Belzec, the major killing centers in Poland, and start the mobile van gas chambers at Chelmno, all get ideas here.

We do not get to go inside, but it is a fine summer day and we hike up to the top of the hill behind the facility. There are flowers, memorials, and a mass grave. Families might have been notified by post that their loved one had passed away suddenly, of some natural cause that made no sense. Appendicitis? The child had had the appendix out long before heading to Hadamar.

Did anyone speak out? After a sermon denouncing the T–4 program by Catholic Archbishop Clemens Von Galen in August 1941 was publicized, Hitler quietly ordered a suspension of the gassing program, though valuable lessons in mass murder had been learned. The killing of children and other undesirables resumed a year later under more decentralized circumstances, with perhaps 200,000 killed before the end of the war.[17]

Later, in deconstructing today's experience, I'm reminded that there is also a danger in untempered and unbalanced curricula and in a system of education that increasingly crowds out discussions of morality and ethics in the classroom in favor of massive testing and technologically radicalized data-driven 'goal setting,' when the goal is squarely focused on high-stakes exams that determine a teacher's worth and create the entirely wrong message for young people about what we should be valuing as a society. And I am reminded of these good doctors and nurses, damn good test takers, mind you, and leave you with this note from an enlightened principal to his teachers:

> *I am a survivor of a concentration camp. My eyes saw what no person should witness—gas chambers built by learned engineers. Children poisoned by educated physicians. Infants killed by trained nurses. Women and babies shot by high school and college graduates.*
> *So, I am suspicious of education.*
> *My request is this—help your children become human. Your efforts must never produce learned monsters, skilled psychopaths or educated Eichmanns. Reading, writing, and arithmetic are important only if they serve to make our children more human.*[18]

July 6, 2013/Wannsee

Berlin. We arrived here late in the evening on the 5th from Hannover by rail, and set up headquarters in the Marriott Berlin, which is very nice, for a few days. Our bus passes Jesse Owens Allee on our tour of the Olympic Stadium, built by the Nazis for the Berlin Games of 1936, a monument to the grand vision of the Imperial Germania of the

Third Reich, where sport for sport's sake was fine, but sport for the conditioning of the super race was better. An Indian cricket team practices on the field; the fields are still in use today. We continue down into the elegant southwestern Berlin suburb at Lake Wannsee, and enter the gates of the infamous Wannsee Villa, where on one day in January 1942, decisions were made that would ramp up the fate of European Jewry, and to use the language of the perpetrators, the 'Final Solution to the Jewish Question' would be decided once and for all.

But make no mistake. The genocide of the Jews was already very well underway. But it was with the invasion of the Soviet Union that for the Nazi hierarchy, efforts among various government bureaucratic agencies would have to be coordinated. Here, at this beautiful mansion on a sailboat-dotted lake, with its manicured grounds and gardens, the intentionality of the Holocaust hits you square in the face and takes your breath away.

Wannsee Villa, July 2013. Source: Author

A troubling photograph is on display here—*'Einsatzkommando 12b of Einsatzgruppe D kills Jewish women and children in a pit, Dubossary, Moldova/Transnistria, 14 Sept. 1941.'* Twenty or so soldiers with rifles are shooting down into a ditch; through the tall grasses we see the target figures, as officers stand on and watch, or walk past in the foreground. It was taken just seven weeks after the blitzkrieg steamrolled into Soviet territory in the largest land and air invasion of the history of the world. Now that the Soviet Union had been invaded, there were millions more Jews in the path of the genocidal war machine; the Holocaust here was carried out by Germans with bullets. Entire villages and districts were murdered, with over 1.5 million victims. The dirty work gets done; the earth atop the covered-over pits undulates for three days.[19] It is remarkably 'efficient'—between June and December 1941, 3,000 men have killed between 600,000 and 700,000 persons[20]—but given the 'trauma' for the shooters engaged in face-to-face mass murder, the thinking is, 'there has to be a better way.' And to dispel another myth, there is no known instance where those few Germans who refused to take part in the killings were shot or otherwise severely punished—because some did ask to be relieved, and they were.[21]

The SS bought the mansion in 1941 for a series of planned rest and recreation centers for its officers. Reich Security Chief and SS General Reinhard Heydrich took a fancy to it, and on January 20, 1942, fifteen German military and government heads met for a day to discuss the Jewish problem. As scholars have noted, the Wannsee Conference was not called to decide the fate of European Jews, but to clarify all points regarding their demise. To put it another way, the intent was there, but with events on the warfront ratcheting up, the fact was highlighted that there was no blueprint for the murder of millions—and that because there was no precedent like this in history, on some level the Germans had been 'making it up as they went along.' Mass murder was already underway, and the process now needed refinement, decision making, and coordination.

On that January day, Heydrich and his henchman Adolf Eichmann indicated to the gathered group that approximately 11,000,000 Jews in Europe would fall under the provisions of the 'Final Solution.' Deploying carefully coded euphemisms—'evacuation,' 'resettlement,' 'special treatment,' and so on—logistics were discussed as plans were made for major gassing centers in occupied Poland. Once mass deportations were completed, the 'Final Solution' would be under total SS jurisdiction. With that matter 'settled,' secondary decisions revolved around revisiting the legal definitions of degrees of 'Jewishness' established at the Nuremberg Laws of 1935.

The conference lasted perhaps 90 minutes. Just one copy of the carefully coded minutes turned up after the war and was subsequently used at the Nuremberg Tribunals. We may have been in the building longer than the criminals who plotted the destruction of European Jewry 75 years ago. And Heydrich almost got what he wanted.

July 7, 2013/Ravensbrück

A couple of hours north of Berlin, in the former East Germany, we come to the memorial at the site of Ravensbrück concentration camp. It is notable for many reasons, probably first that it was a camp for women, and also a training facility for SS camp guards—3,500 women guards were trained here. Survivors corroborate that when new SS female guard recruits would come for training, initially they did not know how to deal with the new job. Industries wanting slave labor also had to send their own guard recruits. The trainees were not kind, but they did not seem possessed with the will to carry out this abhorrent work. Former prisoners would say that always within about two weeks, new staff would have overcome any 'cognitive dissonance' that would have prevented them from doing their jobs. They became 'hardened'; they 'got over it.'

One hundred and thirty thousand women prisoners passed through Ravensbrück, and towards the end of the war, so had another 20,000 men. No inmate barracks are standing today—in the immediate aftermath of the war, the barracks were dismantled and the building materials given to German refugees who had fled the Eastern Reich as it collapsed. Many of the houses for the SS leadership remain just outside the camp wall, where they lived with their families. The housing for the SS women guards is used as a youth hostel education center today—the memorial even has a program where survivors interact with the students for about four days, and they all sleep here at night.

Each day the camp gates would open and thousands of prisoners would stream out past the SS homes into the community for their slave labor assignments, which made it kind of hard to hide it from the kids. I suppose the attitude was that it was difficult, distasteful work, but the kids had to realize that it had to be done for the wonder world that they were creating for the children's future.

Our guide here is the historian Matthias. He appears to be in his 40s and is passionate and knowledgeable, as are all of the German historians I have met thus far. He walks us through the main camp entrance, where thousands of prisoners would pass every day, explaining that for years as a guide he would avoid the single-door entrance that the SS guards used—until one day a survivor he was leading on a tour walked through it to symbolize her victory at this place.

Ravensbrück was built for 3,000 prisoners. At its height it held 35,000, 30,000 of whom were killed here. From the beginning, the SS did not want women with children in the camp; but as more and more territory was overrun, the camp swelled. After the Warsaw Ghetto uprising in 1943, hundreds of pregnant women were deported here. Some are forced to abort; as numbers grow, women give birth and the babies are taken to a 'hospital' where they are slowly starved to death. The crematorium worked nonstop. Ash piles were dumped into the nearby lake as the Russians closed in. When the camp was overrun by the Red Army, 2,000 women and 2,000 men, mostly too infirm to be death-marched out of the camp, were found.

Here in Germany, we turn to the question of the role of the ordinary German person in Nazi Germany. In Matthias's opinion, the majority of Germans at the time supported the master race theory. What disturbs him today is that in his opinion, few of his fellow countrymen seem conscious of this. It is a very complex topic. The historians talk about the mass crimes, and in Matthias's words, they work on thin ice; the responses to the Holocaust run in a range. Some people want to know more—after all, many of them learned nothing about it from their teachers, many of whom were bystanders or even perpetrators.[19] Some quietly deny the

---

[19] *some people want to know more-* In July 2016 the author received the following comment from a German visitor to my website: *'Everything I read or see about this horror scenario of our German history makes me feel so sad and guilty, although I wasn't even born at that time (I was born in 1971). My grandfather was a German soldier who had to go to war aged 19, without*

extent—but as I am careful to lay out in this book, a person will find that the more he or she is willing to study it, the more he/she will learn how vast and almost unbelievable the topic is in scope. Others are tired of the topic—'*Yes, it happened. So what? Enough…*'

For Matthias, herein lies the greatest danger. It is important to have the past in front of you—not in the rearview mirror, as one moves forward. The message may be simply how to 'behave,' and not just for Germans, but for everyone.

The Butcher's Son

One of the most powerful moments here in Germany was when Matthias related the following story, about an ordinary German boy running errands for his father.

The butcher's son delivered fresh cuts of meat almost daily to the SS mess hall, which still stands

---

any alternative. He had to fight in Russia for so many years, hardest circumstances, and only survived because of his desertion at the last moment.
It is so important not to forget, but to remember what happened during those days. My son, aged 10, will not be able to meet any contemporary witnesses anymore and it will be my turn to teach him all aspects of that cruel war and the Holocaust. I'm thankful for everyone who takes his time to account for this past.'

here. Late in life, the old man tells Matthias of his feeling as a young teen, going through the camp gates to deliver the meat, seeing the emaciated and foul-smelling prisoners, and believing fully all he has been taught—that these people are indeed sub-human, vermin. Just look at them—just smell them. It's true and it's disgusting to have to walk past them. Every day it is the same. They even march through the town to the labor sites; best to keep a distance from them.

It's always the same, until on his rounds one cold morning he encounters the arrival of a new transport of women. They appear healthy but are now stripped naked, humiliated, shivering, crying, shocked, and trying to cover themselves in the plaza. Now it is his turn for a shock. Here are the enemies—not subhumans, but girls his age and older, in distress.

And they are naked. He has probably never even seen his mother or sister undressed before. And it is at this moment that he realizes that his teachers and the adults in his life are wrong—that what he is witnessing is a crime. And now, a lifetime later, he unburdens himself.

July 7, 2013/Sachsenhausen

We followed our visit to Ravensbrück with a visit to Sachsenhausen, though Sachsenhausen was known earlier as Oranienburg, the name of the nearby town. The model SS camp was built between 1936 and 1938 and served as an SS military training facility. Here also was the headquarters for the Inspectorate of Concentration Camps, the closest to the center of power, about 40 kilometers outside of Berlin. In March 1933, Oranienburg became one of the first 'KZs'—Konzentrationslagers, or concentration camps. Due to its proximity to the capital of the Reich, local political opponents were imprisoned and tortured here. As a simple matter of natural progression, the Gestapo would also shoot political prisoners here in the 'shooting pit,' which they 'perfected' over time.

After the invasion of the USSR, Sachsenhausen was used to murder Soviet POWs as well. In the infamous 'neck-shot facility,' unsuspecting prisoners would be seated individually facing away from a hidden port with a rifle being aimed at them; over 10,000 were murdered in ten weeks in 1941. And it was here at Sachsenhausen where crematorium ovens were developed, and also here that scientists and engineers perfected gassing vans and facilities. Doctors experimented on live subjects. Always testing.

Later in the war, vast shipments of stolen property from the death camps in the east were also unloaded and warehoused at Sachsenhausen. A brick factory was opened, making bricks stamped 'GERMANIA' to be used in the new Reich construction in Berlin. Life expectancy in the brickyard was six to eight weeks.

Sachsenhausen, July 2013. Soviet POWs. Source: Author.

And as we know, major corporations had their hands in it as well, profiting from the slave labor that left the camp each day and, like at

Ravensbrück, paraded through the surrounding community. After 1936, authorities toned down the visibility/profile of the camp, due to these sinister applications of state policy. But again, nearly 200,000 persons passed through the camp gates. Hiding in plain sight? 'We did not know,' becomes the familiar refrain after the war.

Track 17

Our state-of-the-art bus brings us to a place seemingly on the edge of nowhere in Berlin. We are at the Gleis 17 Grunewald Railway Station Memorial, the major site of the deportation of Berlin's Jews. There is no train station that we can see, just tracks that end abruptly, loading platforms, one spur of rails below, but no train.

Gleis 17 Grunewald Railway Station Memorial Berlin. July 2013. Source: Author.

Then we notice the stepping grates at our feet on the edge of the tracks. You look down:

Oct. 18, 1941. 1251 Jews. Destination: Lodz Ghetto.

What does this mean? On that day, the first of the mass deportations from Berlin, 1,251 people, were rounded up and sent to board the trains of the Reichsbahn. The police and SS had assembled the people for this transport in a local synagogue, and then herded the men, women, and children by foot to this site of their deportation east. For two and a half years, about 180 transports shipped Berlin's Jewish population to ghettos and annihilation centers. And who is going to pay for all of this? After all, there is a war on. Well, who do you think? 'The conveyance of the Jews was billed to the Jewish community: 4 pfennigs were charged per kilometer for adults and 2 pfennigs for children above the age of four.'[22] The Jewish community of Berlin is essentially forced to buy tickets to its own annihilation.

And this all brings to mind another incident that took place as the deportations from Berlin were being orchestrated, little known but highly illuminating and important. Between February 27 and March 6, 1943, a large group of non-Jewish German women publicly protested in the cold for the release of nearly 2,000 Jews—their husbands and the male children of these 'mixed marriages.' These couples had held special 'exemptions' from the ongoing racial laws, tabled even at the Wannsee Conference, but with the defeat at Stalingrad, these male Jews were ordered to be rounded up. Outside of the site of their incarceration at Rosenstrasse 2–4 in Berlin, despite being threatened with lethal force, the women and children gathered here chanted and yelled in the belief that their loved ones were to be deported to suffer the same fate as those other Jews shipped to the East. News of the protest spread, and the regime did not carry out its threat and the men were eventually released (though most were picked up again to work in labor camps).[23] It was the only German public protest against deportation of Jews, and not one of the protesters was shot. No government likes bad 'PR,' even the Nazis at home, especially as the tables began to turn on the war front.

I also recall a dinner I had with some lovely people who were impressed by my work and filled with praise for the job I am doing with my students in preserving the past. Near the end, though, the conversation turned to some of the postwar German émigrés that they had known. One person insisted that the folks she knew who grew up in Germany during the war had had the 'gun to their heads' if they did not join the Hitler Youth as children—'they had to do it, or they were dead.' By her extrapolation, Germans were forced at gunpoint to carry out the policies of the Third Reich. I politely explained that that was most likely not the case. It's not a simple issue, and it is probably not my place to pass judgment on German teens in Nazi Germany 70 years ago, but the simplistic 'gun to the head' mythology persists.

Track 17, Berlin. July 2013. Source: Author.

As we prepare to board the bus to our final stop for today, I pause by myself. It is a beautiful summer day. A breeze ripples gently; the trees reclaiming the site shimmer and whisper. A whistle blows; nearby, an unseen train is passing, the clicking on the tracks steadily growing louder, then trailing off slowly in the wind. I look down. March 27, 1945; the last transport out of Berlin—to Theresienstadt, in Czechoslovakia.

July 10, 2013/Theresienstadt, Czech Republic

At the Berlin train station, we begin our journey to the south, the Czech Republic. The train meanders past Magdeburg again and alongside the Elbe River, passing through the beautiful mountains of the Sudetenland.

After a tour of old Prague and the Jewish synagogue and cemetery here, we move on to Terezin, or Theresienstadt. Forty miles northwest of Prague, it was originally built in the late 18th century as a fortification and garrison town by Emperor Joseph II and named after his mother, Empress Maria Theresa. I will be at the site where the 'Train Near Magdeburg' was destined to arrive—but never did, thanks to the US Army. But why there?

In the closing days of the war, as the Reich collapsed in the East and began to be rolled up in the West, Theresienstadt was the destination of the three transports hastily evacuated from Bergen-Belsen. Only one train made it there; the other was liberated by the Americans and the third by the Russians. It is known that as thousands of prisoners from other camps flooded into Theresienstadt in the last month or so of the war, typhus and other epidemics broke out.

First we toured the Small Fortress, which later became the prison, and then moved onto the former garrison town which became the infamous 'model ghetto.'

Theresienstadt served several purposes. It was a transit camp for Czech Jews whom the Germans deported to killing centers, concentration camps, and forced-labor camps soon thereafter. It was a holding pen where thousands would be eliminated in the poor conditions that would bring about their deaths. It was also the ghetto-labor camp where the SS deported certain categories of German, Austrian, and Czech Jews, 'based on their age, disability as a result of past military service, or domestic celebrity in the arts and other cultural life.' This helped to sustain the fiction back home that deported Jews would be employed at productive labor and not annihilated, made all the more obfuscated by propaganda efforts.[24] Succumbing to pressure following the deportation of Danish Jews to Theresienstadt, the Germans permitted the International Red Cross to visit in June 1944. It was all an elaborate hoax.

Theresienstadt, July 2013. Source: Author.

The Germans intensified deportations from the ghetto shortly before the visit, and the ghetto itself was 'beautified.' Gardens were planted, houses painted, and barracks renovated. The Nazis staged social and cultural events for the visiting dignitaries. A propaganda film was even made for show back home—'The Führer Gives the Jews a City.' And this is the real Holocaust hoax.

Jewish children in the Theresienstadt ghetto, taken during an inspection by the International Red Cross. June 23, 1944. Credit: USHMM, courtesy of Comité International de la Croix Rouge.

Once the visit was over, the deportations resumed with a vengeance. Fifteen thousand children passed through Theresienstadt, and ninety percent were murdered; many of the children were deported to Auschwitz soon after they smiled for Nazi cinematographers.

On May 5, with the Führer dead nearly a week, and the Soviets approaching, the guards left. On May 8, the last day of the war, the Red Army arrived.

We light candles. We wind up our day, like all visits, with a group prayer for the dead and with solitary reflection for the living. We quietly make our way back to Prague, where life goes on. People hurry about their business on the streets. But step lightly, lest your stride be interrupted, so that you must pause and look down. Then you may see the four-inch square brass *stolperstein* 'stumble stone' embedded in the sidewalk, engraved with the name of the former occupant of the dwelling here who was deported to his/her death.

Yes, life goes on. But you stop and wonder—what was, what is, and what might have been.

Major concentration camps mentioned in this book.
Credit: Susan Winchell.

CHAPTER FIVE

The Ash Yards of Poland

People walk around at their wits' end, as though they had gone mad. They wander about in the streets, searching for a way out.
— ALIZA MELAMED VITIS-SHOMRON, WARSAW GHETTO, 1942

I want to thank you with all my heart for what you did for me, by taking my letter and putting it on the ground where my mother's bones are spread.
— ARIELA LOWENTHAL MAYER ROJEK, 2013

As the world went about its business, the clouds of war gathered. German troops had swallowed all of Czechoslovakia by March 1939; Hitler continued to demand the area known as the Polish Corridor and the outlet to the Baltic Sea at the city of Danzig, which had been lost after World War I. Secretly, he directed his foreign minister to enter into clandestine negotiations with the Soviet Union. Strange fellows bedded down in a 10-year pact of nonaggression, and the secret protocol called for the division of Poland between the Germans and the Soviets, the fascists and the communists. On September 1, 1939, Hitler rolled the dice once more as Germany invaded Poland on false pretenses of Polish aggression. The Polish Army fought valiantly but was no match for the mechanized warfare of the blitzkrieg. In short order, the nation found itself submitting to the heel of the German jackboot.

Ariela Lowenthal was an only child living in the city of Przemyśl (pronounced 'Shem-mi-shuhl') in the southeastern portion of Poland, near the border with the USSR. Following the German invasion, her city was divided between Nazi and Soviet forces in accordance with the secret protocol.

Ariela Lowenthal Mayer Rojek

I was born in Przemyśl, Poland, on September 21, 1933. I was an only child, but I had my grandparents from both sides, aunts and uncles, and three cousins. I lived in a very nice area; we lived in our house, which was my grandfather's building, three stories; we lived on one floor and my grandparents lived on the other floor. Downstairs my grandfather had a restaurant, so I guess we were well off—I had everything that every child had normally; I had a very good life.

My father was working in the family business. He had finished economic and accounting school but even before the war, it was very hard for a Jewish person to get a position in a bank or financial company, so he was working for my grandfather. My mother was at home, she was doing the usual, you know, a housewife. My father was a very quiet man. One thing that I remember is that his hobby was reading; he was a big reader. We had a big room full of books in our home; he had 2,000 books in his collection. My mother liked to crochet, to knit, and to sew. They were quiet, loving people. We were very close. I loved them dearly, from what I remember of them. I don't remember their faces now because it's been a long time. I was only eight years old when they were killed, but, this is what I remember from before the war.

My mother wanted to go to Palestine, but she never went. They were teaching me Hebrew and even my name 'Ariela' is a Hebrew name, because she was always dreaming to go to Palestine. My parents met in a Zionist movement when they were young. When they met, they fell in love, but they were going out [many] years before they got married, because my father had two sisters who weren't married, and in those days, you couldn't get married before your older sisters, so they were waiting. They got married in 1931, and I was born in 1933.

I was six years old when war broke out. In 1939, when the Germans invaded Poland, right away our city was bombed and a lot of houses were burned. We were hiding, and everything changed. My father ran away because there were rumors that the Germans were going to take the Jewish men; most Jewish men ran away, but after a few days he came back because he didn't want to leave us alone.

Then the Germans came in, they occupied our city, but we were only with the Germans for six weeks. After six weeks, they signed the agreement with Russia and divided Poland in two; they took some Jewish people and killed them, but our family wasn't touched then. Most of my aunts and uncles who lived in the small cities ran away [in the German invasion] and came to us, and we were all together.

The Russians came here into our city. Our city was divided in half—this was at the river San. One side of the city was in German hands, and the other side, the Russians. We were in the part where the Russians came in—the Russians were in our place for almost two years. Of course, we were happy that at least they didn't kill the Jewish people, [but] our life wasn't easy, because right away they took our business, the restaurant, and forced us to close it. They were claiming that we were rich people, and in Russia, you know, you're not supposed to be rich! But I remember my grandfather had humor, and he told one Russian [officer] that 'If I knew fifty years ago you would come, I wouldn't have built a house and I wouldn't have a business!'

They wanted our money, so right away they took our apartment, and our business. We had to move upstairs with my grandparents, so we were all together; everyone had to live in one room but we managed, because we were still together.

I can remember the war broke out between Germany and Russia in 1941, I believe it was in June. Right away and right in the middle of the night, the Germans attacked our city because we were [just across the river]; we heard shootings and bombs right away. The fighting was very, very hard. They were fighting from street-to-street and from house-to-house—I remember we were hiding in our basement in our restaurant building, and they were even fighting in our house from floor-to-floor! There were German and Russian soldiers all over the inside of the house, because it was a really big struggle. It took a few days, maybe two days, until the Russians ran away and the Germans came in.

Right away, the Germans started with [the persecutions]; you couldn't do whatever you wanted [if you were Jewish]. There was no more school, and you had to wear those white armbands with a

Jewish star. [And] right away, the first tragedy happened. My cousin was studying at the university, and just before the war broke out between the Germans and Russians, they went on some trip from the university. The war broke out, and the students were on the train to go back home. The Germans took out all the students and checked their papers. There were two Jewish students; in their passports [it was stamped] 'Jew.' They took my cousin and another boy out of the whole group, letting the others go home. They got killed…They shot them right away on the spot.

After a few months, I think it was November, or December, 1941, I went with my mother to visit her family and when we came back in the evening, we were going up the stairs up to our apartment, when we saw two men in civilian clothes. We knew that they were Gestapo. They were dragging my father down the stairs, and my mother started to scream, 'Where are you taking him?' They didn't answer, they dragged him, and she ran after them. She held onto this Gestapo man and said, 'Let him go, where are you taking him?' I was on the stairs and I'll never forget it. He kicked my mother and threw her into the other corner of the wall, and she fell down. They dragged my father away and we never saw him again. Our life wasn't the same. We were crying; my mother [wanted] to do something; nothing could be done. Of course, we were very depressed...One day we got a telegram cable. It was from Auschwitz, to let her know that he died in Auschwitz and they are going to send his last belongings; we never got anything. This was the end of my father. This was May or June 1942.

The Przemyśl Ghetto

The Germans decided to open a ghetto, which is a special place in part of the city only for the Jewish people. We had to move to the ghetto; of course, we had to find an apartment there—I think that the Polish people who lived there had to move out, so we exchanged, they would go to our house and we moved there. We couldn't take anything because we were moving to two little rooms. The whole family moved, what was left—it was my mother in one room and my uncle, the doctor, and my aunt. We were in one room; in the other room we had my grandparents, one of my aunts, and my great-aunt. She was in her eighties and had broken her leg, so she was lying down the whole time of the war.

We didn't even have a washroom in our apartment, you had to go downstairs and a few families shared it together. It was crowded, but you adjust, because you have to adjust. We knew that something was going to happen. We lived with a fear from day to day because everyone was saying that they are going to deport, deport, [that there would be] deportations. We knew it was going to come.

[Before the ghetto was sealed] my aunt was going out of the ghetto to work, in a German kitchen. She used to take me with her because I wasn't registered with any papers, and the Germans used to come and take the children that were left orphaned without papers, so they used to send me with her, [when my mother was gone]. I remember I went out with her two or three times. One time we went to the gate and the policemen were counting, saying, 'What is she doing here?' She said, 'Oh, she is going with me.' They said, 'No, she is not, send her home.' My aunt told me it was not far. I went down the street, and when I came close to my house, suddenly I heard a German soldier screaming, '*Halt! Halt! Stop! Stop!*' And I felt his rifle on my back; I started to run to my house and he was running after me! I don't know what happened; something happened, probably in his heart he didn't want to shoot me. He would shoot if I was running away from the transport [but I guess I was running towards it]—my house was right where they had the assembly for the transports. I managed to go to the door and knocked on it. Someone opened it and I went in.

Then in July, rumors started that they were going to evacuate people who did not have a job. There was a card, if you worked or something, and you could stay. All other people were going to be evacuated. They didn't know where, but they were saying that it was going to be another place to get work and good conditions. These were the rumors. People started right away to think that they weren't so true, that they were going to kill us, but people didn't know exactly.

Then the time came, and we knew that we had to go. My mother [who did not have work in the ghetto] decided she couldn't stay. She didn't have permission. My uncle the doctor and his wife, they had permission to stay in the ghetto. My mother decided that she was going to leave me with them because she said, 'I know they take the children right away and they kill the children.' They knew that the children would not survive. Of course, I didn't want her to leave—who wants to let their mother go, while they stay? I was crying.

When the time came, it was July 27, 1942. They had to go to a [gathering] place. We lived in the center of the ghetto and there was a big place and all the Jews were supposed to go there. The transport was supposed to come there in the morning, so my grandparents and my mother went to this place. I said goodbye and I was crying. They took my grandparents and my mother. The Jewish policemen came upstairs; they did most of the dirty work that the Germans told them to. They knew that my great-aunt was still with us.

I have to tell you something that I just remembered. Some people committed suicide. The day before, my uncle the doctor said, 'She can't walk, and they are going to kill her.' So they gave her cyanide in her coffee—they gave her this to drink and she said, 'Why is it bitter?' She knew something was wrong with it, so she spit it out and she swallowed some, but nothing happened to her. The next morning, the Jewish police came, and they had to take her in her chair because she was a heavy woman, and they couldn't even drag her. Right away they took her on a truck, and I think they shot her. They used to shoot people in the city, in the Jewish cemetery. The [empty] chair [that they had carried her out in] was standing there out in front of our house for a few days.

After a few days, my mother came back and she told me that when she was waiting there, ready for the transport, some Polish people came for a work group to work in the fields. They called out the names on a list. They called out a name, and that woman wasn't there, so someone pushed my mother and said, 'Go, go!' They took her with the women, and after two or three days, they released her to go home. She came home, she came back! Of course, I was very happy. After two days there was another deportation and another… After a week my mother was still in the ghetto, but she had to go—she didn't have any papers to stay. She decided to go with her mother and her sister—they were supposed to go on this transport. The evening before she left me again, she said I had to stay, but again, I didn't want to. The same thing repeated itself after a week! I was crying, and in the morning, my mother, my grandmother, one of my aunts, and another uncle came in the doorway while we were sitting downstairs. My mother came and said goodbye to me. I held onto her, and I was holding her, and she was pushing me away... [*Cries*] My aunt was pulling me to her side. They pulled me off her; of course, they didn't let me go with her. That was the last time that I was with my mother.

They went to the gathering place before our house. It took half a day before they collected them and marched them to the train. We were living on the second floor, so my aunt picked me up; she said, 'Look, this is the last time that you will see your mother.' [*Wipes her eyes with a tissue*] I was crying and crying, but you get used to it... My father's sister, my aunt, was Klara Mayer. Her husband, Doctor Edmund Mayer, had some connections outside the ghetto, and they decided right away to adopt me because they were afraid since I didn't have papers that the Germans would take me, too. I stayed with them, and the ghetto life was very hard. We had food but we didn't have a lot, but we managed; he was a doctor so he worked in the hospital and he took care of some patients at home. That didn't last a long time.

People were trying to find hiding places, mostly to go out of the ghetto, to hide on the other side of the ghetto with the Polish people. My uncle said, 'We can't survive together, we have to divide up, and we have to find a place to hide.' They tried to give me away to a [convent] where the nuns are; they bought me special papers and clothes, they taught me how to pray and everything. I didn't want to go. I said, 'No, I look Jewish, it won't work!' I was crying all night, but again, I didn't have a choice. In the middle of November 1942, there were rumors that the next day there would be a big deportation. The rumor was that the workers on the railway knew that they took people to a place called Belzec, and the Germans gassed them there. Right away rumors came back in the ghetto that you would not come back, wherever they take you.

They tried to give me away then. [They arranged it so] a woman had to take me out of the ghetto and give me to another woman. [The day before the deportation] people were running and rushing everywhere—everyone wanted to get out of the ghetto, and it was very crowded beside the gate! We went with this woman, me and my aunt and uncle. I was holding my aunt's hand with one hand and this woman's hand with the other. At the last minute, this woman lost my hand and we couldn't find her! We couldn't find her, and I was left again in the ghetto. [But] it was like from G-d or something; later we heard that the nuns from this convent took those Jewish children and gave them to the Germans, and no one survived.

[But at the time], my uncle said to my aunt, 'You didn't want to give her away, look what happened, now we are going to be killed tomorrow!' We came back to the house, and the people in the house had managed to dig under the ground, like a basement [hideout]. There was a room to hide. Everyone was looking for some place to hide, but they agreed to take us because my uncle was a doctor. We had my other aunt with us and her little baby, a year and a half old; her husband was out of the ghetto working and he couldn't come back, because the ghetto closed before the deportations. The people didn't want to take them, because babies cry… my other aunt said to the people, 'If you want my husband as a doctor, you have to take her,' the condition being that he was going to give the boy something to sleep. He gave him something and the baby fell asleep and they took us.

We were in there for three days and three or four nights. We were sitting in a small room with maybe 50 people. There was no oxygen, you couldn't breathe. You wanted to light a match or candle, but it wouldn't burn because it didn't have oxygen. After two days, the baby woke up and he was very weak and my uncle was afraid to give him more [medicine]. The baby started to cry and they forced my aunt out in the middle of the deportation; they opened the hole in the wall (it was closed with bricks) and they kicked her out in the middle of the night with this baby! We didn't have any choice—she went out, and we stayed.

We stayed for about another day. Everything went quiet, so we managed to go out from there and she was there in our apartment! She was upstairs and the Germans didn't come searching, or they had been through it before. She had survived with her baby, and her husband came back from outside the ghetto [after the deportation].

One thing that I remember that I have to tell you is that one day, some Jewish guy picked off a German. They came into the ghetto and they took three young boys and hung them in the middle of the ghetto. They forced everyone to come and watch it. My uncle went, and closed me and my aunts in the room and said, 'You don't go.' He went because everyone had to go. I remember there were hangings like this for maybe a week or two. When I went out into the street, I saw them hanging. This was the first time I saw dead people, and hangings.

Now it was July 1943. We didn't know what to do, we didn't have a chance. [But] one day the Judenrat, the Jewish council in charge of the ghetto, had an announcement that people who had foreign papers to immigrate to the United States,

England, or South America should register with them because the Gestapo was going to arrange something for them. My aunt and uncle, in 1938 before the war, wanted to immigrate to the United States—we had some relatives there. They got some papers and my aunt said to my uncle, 'You go to the Judenrat with something like this, and maybe something can be done.' He had some friends with the Judenrat…I wasn't registered at all in the papers, so they added my name. The next day, they came and said to my uncle, 'You know what, they agreed to take you all, and you have to be ready in 24 hours.' They said that we were going to go to be exchanged for some prisoners of war, but we didn't know; it was a gamble. You couldn't take anything, only a few belongings—no jewelry, no pictures, nothing. My aunt hid a few little pictures and some jewelry, not much, and she put it in her clothes, so my uncle wouldn't know—he wouldn't have allowed it. We went and my other aunt, my mother's sister with her little two-year-old boy, said, 'You don't have to go. If you want, you can stay with me.' Luckily I didn't, because they didn't survive. This was the last time that I saw them in the ghetto.

The Prison in Kraków

My aunt and my uncle and I went with thirteen other people. We went out from the ghetto and the Gestapo took us on the train during the night and they brought us to Kraków. So they brought us to the jail, and there were quite a few people from other cities, [people] with the same papers to immigrate to the United States and all kinds of foreign countries. They put the women and children in a separate jail cell and the men in another one. But before they put us there, they told us to take off all our clothes, and they put us in a little room, and there was a ceiling that was like showers, but we already knew that the showers meant gassings. So we didn't know, they closed the doors, and they let us stand like this for five or ten minutes [before the water came on], not knowing... can you imagine the fear?

We were in that prison for ten days.[20] During the night we heard people [screaming]; they were

---

[20] *We were in that prison* -Kraków's notorious Montelupich Prison.

shooting people outside in the courtyard, killing people. On the walls [of the holding cell], there was writing all over the walls, 'Don't forget us, we are going to Auschwitz.' 'Don't forget us.' 'Remember us.' The whole wall was written in Polish and all kinds of languages, and we were there in this condition, and we didn't know what was going to happen to us….

After 10 days, they came in the room, and they came with a list with names. It was very frightening and they took us down to the courtyard and they put us against the wall surrounding the jail, and ordered, 'Turn around with your face to the wall!' They were going to shoot us in the back. They held us like this for, I don't know, for maybe fifteen minutes, and then they said, 'Turn around!' and they marched us to the train station. Why they did that, I don't know, it was only for their enjoyment, for their pleasure.

They took us by regular train, not cattle trains, you know—but we didn't know where we were going. After three days, we were passing Berlin! And [after more days] they brought us to a new place, the train stopped in the middle of the forest;

we didn't see anything. They opened the doors and right away we saw the Germans with big dogs, shouting, screaming, *'Raus! Raus! Out! Out!'* They took us out of the train, and they marched us into Bergen-Belsen.

July 14, 2013/Belzec Memorial

We arrived in Poland from the Czech Republic a few days back. We met our Polish guide Waclaw, a treasure who will be masterful in his empathetic recounting of what we will witness here, beginning in this beautiful, revitalized city of Kraków. And like the city, the Jewish community here is also trying to revitalize; there is even a Jewish cultural festival coming up soon in Kraków. Our non-Jewish Polish guides have certainly been passionate about not letting the past die, as were our German historians encountered on our trip. Gosia takes us to the Jewish Community Center, and Jakub gives us a guided tour in the new Jewish Heritage Museum. He reaches 12,000 schoolchildren, doing outreach, and works with others to resurrect desecrated Jewish cemeteries—as he reminds us, it is Polish heritage as well as Jewish heritage. In the 15th and 16th centuries, Poland was the center of European Jewish life. In fact, at the end of the 18th century, 75% of the world's Jews lived in the former Galicia, where we are, once part of Poland, Ukraine, and the Austro-Hungarian Empire. Still, in most places in Poland there is nothing left of this heritage; out of what was once millions, today only between 12,000 and 14,000 Jews call Poland home. And let's not forget that after the war, Jewish survivors were not exactly welcomed back by their neighbors with open arms. And the Communist regime conducted its own purges of Jews as well; all the more reason to embrace the work of Gosia and Jakub and other dedicated Poles.

*

The bus ride from Kraków to Belzec (pronounced 'Bel-zich') Memorial site is five hours. Imagine what it was like traveling in a packed railcar. Well, we can't.

I carry a letter with me written by my friend, survivor Ariela, who, like many friends, is supporting me in my travel here. It has been in my pocket for weeks. Ariela was eleven when she was liberated with her aunt on the 'Train near Magdeburg.' She had also survived the ghetto, and done time in the infamous Montelupich Prison in Kraków.

A little girl. In a political prison.

So, I am kind of quiet as we approach the memorial site. Ariela's mother, only 36, both of her grandmothers, her grandfather, and two aunts were murdered here in 1942. Her father, other grandfather, and uncle were murdered in Auschwitz.

The annihilation camp in the small town of Belzec was sited for its good connections to rail lines and, obviously, relatively close proximity to large Jewish populations. Operations began with testings on small groups of Jews in March 1942 and expanded thereafter. Railcars jammed with up to 100 people were uncoupled from larger transports of forty to sixty cars in units of 20 cars at a time for 'processing.' The deception included time for the victims to turn in all valuables, as they were told they had arrived at a 'transit camp.' In the early days, the men were separated from the women, and according to the SS method, they were eliminated first to forgo any attempt at resistance. Later, when the numbers increased and Jews increasingly became aware of the true ends of the Belzec camp, organized chaos reigned as the victims were forced to undress and beaten down the 'tube' pathway that led directly to the gas chambers. Once sealed inside, the engine was started and carbon monoxide was pumped in, the bodies removed by Jewish slaves and buried in mass graves. In October 1942, the order was given to exhume the bodies and incinerate them on mass pyres using railroad rails as makeshift grills. The murderers also employed a bone crushing machine to pulverize the evidence, and plowed over all traces of the camp after its dismantling in the spring of 1943.²⁵

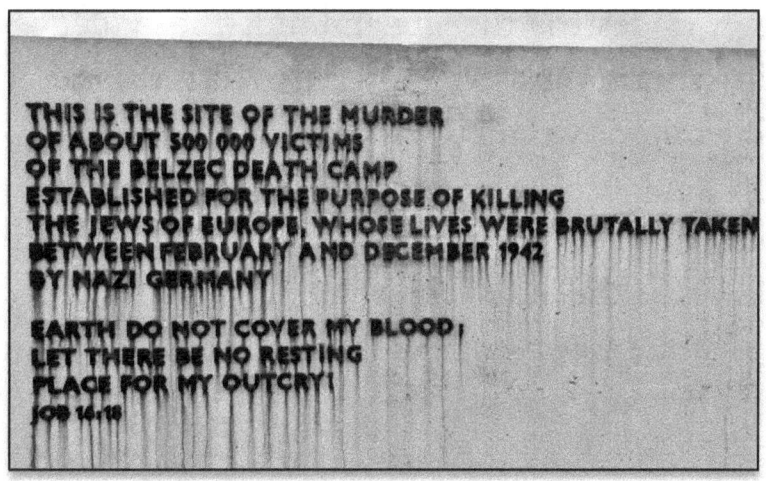

Belzec, July 2013. Source: Author.

Open-air ovens. Rail track. Bone crushing machines. Bone powder.

There was no memorial here at Belzec for nearly 60 years. When Ariela visited in 1993, there was nothing here; it had reverted to forested hillside. The women in our group enter the memorial for a private ceremony. The seven men walk the perimeter, near the hillside. It's said that during the actions, some of the locals would gather on the hillside behind us as transports pulled in to discharge the terrified and doomed victims.

They would watch. And after the German attempt to destroy the site and hide the evidence of half a million gassed and cremated, this site, like many others, would be rifled for gold, pockmarked with shovel pits by the local population. *Surely those Jews had gold with them when they were killed.*

I unfold the letter and step out into the acres of dark molten stones imported here to build the memorial. I am setting up my own memorial. My friend and fellow traveler Alan snaps a photo.

Later, the group boards the bus in silence. I had kept the letter to myself, but now Alan asks, gently, if he may see it. It gets passed around in the back of the bus on our way to the hotel in Lublin. After what we have seen today, I think it makes an important impact on all.

Belzec, July 2013. Source: Author.

My father asked in his last letter from jail that I should pray for him and believe me that I do. You asked how I was left with my aunt, it is a long story, one of those that hurts me to this day. But in short, my mother pushed me physically to my aunt, and my aunt pulled me from my mother.

Once home, Alan sends his photograph of me placing the letter on the memorial to Ariela, in Toronto. She is touched and writes back:

I want to thank you with all my heart for what you did for me, by taking my letter and putting it on the ground where my mother's bones are spread. When I saw the picture, I cried. It is already 71 years but my heart still has feeling for all my family.

I've been with Ariela many times, at reunions and during a visit to her daughter's home in Toronto. We sat at the table, and went through the photo album of her family, surrounded by her two daughters and their spouses, and the grandchildren and a great-grandchild. Her beloved husband, Moshe Rojek, another survivor, passed a few years ago. Ariela is one of my staunchest supporters, and sends me wishes for a long and happy life on a regular basis.

Yes, it was another tough day, but somehow I feel like we are making a difference by coming here. I come with no agenda other than to see what happened, though obviously I too feel a personal stake in it all. Ariela was born the same year as my own mother.

*

Warsaw

A teenage girl began to keep a diary and recorded her impressions of living on the edge of Warsaw, a city of 1.3 million and the capital of

Poland. She was just eleven when the war broke out; comfortable and innocent, she and her younger sister lived with their parents, and she had extended relatives all around: cousins, aunts, and uncles. Her recollections reflect how quickly her upper-middle-class world came crashing down, bringing girlhood to an abrupt end.[26]

Aliza Melamed Vitis-Shomron

I was born in 1928 in Warsaw, the capital of Poland. I was one of many Jewish girls from a good family. I did not have to struggle for existence; my parents had taken care of that. It was that stormy period between the two world wars, during which two totalitarian regimes emerged, arousing illusions of happiness, national vitality, and development, on opposite ends of a view of society: the communist Russian Revolution and the fascist Nazi regime in Germany. And at the same time, there was an amazing burgeoning of the Zionist idea of return to the ancient homeland.

The close of the summer holiday in 1939 brought her parents rushing from Warsaw to the country retreat the family typically enjoyed outside the city.

The End of August, 1939

My parents, who continued to work in our family business, only used to come to us in the country for the weekends. Suddenly they appeared with a horse and cart. 'We must go home to Warsaw immediately, they say that the war is about to break out.' The harsh, incomprehensible words hit us like a hard blow.

Within a week we were already in the midst of heavy bombing from the air. The Germans invaded Poland. It was a nightmare, lasting three weeks, during which almost all of Poland was overrun, and only the capital resisted heroically. Thousands of fires were burning in the encircled city, but it did not surrender. For three weeks, we lived in a cellar, lying on mattresses, in terrible fear of the Stuka planes, diving with earsplitting screeching; and fully aware that when all that was over, the Germans would be inside Warsaw.[21]

---

[21] *Stuka planes*-German dive bomber and ground–attack aircraft.

After those three terrible weeks, during which a large part of the city was destroyed, and there was no water in the taps and no more food, the city surrendered.

I went to see the German victory parade in the city streets. I can still hear the deafening sound of their boots pounding the cobblestones as they marched in unison. A faint echo lingered in the air. The inhabitants of the city stood by in silence. The Nazi occupation, which was to last six years, had begun.

Before World War II, Warsaw was the epicenter of Jewish life and culture in Poland; 350,000 Jews made up its prewar population. This vibrant Jewish community was the largest in both Poland and Europe, and was the second largest in the world, second only to New York City.[27]

Autumn, 1940

It was the golden Polish fall of 1940. As usual, the streets of Warsaw were covered with rusty leaves. The merry chatter of children in the city parks, looking for ripe chestnuts fallen from the trees, had died down. School children began to prepare for their studies after the summer vacation.

But the autumn was different that year, in particular for us Jews. The golden fall was clouded. A strange unease hung in the air, the nights were suffused with dread, and fearful premonitions lurked in the morning, especially in the Jewish neighborhoods. Only one year had passed since that fall when the war broke out, and I felt as though that good life we had before had never actually existed; it appeared to me as a pure sunlit memory of something never to return. That summer I had my twelfth birthday, and I felt very grown up. Everything had changed.

We didn't celebrate my birthday that year. Mother made it quite clear, in her usual tone of voice when she wanted to lecture me: 'I hope you are by now old enough to understand certain things and to come down from your Olympian heights.'

Father brought a box of cakes for the occasion. Before the war, sometimes Father used to surprise us by bringing a box of cakes, tied up with a thin string, from Kapulski's store in Marshalkovska

Street. But now Jews were unable to get there—these areas now belonged to a different Warsaw, the Polish Aryan part. And Father did not want to humiliate himself by stepping off the pavement whenever a German soldier passed by.

My birthday marked the day when I had to begin wearing a white band with a blue Star of David on my arm, like all adult Jews. 'Yes, Mother,' I said to myself, 'I understand far more than you imagine.'

I saw the anxiety on my parents' faces; they worried about making a living. Our family workshop was idle, since most of the women working there were Polish—and Poles were not allowed to work for Jews, and every day we worried about Father. All Jewish men, aged 16 to 60, were forced to work, but none signed up of their own free will. They were kidnapped, beaten, and humiliated. At night, German regular army soldiers and the SS drove around in cars and broke into houses, apparently to commit robberies or just out of hooliganism.

Throughout 1940 we stayed in Warsaw, among its dusty ruins. Jewish children were no longer allowed to go to school. Before the war started, I was able to complete the fifth grade and my sister was about to start the first grade.

As a young teen, Aliza joined a youth organization which would become attached to the underground resistance movement in the Warsaw Ghetto. The ghetto was established that fall of 1940 and sealed off from the rest of the city with a ten-foot-high wall topped with barbed wire. Over 400,000 people would be crowded into an area of only 1.3 square miles.[28]

The Warsaw Ghetto

I want to tell you about the Warsaw Ghetto.

Will I be able to describe it, the largest ghetto in Europe? The overcrowding, the feeling of humiliation, the raging typhoid epidemic, the filthy gray sidewalks, and the houses crammed with masses of refugees from the country towns? Hundreds of thousands of people wanting to survive, running around like mice, trapped in a maze?

The Warsaw Ghetto was a 'Jewish State' under fascist control—an accumulation of all possible contrasts.

In the beginning, stores sold food smuggled into the ghetto, where one could buy anything—even eggs and milk. And outside lurk the snatchers, girls and boys in rags with feverish eyes, lying in wait for people leaving the store, grabbing their food and at once plunging their teeth into it, right through the wrapping paper. People crowd around, kicking and shouting, but the child does not care as long as there is food, no matter what it is. The coffee houses are full of smartly dressed women, wearing elegant pre-war hats. There are also rich smugglers, the new ghetto aristocracy, and all kinds of people getting rich at others' expense; in front of the houses on the sidewalks lay human skeletons covered by newspapers.

Winter, 1942

The winter of 1942 was a hard one. Famine increased and so did the deaths in its wake. We stayed in bed for hours, trying in vain to keep warm. The evenings were dark—there was no lighting. The news of German victories in both the east and west and the news of mass deportations of Jews from the smaller towns preyed on our minds. It was dangerous to pass by the gates of the ghetto.

Sometimes shots were heard from there; they fired into the crowds.

About this time, the news first came in from the Vilna Ghetto.[22] Messengers were sent to Warsaw to tell what was happening there. We all sat on the floor, facing a young woman of about twenty-two, whose hair was already sprinkled with gray. In the twilight she looked beautiful and impressive, and her eyes were devoid of emotion. She spoke fluently, but sometimes her voice broke down and an oppressive silence fell.

> It was a ghastly night. We members of Hashomer Hatzair were hiding together in one apartment.[23] We listened to the noises in the street. German trucks stopped and we heard shouting, firing, heartbreaking weeping. That's how they emptied street after street. Where did they take them? To a forest

---

[22] *Vilna*–Capital of German–occupied Lithuania.
[23] *Hashomer Hatzair*–Oldest Jewish youth movement, ideologically progressive, a source of spiritual strength and resistance for members during the Holocaust and after. Aliza was a member of the Warsaw branch; the resistance would be commanded by their leader, the young Mordecai Anielewicz (1919–1943).

in the vicinity, Ponar—apparently a scene of mass murder.²⁴

Thousands of Jews have already been taken there. There are witnesses who escaped from the trench and said that they make men, women, and children stand in rows beside the trench and they shoot them. We are living in constant fear. I came here to tell you and warn you. We have reliable information about the liquidation of ghettos throughout eastern Poland, in the Ukraine, and in Lithuania! We've decided to defend ourselves. Half of us will stay in the ghetto, and the rest will try to find a way to reach the partisans. Abba Kovner has written a proclamation calling on Jews to fight back, calling for armed resistance against the Nazis: We shall not go like sheep to the slaughter!²⁵ We've decided that when our end comes, we shall not die without defending ourselves. And if we have no more weapons, we'll spit in their faces; at least we'll show

---

[24] *Ponary Forest*- eight miles outside Vilna; out of perhaps 100,000 people shot to death here through the summer of 1944, 70,000 were Jews.
[25] *Abba Kovner*–partisan leader; later, acclaimed Israeli poet and writer.

them our contempt, before we die. But our deeds shall not be forgotten.

We were in shock. It was hard to believe—can they be murdering women and children? Is this what awaits us? They can't kill innocent people just like that! The world will hear about it and cry out against it!

*

The occupants of the ghetto saw conditions decline steadily, with surprise raids targeting supporters of the underground, those engaged in various illegal activities such as smuggling, and with random terroristic executions, leaving bodies in the streets for all to see. Shortly, the highly orchestrated 'aktions,' great deportations to the newly constructed mass murder centers in Poland, would commence.[26]

Summer, 1942: The Great Deportation

In all the streets of the ghetto the Germans have put up large notices, in German. A proclamation on behalf of the German Reich states that all inhabitants of the Jewish quarter in the city of

---

[26] *aktion*—'action,' or assembly and deportation of Jews to mass murder camps.

Warsaw are to be transferred eastward, to work camps. The expulsion will be carried out according to plan: *six thousand people every day.*

Every person is permitted to take five to ten kilograms of belongings and valuables. The responsibility for the execution of the decree is delegated to the Judenrat and the Jewish police, by order of the SS.[27] Exempt will be the people employed by the authorities—the Jewish police, the Judenrat, and hospital employees, as well as all those working in workshops for the Germans.[28]

I stood in the crowd and read the notice again and again. I didn't get the full meaning. People were arguing as though they had gone crazy, trying to understand how many will be expelled. All the inhabitants of the ghetto are out in the streets, asking each other, trying to grasp the significance of the orders.

People walk around at their wits' end, as though they had gone mad. They wander about in the streets, searching for a way out. In the meantime,

---

[27] *Judenrat*—Jewish councils of elders pressed by the Germans into administrative service in the ghettos.
[28] *Workshops for the Germans*—German industrialists with German army contracts set up workshops, exploiting the slave labor of the ghetto Jews.

the managers of the workshops, the workshops working for the Germans, are issuing new work cards. These become a matter of life and death. Whoever has protection—acquaintances close to the workshop managers—have a chance to buy such a document for money and jewels.

On that same day, they descended on our street and began to pull people out of their apartments by force. In the evening, I returned to the apartment with my father, and we only found a few of our neighbors. The building looked as though there had been a pogrom. The neighbors told us that they had given the Jewish policemen money and jewels, and in return, they were allowed to stay at home. The others were pushed onto carts and taken to assembly points. During the first days they also took the poor people lying about in the streets and patients in hospitals. Only those in hiding remained in the houses.

The Germans also published a declaration that all those who come on their own to the Umschlagplatz would get three kilograms of bread and one kilogram of jam.[29] Quite a lot of people gave in, as they had no strength left.

Distribution of the Leaflets

At six o'clock in the evening, after working hours, I reported in the attic of one of the youth movement houses, trembling all over with excitement. We gathered there, about ten boys and girls; no one knew why we had been summoned. When our leader Merdek arrived, I calmed down. I loved and admired him.

He brought many printed leaflets, signed by the Jewish Fighters Organization.[30] They warned the Jews to avoid being sent away at all costs—by escaping, by jumping from the railway coaches—for the destination is death, not a camp to live in. 'The Nazi beasts want to exterminate all European Jews. That is the bitter truth. Do not give in! Fight them in any way you can!'

*

---

[29] *Umschlagplatz*–the assembly point at the railway station in Warsaw, for deportation.
[30] *Jewish Fighting Organization*–the Jewish resistance fighters (Zydowska Organizacja Bojowa, or ZOB), founded in the summer of 1942 in the Warsaw Ghetto. Led by twenty-four-year-old Mordechai Anielewicz, who died in action; 'Our slogan must be: All are ready to die as human beings.'

In the aktions of the summer of 1942, Aliza lost many of the teenage friends in her youth movement group.

An intense feeling of being orphaned engulfed me. It was maybe the first time in my life that I mourned deeply, a feeling I shall apparently have to cope with all my life. I was in despair, a state of apathy, feeling helpless. I'll never see them again, never, ever. By what right am I still here? How am I better than they are?

I have no words to describe all the blockades, the hardships and wandering from place to place, the lack of food, the sanitary conditions, the nights in cellars on the damp floor, the suffering dulling the senses and leading to apathy in the face of the death of others. At that time, we lived like animals, fighting for our lives by means of a primeval urge for survival. This existential urge made us act instinctively. We had shed almost all the veneer of civilization, driven to flee by fear; but defeat in this battle came closer with every passing day…

*

Rumors began to circulate of a camp called Treblinka 100 kilometers northeast of Warsaw.

Most of the other members were pessimistic. They ceased to believe that it was possible to survive and began to prepare mentally for death. Black jokes hung in the air. A few called for vengeance and resistance immediately, but the older members persuaded the others to wait and consolidate the fighting organization that was being set up. This was veiled in great secrecy.

Again we distributed leaflets; the name *TREBLINKA* spread quickly.

*

July 16, 2013/Treblinka Memorial

We are in Warsaw now, my study group of 26 teachers of the Holocaust and our scholar-leaders Elaine and Stephen, and our wonderful guides.

We are booked into the top digs in the town. In fact, our hotel, the Bristol, is right next door to the Presidential Palace. This hotel was of course occupied by the Germans during the war, indeed mentioned in Leon Uris's classic *Mila 18*. We go out occasionally at night, to purge some of the madness that, if you are not careful, on a study tour like this can begin to accumulate like a toxin in the soul. Light, refreshing conversation. Good Polish beer. And yes, laughter with fellow travelers, taking in the sights and sounds of a lively and resurgent Warsaw. There are many important places to visit, but little of the prewar Warsaw remains. We tour Jewish Warsaw and finally the remnants of the ghetto wall, and also the Umschlagplatz, the assembly point where upwards of 10,000 a day were forced to wait in the sun; it is here where the mass deportations to Treblinka took place.

Warsaw Umschlagplatz, July 2013. Source: Author.

And today we are bussed to Treblinka, about 50 miles northeast. The primary roads turn onto secondary roads. Towns become villages, villages become hamlets as we make the final approach on tertiary roads that are dirt. But now, there are railroad tracks that we cross, and then follow.

Treblinka I was a forced labor camp. Soon enough, orders came down to construct Treblinka II, a full-blown killing center authorized, like Sobibor and Belzec, within the parameters of Aktion Reinhard. The signage in English refers to it as the 'Extermination Camp,' like human beings were pests or vermin. Of course, to the perpetrators they were, and though they communicated with carefully camouflaged euphemisms ('special treatment,' 'final solution'), it still feels like we are using the language of the murderers. Most of the Warsaw Ghetto occupants were murdered here, including, again, relatives of survivors I am close to.

When we arrive here, we go to a tiny museum where our guide Waclaw gives us the layout of the camp, overlooking a huge scale model, complete with the SS guard vegetable garden in the front. The trains would roll in like clockwork, at mostly 'regular' times, normal working hours; eight to one, break for lunch, then another transport to be processed. The morning group often waited overnight, and given the heavy rail traffic prioritized for the German Army, it sometimes took days to travel the relatively short distance to Treblinka.

The deception reaches its height at Treblinka. There is a false station front complete with a large clock and a suspended station sign—TREBLINKA—in capital letters. The barbed wire double fence is cloaked in trees, some branches even woven into the fence itself. New arrivals in transports of up to seven thousand, though sometimes just twenty railcars at a time, are uncoupled and shifted forward for 'processing.' The victims are sometimes greeted with a short speech by the camp commander, and then are directed to step down and disembark, to hand over all valuables, as they are at a 'transit center.'

They undress in segregated areas, and are then forced to run naked down the 'tube'—a camouflaged fenced-in path that led to the gas chambers. They are beaten by SS men and specially trained Ukrainian guards. The clothes are searched by the members of the sondercommando and sorted, to be shipped back for reuse in the war economy of the Reich.[31]

We move on to the site of the gas chambers. Even the 'bath house' has a Star of David, a Hebrew inscription that reads, '*This is the gate through which the righteous pass.*' Once inside, the doors are sealed, and a captured Soviet T-34 tank engine is started, pumping choking carbon monoxide into the chamber.

After a quarter-hour, the people would be dead. Bodies would then be pulled out and cavities searched for gold or other valuables. The disposal of the corpses evolved, almost as a science, at some of these centers. Buried at first, near the end of the camp's existence Himmler ordered that bodies be exhumed and cremated, to destroy the evidence of their crimes. Iron railroad rails would be set up and huge pyres would be created. Ashes were scattered, mixed in with the sandy earth, and plowed over. Treblinka was so far off the beaten path and so well hidden that for years the general public, outside of the locals, had no knowledge of it. It was

---

[31] *sondercommando*– unit of Jewish prisoners whose job was to dispose of the remains of the victims.

pretty much gone by the time Soviet troops overran the area in late July 1944.

Between July 1942 and November 1943, probably near 900,000 people were murdered here. But a little-known part of the story focuses on the uprising that led to the camp's demise, documented in narrative style in Jean-François Steiner's 1966 book *Treblinka*. Under the noses of the SS and Ukrainians, a secret revolt manifested among the slave laborers. On August 2, 1943, six hundred attacked the guards, burned parts of the camp, and about half of them managed to escape into the forest. Most did not survive, but a few dozen did.

Memorial at Treblinka. July 2013. Source: Author.

So we are at the scene of the crime, educators from across the USA, sharing this special bond, only 70 years later. Jagged upright memorial stones, 1,700 of them, emerge out of the landscape—one for each shtetl, town, and city purged of its Jewish population in Poland during the Holocaust.

Talli says, in between the tears that trickle down her face, 'I feel such a presence here.' I feel it with her.

Alan knows. A widower, he has become close to many on this trip—it is the presence of absence. 'Treblinka manifests the presence of absence, and the absence of presence.'

We gather at the site of the gas chambers. Mindy is reading her poem. Talli is crying. Beryl shares a special story. Back on the bus, Elaine cups my face with her hands when I ask her if there is anything I can do for her; her eyes are overflowing with an anguish she must feel every time she comes here, but also a special kind of love for us as teachers, as witnesses. Her parents were survivors, and as an educator she's led hundreds of teachers on this journey, but today is just as hard as the rest, maybe more so as time slips by. After the prayer for the dead, I go to the perimeter by myself, to wander along the vanished fence line. It's not a huge place. It only had one purpose.

We are here for a couple of hours, and our group is alone, or so it appears. The wind sings and the pines sway with the presence of the dead.

I try to capture my thoughts and write in my journal on the bus ride back from Treblinka to Warsaw. My handwriting is nearly illegible due to the poor bumpy roads, underscoring the remoteness of this place where nine-tenths of a million people were murdered, burned, and plowed under the earth.

*

The Cauldron

Aliza Melamed Vitis-Shomron

The 'kociol' ('cauldron') began on the 6th of September, 1942. In the evening policemen went from house to house, from workshop to workshop, and ordered all the Jews to report the next morning at ten next to the workshops where they were registered. By then all must be in this small area enclosed on all sides by ropes, secured by the Germans.

What's happening? Family members are debating: Should we go, or hide in the hiding place we've prepared? If we don't go and they find us, the order is to kill anyone on the spot. And if we do go, maybe there will be some kind of selection and some of the residents of the ghetto will survive…

Father and Mother decided to go. My parents were promised a worker's permit by the large shop of the German industrialist Töbens.

We walk with our usual backpacks to Lesno Street and join the line of thousands of fortunate people belonging to those workshops. The weather is hotter than usual, stifling summer heat, and we are wearing everything we were able to put on. Of course, one dress on top of another and a winter coat as well, for who knows where they'll take us from here. Each one of us is afraid, but also believes that he'll get through this selection.

I look at my mother, a young, beautiful woman, but her hair has gone white and her face is haggard. I have scissors in my backpack and I suggest that I'll cut her hair short, to make her look younger. Father, a young man, very thin, his face is pale and drawn. He feels the responsibility, he is anxious about his family; my dear father, unable to help his children, me and my sister, aged nine, but looking much younger. Her hair is fair—she doesn't look Jewish. She is clutching her mother, she cannot exist without her. She believes in Mother and Mother's ability to save her.

I feel terribly hot and thirsty. We are approaching the line forming in front of the German manager. Next to him stands the Jewish manager of the plant, and he whispers to the German, telling him to whom to give the worker's permit. Father and Mother receive the worker's permit; my sister and I, of course, do not. The endless procession is approaching its destination, on order by the Germans. We are already in Mila Street. Now we are pushed from the lines of the Töbens factory people, pushed into the crowd; we hold onto each other with all our strength.

God! We mustn't get lost among the thousands of people, sweating like us, totally exhausted by the tension, the heat, and the thirst. The silent question is reflected in their eyes: What do they mean to do with us here, in this cage? In this human 'cauldron?' Why did they concentrate tens of thousands of people here?

The commotion in the street increased. The Töbens workshop people were called to stand in lines, to go through the selection process, and then return home. The heat got worse. I threw my winter coat on a pile of things lying in a corner. I went with my family.

And now we are at the large wooden gate, built across the street. I go with my father as though in a dream. He is holding the worker's permit in front of him. Two rows of Germans stand in front of us. Suddenly I hear a voice, asking in German:

'Deine Tochter? Ist sie auch eine Arbeiterin?' 'Your daughter? Also a worker?' 'Yes,' Father answers. A hand motions us to turn back and the same hand takes the worker's permit from my father. Mother feels instinctively that something is happening to us and drops out of the line. Meanwhile the crazy procession moves on. I step aside, right up to the fence, and peep in to see what is happening on the other side—two rows of Germans, motioning to

the people to go right or left. I see a mother with a little girl. They separate the girl from the mother. The mother, to the right—the child, to the left. The girl holds her hands out to her mother, crying bitterly and calling her desperately. The mother stops, tries to free herself from the German policemen holding her, wants to run to the other side, to the weeping child. Blows rain on her from all sides and in the end they drag her to the right. Now there goes a father with a baby in his arms. The German grabs the child from the father's arms and throws it with all his strength on the ground. They beat the father with a rubber truncheon, until he loses his balance. The corpse of the baby is disposed of quickly.

Now I understood that they were taking all the children to be killed. What a miraculous instinct warned my mother so that she did not follow us, but moved back.

The evening fell. The gate of the selection was closed. They said that most of the people with worker's permits had already passed through. Yet tens of thousands still remained in the 'cauldron.' Mother went up to me: 'Liza, you are young…

fourteen… my darling, take the remaining worker's permit and try to get through tomorrow. Maybe people will help you and you'll survive.'

Stunned, I looked into Mother's face, grown so old these days, yet still full of boundless love and the willingness for self-sacrifice. 'Surely you understand,' she continued. 'We'll go together with Mirka. Why should you sacrifice yourself in vain…?' I look into Father's face, it expresses determination… I fall into my mother's arms.

'No! Don't say that! I won't go on my own!'

It was a great relief to be together again. We stopped talking about it. Now my mind started to work, to search for other solutions. I felt that my parents accepted the idea of death; they were quiet. I did not. I had come to my senses and began to think logically. I wondered why did the German during the selection send my sister and I back with my father into the crowd and not order us to the left, as they did with all those without a worker's permit? Does that mean that there will be another selection tomorrow, but this time not according to the work permit or any other document, but according to some other criteria? It was already evening then, and after us the selection was over for that day.

I try to explain to my parents that we can attempt to get past tomorrow as well, we must not despair. One of us suggests that we empty a backpack, put Mirka inside, and Father will carry her on his back. I'll hold the only worker's permit we have, as I am still in danger, and my parents will try to get past, declaring they work for Töbens and were late yesterday. We calmed down a little and looked for a place for the night. We entered an apartment, already full of people lying on the floor. The atmosphere was full of tension and the people were nervous, but we sensed wonderful, friendly warmth; they even made room for each other and for us too. *Last minute charity, fellowship of the condemned to death*, I pondered.

At five o'clock in the morning, after a sleepless night, we again stood in rows in the street, waiting for the selection. The people of the Schultz workshop passed by, holding out green numbers, attesting to their status. Many children were among them, going to their death. Suddenly, in one row, we saw Uncle Leon, Father's brother, his wife, and two sons, without their six-year-old daughter. Father asked: 'Where is Hanale?'

'We've hidden her in a hiding place with grandmother,' Uncle answered.

'Where is it? Tell us and we'll take Mirka there. Do you know that they are taking all the children?' said Father, agitated.

Aunt Irena answered: 'That's impossible, there isn't any more room there for anyone.' They strode on in wide rows in the direction of the wooden gate. We stood there, stunned.[32]

We had another significant meeting during that march to the selection in Mila Street. Fate again brought together two brothers—my father and his older brother David and his family. Fate had wished him to meet his other brother as well, before their final parting.

Uncle David was unshaven, emanating despair. Beside him walked Aunt Guta and their two daughters, ten-year-old Helenka and nine-year-old Milka. The two brothers embraced. Uncle

---

[32] *We stood there, stunned*-Hanale and the others hiding in the cellar were betrayed two days later by a man who was caught in the German roundup. In exchange for the lives of his wife and son, the cellar was revealed, and eight-year-old Hanale and the others were transported to Treblinka.

David said: 'There's nothing we can do, Shimek. That's the end for us.' They had no work identity card; they went along with their little daughters; they went with them to the end. There was nothing to say to each other. We were also going into the unknown. I looked at the little girls. My uncle's daughters had blue eyes, so light blue. Did they understand what awaited them?

Father's backpack was heavy for him. He made a hole so Mirka could breathe, and through it he occasionally gave her water to drink from a bottle. I supported the precious backpack from below. How can the poor child sit there, with her legs folded under her, her back bent tightly, without air? Will she be able to remain like that? And what if they beat Father with a whip, as they often do, and Mirka is hit and cries out? And anyway, how much chance do we have?

We agreed that I'd go first and Father would follow me. If he sees that they order me to go to the left, to those condemned to death, he'll go there too, and Mother will follow him. But what will happen if I get through and they don't?

My head is throbbing; it's hot. I must remain calm. Mother comes close to me and whispers in my ear. I feel her hot breath. She kisses me, she gives me strength.

Now it is the turn of the rest of the people belonging to the Töbens workshops, left over from yesterday. Suddenly, the people in front of us draw back, and we are facing the gate. Father pushes me to go first; I hold the worker's permit firmly in front of me and go straight to the right, pushing aside the rubber truncheon in my way. I turn around. Father follows me with the heavy backpack. Mother, where is she? And then I see her, head held high. Walking erect in a dignified way, she follows Father. We've made it!

A miracle! The people in front of us drew back because they began to take everyone to the left, and yet we passed. We stood in a long row with the other fortunate people and watched what was going on: There were no more workshop people. The Germans let us go to the right for no particular reason. They took others to the left according to some blind game, according to rules known only to them!

At noon, exhausted, we begin to move in a long procession back to the ghetto. It is hot, terribly hot; we are covered with sweat and very thirsty. Mirka peeps out of the backpack; people are surprised that a whole family was able to pass. Most of them have remained alone.

We are escorted by Jewish policemen. They are also tired and worn out. In the streets, corpses are lying about, of people who were discovered in hiding places and did not go to the 'cauldron.' The roads are strewn with household utensils, clothes, cutlery, undone quilts—the ghetto streets, brimming with life only a few days ago, are deserted. A deathly silence permeates everything. Only the open windows bang in the wind, and belongings bereft of their owners lie around; the blood of the unfortunate people, lying on the sidewalks—only the stillness is calling for revenge. Everything cries out for vengeance! We drag our feet in silence, not as though we had been set free, but like slaves granted a respite. A thought reverberates in my head: *why not me?* We returned to our street, to the houses allotted to the Töbens workers.

*

In the course of time, I found out the extent of the catastrophe. The selection and the search for people hiding in the ghetto lasted four days. The first stage of the extermination of the Warsaw Jews was over. During those days they took more than a hundred thousand people, among them almost all the children in the ghetto. The ghetto was now *kinderrein*—'unpolluted by children.' At the end of the great 'aktion,' on September 12, 1942, only about 50,000 Jews out of a population of over 300,000 remained alive.[29]

As 1943 dawned, the SS returned to the ghetto for another major deportation. They encountered the first armed resistance from the ghetto fighters and beat a hasty retreat, leaving behind wounded and weapons, and calling off the operation. For the next three months, the ghetto fighters organized and prepared for the final struggle. On the eve of Passover, April 19, the Germans returned again, this time with the aim of liquidating the ghetto once and for all, in time for Hitler's birthday on the 20th. By then, there were between 300-350 active fighters; the young were now the real leaders of the ghetto, having decided not between life and death, but rather, how to die.[33] *Aliza recorded her observations of the preparations for the final battle they all knew was coming.*

Spring, 1943

As spring approached, the atmosphere in the reduced ghetto changed. We waited for the final 'aktion,' for the final extermination of the Jews of Warsaw. People began to build bunkers. Experts turned up, engineers who built bunkers with electric light, in wells and toilets. Most of the bunkers were dug in cellars. There were various ways to enter the bunkers from the ground floor: by raising a cover in the kitchen stove or through an opening in the large stove attached to the wall, or in many other strange ways, according to the fertile imagination of the builders. The ghetto was preparing for a struggle.

*

March passed, and April came. Talk about the approaching final liquidation of the ghetto

---

[33] *By then, there were between 300-350 fighters-* Bauer, Yehuda. *'Current Issues in Holocaust Education and Research: The Unprecedentedness of the Holocaust in an Age of Genocide.'* Lecture notes, International School for Holocaust Studies at Yad Vashem, Jerusalem, Israel. July 21, 2016.

intensified. The ghetto was fully aware of it and prepared. It was the calm before the storm, suffused with energy and tension. Frequent shots near the ghetto and sudden evening searches by the SS command cars heralded what was to come. Sending off the people working for Töbens and Schultz factory workshops to Poniatow and Travniki caused apprehension, even though they had gone of their own free will.[34] If they are sending out the workers, what will happen to all the rest? The companies of the SS General Globocnik, in charge of extermination, again arrived in Warsaw.[35]

*

The only possibility left is to escape to the Aryan side, to dress up as a Pole and look for acquaintances or people willing to hide Jews in exchange for money. For a few thousand zloty, one could get a Polish birth certificate and a ration card. People handed over their children to Christian clerics, to monasteries, and to peasants in the villages. Sacks

---

[34] *Poniatow and Travniki*– forced–labor camps for Jews in Lublin District near the concentration camp Majdanek.
[35] *SS General Globocnik* –SS and police leader who directed Operation Reinhard between autumn 1941 and summer 1943.

were thrown over the walls daily and openly, at least on our side. People paid bribes to the foremen of the work crews to be able to join them going out to work on the Aryan side. Some of them did not look Jewish and were lucky enough to find 'good' Poles. Women dyed and oxidized their hair, and created curls by rolling their hair in pieces of paper, to look like blonde gentile girls. But they could not change the color of their eyes, or their dejected and pallid look. A Jew could also be picked out by his hesitant walk, his bent back, and his eyes constantly darting around him. We were so preoccupied by our aspiration to look like 'goyim' that we examined ourselves and others: Does that man look like a Jew? Will they recognize him in the street?

Of course, a new profession cropped up among the simple Polish people, with many demanding a bribe, or being paid to be an informer, a blackmailer. We were deeply disappointed; we thought that as witnesses of our tragedy, our compatriots, sharing the same language and culture, would hold out a hand to save us. But it did not happen. A few of them hid Jews for large sums of money;

these were mostly people connected to socialist activities and the left-wing parties. Many devout Christians and religious scholars did so without taking money, out of true nobility of spirit. Many others, from among the simple folk, made a living by informing on Jews to the Gestapo, and collaborated willingly out of pure antisemitism. They walked around in the streets close to the ghetto, spied by the gates and the places where Jews worked on the Aryan side, and looked for victims. Thousands made a living in this way.

*

The state of our family grew worse. We began to suffer from hunger. There were no clothes left to sell, we lived on the food we had received in the workshop, distributed by the Germans.

*

Aliza's family decided to split up to increase chances of survival. Her more 'Aryan-looking' mother and younger sister, with a great deal of bribery, subterfuge, and nerves of steel, went into hiding on the Aryan side. Her father decided to take the chance and volunteer to go to the work camp near Lublin. Aliza herself wanted to stay and fight in the ghetto, but now only fourteen, she was deemed too young and was directed by the leadership of the resistance to make her way to the Aryan side as well, to live to tell the story.

Leaving the Warsaw Ghetto

We stood at the entrance of the house. Father was to leave me there and go off. He was pale and had a tormented look. He could not move. He hugged me, kissed me, and went off. He came back a moment later, and we embraced again. I did not cry. I clung to him. Again he left. No, I saw him come back to me once more. I felt I wanted him to leave; I couldn't bear it any longer.

'Daddy, goodbye, see you again. You'd better go!'

One more hug, and he left.

Left altogether.

A long time has passed since I saw him disappearing into the distance, turning again and again to look at me. I was naïve enough to believe we would see each other in a week's time. I did not know, nor did Father, that at that very moment the order to surround the ghetto before the final liquidation was already in the works.

*

July 15, 2013/Majdanek

At each new authentic site, where these unspeakable horrors were perpetrated, some kind of invisible hand pushes me just a little bit harder. It's tough to explain. But this evening, as I write into the early hours on the laptop from my bed in the splendid Grand Hotel, perhaps Lublin's most celebrated and storied, I am troubled. We teachers are being handled with the finest accommodations, something which teachers are rarely afforded. My roommate Tim and I appreciate this, and talk about it when the lights go down, lying in the dark. We bounce theories and ideas off each other about what we have witnessed during the day, trying to process what we have experienced. Yet I fall asleep fitfully, for outside of our room not so long ago, Nazi jackboots echoed on the staircases.

Lublin, for centuries an important center of Jewish life and culture in Europe, became the seat of SS power in this part of the Generalgouvernement, that large area in Poland that had not been annexed directly to Germany, German East Prussia, or after 1941, the German-occupied USSR. The month after the invasion of the Soviet Union,

Himmler ordered the construction of a new concentration camp on the outskirts of Lublin. The original purpose of the camp, to be known as Majdanek (pronounced 'My-don-ek'), was to provide forced labor for the construction of SS and administrative centers in the planned eastern territories.

Majdanek, July 2013. Source: Author

Majdanek holds a central role in the administration of Operation Reinhard, the code name for the plan for the physical annihilation of the two million Jews still residing in the Generalgouvernement. Named for Reinhard Heydrich, who was assassinated six months after presiding over the Wannsee Conference, it took planning and it took deliberation. Within this framework, Majdanek primarily served to concentrate Jews whom the Germans spared temporarily for forced labor. It occasionally functioned as a killing site to murder victims who could not be killed at the Operation Reinhard killing centers: Belzec, Sobibor, and Treblinka II. It also contained a storage depot for property and valuables taken from the Jewish victims at the killing centers. And like other concentration camps in the Reich, Majdanek also served as a killing site for targeted groups of individuals, including members of the Polish resistance, hostages taken from the Security Police prison in Lublin, and prisoners in the camp itself who were deemed no longer capable of work.[30]

To witness Majdanek is to see the first concentration camp to be captured when it was overrun relatively intact by the Red Army in July of 1944. All of the evidence is here; buildings intact, stuffed with original artifacts that were left here. Himmler must have been angry about that. The barracks here are the original intact wooden shacks. Do you know how a sound, or a smell, can instantaneously trigger a memory long buried? These buildings reek; I know that heavy gasoline-like smell. My late father is before my teenage eyes on a hot July day like today, in his white T-shirt, layering on this thick petroleum-based wood preservative with his paintbrush at our hunting shack in the Adirondacks, before the version he favored was banned for public use. The authentic guard towers menace like outer space creatures from The War of the Worlds. On top of that, the bizarre science fiction 'unreality' of the place is enhanced by the Soviet memorial in the far-off distance, which resembles a flying saucer hovering over an unknown object.

Did you know that an undestroyed gas chamber as well as crematorium ovens still exist at this site? So why not see it? Go in it? The intact gas chamber building is still labeled outside as 'Bath and Disinfection I.' I enter. Low ceiling. Dark. Concrete floors with gutter channels. Sinks.

Pushing a bit deeper into this claustrophobic 'assembly line,' I feel a deepening pressure in my chest—I don't like it here. Another doorway beckons, summoning me forth into a small room with showerheads above—all connected, all so orderly.

Majdanek, July 2013. Gas chamber I. Source: Author.

I'm trailing behind the group now. To continue moving forward with the group will bring me to the gas chamber; I turn around and my feet carry me back through the entrance, and I exit this wooden building. I'm just not going there; I wait outside. I am conscious of a pull to witness, but today I am just not going to go in.

The next building is the storehouse for clothing and other personal items taken from the Jews of the combined killing centers.

Walking in here you are overpowered again by the nauseating smell of the creosote, and then your eyes try to take it all in—row upon row of piles of shoes, all behind chicken-wire cages holding them back from spilling at your feet. Leather, different colors, different materials and designs; men's, and women's, and children's shoes of all sizes and shapes, and all now taking on the brownish hue that channels the temporal spectrum of the passage of time. Mountains of shoes, voiceless yet vociferous messengers from the past that scream out to reclaim lost dignity—***Remember Us***.

Majdanek, July 2013. Shoes and lost dignity. Credit: Alan Bush.

We exit the building. Two young Polish women with a stroller casually pass us, chatting—they are cutting through Majdanek to take a shortcut to the Catholic cemetery on the outside of the camp memorial complex. The irony is not lost on the group.

And it is going to get a hell of a lot more ironic in the next 20 minutes. In the barracks area, we have a stop and a discussion; we move on to the Soviet memorial, that futuristic hovercraft, and the crematorium. The crematorium is intact, too. Again I hang back. Instead, I go over and check out a memorial stone with a plaque near the steps to the Soviet memorial. I note the trench-like undulating terrain behind the memorial stone. I read what happened at this spot, and I think I need to sit down.

Nervous about the recent uprisings at Treblinka, Sobibor, the Warsaw and Vilna ghettos, and elsewhere, the SS chief Himmler ordered the murder of the Jewish slave laborers in and around the camp, including the camp at Poniatow.

Code named 'Aktion Erntefest' (Operation Harvest Festival), the SS and police auxiliaries shot them in the ditches I am standing before; they played loud music through loudspeakers to drown out the noise, to disguise the gunshots for the folks back in the town. The shootings went on all day, the largest single-day and single-location massacre known to have occurred in the Holocaust.[31] Over 33,000 were murdered on that chilly Wednesday in November, 18,500 right here, right before me.[32]

I take a seat alone on the concrete steps in front of a memorial stone, right in front of the execution ditches. I have my journal out, but I don't even know what to write, so I pretend to write, because I really do not want conversation right now.

When the group does trickle over to the steps of the Soviet memorial with the saucer-like dome, we ascend. Someone who noticed that I avoided the crematorium and gas chamber tour today asks if I am okay.

Yeah, I'm fine. Eighteen-thousand, five hundred. Murdered, shot right here in front of me. In one day. That is twenty times the population of our high school.

Now we are under the dome, that stupid-looking flying saucer. We are in it, looking down on a mound the size of a small house. And as the realization dawns, now comes the shock that nearly knocks me over, the high-tension electrical jolt that poor saps must feel when they realize they are suddenly in a very personal episode of *The Twilight Zone*—this dumb-looking saucer roof is covering something I instantly recognize—and I don't need a sign for this. As a trained avocational archaeologist, I have excavated this material more than a few times, though not the human type, or anywhere near this magnitude.

Majdanek, July 2013. Source: Author.

Calcified bone fragments, bone powder, and burned earth. Literally tons of it; I am looking at a mountain of burned bone. It's a giant urn, an open-air mausoleum—I am face-to-face with cremated human remains. Bleached white and gray from superheat.

How many thousands of human beings are in front of me? One of the most respected Holocaust scholars has suggested 50,000. A guess. There is a Catholic cemetery across the way, outside the gate. I suppose you could get an accurate count of the dead who lie there.

I don't know why, but I don't participate in the Kaddish here. I don't speak. I don't pocket a rock for a memorial memento today, either.

Today was like a bad dream day. And later I learn that Aliza Vitis-Shomron broke down leading a tour of high school kids on the very steps where I just had to sit. You see, her father had been one of those shot to death on that November day, as the music played.

And if there are any words to be spoken here in Majdanek, they would be outflanked and interrupted in some kind of twisted irony by the squeaking of the wheels of the baby stroller trespassing its way through the camp—yes, maybe a symbol of life in this monument to the dead, but more aptly a metaphor for the present, willful yet oblivious, dodging and darting the presence of the past.

*

Aliza Melamed Vitis-Shomron

The Warsaw Ghetto Uprising

He came in the evening. I look at my cousin Lazar [the former Jewish policeman whom I resented], a young man of twenty-eight; sunken eyes, a thin, pale face, eyebrows and his hair singed, his hands covered with blisters from burns. I am writing Lazar's story; maybe someone will find my diary.

Everything was ready for the Passover Seder, which was to begin the next day, on Monday, April 19. But on Sunday night, we heard a stamping of boots on the sidewalks. When my father-in-law went out to see what was going on, several neighbors rushed in, their faces pale: The Z.O.B. guards told us that the ghetto was surrounded.[36] On the roofs of the houses all-round the ghetto, we can see machine guns and suspicious movements around them. The clock struck midnight. So

---

[36] *ZOB*– Jewish Fighting Organization, the Jewish resistance fighters.

that's it. The last, final 'aktion' will probably start tomorrow morning.

We got ready quickly. Our hiding place was in the cellar. We had prepared two rooms under the cellar, with the entrance well-camouflaged. We had an opening for air, a well for water, and even electricity. In one room, there were personal belongings and food, in the other, wooden bunks to sleep on. We intended to survive for two or three months in this way; maybe the war will have ended by then. All the occupants of the house ran around, gathering their essential belongings. People were not afraid to go out into the street to visit their families and friends, to say goodbye.

In the morning, we heard dull sounds of firing and explosions. In another house, in Swentojerska Street 34, the Z.O.B. had their positions. People from the organization told us about a mine they had detonated when the Germans decided to penetrate into our area; about battles leaving ten Germans dead; about a 'peace delegation' of SS officers who came with a white flag asking for an armistice to pick up their wounded, and how they fired at them at once. The fighters were elated, exhausted—but looked happy.

The battle in most of the houses in that area lasted two days. They ran from house to house. The leader of the group was the commander Marek Edelman. Dozens of fighters took part in the battle; some of them were killed. They went out at night to try to make contact with their friends. They told us that the battle inside the ghetto was still going on, that the fighters had delayed the entry of the tanks and set fire to them with homemade Molotov bottles. They were stationed at windows and changed their positions by moving across the rooftops. We in the shelters decided to open fire only when they discovered us. We made up our minds to defend our families to the end, not let them take us to Treblinka.

Photo from the infamous Stroop Report, 'The Jewish Quarter of Warsaw is No More!' Credit: NARA.

On the third day, fighting also broke out in the area of the workshops of Töbens and Schultz. At the last moment many people preferred to move to the Poniatow camp. In the meantime, the Germans began to set fire to the houses. On the second day of the uprising, the fighters told us about fires in the ghetto. We sat in the crowded shelter, praying that they wouldn't get to us. We had expected the worst, but not fires. The people in the shelter said goodbye to each other. We were in despair, expecting certain death. We could already smell the smoke. Someone came from the neighboring house; people were fleeing from adjacent houses. There were no Germans around. After a night full of dread, just before dawn, we did hear German voices in the courtyard. They were calling to the Jews to come out at once, or else they'd burn us alive.

The artillery was constantly firing incendiary bombs. Whole blocks of houses were on fire. The shelter was not damaged, but the water stopped running. The electricity went out. The walls of the shelter became unbearably hot, smoke penetrated the cellar. We sat there, coughing, wrapped up in wet sheets. People wept, dragged themselves to the courtyard with the last vestige of strength. We had no choice, we would defend ourselves in the yard. The men cleared the opening and gave the order—'wrap yourselves up in sheets soaked in the remnants of water, lie in the middle of the courtyard, in the garden.'

The yard is full of people, smoke covers everything, the top floors are in flames, the fire is running wild without any interference, parts of walls are collapsing and falling into the yard. People lying on the ground are groaning with pain...

Suddenly, we hear German voices in the street. God! We thought it was all over, that they've left us here. What shall we do? Several Germans burst in through the gate...

Lazar was captured and beaten, but managed to escape deportation, and made it to his cousin's hiding place on the Aryan side.

I saw a different Lazar before me. He used to be arrogant, a show-off. The person sitting here now was thin, withdrawn; he stammered slightly when he spoke. We'll have to live together in that small room in the cellar. Who knows how long? Until this damned war is over?

Photo from the infamous Stroop Report, 'The Jewish Quarter of Warsaw is No More!'[37] Credit: NARA.

The Beginning of May, 1943

They say that the ghetto no longer exists. The wreckage of the houses is still standing; the piles of cinders still crackle, and at night, shadowy figures, seeking food and shelter, still move about in there. But the ghetto no longer exists; 500,000 people have gone up in smoke. And those still alive bleed

---

[37] *Stroop Report*-The Stroop Report was an official report prepared by SS General Jürgen Stroop for Himmler, detailing the suppression of the uprising in text and photographs. Only a few copies exist. The boy in this famous photo was the subject of a book by Dan Porat, who contacted the author because one of the four persons who thought they may have been the boy in the photo was a person liberated on the Train near Magdeburg (Tsvi Nussbaum). See Porat, Dan. *The Boy: A Holocaust Story*. New York: Hill & Wang, 2010.

inwardly; their deep wounds will never heal. And maybe there will be no one left when freedom comes? Why are human beings so cruel and evil? They speak about the future, about truth, about Man as proof of God's great wisdom, and it's all lies, lies!

I know there are also good people, but they are persecuted; society rejects them as weaklings. Why am I prevented from seeing the wonders of nature and the world, from breathing fresh air?

The Hotel Polski

After the liquidation of the ghetto, the situation for any Jew still alive was growing increasingly precarious. Rumor was circulated that at Warsaw's Hotel Polski, foreign certificates or even passports could be obtained at a price for a complicated exchange for German nationals or prisoners interned by Allied nations abroad. Many of these were papers from South American governments that had arrived after the great deportations had begun, and their original owners had been killed.[33] Additionally, any Jews holding legitimate foreign certificates began to consider the prospect of taking refuge at the hotel.

Reunited with her mother and sister, and hiding in the home of a devout Christian, Aliza now recorded another dilemma in her diary.

July 8, 1943

Today, Mother met Mr. Wosz upon his request. He told her some exciting news. Jews, hiding in various places on the Aryan side, are gathering in Hotel Polski. It is not clear who is organizing it, but it appears that the Germans have a certain number of permits to go abroad. They are selling them by means of Jewish middlemen, and for a large sum, it is possible to obtain a 'promesa'—an entry visa to a South American country. There are also 'certificates' to Palestine, and for these one can register for a smaller sum. All the people who register will be exchanged for German citizens, living in those countries, and until then, the Jews will be kept in camps for foreign nationals.

[But] what about Father?

July 11, 1943

Something very important has happened. We've decided to go to Hotel Polski. Uncle Leon and his family are already there. We are taking the risk of our own free will. Shall we get to Palestine? Who knows? If it were true, I would be happy. I am dreaming about that country, about freedom, studies… I am sure there are hard times ahead until then, but at least we'll finally be doing something! No longer sitting around doing nothing in these hiding places, in apartments belonging to good people, who, with all their kindness and courage, look at us anxiously, begging us silently—leave, leave soon!

The tragic part is that we have not been able to bring Father out![38] Leaving without Father, abandoning him there, that's terrible. What should we do?

What can we do?

*

July 12, 1943

We are already in the hotel. We parted, weeping, from young Mrs. Maria and thanked her from the bottom of our hearts. Maybe her savior, Jesus,

---

[38] *we have not been able to bring Father out*- a plan by the family to bribe a railway worker failed; the money was not returned.

will see her good deeds and reward her for saving a family belonging to our people.

There are many Jews here. They are all running about, excited and tense, talking loud. We have registered for a 'certificate' to Palestine, shared by 250 people. Uncle Leon has apparently paid for us. The excitement is tremendous: We are allowed to speak Yiddish, people are meeting acquaintances and friends, telling each other their experiences, and how they escaped from the ghetto. They say one transport left a week ago and we may leave tomorrow. Another transport will leave next week.

I listened to everything, and believed our luck. It may have been just childish.

*

July 13, 1943

We set out. We went on trucks to the railway station. We passed the walls of the burnt ghetto on our way. We were able to see the destruction and hear the deathly silence.

We traveled in silence. We all parted from the life we had led there, in the city of our birth. I also said goodbye to the ruins of burnt-out houses, the place where I had spent my childhood, a time never to return. I left my weeping soul among those ruins, still issuing a terrible smell, a huge graveyard of half a million of Poland's Jews. *Wait for the avengers, for the day of reckoning, you damned ruins!* Germany will never be able to atone for its responsibility for the death of hundreds of thousands of innocent people!

Farewell Warsaw, the city of joy and anguish, we shall never return! You stood uncaring when we cried to you for help in our despair. *I hate you, you let a third of your inhabitants die before your eyes, without a word of protest against that terrible injustice!*

The ghetto was lit from above by the bright summer sun, but darkness, the smell of burning, and stench of corpses reigned inside.

*

Most of the more than 2,500 Jews who had purchased passport papers of others murdered by the Germans were murdered themselves. On the day Aliza and her family departed on the route to the exchange camp at Bergen-Belsen, over 400 others were transported to a nearby prison to be shot.

Aliza Melamed Vitis-Shomron

Many years now have passed since I wrote those sad words of parting from the city of my birth. I always felt a powerful urge to revisit it, to see the ruins again with my own eyes, to connect again with the period of my life that had become so important to me, and maybe to find relief from that heavy burden! Throughout all those years I wanted to find out –I craved to hear and read—all I could about that final 'aktion' and the heroic uprising. It was only in 1983 that I went with my sister to Warsaw with the first delegation to participate in the official Remembrance Day held by the government of Poland in memory of its Jewish citizens. By now an elderly woman, I told my story to youngsters who were at the age I was when I experienced those events. I looked into their eyes: Do they grasp what happened here? Does our story touch them, are they capable of identifying with it, or maybe they find it repulsive, too strange and horrible?

In September 1943, the slow-moving bureaucratic machine of the SS Reich Main Security Office finally caught up with most of the South American certificate holders at Bergen-Belsen when it realized that most of these 'Hotel Polski Jews' were not the original passport owners. Of the entire group, only about 260 people survived; the rest were sent to Auschwitz.[34]

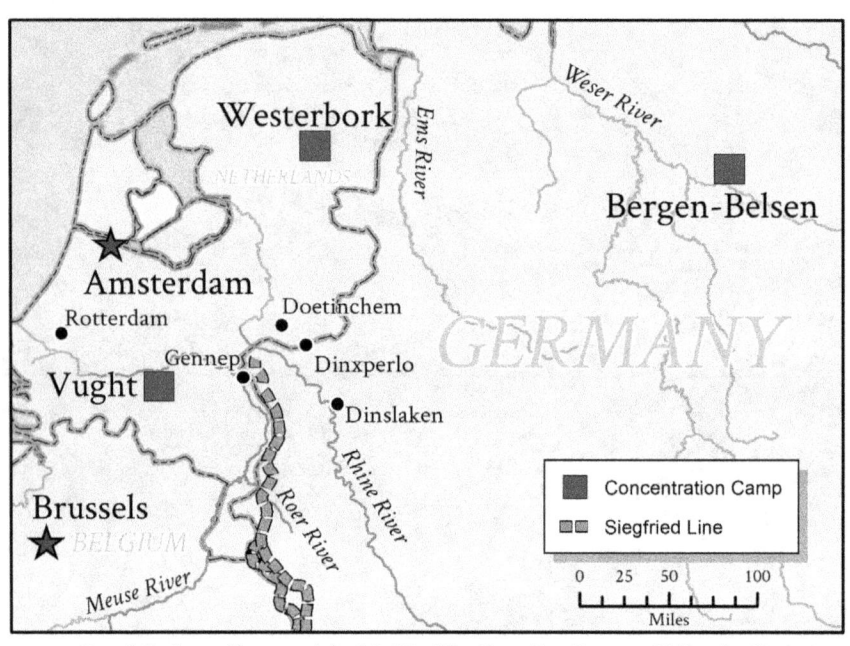

Fred Spiegel's world, 1940-45. Credit: Susan Winchell.

CHAPTER SIX

A Child in Holland

With the fall of Warsaw on September 28, 1939, the German blitzkrieg planners had completed their first task in Poland in all of four weeks. In accordance with the secret protocol, the Soviet Union swallowed up the coveted eastern half of Poland, which they would exploit and use to buffer themselves from the fascist threat, for the time being. As for Hitler, he could carry out his conquest of Western Europe, and then turn his armies eastward.

Perhaps to Hitler's surprise, World War II finally commenced with the British and French declarations of war against Germany on September 3. It now seemed the western democracies might fight, after all. The United States proclaimed its neutrality, but the president authorized moderate increases in the American armed forces; frighteningly, it had recently lagged behind Bulgaria as the 18th placeholder for the largest army in the world.[35]

For seven months the western front remained relatively quiet. In Britain the press began to dub it 'the phoney war.' For the tormented victims in Poland it was anything but, and reports trickled in to the rest of Europe about the savagery of the blitzkrieg and the early treatment of the Jews during wartime. In desperation, most European Jews had found their paths to move hopelessly blocked; the appeals for sanctuary went unheeded even as the blitzkrieg in the west began in earnest the following spring.[39] One by one western democracies

---

[39] *appeals for sanctuary went unheeded*-A highly noteworthy exception was the Kindertransport, a series of informal rescue efforts which brought nearly 10,000 Jewish children to Great Britain from Nazi Germany for a short period after Kristallnacht. Parents or guardians could not accompany the children; most of them would never see their parents again. Many of the

were rolled up on German terms; Denmark and Norway in April, and the Netherlands, Belgium, Luxembourg, and France in May and June of 1940. The United States, Canada, and Australia had formidable immigration barriers in place, and while the British had admitted 80,000 Jewish refugees, all of that essentially ended after the declaration of war.[36] British-controlled Palestine also began to turn back ships of Jewish immigrants, a policy they would continue all throughout the war and beyond, sticking to strict Jewish immigration quotas to appease the non-Jewish residents there. The doors slammed shut in a cascading crescendo of foreboding.

In Holland, however, Jews had generally enjoyed a level of secularization and equal rights following the ideals of the French Revolution and the establishment of the Kingdom of the Netherlands in 1814. While their integration into Dutch society, culture, and secular values was very well established, many still retained a Jewish identity. The German invasion of 1940, therefore, was an

---

children saved ultimately became citizens of Great Britain, Israel, the United States, Canada, and Australia. See USHMM article, 'Kindertransport, 1938–1940'.

unforeseen and unmitigated disaster for the Dutch community, and the 15,500 Jewish refugees from Germany that they harbored; there would also be the shock of neighbors turning upon neighbors in this terrible new world.[37]

After Kristallnacht in Germany, young Fred Spiegel had been delivered out of harm's way with his sister Edith to stay with relatives in Holland, as his mother tried to make other more permanent arrangements for the family. In the beginning, the children were happy with an aunt, uncle, and cousins. But soon the children could sense the danger returning all around them.

Fred 'Fritz' Spiegel

After Kristallnacht, November 9 and 10, 1938, my mother tried desperately to obtain visas for us to leave Europe. Nothing was available. The United States had closed its borders to immigration, especially German immigration. Palestine, which today is Israel, was a British Mandate.[40] The

---

[40] *British Mandate* –(1922–1948) Following the defeat of the Ottoman Empire in World War I, Great Britain was called upon to facilitate the governing of Palestine. As tensions between the local Arab population and Jewish

British Government had issued a 'White Paper,' an official government document stopping any further Jewish immigration into Palestine. However, in August of 1939, my mother obtained a visa as an au pair, a foreign maid, for England. Unfortunately, this visa did not allow her to take us with her. During World War I, Holland had been neutral, a policy it could presumably pursue in the event of another war in Europe; my mother thought we would be safe staying in Holland for the time being, until she could make arrangements for us to join her in England.

On the way to England, she decided to visit us for one week in Gennep. She was due to arrive on September 1, 1939. I was seven years old and had not seen my mother since November 1938, and so I was tremendously excited, looking forward to seeing her again. I had such a lot to tell her. When my mother arrived, I ran into her arms and cried. Then my uncle came, gently pulling me away. He urgently needed to speak to her for he had just heard the news on the radio that the German army

---

emigrants grew, the British severely restricted Jewish immigration right on the eve of World War II.

had invaded Poland. He tried to explain to my mother that it would be better to leave immediately, as otherwise he feared that there would be no more passenger ships to England. He believed that Europe was going to be at war after the British and French ultimatum expired on September 3, 1939. I was very disappointed and upset when my mother told me she had to leave within the hour. How could I tell her everything that had happened to me since I left home about my new friends and school in one hour?

After too short a time, I said goodbye to her again. Little did I know at the time that not only would I not see her for more than six years but also what would happen to us and the terrible times that lay ahead. I am sure she could never have imagined the terror we would experience before we would be reunited. My mother did manage to take the very last passenger ship from Holland to England on September 1, 1939. As she left, she promised that as soon as she was settled we would be reunited with her in England.

The German Invasion

May 10, 1940, was a day of infamy in Holland. The German army invaded without provocation because Holland had declared its neutrality in the event of a war in Europe. The official start of the war on September 3, 1939, had not affected us in Gennep. However, some trenches were dug around the school, and we had air raid drills in case of an attack.

The dawn of May 10 brought a beautiful, bright sunny morning, a typical Dutch spring morning. The day before I had done all my homework for school and had spent the evening playing with friends. But then I had woken up at night and heard some noise like airplanes in the sky. I did not pay much attention to this, almost immediately going back to sleep. The rays of the sun woke me up. I heard some strange and loud noises coming from the sky and also the street below. The sky was full of airplanes and some of them were flying quite low. I could see the German markings, including the swastika. I looked down from my second-floor bedroom to the cobblestone street running through the little town. German soldiers in full battle dress, helmets, rifles, and gas masks stood there with several tanks and trucks. Downstairs, I heard my aunt speaking German, and I heard a male voice answering, but it did not sound like my uncle. My sister and cousins were in the living room, looking out the window at the German army. I went to the kitchen and saw my aunt talking to a German soldier who was sitting at the kitchen table waiting for her to brew him some coffee. My uncle, however, was nowhere to be seen. Apparently this German soldier had knocked on our door early in the morning and asked to come in for a cup of coffee, as if this was the normal thing to do. Oddly, he had brought his own coffee to brew and refused to let my aunt take coffee from our pantry. He asked my aunt, 'How come you speak such flawless German?' She told him that she was originally from Germany but had come to Holland because she was Jewish, and it had become increasingly difficult for Jews to live in Germany. He said that was very true, but that he had no problem with the fact that she was Jewish and we should not be afraid—the German army would not harm us. Then he turned around and asked me my age. I told him, 'Eight years old.' He told me that he had a son my age. After this he explained that he was part of a motorcycle unit parked across the road. He asked me to look out of the window and let him know when his unit started to move. Even though this German soldier was very polite and civilized, I was hoping that his unit would move soon because I did not like him in the house. Because of Kristallnacht, I sensed things would be bad for us Jews now that the Germans had invaded Holland. A short while later, when the soldier had to leave, he said, 'Goodbye and good luck.' I have often wondered at his politeness, going as far as bringing his own coffee and wishing us well. My experience with German soldiers, with few exceptions, would be that, at best, they did not care, but usually they would be very brutal and uncivilized. For a child, these experiences were confusing; I was never sure what to expect from my encounters with German soldiers.

Gennep was under German control almost immediately. Because the Netherlands was supposed to be a neutral country, it had only a small army, and after five days the army surrendered.

Rotterdam had been bombed, with many civilian casualties, as a warning not to resist the invaders. At the Grebbe Line, a defensive line to protect the major northern cities, there had been heavy casualties on both sides. The Dutch government and the Queen fled to England after the commander-in-chief of the Dutch army warned them that he could no longer protect them, leaving instructions to government employees and the civil service who remained to cooperate with the Germans in order to make life easier for the local population. In Gennep, Dutch soldiers were surprised by the sudden and ferocious onslaught of the German Army. Many left their posts and, in order not to be captured and to fight again another day, took off their uniforms and put on civilian clothing borrowed from the local population. I remember seeing young men in ill-fitting street clothing standing around and staring helplessly at the German invaders. The Germans laughed at them when they saw them because they did look very strange; I have often wondered whether they suspected that these young men had been Dutch soldiers.

My own uncle had disappeared during the night. He went into hiding the day of the invasion because he knew that the Gestapo, the Nazi secret police, would be looking for him because he had been on their 'most wanted' list before he fled Germany. Sure enough, just three days after the invasion, there was a different kind of knock on the door. It was the Gestapo looking for my uncle. They searched the house for him. When they could not find him, they took my aunt with them to question her at Gestapo headquarters. My uncle managed to survive by always being a few steps ahead of the Gestapo and changing hiding places many times. My aunt was released by the Gestapo after they had beaten her, and once they realized that she really did not know where my uncle was.

On June 6, 1940, my grandfather, Louis Spiegel, who had been living with us, suddenly died. I remember being very upset and going to the funeral at the small Jewish cemetery. I had to say Kaddish, the Jewish prayer for the dead; I was the only male relative at the funeral, for Uncle Adolf had already gone into hiding to avoid capture by the Gestapo. I had difficulty saying the prayer because I was crying so much. Then my cousin Alice, eleven years old at the time, was sick again, only this time it seemed even more serious.

The Soldiers' Song

More than sixty years after the invasion, I can still hear the German soldiers sing their songs. The invasion and conquest of the Netherlands had been easy, relatively bloodless—all over in five days. The German soldiers were happy and content, hoping and dreaming that the war would soon be over and they could go home. Those first few weeks after the invasion, thousands of German soldiers were stationed in or near Gennep. I was eight years old, and to me, it seemed that the whole German army was encamped in and around Gennep. It was late spring and the days were long. We could hear them sing, especially in the evening when it was quiet. Of course, they sang in German, which I understood well. Somehow I remember part of one song, because it was always sung a lot towards the end of the evening: *'Lebe wohl mein Schatz, lebe wohl, lebe wohl, denn wir fahren gegen Engeland.'* "Be well my sweetheart, be well, be well, because we will be marching against England.' This would be repeated several times with much enthusiasm. As young kids do, we would approach the nearest encampment and watch and listen to the soldiers singing. Usually one of the soldiers would get up and give each of us a piece of chocolate or a candy.

Those first few weeks were like a honeymoon. The German occupiers treated the Dutch as 'favorite cousins.' Once England surrendered they thought everything would be fine and soon the war would be over. Life seemed almost normal except for the German troops, and even the Jews, especially the Dutch Jews, thought maybe our fears were exaggerated. I even remember one evening going with some friends to a German encampment, and while one of the soldiers was giving us some candy, one of the kids pointed at me and said, 'You know he's a Jew. Don't give him any candy.' The German soldier answered, 'Mind your own business,' and gave me an extra piece of candy.

After a few weeks, most of the soldiers left, not to march against England as their favorite song went, but to march east, to prepare to attack the

Soviet Union. We did not know this at the time. Other things also changed; the 'honeymoon' was over very quickly, especially for us Jews. I was very unhappy about the German invasion, and despite my curiosity, I did not like seeing all those German soldiers. Yet, despite all the traumas I suffered in the years to come, I often wondered what happened to them, so happy at that time. How many, if any, survived the war? It is difficult to understand that many later took part in the atrocities committed against not only the Jews but also the general population of Europe controlled by the Germans.

After the German invasion in May, and my grandfather's death in June, and also because my Aunt Martha and cousin Margot were very busy trying to take care of my cousin Alice, my sister and I were sent to our Uncle Max and Aunt Paula in Dinxperlo in the middle of June 1940. Alice died in July of 1940, just a few months before her twelfth birthday. After Alice's death, my uncle arranged for Aunt Martha and Margot to go into hiding.

*

Meanwhile, the Germans continued to add new anti-Jewish laws. Everybody in the Netherlands had to have an identity card, but ours had a big 'J' for Jood, or Jew, stamped on it. We could no longer shop in non-Jewish stores. Two houses down the road from us was the village bakery, where we had previously bought bread and rolls. Now, we had to do this surreptitiously through the back door early in the morning. In addition, we were not allowed to use public transportation except by special permit, we had to surrender our bicycles, we could no longer go to the cinema, and on park benches there were signs—'Jews and dogs not allowed.' Then on May 3, 1942, we had to start wearing the Jewish star, the six-pointed yellow star with the word 'Jood' (Jew) written on it. Jews could no longer go to the same school as non-Jews. Jewish teachers had been expelled before that because they did not want Jewish teachers to teach non-Jews. Dinxperlo had a small Jewish community with a synagogue, but it was too small to support a Jewish school. Therefore, we had to go to the nearby town Doetinchem, where a Jewish school was established for the town and the neighboring villages.

The Prins Family

When I was still traveling by bus to Doetinchem to the Jewish school, I had a strange and terrible experience on one of those trips in the early fall of 1942. I have never forgotten this bus ride.

On this particular morning, I arrived at the bus station and got on the bus. There sitting in the back of the bus was Mr. Prins, his wife, Bertha, and their three children, Philip, Caroline, and Jannie, each one sitting next to a policeman. Apparently at dawn the Gestapo and the local police had raided Villa Pol, where the Prins family lived. They had to leave their home immediately; they were not allowed to take anything with them or even to wash and dress properly. The police then decided to take them by local bus to Doetinchem. The ride was at least an hour because there were many stops and the bus went very slowly. I managed to sit in the seat just in front of Jannie. I knew the Prins family well because Villa Pol was opposite my uncle's house. I was friendly with Jannie, a few years older than I. I remember talking to her all the way to Doetinchem, and she kept reassuring me that all this was just a big mistake and that she and her family would be back soon once everything was straightened out. The policeman sitting next to her never said a word, but Jannie complained that she had not even been able to wash her face and put some makeup on. Upon arrival in Doetinchem they got off the bus after us, and I watched them slowly walk away towards the police station. I did say goodbye to Jannie and that I hoped to see her that evening or the next day back in Dinxperlo. But I never saw them again. A few days later some of their workers came to the Villa Pol to pack some clothes for the family, who by then were in Westerbork.

In contrast, on this same day, the family of Leopold Prins, a cousin of Mr. Prins, who also lived in Dinxperlo, was picked up and put in a truck. Then they were taken across the border into Germany to be interrogated before being sent to Westerbork and then later to Auschwitz. Apparently they had been planning to go into hiding but somebody in the village whom they trusted had betrayed them.

The events of that day will always remain with me, especially the memory of sitting on the seat in front of Jannie; she was trying to reassure me and probably herself that everything would be fine and that I could come and see her at home that evening or the next day. For over fifty years, I have wondered whether my memory of this event was correct, whether this incident really happened this way. Usually the police would come to Jewish houses or apartments and take them by trucks to an assembly point, and when they had a big enough transport, would send them by train, usually to Westerbork. So it is still a mystery to me what happened that day, why the Prins family had to endure this special kind of torture, to travel on a regularly scheduled bus full of regular passengers to their doom.

Jannie, her sister, Caroline, and their mother, Bertha, were killed in Auschwitz on October 26, 1942. Mr. Prins died in Neukirch on June 30, 1943. His son Philip died in Ludwigsdorf on January 1, 1944.

*

In April 1943, a new law went into effect that the provinces of the Netherlands had to be 'judenrein.'[41] Except for those few who managed to go into hiding, most of the Jewish population of Dinxperlo was sent to the slave labor/concentration camp Vught in the south of the Netherlands. From Vught, nearly everybody was sent to Westerbork and then on to the various concentration and death camps. Of those, only four survived. The Dinxperlo synagogue was destroyed during a bombardment, and no Jews live there today. A congregation of fifty to sixty members disappeared.

On April 10, 1943, Edith and I were forced to leave Dinxperlo. Together with my Uncle Max's family, we were sent to Vught. We were picked up early in the morning and taken by truck to the railroad station in Nijmegen. From there, we went the rest of the way to Vught by train. When we left Dinxperlo for Vught, most of the rest of the population of the village stood there and watched. Many of them were 'bystanders.' Although a few

---

[41] *judenrein*- Jew–free, or cleansed of Jews

by then were active in the resistance, they could have done very little to help us, except to hide us, which would have been too dangerous.

My sister was almost happy to leave the constant Allied bombardments. She had no idea what lay ahead.

The Missed Transport

We had arrived in Westerbork late Monday afternoon after about a six-hour train ride, and we were immediately separated, my cousin and I in one huge barrack, my sister elsewhere, and my uncle and aunt also in different barracks. Most people in our barrack had arrived together with us. Yet our first night in Westerbork was uncomfortable. Nobody was able to sleep much that night. The barracks were huge, noisy, and very crowded; each barrack held about 500 to 1,000 people. Bunks were stacked three high. Very early in the morning, the barrack leader started to read out the names of the people to be put on the train that day. As my name and my cousin Alfred's name was called, we walked towards the train, carrying the few belongings we were allowed to take with us. It was dawn and the walk to the train was very scary. Nearly everybody was crying, especially the little children. The people not going on that train were under total curfew and could neither leave their barracks nor look out of the few windows. The only people we saw were the German SS guards with their dogs, Dutch policemen, and the Jewish camp police, or Ordnungsdienst (OD). I saw nobody I knew, nor anyone from my family, except Alfred. When the OD started to push us on the train, I panicked. Everything was so crowded. Some people cried, but most went quietly onto the train. I screamed loudly, 'I don't want to go onto this train!' When Alfred heard me screaming, he also started to scream. This caught the attention of an SS guard who asked a Dutch policeman what the screaming was all about. He apparently answered, 'I think the children are afraid and do not want to go on the train.' The SS guard then immediately gave the order to take my cousin and me off that train. The same OD, who had been pushing us on, took us off, and we were put in a small room isolated from everybody else until after the train departed—without us.

I did not realize at the time that I had narrowly escaped death. As I found out years later, this was very unusual. There was always commotion when these trains left because nobody wanted to be crammed on the trains going to an unknown destination eastward. However, it was indeed a rare occasion when a German guard ordered a Jew to be taken off a train destined for the gas chambers. The Germans preferred that the Jews went quietly and orderly. Apparently my screaming did not fit in with their plans.

Years later, I also found out that nearly everybody who had arrived from Vught the day before was on this train and sent to the death camp Sobibor in Poland. There were no survivors. Between March and August 1943, about 35,000 Jews were transported from Westerbork to Sobibor. Only nineteen people are known to have survived.

Uncle Max and Aunt Paula had not been aware that we were almost deported. Immediately upon arrival in Westerbork, Uncle Max had applied for an exemption, not to be sent on one of those trains east. He had been a soldier in the German army in World War I, and for this, for the time being, he had received an exemption. He thought this would keep all of us safe from being deported. However, he soon realized, especially after what nearly happened to us, that his deferment would not apply to my sister and me because we were not his children. He felt it was his responsibility to try and save us. My uncle consulted with Kurt Schlesinger, the head of the Jewish council. Schlesinger suggested that my uncle put us on the so-called Weinreb deferment list. For a large amount of money paid to Weinreb, a German Jew living in the Netherlands, people were put on a special list of people who would not be put on those transports east. My uncle was ready to do this, even though it meant that it would cost him almost all the money he still had hidden with non-Jewish friends.

Weinreb had been highly recommended because he was able to pay off the Nazis to save himself, his family, and other people who were willing to pay. My uncle decided to go ahead, but somehow, at the last moment, changed his mind. He then decided to go and see the German SS Camp Kommandant, Albert Gemmeker, even though everybody, including Kurt Schlesinger, strongly advised him against it, as this was considered very dangerous and might cost him his life. But he saw Gemmeker and tried to convince him that my sister and I were British citizens and as proof he brought with him the Red Cross letters we had received from my mother who was living in England at that time. We were foreign nationals. I was never quite sure what transpired, whether we now had deferments as British citizens or if we were still on the Weinreb list.

About six weeks after this incident, my Uncle Max's exemption expired, as all exemptions and deferments eventually did in Westerbork. My uncle, aunt, and Alfred's names were on the list to be sent east to one of those 'work or resettlement' camps. I spoke to my cousin before he left and I said to him, 'I will see you soon.' I believed that my sister and I would probably follow them, being sent on a later transport. Alfred seemed to have a premonition that this would not happen. He was crying and said, 'I don't think so.' Unfortunately he was right; as I found out after the war, they were deported to Sobibor and killed in the gas chambers on July 2, 1943.

Even though he would never know, my uncle's maneuvering had succeeded in keeping us off those trains to Sobibor and Auschwitz and allowed us to stay in Westerbork. We could remain in Westerbork for the time being, as we apparently were considered 'Foreign Nationals' because our mother was living in Leeds, England, as an au pair, a foreign maid. We would now live in the orphanage of Transit Camp Westerbork, which was still under the jurisdiction of Kommandant Gemmeker.

*

The Orphanage

The orphanage in Westerbork was established in 1939, by Mr. Jehoshua (Otto) Birnbaum, an educator from Berlin with six children of his own. By the time my sister and I came to the orphanage it was crowded with orphans. Sometimes the Gruene Polizei, police in green uniform, in the bigger cities, especially in Amsterdam, would pick up Jewish children on their way to or from schools, without their parents! Also many times children in hiding with non-Jewish families were betrayed and these too would arrive in Westerbork without parents.

Mr. Birnbaum was allowed to take children up to the age of fifteen. A lot of very young children lived in the orphanage. Mr. Birnbaum had access to the lists being prepared every week for deportation east because the Jewish Camp Council prepared these lists. If he found the name of any of 'his' children on the lists, he would run to the German Kommandant Gemmeker and plead with him not to deport the children. Birnbaum would tell Gemmeker that the children were much too young to go to a work or resettlement camp in the east and that he would take care of them. So, for a while, the kommandant relented and took the children off the lists. The Jewish Camp Council created special exemption lists for the children; they were put on the so-called Palestine lists, Jews selected for possible exchange with the British for German nationals. If chosen, these Jews would later immigrate to Palestine.

This was the situation in the orphanage, and it continued for several months. It was a safe haven for us; I got used to the life there. We received a little more food than the rest of the camp, and we were allowed to receive parcels from the outside. We received non-perishable food parcels from Dinxperlo, from Mimi Otten, who was working for the resistance. My uncle had given her money before we were deported to send the food to us. We shared our parcels with the other children. Also many prominent professors, teachers, and musicians came to help in the orphanage, before they were themselves deported. The one I remember best was Mrs. Clara Asscher Pinkhof, a well-known Jewish Dutch author of children's books. She was the widow of the rabbi of Groningen and became an author after his death. I remember her especially well because she was a good storyteller.

Then came November 16, 1943. The camp was very crowded, with about 25,000 people. It was Monday evening and the train stood ready to go east the next morning. About 2,500 Jews were supposed to be deported that day. However, nearly everybody in the camp had some sort of exemption. So this time there were not enough people to fill the train. The head of the Jewish council, Kurt Schlesinger, went to Gemmeker and told him,

'There are not enough people without exemptions.' Then the kommandant canceled all exemptions, including most Palestine lists. This meant that nearly all the children of the orphanage were put on the deportation lists, despite Mr. Birnbaum's efforts. Most of the children in the orphanage, many of whom were very young, went on this train to Auschwitz and to the gas chambers. Many people working in the orphanage, including Mr. Birnbaum, volunteered to go with the children, even though they were not on the deportation list; they wanted to take care of the children once they had arrived at these resettlement or work camps. The kommandant would not allow Mr. Birnbaum to accompany the children. So he stayed behind, as did Edith and I, among the few other children who were left. But my sister and I were saved, I assume, because my uncle, at the last moment, had changed his mind, as noted earlier, and had decided not to put us on that Weinreb list, but instead to stress the fact that our mother was in England.

This was a terrible night for all of us. Many of the children were very young, and all of us were unhappy. We did not know what their fate would be. In the morning, the train left with most of the children packed into cattle wagons. Those of us left behind felt very sad, as we had lost most of our friends. Despite the circumstances, we had been like one big family. Upon arrival in Auschwitz, all the children, with the people accompanying them, were sent to the gas chambers. There were no known survivors.

*

Exchange Camp

After November 16, 1943, there was a short pause in deportations to the east. No transports left until January 11, 1944, when the first transport from Westerbork went to Bergen-Belsen. After eight months in Westerbork, Edith and I were placed on this transport. While we were walking towards the train, we saw Kommandant Gemmeker standing there. Usually he came only when the transports were about to depart. This time he was standing there from the beginning, telling everybody who walked past him, 'You people are lucky. You are going to an exchange camp in Germany called Bergen-Belsen.'

We noticed that the train was not the usual boxcars or cattle wagons but a regular, if very old, passenger train. We arrived at the railroad station of Bergen early in the morning. I was almost twelve years old. SS guards, yelling and screaming, stood on the platform to receive us. They stood shoulder-to-shoulder holding big dogs. Yet, I don't think anybody dreamed of escaping; we knew that we were in the middle of Germany, somewhere between Hannover and Hamburg. Even though Westerbork was not a concentration camp, food had been sparse, and we looked pale and thin, sickly. I am sure the local population would not have been friendly to anybody trying to escape.

We had to walk to the camp, several kilometers away, under the watchful eyes of the armed SS guards who threatened us with their rifles. This frightened me, and I am sure also the other children from the train. The parents tried to comfort some of the smaller children who were crying. Some of the young men and women also tried very hard to comfort the children, especially my sister and me because we were without parents. We were made to stand for roll call several hours, awaiting our assignment to the barracks. All the time, there was the sound of rifle fire in the background, seemingly coming from one of the many watchtowers around the camp. I was very concerned that they were aiming at us and maybe wanting to shoot some or all of us. After a while, we found out that they were not firing directly at us; they were shooting to scare us. This was our reception at Bergen-Belsen and it caused me nightmares for many weeks later.

Our segment of the camp was called the exchange camp by the Germans, but Sternlager, or Star Camp, by the rest of the inmates. In the Sternlager, we wore our own clothing, by then more like rags, with the Jewish star sewn on.

In February of 1944, the Birnbaums and the few other children remaining at the orphanage arrived in Bergen-Belsen. Hannah Goslar and her little sister Gabi, then four years old, came with them. I had first met Hannah at the orphanage in Westerbork where she had occupied a bunk right next to my sister Edith and the two had become very friendly. By the fall of 1944, the first transports arrived from the east because the Germans were evacuating the eastern camps as the Soviet army advanced across Poland. Several transports of women, about 8,000 from Auschwitz-Birkenau, arrived at the end of October or the beginning of November. They were put into tents next to us. However, the tents collapsed because of the strong autumn winds. Therefore, half our barracks was taken away to accommodate them. Barbed wire was put up to separate us. We were forbidden to talk with them.

As I found out years later from my friend, Hannah, or Hanneli, as she was known in Anne Frank's diary, her friend, Anne Frank, and Anne's sister, Margot, were among those women. I never knew that Hannah had been Anne Frank's close friend and had lived close to her in Amsterdam. I also did not know at the time that Hannah had talked with Anne several times in Bergen-Belsen. Hannah had been surprised and shocked when she found Anne and Margot among the women who had arrived from Auschwitz-Birkenau. She had been under the impression that Anne and her family were safely in Switzerland, a rumor circulated by the Franks when they had gone into hiding in the Annex.[42]

It is still difficult for me to comprehend what happened, how it was possible that people could be so cruel and utterly inhumane, to allow tens of thousands of people to die of starvation and disease, cooped up behind barbed wire, living under the most terrible conditions.

---

[42] *Hannah had talked with Anne several times-* The author met Hannah Pick Goslar in Jerusalem in July 2016. She related the story of seeing Anne in the women's camp and of trying to smuggle bread to her in Belsen in February 1945; Anne's sister Margot was too ill to move to the fence with Anne. Anne remarked, in a weak and sad voice, 'We never went to Switzerland,' and 'I have nobody anymore,' not knowing that her father was still alive. Hannah was later liberated on the third transport to leave Belsen, the so-called 'Lost Transport,' by the Russians across the Elbe at Tröbitz, Germany, on April 23, 1945.

CHAPTER SEVEN

'Hungary is Judenrein'

Why is the sun not shining in my soul anymore?
Why can't I feel what happiness means anymore?
Why has darkness struck at my world?
— IRENE BLEIER MUSKAL, 1944

By the summer of 1944, the time American soldiers had fought their way ashore at Omaha Beach and beyond, the net had closed in on Hungary's Jewish population. By the time the Allies crossed over into Germany itself, most of Europe's Jews were dead.

Hungary's Jews had been spared the horrors that unfolded as German troops moved into conquered territory, as the Hungarian government had made an alliance with Hitler in 1938. Antisemitic legislation began in earnest in 1939, but many of Hungary's Jews saw this only as a measure to appease Hitler. The Hungarian Army joined the attack on the Soviet Union, but their commitment began to waver after heavy losses in early 1943. On March 19, 1944, the German Army occupied Hungary, with SS-Obersturmbannführer (lieutenant colonel) Adolf Eichmann arriving with his orders to make Hungary 'judenrein.' The swiftness of this action was stunning: by the middle of the summer that had brought American, British, and Canadian liberators to the continent, 440,000 of Hungary's Jews had been rounded up and deported, most to be murdered immediately at Auschwitz.[38]

Leslie Meisels was born in 1927 and was just entering his teenage years when the changes began.

Leslie Meisels

My childhood in my hometown of Nádudvar felt normal, unmarked by special events, although being Jewish meant certain differences. While my neighbor's children were spending their time in whatever way they wanted, from the age of five I attended cheder several times a week to learn about being Jewish, our history, and how to pray.⁴³ At cheder, the teacher taught us to read Hebrew and explained, in Hungarian, the basics of the five books of Moses. When I turned six, I attended

---

⁴³ *cheder*-early religious education studies

public school, as did other Jewish children, because with so few of us, there was no Jewish school.

In such a small town, everybody knew all the Jewish people, and all the Jewish people knew, if not by name, by face, most of the people in town. When I was growing up, we identified ourselves as patriotic Hungarians who practiced the Jewish religion. I felt like our Jewish community was entirely integrated, accepted, and respected in town. However, there were times that I was on my way to or from school when a child, who might have been angry with me, called me a 'dirty Jew.' It was unpleasant, but it didn't go any further than that.

[A turning point came] in 1939, one year after the first anti-Jewish law that the Hungarian fascist government, which politically supported the German Nazi regime, had independently implemented. The law restricted the number of Jews who could participate in businesses and commercial enterprises. In spite of this, my family and I were not yet experiencing any major changes, but on May 5, 1939, the government issued a second, more severe anti-Jewish law that further restricted the number of Jews in certain professions, restricted admission to higher education, and forbade Jews from operating large businesses. They could only continue working if they officially transferred management of their businesses to non-Jews. Although Jewish businesses and tradespeople in Nádudvar suffered from these laws, many had trustworthy gentile friends and acquaintances who allowed their names to be used for the government requirements, sometimes for a fee, allowing the Jewish owners to continue managing their own businesses. That same year, government-organized anti-Jewish propaganda suddenly started to appear everywhere. Although we were afraid to a certain extent, we still thought that nothing worse than the curtailing laws would happen to us. We considered ourselves to be patriotic Hungarians first and Jews second, [having lived here for generations]. Soon enough, though, we found out that our beliefs were just sweet dreams. In the regime's eyes, not only were we not Hungarians, our lives were not worth anything.

The atmosphere in Nádudvar began to change. The town electrician was also the local leader of the Nyilas, the Arrow Cross party, which was the

Hungarian version of the German Nazi party. The Arrow Cross had adopted Nazi beliefs, although in its early days, its followers only verbally abused Jews in confrontations on the street; their actions didn't go any further until later.

I was scared of one of my classmates, a butcher's apprentice. He was about two years older than me, six-foot-five and more than two hundred pounds, and a member of the Arrow Cross Party. Although he didn't pay too much attention to me, he made it clear, often and vehemently, that he didn't like Jews. I avoided stepping in front of him or provoking him, worried about being beaten up. One wintry Friday night, however, he decided to show off, saying, 'Hey, guys, take a look. I'm going to scare the shit out of this Jewish boy.' And as soon as these words were said, his butcher knife flew through the air and stuck into the top of my desk, vibrating, just inches away from my chest and face. He didn't beat me up, but it scared me enough to want to stay as far away from him as possible. My tormentor was amused, and some of my classmates laughed, cheered, and clapped. Others kept quiet, and some expressed their disapproval and support for me by looks and later on by words, but they certainly didn't do anything to stop him. The atmosphere in class was much divided—like the rest of Hungarian society—between verbal antisemites, sympathizers who didn't act on their beliefs, and the majority who just remained silent. People let Jews be antagonized as long as they themselves were left alone.

That winter, the butcher's apprentice was part of something more deadly. One evening, when my old teacher from cheder was going home from the grocery store after work, carrying a bag of potatoes, he encountered the butcher's apprentice, who stabbed him in the back with his butcher knife, killing him. His excuse was that a Jew was gathering food at night, taking it away from the gentile population. When the gendarmes took him in, there was no question that he had committed a crime—he didn't deny it and there were witnesses—but he had only killed a Jew. Although there must have been a trial, he wasn't imprisoned. He may have received a warning but continued living in town as if nothing had happened.

The Yellow Star

Many Hungarian Jews were ordered up into labor battalions as the Hungarian government threw its lot in with Hitler's forces in the June 1941 invasion of the USSR. After the crushing defeats suffered by the Hungarian Second Army at the end of the battle of Stalingrad in early 1943—out of 200,000 Hungarian soldiers and 50,000 Jewish forced-laborers, over half were killed[39]—followed by the defection of Italy in the summer of 1943, the Hungarian government began to make peace overtures to the western Allies. Incensed, Hitler immediately ordered the German army into Hungary.

Leslie Meisels

The German army occupied Hungary on March 19, 1944. Within weeks, they decreed that Jewish people put a cloth yellow Star of David on their garments, which had to be visible so that everybody could see that we were Jews. My paternal grandfather, sadly, experienced this degradation. A Hungarian-looking gentleman whose forefathers were born in the town and who had lived respectful lives there, Grandfather said that he wouldn't be humiliated; he wouldn't wear the yellow star. He brooded about it for two days, not leaving the house. Then, he had a heart attack and passed away a couple of days later. He died without ever putting that symbol on his clothing. We were permitted to have a funeral; in April 1944, he was the last person buried in the Jewish cemetery of Nádudvar. After the war, my father erected a concrete cover on his grave that couldn't be removed or destroyed. It was a good thing that he did because even today, with no Jews living in town, the grave is untouched. My grandfather's death was our immediate family's first real tragedy from the Nazi occupation.

Irene Bleier Muskal was also born in 1927 and lived in the same small town in Eastern Hungary as Leslie Meisels, later moving not far away to the slightly larger town of Püspökladány, where her father could conduct business with less competition. She wrote her memoir in 1989, recalling her experiences and incorporating notes from diary fragments.

Irene Bleier Muskal

April 4, 1944

The Hungarian government introduced a degrading law forcing us to wear a yellow star on the left side of our clothes. Whoever disobeyed would be punished. My father prepared perfect yellow stars for each of us. Sad reflections overtook his face as he worked.

My father's instruction that I put on the yellow star filled me with enormous hatred and depression. We always showed great respect and love to both our parents—especially to our father—but now I had to refuse. 'I cannot wear the disgracing badge,' I told my father. My father answered that I should wear the star with pride. 'Show them that you are proud to be a Jew,' he said. 'I am proud to be a Jew,' I told my father. 'But that pride does not mean that I will let them degrade me and make me a laughing stock.' Those barbaric demands deeply hurt my self-dignity. The first day I wore the yellow star fell on my seventeenth birthday. Instead of marking the spring of life, my birthday turned into a dark omen for many more hopeless days that followed shortly.

Parents also worried that brutal Nazi soldiers would harm their unmarried daughters. My father proposed that I fictitiously marry a local boy, but I became suspicious and did not consent. I also told my father that I could not marry this boy, as I already put my eyes on the boy's younger brother. My father thus abandoned his plans to find me a husband. He continued to fear that German soldiers would attack me and suggested I stay indoors. I could not do that—I just had to walk about outside and feel the atmosphere.

I promised my father that I would not let anyone harm me so long as I was alive—just over my dead body. Thanks to the Almighty, nobody harmed me this way. I once had a close call when a childhood archenemy of mine came to enjoy the sight of Nazi invaders in our town and noticed me near an SS soldier who stood guard by city hall. He tried as hard as he could to get the SS soldier to harm me, but being a stupid ignoramus, this teenage boy did not know German. So all he could do was point at me and repeatedly yell, 'Juda, Juda.' The Nazi soldier completely disregarded the peasant boy as I quietly walked away.

The Allied air forces started conducting air raids since the Nazi occupation began. Looking up at the planes in the sky, I wondered why the free countries don't do something to help us Jews before the Nazis exterminate us. We were innocent victims, and they could have helped us if they wanted to. My soul directed a silent prayer to them—please help us escape the devil's clutches.

Leslie Meisels

Near the end of April 1944, my father was instructed to report for forced labor on May 1. At this same time, all the Jews of Nádudvar were ordered to abandon our homes, take whatever we could, and move into a ghetto. All young gentile men born before December 31, 1926, were called up for military service, and all Jews born before that date were ordered to report for forced labor. Since I was born in February 1927, those two months saved me and made it possible for me to stay with the rest of my family in the ghetto.

Irene Bleier Muskal

Another anti-Jewish law shortly passed, forcing us to leave our homes and be concentrated in a ghetto. On that very same day, my father left us forever. The army called him up, and he had to present himself at the army headquarters for forced labor service. This was a very distressing period for us. Jewish men had been called for this purpose several years back; most had already died from hunger, been beaten, or froze to death.

Unspeakable sorrow filled our deeply shocked hearts as we left our warm homes. With a gloomy face that reflected how we all felt, my father put on his backpack and said his last farewell to us. I silently escorted my father to the train station. We walked side-by-side for thirty short minutes before he arrived at the appointed place. My father met other forced laborers there, including a childhood friend of his. A pair of local gendarmes yelled at me and told my father to board the train which was already waiting. I choked back the tears as I parted from my father. I stayed on to see him take a seat in the train, a cigarette in his mouth and his reddish-brown face with a very sad expression.

This was the last time I ever saw him. He was transferred to Debrecen, where he met his tragic death.

Restless and depressed, we could not stay at home. I tried to think if there was some way to stop the pending disaster. But I could not come up with any comforting answers as I walked the familiar streets of Püspökladány.

Why is the sun not shining in my soul anymore?
Why can't I feel what happiness means anymore?
Why has darkness struck at my world?
Why is the devil ruling human souls?
Why is he turning them into cruel forces?
Why are the hopes of innocent people being shattered?
Why has the world kept silent at our loss?

*

Peter Lantos was a four-year-old boy living with his parents in the town of Makó in southeastern Hungary. His brother, fourteen years his senior, had also just been called up to serve; Peter would never see him again. In his 2005 memoir, he recalled the trauma in the days that followed from the perspective of the small child that he was.

Peter Lantos

Unexplained activity in the house was a sign that something was afoot. My mother was carrying out what appeared to me to be a second spring cleaning, systematically going over the rooms, turning out wardrobes and rummaging through drawers. The whole exercise was unnatural since the annual spring cleaning had been completed only a few weeks earlier, and I expected some explanation, but none was forthcoming. I found my father's involvement even more ominous, since he never showed the slightest interest in any domestic work. Now, he stood by mother's side, and although he was doing very little, I could hear him saying: 'Take this coat' or 'No, I do not want this jacket.' After a while, I realized that this was not spring cleaning but a careful process of selecting clothing. My mother pulled out each drawer, emptied its contents and, lifting each item, paused for a moment, as if assessing each garment for its quality. A few items were collected in a small pile, ready to be packed, while the rest were hastily replaced in the drawers. My first thought was that we must be going away for a summer vacation, although summer had not yet arrived. My hopes were shattered and replaced by suspicion, however, when I noticed a couple of the items earmarked for packing: they were heavy winter overcoats rather than flimsy shorts and cotton shirts for a summer holiday. I plucked up my courage and asked: 'Are we going on a holiday?' 'Yes,' said my mother, 'we are going away, but not for a holiday, and we are not going very far either.'

She looked at my father and asked me to sit next to her. She explained that the following day we would have to leave the house and that we were going to live, for a short time, in another house with some other people, also Jews, but we would not have to leave the town. Other people, many we knew, including my grandmother and other cousins and relatives, would also be leaving their houses. She consoled me with the promise that the three of us would remain together and that I would be able to play with other children. But I would not have any of it; I was adamant that I was going to stay and would never leave our house. I wanted to play with other children in our garden, not in some other place I did not know. Nor did I want to share a house with other people, even if I knew them. And to give weight to my objection I started to howl—my ultimate act of disobedience, but used this time to no effect. My father put his hand on my head and said, 'We do not want to go, but we have to.' I did not understand why we had to leave the house where we had always lived. I did not understand who had ordered us to do so, and I did not understand what wrong we had committed, to be punished in this way. But I knew that further protests would be in vain.

My mother finished selecting the belongings we were allowed to take and prepared everything for the next day. My whole world seemed to come to an end. The everyday routine and the security of our lives, all of which had been taken for granted and never questioned, had gradually been undermined by forces I neither knew nor understood.

The increasing tension at home, the secret sessions of listening to the radio, the deterioration in our food, the wearing of the yellow star, the departure of my uncles and my brother all had increased my suspicion, which gradually turned into fear that despite the protection of my parents something terrible would happen. And now this fear grew into terror, prompted by this latest catastrophic event: we were leaving our house, the final anchor of certainty that tied us to the world we knew. And in the morning we left—a short, bald man of fifty-one, an elegant woman of forty-four, and a boy not quite five years old.

Life in the ghetto for Meisels and Bleier was crowded, as it was only a few dozen fenced-in houses and a synagogue, 250 people in all, guarded round the clock by police. It would also be short-lived. A few weeks later, deportations would begin. Irene Bleier was working with other girls from the ghetto as a farm laborer when the order to return to the ghetto came.

Irene Bleier Muskal

An order to pack our belongings and return to the ghetto came suddenly one afternoon. We had to quit work and go right away. Some of the girls cried hysterically, fearful that we would now all be taken with our families to Hitler's death camps. I was scared stiff and overcome by tears, my brain stiffened by the worry. With great pain, we boarded the horse-cart.

Six horse-carts filled with fifty young Jewish girls made their way through town. Some of us cried uncontrollably, the tears streaming down our faces. The others just cried inside in their hearts. Starting at the outskirts of town, we passed by the Jewish cemetery. Two girls wailed bitterly at this point, bidding farewell to their dead—one to her late mother, the other to her late father. Many people stared at the pitiful sight. If they felt sympathy to the humiliated girl prisoners, none showed any signs.

June 18, 1944

Early afternoon. All the Jews of the ghetto stood by the gate in the schoolyard. Those of us who owned goats had to hand them over to the gendarmes—I still recall how our goat cried. Even animals have feelings.

A local Christian midwife had to undress all us women over 16 years old and check our bodies for hidden gold or jewelry. We all crowded into a classroom for this degrading event, but the woman did nothing to us. We just lingered there for a few minutes without being molested. Girls with long hair had to have their hair cut.

We stood in the courtyard with our meager possessions in the one backpack we were allowed to take. The gendarme officer asked if anyone still had any valuables—there were none. Then he shouted that if one person tried to escape, ten people would be shot dead. An old man cried out, 'Someone please give me rope so that I can hang myself and die here. I do not want to go to a death camp to be killed by Hitler. I would rather do it with my own hands.' Mrs. Grunfeld, a mother of four small children, quieted him down and asked him not to stir up a panic.

Contradictory thoughts overtook me. On the one hand, I very much wished to disobey these inhuman decrees, run away and hide somewhere. On the other, strong fears stifled my feelings and paralyzed my body, leaving me unable to resist those devilish decrees. I am sure that many others also felt this dissonance. We lived under great mental pressure, paralyzing fear. Our feelings were stifled, and our brains were unable to think clearly—as if dark clouds floated in our heads.

Leslie Meisels

At the end of the day, when we were marched from the ghetto to the railway station, I was unprepared for what I experienced out on the main street. It was lined with people, several dozen of whom were members of the Arrow Cross and were laughing and clapping loudly, showing their happiness that the Jews were being taken away and yelling insulting, derogatory remarks. Perhaps they were already thinking how wonderful it would be the next morning to loot our abandoned houses. Behind them, hundreds of people stood silently, which was painfully disturbing. Up until then, I had thought better of most people in my hometown. In central Hungary, there was no uprising against the Nazis or their collaborators, not like there was in Slovakia or Poland. Since the beginning of the 1920s, Hungarian society had been a regulated police state, and people probably didn't dare to risk the wrath of those loudmouth antisemites. Even with that in mind, this behavior was still a blow to us; their silence was a shock that has stayed with me all my life.

Irene Bleier Muskal

We arrived at the railroad station where empty cattle cars waited for us. Ninety people had to crowd themselves into each car. We had to jump down from the platform into the car, and many people badly hurt themselves in the process. It was so crowded that we had to sit on each other, unable to move our legs. The heavy doors soon closed, and we were locked in. An eerie quiet encompassed the gloomy situation.

Our transport traveled swiftly. We had no idea as to our next destination. The following day, a black Monday, at around 5 p.m., the train came to a sudden halt. We heard some cries, fear creeping under our skin. My mother ordered me to get rid of the photographs of friends and family that I brought along. The gendarmes may beat me up if they find them. I promptly hid the photos between the side and the ceiling of the boxcar. I wonder if anyone ever found them.

Leslie Meisels

The next morning, we arrived in Debrecen, where the gendarmes were concentrating the Jewish people from the smaller ghettos before deporting them somewhere else by train. These larger ghettos were brickyards or similar establishments on the edges of the city; we were put into a hide-processing plant, a tannery that was worse than a brickyard would have been. Because the hides were processed by soaking them in bins of water until the hair fell off, the place had only outer walls; it didn't have a roof because rain or snow was a welcome addition to the processing operation. For the Germans and their Hungarian associates, it was a good enough place to keep us in. I cannot recall how many roofless buildings there were, but between three and five thousand people had been amassed. The one we were forced to stay in was so crowded that the five of us were only able to put down our belongings. At night, my grandmother and my little brothers crouched down on them, trying to sleep. My mother and I had to stand, planting our feet among them, leaning against each other to try and sleep or nap, whatever we could manage. On top of this inhumane compression, it started to rain on the first night and continued to rain steadily for two days and nights. We stood in mud, soaked to the skin.

In the daytime, we were permitted to roam within the enclosed area. I saw terribly sadistic gendarmes, strangers who had been brought in from other parts of the country to eliminate the possibility of leniency toward people they might know. They beat people, punishing them for even the slightest infraction. On the first day I saw one of the oldest people from my town, a man I knew who was very hard of hearing, feeble, and near-blind, walking with a white cane in the middle of the yard where freight cars stood with open doors. While he shuffled around in the yard, a guard yelled at him to stop, but since he didn't hear, he kept walking. After the third yell, they grabbed him, beat him, and hung him up by his wrists from the corners of one of the freight car's doors. He lost consciousness within minutes and they didn't even take him down. They left him there to show others what would happen to those who didn't obey orders. They did this only because we were Jews.

Irene Bleier Muskal

A gendarme, shouting and cursing, greeted us as the heavy doors opened. He ordered us to quickly get out with our backpacks. We then witnessed a bloodcurdling sight; a gendarme was brutally beating up a good friend of my father, and his sister-in-law.

The gendarmes ordered us to line up five to a row to be counted. Then we marched into a big building with no roof. A young girl from our town was being hanged from the building by her hands and legs. A couple of gendarmes beat her all over her body with their hands and guns. The girl screamed and cried bitterly. The gendarmes poured many liters of water over her so that she would wake up after fainting, and then kept beating her. Blood and tears streamed down her crucified body all the while. Oh, those barbaric, ruthless beasts. It was a miserable sight.

We crowded into the roofless building, sitting on top of each other and stepping on each other's legs as we tried to walk around. As we all took our places, a heavy rain poured down on us, soaking us down to our bones. Our belongings were also soaked, spoiling the food and leaving us with almost nothing to eat for the next two weeks.

Agnes Fleischer Baker was ten years old and was to be taken with her mother and younger sister.

Agnes Fleischer Baker

When the Germans came, within a month and a half we were in the ghetto, then we were assembled in the place that turned out to be worse than everything that came after. That's when the suicides started, because people realized what's going to happen to them. Our doctor had a six-year-old daughter, so he killed himself and his wife, and the little girl threw up, so she somehow survived. My father was very sick, and I still remember the little suitcase that we had with his medication. My mother said to my father, 'We actually have enough to end it all now,' and my father said, 'No, if anybody will kill these children, let the Germans do it.' He was the first one that really saved our lives. He later died; it was the heat that killed him.

Leslie Meisels

On the third day, there was an announcement that families with five or more children had to report to the railway track, where a group was being assembled for transport. We knew that people were being taken away, but the government's propaganda emphasized that any rumors we heard about Jews undergoing cruelty at the hands of the Nazis was just that, a rumor; they made us believe that for the remainder of the war, which we hoped would be short, we were being sent somewhere for slave labor. As bad as that seemed, we still thought that if they wanted our labor, they would have to give us food and shelter. At the tannery we had nothing, and so we believed that anywhere else would be better. We didn't know at that time about the Nazis' unparalleled, unimaginable annihilation plan, already working full blast in Auschwitz and the other death camps.

Later, there was another announcement calling for families with four children to report to the train. One of my best friends, who had four siblings and was going to be on that transport, came to me saying that they had heard that they needed eight more families with three children to make up the quota and asked if we wanted to come along with their group. I went back to my mother and told her this, even though nobody knew where the people on the transport were going or what would happen to the rest of us. My mother said we shouldn't go because they hadn't called for families with three children. I have to explain that in those days, a seventeen-year-old never, ever said 'no' to his or her parents. Up to that moment, I, too, had never spoken back to my mother, but this time I said, 'We're not staying! We're going!' We argued back and forth until I grabbed my belongings and started to walk. She had no choice but to follow. My father had already been taken away to the unknown, and she didn't want her family to be broken up any further. I didn't know then, and I still don't know now, what made me defy my mother, but it was the first miracle of my survival, [for this was a transport that was shunted away from Auschwitz towards Austria].

Irene Bleier Muskal

We left this miserable hole Friday morning. A uniformed German SS soldier appeared and called on rabbis and families with four children and more to gather at the center of the yard. Our empty stomachs rumbling, we heard this Nazi bawl out instructions to us. We were about to start a long 'walking tour.' For many of us, this would be a death march to Auschwitz. I recall that he told us that there is no need to put up resistance, as we would not be beaten—he has family too, and he is not a human dog.

Thus, after starving for four days, we commenced our march. German SS guards watched from both sides as we marched in rows of five. None of us tried to escape. We were too depressed, our will power broken down, wholly tormented. We soon arrived at a camp overcrowded with other fellow, desperate Jews, stopped for a while, and then continued the humiliating journey. As Jewish men aged 18-48 were long ago taken to forced labor camps, the marching contingent was composed of young girls, mothers, babies, and children, along with many old and sick human souls. Trucks carried our backpacks while we marched for grueling hours in our mournful procession through small towns. The Christian townsfolk stared at us, nobody pouring tears, nobody expressing sympathy.

We arrived one afternoon at a small farm known as St. George Plains, where we were accommodated to empty tobacco sheds. The armed Hungarian gendarmes who carefully watched our frightened moves let us walk outside a fixed distance from the sheds during the day. We saw how a heartless gendarme chased away a Jewish child who tried to pick up some food he spotted on the ground.

The weather was beautiful this June afternoon. Ordinarily, an early summer day such as this would elevate my soul and give joy to my body. Soft warmth full of promise. But now all I felt was immense sadness, no joy could penetrate me. At nightfall, we were all herded inside the sheds to lie down on the bare earth. We were cold and hungry, sleep did not come easily.

Another day of beautiful, joyous sunshine came Saturday morning, but not for us on June 25, 1944.

By Sunday afternoon, we packed our backpacks and prepared to board the nearby train trucks. When we entered the strongly chloroformed boxcars, many people became dizzy or fainted.[44] Ninety people crowded into each boxcar, and we were each given half a slice of tasty dark bread and a little water, which we quickly consumed. Quite a few people died during this weeklong journey.

We were too exhausted to cry about the present or worry about our future. Subconsciously, though, we feared the worst. Indeed, we later found out that our premonitions were well founded. We later found out that not only did the Hungarian government give us away to the Nazis for annihilation; they also paid the full cost of transport to the death camps.

---

[44] *strongly chloroformed boxcars*-it is assumed that these railcars had previously been used to deport the sick and dying and dead and had been recently 'disinfected.'

'Water, Water!' Watercolor completed by Hungarian survivor Ervin Abadi at Hillersleben DP camp, May 1945. Soldier Monroe Williams collection. Abadi was probably on the train described in this section of the chapter.

As the Jewish transports did not appear on the regular railway schedule, we were often stranded for hours under the blazing sun waiting for our turn to travel. We received no food or water. People urinated and took care of their natural needs aboard the train, spreading a putrid odor. Small children and babies cried themselves to sleep out of sheer exhaustion, from hunger and thirst, from the wholly wretched situation we were in. Some of the men donned their tefillin and fervently beseeched the Almighty to save us, 'Look upon your forsaken children, see what the world is doing to them and send help; pull us out of this catastrophe before it is too late—if it isn't already.'[45]

The transport hurtled along mostly at night, rocking us to sleep. We dreamed of freedom, of home, of plentiful food and water. Each time the train stopped, so did our dreams. We sadly woke up to the dreadful reality. During air raids, the cowardly SS guards locked us inside the train, taking cover themselves in bomb shelters.

Our transport stopped one day by the train station, with many Hungarian soldiers and civilians all around. My cousin Magda peeked out of a tiny window at the side of the boxcar and begged a Hungarian officer for a little water. He promptly denied Magda's request. How could anyone be so cruel? Even dangerous criminals condemned to death receive their last request. Why are innocent Jews treated even worse? Is there no more justice left on earth?

My mom and us children resided just beneath a small window, so we saw much breathtaking scenery as the train swiftly raced along. Normally, this

---

[45] *Tefillin-* or phylacteries, are two small leather boxes that contain verses from the Torah. They are worn by observant Jewish men and boys on the head and on one arm with leather straps while praying.

would be uplifting, but now we were engulfed by depression.

Our journey reached a turning point on Thursday afternoon as we left Hungarian territory, soon arriving at a nearby small Polish town. Our transport was delayed at the station and another transport with Jews being deported to annihilation centers stood nearby.

July 11, 2013/Kraków, Poland

We are picking up speed along the tracks, night train to the East. Hours and hours of clacking and swaying in the dark, in cramped and claustrophobic compartments across the Czech Republic from Prague to Poland. A little unsettling.

We arrive in Kraków, Poland, in the morning. The German Army arrived on September 6, 1939. We will be here for a couple days. They stayed for several years. We rest up, tonight. For tomorrow, the tour continues. We are heading to Auschwitz, 50 miles to the west.

July 12, 2013/ Auschwitz-Birkenau

So the day that many of us approach with a bit of apprehension is finally here. We are on the bus from our hotel in Kraków to Auschwitz.

As we roll southward, our tour leader Stephen points out an impressive large building on the top of a hill that looks like a five-star hotel. Built after the German invasion in 1939, it was a rest and relaxation villa for Wehrmacht officers rotating off the Russian front to unwind for a bit, as industrialized mass murder was unfolding every single day less than an hour away.

Soon we see the road signs for Oswiecim, the small Polish town at a railroad hub that has become one of the most visited tourist sites in Poland. Most of the world knows it by its German name—Auschwitz.

The bus lumbers into the overcrowded parking lot and docks in the slot. The driver kills the engine. And it begins to rain as our other leader, Elaine, relates the story of her mother's family, the idyllic childhood in this beautiful prewar country, a young teen when the nation is invaded, the oldest of four children. No one on the bus makes a sound. It is now raining very hard, pounding out a terrible rhythm as she reconstructs the sequence of the destruction of her family.

What is this place? Our guide Alicja is a top-notch scholar, and she leads us on a day-long tour that is hard to put into words.

We begin at Auschwitz I, the first camp. This place is centrally located, a railway hub dating back to the turn of the century.

The first prisoners, after it is converted from a Polish military facility, are Soviet POWs and Polish prisoners and other 'security risks' who will be worked to death slowly expanding this camp, and the much larger Auschwitz II-Birkenau. She walks us through the exhibits and the displays at the various blocks. Block 4 is the 'Extermination Exhibit.' We think about the words, the language. 'Extermination'—as if the victims were vermin. Over 1,100,000 human beings were killed here, most of them Jews. Now, 1.4 million people visit here every year.

We see the map with the spiderlike rail lines radiating outward from Auschwitz like tentacles, from northern Poland, from Germany, Hungary, as far south as Greece and as west as Paris and the Netherlands. In the summer of 1944, tens of thousands were murdered here, per day; Primo Levi put the record at 24,000 on a single day in August 1944.[40]

We see the large-scale terra cotta model of the process, which the German engineers had perfected at Auschwitz II-Birkenau—the arrival of the transports, the undressing rooms with signs admonishing bewildered people to hang their belongings carefully and to remember the number of the wall pegs where they left them for quick retrieval later. We peer into the shower rooms that could fit in some cases entire transports, which were in fact the hermetically sealed gas chambers. The figurines of the Germans stand above them with their gas masks, waiting for the proper temperature to be reached through body heat, just the right humidity to be achieved before dropping in the pellets so the gas released would work more effectively. The anguished death throes of the thousands of naked figurines assault our senses. The process is not complete until the corpses are carried out by the sondercommando slaves, defiled for any gold fillings, the hair shorn from the women, the bodies then burned in the open air behind or cremated in the ovens.

But the experience is just beginning. Minutes before, we were looking at a terra cotta model. And now in Block 5 we will be presented with the evidence. This is an exhibition, after all. Exhibit A is about to slap us in the face. Hard.

It is a room, 50 feet long, with nothing but human hair piled several feet back and as many feet tall. My heart skips a beat.

What do our eyes perceive? Now we see a photo of stacks of bale bags, carefully labeled, packed, and stacked, awaiting shipment back to the Reich for use in various products for the German war effort. Slippers for submariners so they can walk quietly aboard ship to evade Allied sonar. Stuffing for the seats of German pilots.

We shuffle on in silence with hundreds of others past the mountains of spectacles, the pots and pans, the suitcases carefully labelled by their owners with chalk on the orders of the perpetrators, again, for 'quick retrieval after disinfection.' And the shoes. Sorted. Case after case of women's shoes. Men's footwear. And then, the children's shoes.

Our knowledgeable guide takes us into Block 27, the new exhibit on the Shoah. This is a temporary relief of sorts as now we see faces, film and stills, of prewar Jewish life, projected on the walls. We hear songs and voices.

At the end is the Book of Life, rows of giant suspended volumes containing four million names compiled thus far. A moving moment when Elaine and others in our tight-knit group find entire pages with the names and dates of family members murdered during the Holocaust. There are gasps. And tears.

And now it is on to Auschwitz II-Birkenau.

*

After the 'tour' of Auschwitz I, we have lunch on the bus in the parking lot, and then drive the three kilometers through town to Birkenau.

Auschwitz, July 2013. Source: Author.

The entry tower is the iconic symbol of evil, menacing and devouring as we are pulled closer on this overcast day. We follow the guide up the stairs in the tower. From here we can see the sheer vastness of the camp.

Dozens of long, narrow women's barracks, brick, still stand, albeit some braced with wood on the gable ends to keep them from toppling until they can be re-pointed. Alicja indicates that historic preservation here is a major concern.

The rest of the camp is many square kilometers of row upon row of foundations and brick chimney stubs, surrounded by the intimidating curved and tapered concrete posts dotted with white insulators and strung with miles of parallel lines of barbed wire. In the summer of 1944, when hundreds of thousands of Hungarian families were deported here, the rail lines came right into the camp. Following the German invasion of Hungary in March 1944, over 400,000 Hungarian Jews were deported and murdered at Auschwitz.

*View of the ramp at Auschwitz-Birkenau showing the SS selection
of Hungarian Jews, summer 1944. Credit: USHMM.*

The Walk

Our guide leads us along the path through the camp that leads to the gas chamber and crematorium. We walk in silence along the roadway, the only sound the crunching of brick fragments and gravel underfoot. It appears to have been paved with brick, slave labor of course, though in some spots it is hard to tell anymore. No one speaks, and on and on we walk.

Two minutes.
Five minutes.
Ten minutes.
Fifteen minutes. I've been on historic battlefields that are smaller than this site.

Auschwitz, July 2013. Source: Author.

Finally we reach the end of the camp where the kitchens stood. A round concrete ring rises out of the earth, maybe 6 feet in diameter. Someone finally speaks and asks Alicja what it was. A giant flowerpot. It was for flowers. She tells us that they were also placed near the entrances of the gas chambers.

Flowers at the gas chambers.

We turn left and keep walking past interpretative signage. It seems like we are walking outside of the camp perimeter, but we are not. Beautiful woods of white birch appear, and we are walking on the edge of the woods with the camp to our left.

We stop near another sign and rest for a moment, allowing the others to catch up. Then our guide calls our attention to the photo on the sign, showing Hungarian mothers and children doing the same thing we are doing. Halting and resting.

And a short path through the woods will take us to the ruins of the gas chamber/crematorium Number Five.

Auschwitz, July 2013. Source: Author.

We are resting at the spot they rested at, 20 minutes after walking, immediately after disembarking from overcrowded transports that they had been traveling on for days. Here they waited, anxiously, as their turn to approach the chamber would come. But the victims of the transport ahead of them had to be removed from the chamber first. Some days in the summer of 1944, these victims were backed up for hours.

I pick up a rock from the path and carry it with me past the ruins. At the ash field there is more signage and a memorial asking visitors not to walk through the field. I place my stone on the memorial, looking down to watch where I step. But it is probably a futile gesture—this whole place is an ash yard, a graveyard. So many Hungarian Jews were killed in the Auschwitz camps in that season of murder that the crematoria were incapable of burning all the bodies, so open-air burning pits had to be utilized.

Auschwitz, July 2013. Destroyed crematorium. Source: Author.

We turn again and walk past the remains of crematorium Number Four to the disinfection center for those selected to be worked to death. Again, a system. Disrobing. Wading through disinfectant. Shower. Uniform thrown at you, mismatched clogs or shoes.

Elaine's mother spent two years here. Her grandmother and the little ones were selected upon arrival. Her mom's beloved sister was murdered in the quarry after slipping while carrying a large pot of soup in the ice and snow with three other girls. Today is a hard day. I want to comfort

Elaine, to carry her pack for her. I feel helpless. There is nothing I can do.

Portraits of those killed at Auschwitz, discovered after the war. July 2013. Source: Author.

The Red Army liberated this place on January 27, 1945. At the Soviet memorial constructed near the two destroyed gas chambers/crematorium at the end, we have a remembrance ceremony. Kaddish is recited in Hebrew. I read it aloud in English today to the group. With tears, Elaine tells us that she feels her grandmother smiling down on this extraordinary group of dedicated teachers. A lump rises, again. I swallow hard and try to blink back the wetness I feel welling in my eyes. Glad for the sunglasses, even though there is no sun. The plaque reminds:

'A Warning to Humanity.'

We light candles, turn our backs, and just walk out, which allows for another twenty-minute stretch of quiet, personal reflection. We have come to the epicenter of evil. We have been here; we try to process—but we just cannot.

*

The Hocker Album- Dr. Josef Mengele, Rudolf Höss, Josef Kramer, and an unidentified officer. Credit: USHMM.

In January 2007, the United States Holocaust Memorial Museum acquired a mysterious photograph album which was inscribed 'Auschwitz 21.6.1944' on its first page, and because there are few wartime photographs of Auschwitz, it was a major find, photographic evidence taken by the perpetrators themselves.[46] In one incredible photograph, taken at Auschwitz, you can see some of

---

[46] photographic evidence taken by the perpetrators themselves- The Hocker Album can be viewed online at https://www.ushmm.org/collections/the-museums-collections/collections-highlights/auschwitz-ssalbum/documentary.

the more well-known criminals. Commandant Rudolf Höss was hung at Auschwitz following his trial after the war. Joseph Kramer, whom we met in Chapter 1, was executed by the British after his assignment presiding over the horrors of Belsen following his transfer there. Of course, smiling Dr. Mengele escaped to Argentina and died in a drowning accident in the late 1970s. This is casual shot, a cigarette break; another day at the office.

People did these unspeakable acts to other people. But the 'monster' myth is just that. I suppose it is one way of coping with the unthinkable. Let the perpetrators off the hook, in a sense, labeling them 'monsters,' not humans capable of deeply evil deeds, and move on. But to me, it kind of absolves them of something. They are not 'human,' after all, so what does one expect of them?

Others may choose not to think about such things at all. I certainly do not blame them. But to me, to not think about it is to forget, and to forget is as good as saying that it did not happen. But you can't just talk about the history, the chronology. To really try to understand, one has to know the stories of the individuals who were here. We need the individuals to speak to us. And then, we need to give them the voice that was taken from them.

*

The Bleier and Meisels families appear to have been spared an arrival at Auschwitz in late June of 1945 due to logistical railroad complications and/or other events beyond local control; the transport was shunted back into Hungary, and then proceeded to Austria, where they worked for several months as slave farm laborers, as the mayor of Vienna had made an appeal to Nazi authorities for workers.[41] Little did they know that they were now also pawns in a twisted chess match, a complex late-war scheme involving the exchange of Hungarian Jews by Nazi leaders for economic gain.[42]

Strasshof Concentration Camp, Austria

Irene Bleier Muskal

After a while, our transport's locomotive went to the rear—we were going to travel backwards. We soon went back onto Hungarian soil. At first, we fooled ourselves into believing that the Hungarian government claimed us back, and would not let us be taken to annihilation. It took just a short while, however, for us to face our destiny. Now our transport traveled swiftly. We left behind the country that we mistakenly believed was our homeland.

Leslie Meisels

The doors closed, and the train took off to an unknown destination. In that closed-in, dark, crowded place we were given two 25-liter pails, one with drinking water and one for human waste. The water was soon gone, and the waste pail flowed over. These were changed, refilled, and emptied once a day when we stopped at a station. On the seventh day, we arrived at a town called Strasshof in Austria, about 25 kilometers northeast of Vienna, a central transit station for deportees arriving from Hungary and other places. When the door opened, we heard Germans harshly yelling, *'Raus! Raus!' 'Out! Out!'* As we left our car, I saw several bodies being carried out from each of the wagons. Six or eight bodies were carried out of ours. Many had succumbed from lack of food, water, and ventilation.

We were all sent into a large room and together—children, adolescent boys and girls, mothers, grandmothers and grandfathers—had to disrobe and march naked to a shower between two lines of laughing, pointing, machine-gun-toting SS guards with dogs. Walking to that shower was the very first real dehumanization I experienced. It drove into our minds the fact that we were not who we used to be, not individuals who had our own dignity, respected within our communities, but, rather, people who the SS guards considered to be subhuman. I was stunned, as were my mother and grandmother. All those laws that had existed in Hungary for a number of years and prevented Jews from living a free and normal life, even the German occupation and being forced to wear the yellow star—none of it was as psychologically damaging as this was. It wasn't just a physically and mentally unpleasant experience—this was the ultimate shock from which I don't think I recovered.

Peter Lantos

My parents found out after a while where we were, but they did not know how long we would be staying here or what we would be required to do. I did not understand the language the soldiers were speaking, and my mother explained that it was German, a language both my parents spoke. The soldiers were either German or Austrian, she said, and we were no longer in Hungary. This was a confusing discovery, since I could not understand why the enemy was kinder than our own people. Here we were treated better than at home; we were given food and drink, and they did not beat us. At least, not until we encountered our first Ukrainian guards. They were not prisoners like us—they had voluntarily joined the Germans in their retreat from Russia—but their privileged status did nothing to diminish their appetite for cruelty. They carried thick, long sticks, and these they wielded to devastating effect. Their savagery was unprovoked and indiscriminate: it was not necessary to commit what they could have perceived as a crime, or even a minor trespass against regulations; our very existence was enough to trigger their brutality. Incomprehensible as it was, they apparently enjoyed beating us; they found sadistic delight in crushed bones and bloody faces. Although I did not realize this until much later, it was in Strasshof that, for the first time, I witnessed the practical implications of the concept of punishment without crime or cause: you are guilty simply because you exist. It was also here that I made my first anthropological observation, to be confirmed later elsewhere—that the women guards were the more vicious of the species; in their brutality, they easily outperformed the men. It was a shock to see women beating up defenseless prisoners who could have been their mothers or their children.

Irene Bleier Muskal

We woke up Friday morning in Austria to the sound of the boxcar doors opening, our clothes crumpled from being on our bodies for two weeks now. Spiritually anguished, we dragged ourselves out and discovered that we had arrived in Austria. Many dead bodies were soon spread out in front of the open boxcars. The Austrian policemen took over this 'human cargo.' To their credit, they acted much more humanely than the Hungarian policemen did. No bawling or beating us.

I looked around and discovered a nearby road where civilians—free people—occasionally rode through. Together with my thirteen-year-old sister Jolan, I walked to the roadside, where Jolan begged passersby for bread. We hardly got there when a young bicycling girl stopped and gave us her own sandwich roll with butter and yellow cheese, which we divided among the five of us. This anonymous Austrian girl's kind gesture satisfied our starved stomach and made our souls feel good.

Armed gendarmes instructed us to line up in rows of five. We put down our backpacks in the bare field that was our 'home' for now and breathed some fresh air. We walked around the area, turning over every little bit of garbage we found in the hope of finding some food. I found some moldy, greenish bread, broke it up into five pieces, and shared with my family. Each of us received less than one bite, so we just swallowed it bitterly.

We laid down our starved and tired bodies on the bare earth as dark clouds threatened above us. The clouds soon poured heavy rain upon us. I took this as a sign that God is crying for us. If the whole world keeps quiet and does nothing to help us, at least the faithful Almighty feels for us. The rain poured mercilessly on our bodies as the Sabbath entered on our second deeply sad Friday night.

At daybreak Saturday, the beautiful sun shone brightly in the sky. But we could relate neither to the sun nor to the rain. Our feelings deserted us; nothing penetrated our consciousness.

As we walked about, we discovered some barracks surrounded by barbed-wire fences. In the compound, we see fellow Hungarian Jews, including some friends and relatives from Püspökladány. Their transport left Hungary after ours, going straight to the Strasshof concentration camp in Austria. Our transport was on its way to Auschwitz, but by some miracle was turned back from Poland and arrived here in the Strasshof concentration camp.

In turn, residents of each barrack took their belongings with them to take a shower and undergo a 'procedure.' This meant taking all clothes, including the last bit of clothing which covered our bodies, and presenting them by hand to a Ukrainian man. This man took care of disinfecting the clothes while the people strolled around naked inside a special building for a couple of hours. I could not believe that this unheard of, degrading description was true, but when I went to look, I saw with my own eyes that it was really happening. Naked women lined up and handed their packs to the hands of Ukrainian men.

At once, I felt the pain of the dreadful shame. Oh, such torment, such a miserable spectacle. I just stood there scared stiff, and like a living dead walked to my place. Then a deafening scream woke me up from my lethargy. I looked in the direction of the hysterical bawling and saw a young woman trying to escape this degradation by choosing death. She was about to hang herself on the outer wall of the barrack building, both her parents lamenting and begging her not to punish them.

Sheer desperation encompassed me. As I stepped inside our barrack, the multitude already had their packs on their backs and were starting on their way to the shower for disinfecting. My mother begged me to come with them. 'No,' I answered her, 'I am just unable to go.'

The place soon emptied completely, save for me. Still scared stiff in my dark desperation, I leaned against the wall. A young Ukrainian beast shortly appeared, yelling at me to come. 'No, I am not going anywhere,' I daringly answered. His expression grew angry as he lifted his hand and beat my back with his whip. My mind darkened, my soul deeply injured.

Unable to think, my two legs dragged me to the shower place, where I joined my mother. All of us women stood in line, naked, and handed over all our belongings to a Ukrainian man. Then the real torture began. We were herded from room to room and questioned about many different things, then underwent medical examinations. Then a young male shaved all our body hairs. Oh, how can the earth tolerate so many cruel deeds? Our senses were totally numbed by so many different shocking events. I could not comprehend anything and was paralyzed.

Agnes Fleischer Baker

I can only tell you that probably the worst thing, when we were in a shower, and it wasn't gas, obviously I'm alive, but they used the Ukrainians, and we were naked in the shower, my mother and my sister and I, and I'm ten years old, and one of the Ukrainians came and pinched my naked butt. That was terrible.

Peter Lantos

One day my grandmother died. I cannot recall how; my mother later said she had suffered a heart attack. I do not remember any burial ceremony— my parents said a prayer, and that was all. My mother cried, but I was standing by her side without shedding a tear, numb and motionless, paralyzed by fear. But death did not become my grandmother—it was strange to see her, the commanding matriarch suddenly diminished to a small, silent corpse, lying motionless under a foreign sky. Her silence was anomalous and ominous; there was no longer anyone to order around or quarrel with. She timed her death well, the last act of a resourceful woman with a long and full life—

by dying suddenly in Strasshof, she avoided the later, harder stages of the journey, and saved herself further suffering and humiliation.

Irene Bleier Muskal

We were divided into two groups. Ours became the forced slave laborers of the 20th century. The other group consisted of people unfit to work, either because of age or poor health, but mainly young mothers who had more than two babies with them. Empty boxcars stood ready to ship these miserable saints without delay to the gas chambers of Auschwitz. There, the innocent, defenseless human cargo perished within minutes—their tormented souls returned to the Creator, their remains herded to the crematorium and burned to ashes. The pure souls parted from the bodies through the crematorium chimney in the form of dark gray smoke, on their way to the heavenly tribunal.

Our group boarded boxcars at the same time as the less fortunate group. With deep pain, I can still recall seeing a former neighbor of ours, Mrs. Stern—along with her four young children—board the Auschwitz-bound boxcars. She saw no one except for her young ones. Her eyes reflected the oncoming death. After the war, she and her children never came back, like so many others from our hometown, and from so many other cities and countries.

Leslie Meisels

Our group consisted of twenty-one people from four family remnants—'remnants' because almost all of our fathers had been taken away to the forced labor service. We were with the Bleiers, a widow with four children from my hometown, Mrs. Bleier's sister-in-law with her three children from the nearby town of Püspökladány, and the Leib family of seven from Kaba.[47] As we waited, we saw some of the people who had come with us on the train being led back to the cattle wagons, and we all wondered where they were going. When we saw that our respected rabbi, Yisrael Jungreis, and his wife, the rebbetzin, who were both in their late seventies, were being forced into one of these cattle wagons, my mother gave me a half-full pot of

---

[47] Mrs. Bleier's sister-in-law with her three children-Irene's family.

roasted flour and goose fat we had been saving and told me to take it to them because they might need it. I went right over to the wagon where the rebbetzin and rabbi were and, finding the door slightly open, gave them the pot from my mother. After thanking me, the rabbi put his hands on top of my head and recited the priestly blessing, *'May God keep you... bless you and be gracious to you....'* It was very moving, and I felt touched. He had barely finished the blessing when an SS guard came over and slammed the door shut, pushing me away. This has always stayed with me.[48]

*

Irene Bleier Muskal

Our transport got moving, stopping after a while at a small Austrian town. Here, each of us received a hot meal consisting of mashed potatoes and spinach, compliments of the local mayor. It was a very nice gesture.

Later we arrived in Vienna, where we left the boxcars and walked through some of the city's long

---

[48] *This has always stayed with me*-Thirty-five years later, Leslie had the opportunity to meet the granddaughter of this beloved rabbi, a famous rebbetzin in her own right, and share his blessing with her.

streets, our packs on our backs and in our hands. As usual, armed guards escorted us. I recall being taken over by a terrible sense of humiliation when masses of civilians peered at our column. Looking back, it was they who should have felt the shame, and not me.

Our first day of work turned out to be our holy Sabbath day. The farm owner paid the Nazi authorities some amount in order to use us, but we received no payment, only a meager food supply. We performed strenuous farm work from sunrise to sunset for the duration of our stay, all summer and fall. Sunday became our day of rest. Our captors treated us inhumanely, hitting us on any special occasion they found. We kept track of our holy days, the Jewish New Year and Yom Kippur. The landowner permitted us to celebrate them. We prayed to the Almighty even more fervently than ever, hoping to be rescued soon—to be free human beings with all our loved ones.

In the late fall, the clock ran out on the Hungarian families in Austria. The decision was made to send them to Bergen-Belsen, part of a complicated holding pattern as exchange negotiations went on.

Towards the end of October, we were served a one-day notice to prepare ourselves for a journey; the destination was again unknown. The first station for us was back to Strasshof, where several thousand of our fellow Jewish slave laborers gathered. After a few days, we were again herded into boxcars, ready for shipment.

The boxcar with its human cargo was advancing from Austria through Czechoslovakia in the direction of Berlin, Germany. The human cargo consisted of the Jewish slave-laborers of the twentieth century, stripped of all their human rights, banished from their country of birth by the government, mercilessly thrown to the clutches of Nazi Germany in order to be annihilated. We sat crammed on the naked floor, asking no questions as to our pending destruction. It was pitch dark at night. Under the influence of months of agony, we lost our own free will and just accepted the treacherous instructions and followed the perilous hands wherever they took us. Our minds were in a state of terror, with the effects lingering long after.

Bergen-Belsen

Thus our journey continued, coming to a stop after an unknown amount of time. We dragged ourselves out of the boxcars as the doors were unlatched, the Nazi guard roaring out orders. We had to line up at our destination, the Bergen–Celle train station, a slow and steady rainfall welcoming us.

Since we were chased out of our former homes, dark skies and steady rain greeted us at each new location. Such a marvelous sensation this phenomenon gave me. I was overcome with a special feeling that somehow even managed to uplift my darkened spirit. It came to me as a message from the heavens, which were venting their anger. *The Almighty shares in our tragedy and is pouring tears of sorrow; He is crying on our behalf.* These thoughts planted seeds of hope and faith into my soul against the backdrop of the great catastrophe.

Lined up in rows of five, we set out on our sad march. Army trucks delivered our backpacks. Swab-German SS Nazi soldiers escorted us. The group I was in consisted mainly of women and children, some old people and a few young ones;

men aged 18 to 48 were taken to forced army labor several years before, where most had perished from starvation, from inhuman beatings, or from freezing to death in sub-zero weather.

Our group marched in the middle of the road, with a few stone houses to our left, curious eyes staring at us from the windows. I felt deep humiliation, but the people who should have felt the shame were those staring at us from the houses. We were innocent, defenseless people; they were partners in the annihilation of millions of innocent souls.

BOOK TWO

THE AMERICANS

During the night I realized that I was going to die. When I accepted this, I felt peaceful; there was nothing that I could do.

— Carrol 'Red' Walsh, Age 24

*The author and his father, February 1992.
Credit: Monty Calvert, Glens Falls Post-Star.*

CHAPTER EIGHT

Coming Home

1987/ Hudson Falls, New York

I fire up the Beast on this cold December morning, and retreat to my sanctuary to wait for her to warm. Exhaust fumes drift my way, but I pay them no mind. Sitting on the edge of my bed in a former recreation room attached to my parents' garage, I also fire up the first of four cigarettes, a bad habit I picked up in a previous life in the restaurant business to deal with stress. I am chain-smoking before climbing into the Beast, a hand-me-down gas-guzzling Oldsmobile Delta 88 convertible, to make the short drive to the public high school where I now teach, the school that I left eight years ago as a high school graduate, in the town I told my father I would not return to. In that conversation as a senior in high school, I also responded to his parental 'what are your plans for the future' entreaties with the timeless wisdom and wit of the eighteen-year old—'I'm leaving this town, I don't know what I want to do, but I do know I am NOT going to become a teacher, like you'—a passing shot before I head off to college a few hundred miles away. Take that, old man.

But, touché. He has the last laugh, because at 26, I am now paying him a token in rent, and driving his old car around town. And I am a teacher, a high school teacher like him, and wait—oh, yes—teaching the exact same subject that he has been teaching for thirty years, world history. Even the young can't outrun the karmic wheel, it seems.

Now on the other side of the desk, in my first year in the public school system, my stress levels have me thinking of investing in tobacco stocks. I'm the third history teacher that the students have had this year, and it is not even Thanksgiving. My own high school teachers are now my colleagues—let's talk about weird—and I'm pushing what feels like a shopping cart through the crowded hallways with lesson props, books, and marked-up papers to hand back, all asunder. I'm shuffling from classroom to classroom, like an itinerant peddler of obscure vials of 'wisdom' and 'knowledge' that nobody seems to want. I don't dare turn my back to the chalkboard for I have discovered that a new teacher is also a magician, and can, with this act, make pencils and pens, paper wads and notebooks all demonstrate Newton's Laws of Motion of their own accord. When I walk into the classroom, my young charges seem to rub their hands together in hormonal homicidal glee. For many of them, I am next on the hit parade, hopefully out by Christmas. This is my life and the tunnel I have entered. How did I wind up here? What have I done?

*

Well, for starters, I have to admit to myself that I always liked history. It was easy to annoy my younger siblings by lingering at the museum exhibits and devouring every last word of the descriptions and interpretations, and I supposed I relished that as well. Before the household would wake up on sunny summer mornings, I would ditch them all and head down to the river that flowed south nearby, alone to wander the banks in search of old bottle dumps and remnants of the fighting from the wars of the colonial period and the American Revolution that raged right through here, the confluence of warpaths along the falls of the Hudson River in the foothills of the Adirondack Mountains in upstate New York. In my solitary pursuits I trespassed and looted with abandon, bringing home unbroken glass treasures to my appreciative mother, who would wash them and set them with love on her kitchen windowsill. This went on even after a well-intentioned neighbor spotted the adolescent me crossing the bridge at the river, and placed a call to Mother, who, with characteristic shrugs, made no real effort at interdiction. I also hung out for hours on summer days in the local graveyards, and I was fascinated by the stories and legends of the heroes and villains who played parts in the forging of the United States. My dad taught summer school, and when I came home from my explorations, he would be setting up the slide projector to preview his course materials and here exposed me to other history, particularly the art and architecture of Renaissance Europe. He really loved that, and he was a minor expert because of it. My mother and he were big readers as well, and enjoyed their travel; I suppose it all rubbed off.

In college, I took one history course after the other, but in my curiousness, I did not formally concentrate in any particular area. So, when the time came to graduate, I really knew my history but had failed to consider focusing on job prospects. I may have been distracted a bit by a burgeoning career in the restaurant business, working my way up to running the kitchen on occasion for one of the top restaurants in my college town. And there I was, opening and closing a restaurant on many days, working incredible hours, but also with student loans to repay. So I went back, and studied all the required courses to be a teacher of social studies. I student-taught in a middle school near the college, and hitched a ride with a pretty girl who was my age but had landed a real paying job at the school, right out of college. We kept each other company, and we married five years later, after which I whisked her off her feet once more—

all this can be yours!—to move under the same roof as my parents.

While she was still my girlfriend, I tried like crazy to get a job near her, out in our college town. I came in second in a job pool that had 80 applicants. In desperation, I applied all over New York State, wearing out the old Beast on hundreds of miles to interviews to no avail, until I got the call to go to Glens Falls, the city across the river where my father taught—not to his high school, but the Catholic school in town. I passed that interview, and bid my future wife a tearful goodbye, hoping that somehow this relationship would last. I had my first real teaching job.

On the third floor at the small but prestigious St. Mary's Academy with its big windows overlooking the Hudson, I watched the mist rise over the river as I swept my own floors and prepared for my 7th, 8th, and 9th graders to arrive. I conducted my lessons after long nights of preparation and assignment grading, and though my charges could be goofy, they were also fun. At Friday noon Mass I instructed students to kneel properly, butts off pews, and even the rebel agnostics among them grudgingly responded to my admonitions. There was a pride in a steady job and a steady paycheck, but I was making less than I could have brought home had I stuck with the restaurant job. By happenstance, my dad heard of a sudden opening at my alma mater just as the following school year was getting underway, and duly noting the irony, I applied. I got the job in November but had no idea what I was walking into.

*

'What's your policy on homework, Mr. Anders?'

I'm leaning over the kid's desk, hands placed firmly on either side. In suitcoat and tie, I'm making myself into an imposing presence. I've just attempted to collect written homework assignments from 25 mostly non-committed sixteen-year-olds, and the results are, shall we say, discouraging. Should I assign the entire class to detention with me after school, or choose one to make an example out of him? I decide on the latter.

Big Lenny Anders, a tall, long-haired teenager with a black motorcycle jacket, lifts his head up from the desk long enough to answer coolly.

'Not to do it.' Clunk. Lenny's head returns to the desktop in a disquieting commentary on my attempt to present myself as the new lord and master. Lenny is face down and unresponsive, and I'm left flapping in the proverbial breeze. Best leave him be, though the rest of the class is nearly rioting in an expression of collective admiration over his truthful response.

So how in the world would I make it until June? When I do have the audacity to drop the hammer in the classroom in the next few weeks, I'm notified quite strongly by a young adult that I can consider myself a 'dead man.' Besides the pending school disciplinary action, the office suggests strongly that I go to the police station to 'swear out a complaint' against the offender.

A what?

And for the first time in my life I'm sitting in a police station, in the first month of my public school teaching career, trying to balance in a wobbly chair with stainless steel ankle-shackles affixed to the legs, listening to the officer clack out his report on a typewriter. They say that teaching has its special rewards.

*

Things aren't going much more smoothly after Christmas break. It may be time to rethink and reboot, but new teachers don't have this kind of time. In desperation, I am living day by day. I'm banging out lesson plans, notes, and tests nightly after dinner on the typewriter for hours at a stretch. I try calling parents, but there is no privacy at my house and surely it is a sign of weakness—after all, the old man doesn't have to call parents.

As I struggle to survive in the spring of this first year, a tight budget year when layoffs are being presented as a distinct possibility, I secretly pray that a pink slip will land in my mailbox to end my misery and I will have an excuse to move on to some other occupation. When the layoff notices do come, I am spared, but a co-worker is not. In a moment of duress, a nuclear bombardment of frustration and raw, naked truth is unloaded by the recipient in my direction—*It should have been you, you don't even want to be here!* I keep my silence, because I'm astonished that my mind has been read—

and now I can add guilt to the heap of misery that I think is my life.

I am afraid to ask for help; I would not even know where to start. I did not realize that my private distress showed so much. I don't complain about the troubles I faced each day in the classroom—surely it is a sign of weakness. In my mind, Mr. Third Teacher was hired to be the answer at the plate, and I feel like I am now facing the third strike. Maybe they will fire me at the end of the year, anyway—problem solved. When the door closes, they say, another will open. I am going to nail this baby shut.

I'm sinking like a stone. I want to just walk away—but after avoiding being laid off, I don't know what to do. It is night and fog, a tunnel vision day-to-day miserable slog that I feel powerless to escape. So I go on, because I can only put one foot before the other.

*

On schedule, the principal walked into the classroom for my official evaluation later that year. I had the best lesson planned, but somehow it devolved into a train wreck. The ninth graders were flirting with each other, joking, and throwing things as I tried to bring order and conduct the lesson. The principal was stone-faced in the back of the room, tapping his pencil on his notebook as hormones raged out of control. Mercifully, the bell rang and he gave me a nod; before darting out he told me to make an appointment with the secretary for the post-observation conference. And away they all went, rushing past me for the door, not a care in the world as they left me to contemplate the complete implosion of my career.

*

Sitting outside the principal's office waiting for one's turn to be raked over the coals is not a pleasant experience. The second hand on the clock seems to wind backwards; the hustle and bustle of the comings and goings of students and staff seem to mock me as I wait for the ax to fall, the platform to be opened beneath my feet. The door swings open, and I am summoned forward for the inevitable.

'Sit down. Tell me how your lesson went.' The principal, a big guy, goes back behind his imposing desk and sits.

I try to explain my objectives and which of the mandated bullet points regarding the GDP growth of the Indian national economy since World War II I was trying to instill in my hormone-addled charges, though I'm not sure I'm making enough eye contact.

He leans in, interrupting after a short while.

'You really did not have control, did you?'

Here we are. I shake my head silently, a sickness rising up from my stomach, not really able to talk anymore, anyway. That lump is in the way.

He looks me in the eye for what seems like a really long time. He's got my number, and now I just want to get it over with.

Busted.

Crashed and burning.

Cooked.

Cashiered.

He looks back to the notes that he scribbled in my room that day, crumples them up, and drops them into his wastepaper basket. He settles back in his chair, lacing his fingers behind his head, and with a hint of a smile, says seven words:

When you are ready, let me know.[49]

*

I breathed out with a bizarre mixture of relief and resignation and survived through that first year's end. I left town for the summer to go back to work on my advanced degree, still not sure about whether the path I am on is the right direction for me. Sure, there were some kids I hit it off with, I tell myself. But as a new school year approaches, so does that sense of dread I feel every morning as I reach for the Marlboro Lights. A few days before the start of classes I see my computer-generated roster and I can feel my chest constrict with each name as my finger anxiously traces down the page. The same torturers are to be in my classes—again! I steel myself as they walk through the door, but something unexpected happens. The kids are a 'summer away' older, and they are genuinely glad to see me.

---

[49] *When you are ready, let me know-* There was no such thing as formal teacher-mentoring programs when the author was starting out as a young teacher. That has changed, thankfully. I'm sure all my evaluations were not poor ones, but how I made it through that year was another miracle in life's journey that led to this book.

One of the things I did have going for me in the classroom was that I actually knew a lot about the history that I was supposed to be teaching students. I was a good storyteller; I was enthusiastic, I was passionate. I listened to them. They began to listen to me. Over time, I became their class adviser, orchestrated their prom, and took them on their senior trip. We matured in our own ways, together. I had survived. They spread their wings; I spread mine. Maybe it was time to fly.

*

The months tick by. Springtime arrives again and we wind down the schoolyear by immersing ourselves in the study of the 20th century. I am lecturing energetically about World War II, and I'm getting a response; my enthusiasm seems contagious. In the late eighties, all the students would raise a hand when I would call out for examples of grandparents or other relatives who had served in the war—frequently two hands would go up in the air. Every kid had a personal connection to the most cataclysmic event in the history of mankind—and at that time, many of the soldiers, airmen, Marines, and sailors who came home from the war were still with us.

As the 1990s unfolded, the United States commemorated the U.S. entry into World War II with the 50th anniversary of the attack on Pearl Harbor. After that, we had the 50th anniversary of the Normandy landings, which again attracted much interest. The films *Schindler's List* and *Saving Private Ryan* were released to much fanfare and critical acclaim. The United States Holocaust Memorial Museum, a work in progress for over a decade, opened its doors on a cold April day in 1993. These events signaled to those who had lived through World War II that it was okay to begin to talk about these things, that maybe people were finally ready to listen.

Building on that momentum, I conjured up a simple survey for students to interview family members, kindling something that every teacher searches for—a tool to motivate and encourage students to want to learn more, for the sake of just learning it. We brought veterans into the school for forums with the student body. Young people who despised school stopped me in the hall to voice appreciation after listening to them. I learned a lot about World War II, but I also learned a lot about teaching.

Shortly after the 50th anniversary of the end of the war, we took it a level further, initiating a dedicated project on the oral history on World War II and starting a website for the testimonies we recorded. My students also began to fan out into the community to listen to and record the stories, forging bonds and bridging generational divides, and bringing happiness and companionship to their elders. These students became collectors of memory, improved their 'people skills,' honed their capacity for sustained concentration and analytics, and sharpened their writing chops for college in the process. And besides, it was fun. At some primal level we knew what we were doing was important, but we had no idea what this project would lead to in the years ahead.

Thirty years later, I think back on these moments when I was going to leave teaching before I even really got started. Maybe there is something to be said about persevering and finding one's way.

And maybe, the universe had other plans.

CHAPTER NINE

A Date with the Cosmos

1989/Hudson Falls, New York

My father jiggles the key into the lock of the back door to his school, and we slip in to the back stairwell leading up to the floor where his office is located. I'm meeting him after school, now in my third year of teaching. The old man is intent on giving me notes or filmstrips or some other teaching materials, which I don't really want, reminding me of the times in high school when he tried to hand down his old ties or worse, his Haggar slacks— *'I bought an extra pair, they'll fit you good.'* While he was the style king in his day as a 30-something teacher in the swinging '60s—the first to don a turtleneck in the classroom, the first to sport a beard in the high school—I'll stick to Mom's fashion sense, thanks.

We encounter three young teens kicking a crushed milk carton around. As we move in their direction, they disregard us, absorbed in this mindless miscreant activity, slapping away with their feet in rhythmic passes. I feel like I am doing the old man a favor by meeting him, but I can't get past the fact that these knuckleheads seem to be defying the surprise appearance of authority on their stage. I wonder how My Father the Teacher is going to handle this—would they be sent to the office? Reprimanded? Told to pick up the milk carton and exit the building promptly?

With fluidity that hardly breaks his stride, he leaps in the middle and completes a few passes back and forth. I don't think he even knows these guys, but he does not care. He's in the moment, for the moment, and enjoys the kids more than the power he could probably lord over them. So here is a lesson, after all, even though we never even observed one another teach in the classroom; no pretensions, no airs, just acceptance, trust-building, respect.[50] Dad retired a few years later after 30 years of teaching, and in a 1992 newspaper story that was written on us as father/son teachers he remarked, 'Matthew's very independent....*and if you know your subject and you're fair, it doesn't make any difference what you teach.*'

It was making sense to me that a sense of confidence in the classroom allayed most of the problems that had the potential to arise, and that harnessing my passions with students made all the difference in the world. And so it was that I pursued my passion even outside of the classroom, and set forth on the journey, the manifestations of which would resonate through time like ripples on a pond. I was about to start tossing pebbles.

*

---

[50] *acceptance, trust-building, respect*-As a young teacher, the author acknowledges that such actions described here about his father were beyond his ability to pull off, and probably not recommended. Dad just didn't care about the small stuff, and that was the whole point.

June 2001

My dad passed away in the summer of 2000. As we approached the first anniversary, I arrived to pick up my young children from daycare and struck up a conversation with another dad. Tim Connolly knew of my interest in interviewing World War II veterans, and that we had recently begun publishing the oral history narratives on a class website. He suggested that I come over to his house when school got out for the summer, as his father-in-law, a retired New York State Supreme Court justice and Army veteran, would be in town.

July 26, 2001/Hudson Falls, New York

A pleasant summer afternoon and I am sitting in another living room here in my hometown, talking to a man I have never met before. He is tall and fit, smiling, and has recently turned eighty years old, hands gripping the arms of the rocking chair in his daughter's living room. He is the picture of health, punctuating the air with his infectious, good-humored laugh and with a twinkle in his eye as he is recounting his Army travails as a combat soldier in the European Theater of Operations. I think I know a bit about World War II, and we have a lively conversation, back and forth, for almost two solid hours. I took the time that afternoon to talk to Judge Carrol Walsh, and somehow the universe tilted just long enough for a crack to be opened across time and space. But it almost did not happen.

*

In 1945, Sergeant Walsh was the tank commander of Tank 13, a Sherman light tank in Dog Company of the 743rd Tank Battalion, an armored unit working in tandem with the famed 30th Infantry Division. He had arrived in France in July 1944, and by the time that the Battle of the Bulge had broken out the following December, he was commanding his own tank and crew of four. That July afternoon 57 years later he told me many stories of pitched battles and close calls, of weeks that alternated between the extremes of boredom and sheer terror. As he put it,

I [was] twenty-four. I would have been in combat for ten months. That is a long time to survive—to survive ten months was to survive a hundred years! I could not even remember my former life... I was a fugitive from the law of averages, as it was.

It has been a wonderful interview, really more of a freewheeling discussion with a person who feels like an old friend on a subject of mutual passion. As the conversation winds down, I am confident that I have a gold mine of first-person World War II testimony from the combat soldier's perspective, and I'm almost at the point of packing up the video camera that I have set up; it's summer after all, and I have other things that I need to do today. Judge Walsh's daughter, though, has a final question for her father. I sit back, and listen politely for a few moments more. She puts the question to her father:

Elizabeth Connolly: Did you mention the train at all? That was kind of interesting.

No, I didn't tell him about the train.

Matthew Rozell: What was that?

Well, late in the war, again a nice, beautiful April day—we were shooting like crazy across the top of Germany, and Major Benjamin of the 743rd was kind of out ahead scouting a little bit—he came back to the battalion and he pulled my tank and George Gross's tank [fellow tank commander] out. He told us to go with him. So we did.

We came to a place where there was a long train of boxcars. I can remember pulling up alongside the train of boxcars, Gross and I, and Major Benjamin. As it turned out, it was a train full of concentration camp victims, prisoners who were being transported from one of their camps… I think they had been in Belsen, on their way to another camp…

So there they were. All of these people, men, women, children, jam-packed in those boxcars, I couldn't believe my eyes. And there they were! So, now they knew they were free, they were liberated. That was a nice, nice thing. I was there for a while that afternoon. You know, you got to feed these people! Give them water. They are in bad shape! Major

Benjamin took some pictures, and George Gross took some pictures too…

That was a nice, nice thing.' Later, this will strike me as the understatement of all time.

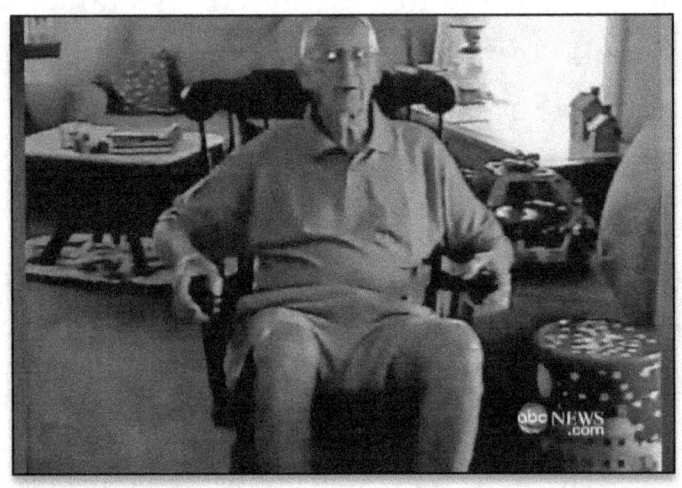

Screenshot of author's videotaped interview with Carrol Walsh, July 2001.

Though we could not know it at that moment in the summer of 2001, we had just had a date with the cosmos. A portal across time and space had just unlocked, and I was about to step across the threshold, changing our lives and the lives of hundreds of other people.

I finished recording the end of the conversation, and with my curiosity piqued, I shook hands with Judge Walsh and headed out the door.

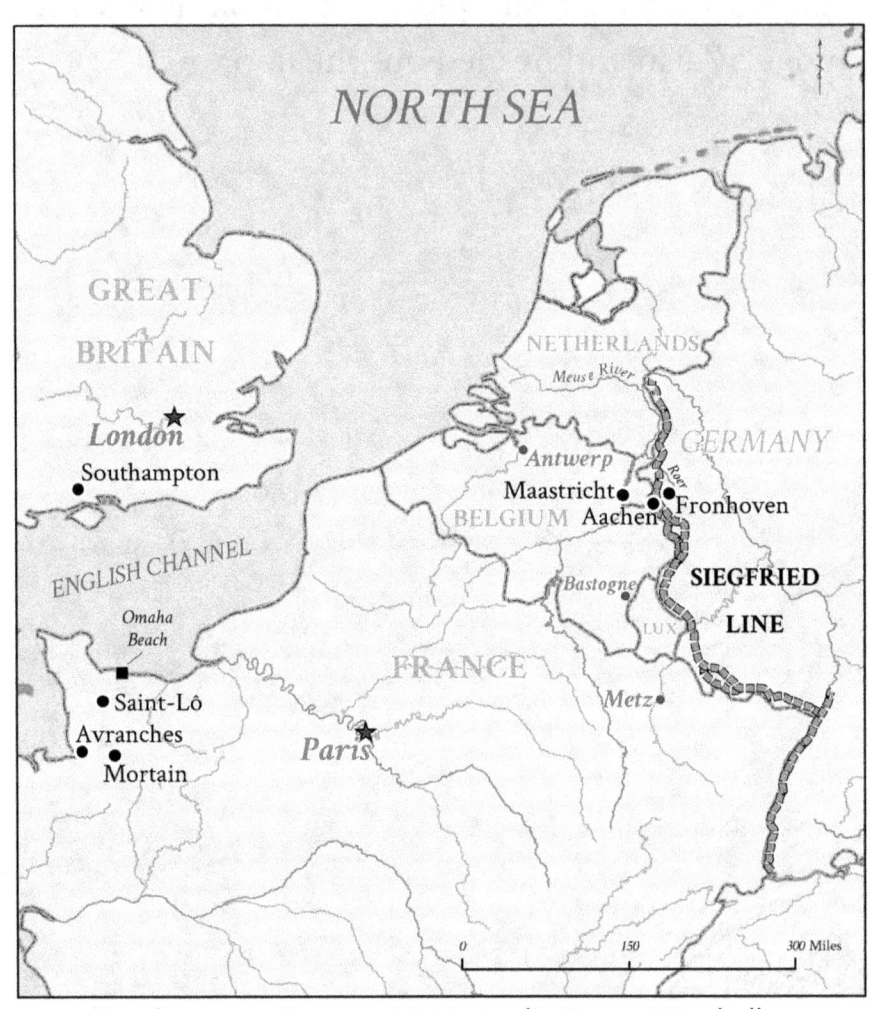

Northwestern Europe, 1944. Credit: Susan Winchell.

CHAPTER TEN

A Time to Die

1945/Fronhoven, Germany

Red Walsh knew he was about to die.

It was his time. The tall, lanky Irish-American supposed that he and his four-man tank crew should have been killed weeks ago in this race to destroy the enemy, who had clearly not gotten the message that they were going to lose the war. Fighting or moving rapidly now for sometimes eighteen hours at a stretch, being shot at or shelled even at periods of rest, had taken a heavy toll; the vow of honor and motto of his 743rd Tank Battalion, '*We Keep the Faith,*' had been upheld. Now he was resigned, serene, and at peace with the realization; he was going to die.

The jump-off time for the attack on the little town of Fronhoven, less than twenty miles into Germany, had been delayed. No wonders there. Army life did not suit the twenty-four-year-old sergeant from upstate New York. He railed, in his own way, against what he saw as the stupidity of regulation and regimentation. Just five months into heavy combat, he knew from experience that sometimes 'the Army way' got men killed.

His real name was Carrol, and with that easy laugh and red hair he had taken to courting a girl named Dorothy after moving to the state capital to enroll in law school, fifty miles from home. He was returning with Dorothy to her home for dinner on that Sunday afternoon when her father met them at the door with a troubled expression and asked if they had heard the news. After the initial shock, they all realized that no one knew where Pearl Harbor was. But the Japanese knew where it was, and December 1941 was not a grand time to be a first-semester Albany Law School student.

His friends were enlisting, and others were being called up. His parents urged him to stay in school. For a while he followed their wishes, but

Carrol was antsy, so he scheduled a physical and enlisted in the Army the following August. The Army put him in the enlisted reserve corps, and told him to stay in school for the time being. He continued with school, but felt funny. They didn't call. His friends went off to war. A bit of shame got the better of him, so he went down to the post office building in Albany, went into the Army office there, and told the officer on duty that he thought it was time that they called him up. 'Listen, buddy, we'll run the Army,' was the reply. 'You don't run the Army. When we want you, we'll tell you!' Privately relieved, he continued his studies, but as his class shrank, he no longer made the trip home to Johnstown. He was too ashamed. He and another student were the only ones left in the class who were not classified as 4-F, or unfit for combat. This was serious. The stigma was such that college girls would not even date the young men who had been left behind. You had to have a really good reason for not being in the service—and even then, failing your induction physical was not a good enough reason.

Finally, the call came. Carrol and his friend took the bar exam at Albany Law School. Two days later they were in the Army and picking up cigarette butts on the parade grounds of Camp Upton, Long Island. He took his basic training and walked guard duty at Fort Knox, studying Army radio code, which he found interesting. He also took tank training, and his group was then shipped to Fort Campbell, Kentucky, for more armored training with the 10th Armored Division—everyone except him and a few others, because alphabetically, his last name did not make the cutoff list. He was shipped instead to Fort Meade in Maryland, awaiting further orders as a future replacement soldier. It was March of 1944. Since late 1942, when the American fight forces landed in North Africa to fight with the British, costly and powerful lessons had been learned as inexperienced soldiers and their commanders garnered hard-earned experience through early setbacks. The momentum of battle was carried into Sicily and now into Italy, where near impossible German mountaintop defenses would be encountered on the road to Rome and beyond. Now, on the eve of Rome's fall, the much heralded second front was about to open on the beaches of Normandy.

At Fort Meade, 'Red' had a final physical, the one that would determine whether or not he would go overseas. He was nearsighted and now required glasses. The kindly older doctor furrowed his brow as he gave him the results.

'Young man, I have bad news for you.' He paused.

Red thought, 'Well okay, he's going to tell me there is a boat out there in the Chesapeake Bay ready to go to Africa or Italy or someplace, and I'm going to be on it in about ten minutes.'

But he said, 'You'll never fight for your country.'

Red thought, 'That might not be so bad, I'm not going to argue too much.'

But then the doctor said, 'I'm going to do you a favor, I'm going to let you go overseas. Now they'll have to find some kind of a job for you, but because of your eyes, you can never be in combat.'

Red nodded and thought, 'Okay, maybe I will survive.'

So Red shipped out, and that conversation was the last time that he heard anything about being a 'noncombatant' even though it was stamped all over his records in bold print. Later, for fun, the 743rd Tank Battalion's company clerk would wave Red's service record aloft to the assembled grizzled tank crews and say, 'Now, gentlemen, I want you to know that we have a real hero among us, someone who does not have to be here but who has volunteered to give his all.' Wise guys. Everyone would have a hearty laugh, and Red would join in. To the Army he was just another warm body—for the time being, at least.

*

The top-secret planning for the 'Operation Overlord' was coming to fruition in a rapid full-scale frenzy of last-minute preparations. A million-plus men and supporting matériel from the United States had settled in Britain, so much that a wit remarked that if not for the barrage of balloons tethered to the ground, the island would have sunk.[43] Part of the grand strategy depended on a steady supply of replacement bodies for those killed or wounded in the Normandy landings, the largest combined land-sea-air assault in the history of the world. For sixteen days, Red and the convoy of soldiers sailing from New York City zigzagged across the Atlantic, wary of submarines and dodging seasickness. Landing in Liverpool, the replacements were sent south to the Salisbury Plain, and then down to Southampton, where they were greeted by nice ladies with coffee and donuts. In July, a few weeks after the initial invasion, they were taken across the English Channel. By this time, the division that his tank battalion was now attached to had fought inland about ten miles. At his landing zone off Omaha Beach, Red and the men waded to shore, which three weeks later had been cleared of bodies and much of the detritus of battle. He looked up and he could not believe it. The bluffs of Point Du Hoc overlooking the beach had been scaled and captured by the Army Rangers with grappling hooks only a few weeks before in the heat of battle. On the high ground overlooking the draws and gullies leading off the beach, the sight of concrete pillboxes and machine gun nests with walls 10 feet thick filled him with a quiet awe for what the men who had landed that day faced and had to fight through.

The night before the D-Day landings, the Allies had dropped 13,000 airborne troops behind enemy lines to secure vital crossroads and bridges for the men who would come in after daybreak. Coastal defenses had been targeted by the air in massive aerial bombardments, though many bombs had gone astray. At dawn, Navy ships opened up and chinked away at the heavily fortified bluffs overlooking the landing areas at Omaha Beach but quieted as landing craft churned the rough surf toward the death zone. Some soldiers slipped over the side of the boats into water that was too deep to touch bottom; others were cut down as they waded in water up to their necks. Engineers were targeted as they tried to fix demolition charges to the various beach obstacles laid down as part of Hitler's Atlantic Wall. Nevertheless, the first tankers of the 743rd Tank Battalion did touch down on that bloody morning, and made it onto the beach and up to the seawall; one recalled hearing the machine gun bullets hitting the tank, a sound he likened to throwing glass marbles at a car. Explosions rocked the crew inside, and of the 15 tanks in

Company A, only his tank and four others survived.[51]

Red and the men continued up the sandy path off the beach, now cleared and taped off in safe lanes where only a few weeks earlier 2,500 men had fallen, taking this ground by the square foot. German signposts on either side mocked him in ominous skull and crossbones declarations—'*Achtung! Mienen!*—as the men carried their packs on towards the replacement depot where they would receive their new orders. By now Red was one of a million men having arrived in Northern France, and the tank he was assigned to was one of the quarter million vehicles which had landed since June 6.

Red received his orders and joined the men of his tank battalion, which consisted of three companies of 15 medium Sherman tanks and one company of 15 more mobile light tanks. Unlike the armored divisions of World War II, the tank battalions were attached to and supported infantry

---

[51] The testimony of Silver Star recipient William Gast can be found in my 2019 book, *D-Day and Beyond: The Things Our Fathers Saw—The Untold Stories of the World War II Generation-Volume V.*

divisions by working in tandem with the soldiers on the ground in fluid combat situations, and many an engagement was turned by the exploitation of the swift-moving and maneuverable Shermans.

Sherman Medium M4A1 tank, Italy, 1944. Credit: US Army.

Light tanks also had a crew of four, instead of the medium's five: the tank commander, who directed all tasks and gave the orders in combat; the driver, who when confined to using the periscope probably found the experience like trying to steer a tractor on the battlefield through a viewfinder; the gunner, who had to accurately fix on a target as the commander called it out and fire the 37-mm cannon; and the bow gunner, responsible for the firing of the .30-caliber machine gun protruding from the front deck of the tank. In Red's light tank, the tank commander also fulfilled the function of the big gun's loader, slamming the shell into the breech so the gunner could ready the cannon to fire. The Sherman was the work horse of the American armor; by the time Red was assigned to 2nd Platoon, Dog Company, production rates were soaring back home in the States, and northern France was dotted with 4,500 Shermans as they tried to break through the German lines. The Germans, by contrast, had one-third the number of tanks available, but it was usually no contest if a battalion light tank, moving swiftly with the infantry soldiers, found itself one-on-one with more heavily armored German tanks; in fact, a light tank like Red's, mounted with its already obsolete 37-mm gun, was known to have its rounds bounce harmlessly off the six-inch-thick rolled steel plating of some of these German monsters. The gasoline-powered Shermans could also burst into flames if an enemy round penetrated the engine compartment, touching off the fuel and rounds of shells and ammunition.[44] The Shermans, and the men in them, seemed to be expendable.

Carrol 'Red' Walsh

We thought we were hit once. We had run into a situation where we did not know there was German armor, and we took cover in some woods. Of course, the Germans had the woods zeroed in! So the Germans are dumping all sorts of big shells into the woods. A shell had exploded on the right side of our tank, but artillery will not hurt you that much in the tank if you are buttoned up, although the concussion can hurt you, if it is close; the pressure created can kill you somehow. Did you know that?

But anyway, the shell came in and struck. Then all of a sudden there was a lot of smoke in the tank. Schultsie, the commander, said, 'Jeez, we are hit! We got to get out of here!'

If a tank is hit, you have about three seconds to get out; the reason is because if the tank is hit, the ammunition in the tank will be set off and the tank will blow up! So we see all the smoke and we know what will happen. Naturally we would have to get out. So, remembering to open the hatch, I started out along with the driver. The tank commander and the gunner got out through the turret and scrambled behind the tank somehow. So Earl Dhanse, the driver, and I start up out of the tank, and here comes another shell! 'KABOOM!' It was very close! So we said, 'Jeez, we have to get back down in! What are we going to do? They are shelling outside and the tank is going to blow up!'

So we backed down into the tank, looking at each other, and we panicked. We figured the tank was going to go up any minute. But it was not hit—fortunately, it was not any kind of direct hit; the shell had exploded next to the tank and had made it lurch. We realized that the tank was not hit because it would have been burning by then. So we just stayed in the tank and sat out the artillery barrage; I think the only casualty from the entire group was a kid from Chicago who lost his hearing because of concussion [*laughs*]. I thought, 'What a lucky guy!' They took him out of combat and he was going home. But he was still alive. You would give your hearing or anything to get out of combat alive! Have you ever heard the expression, 'Million-dollar wound?' You prayed for a million-dollar wound! Anything! 'Well, I lost an arm but I'm alive. Hooray!' [*slaps knee, laughing boisterously*] That is ridiculous, but that was the way it was.

*

The 743rd Tank Battalion was now attached to the 30th Infantry Division, and Red's first major battle with the enemy was at the Norman town of Saint-Lô. The 30th Division originated in the South and was nicknamed the 'Old Hickory' division in honor of President Andrew Jackson. Later christened the 'Workhorse of the Western Front,' it had a history that dated back to the trenches of France in an earlier fight against the Germans, and it was now fully committed again in the ancient Norman hedgerows. With centuries-old sunken lanes and earthen embankments, this terrain was a nightmare of ambush, attack, and counterattack at the hands of a determined enemy well-concealed behind the screen of foliage. The maze of hedgerows was dubbed 'Green Death' for the way it divided the battlefront into innumerable 'small boxes, with each box a separate battle, a lone tactical problem on a checkerboard of fields, each in itself a single objective to be fought for, gained, or lost.'[45] But push on, they did. Casualties were high as they fought towards the west bank of the Vire River, and more replacements were needed.

By July 20 Saint-Lô had finally given way, and the men of the 30th Infantry Division, the 743rd Tank Battalion, and the attached 823rd Tank Destroyer Battalion were gearing up for the vaunted breakthrough just to the west. It would be rough, so the high command decided to coordinate the largest air assault in support of ground troops ever, waves of medium and heavy bombers winging their way from England over the target area five miles wide. At the jump-off point on July 24, soldiers and tankers looked up as hundreds of planes droned overhead and began to release their deadly payloads in response to the red smoke that rose to mark the target area. Tankers started their engines, and the infantry began to deploy. H-hour was here, but so was the south wind which carried the red smoke directly over their positions 1,200 yards behind the target area. Twenty-four men of the 30th Infantry Division were killed and more than five times that number were wounded, but Red and the men of the 743rd were relatively unscathed, though badly shaken. The attack was called off and postponed for 24 hours.

July 25 brought another clear day, and three miles up the bombers appeared again in their stately formations to rip their holes in the German lines. The men on the ground readied themselves and breathed a little easier as the first bombs hit their marks. Soon thereafter the second wave appeared, and the earth quaked as those bombers hit their marks. A sergeant of the 743rd looked up, watching the next wave of medium bombers, and saw that when the bombers were directly over their heads, their bomb bays dropped open and to his horror the bombs began tumbling out like peanuts coming straight down at the tankers. He dived under a bulldozer as the ground shook and the sky grew dark; dense smoke now covered the target area, and the red smoke was no longer distinguishable. As the day turned to night and the bombing intensified, men were buried alive or blown apart, including the Lieutenant General Lesley McNair, the commander of all ground forces who was visiting from Washington, D.C.—the highest ranking American officer to be killed in the European Theater of World War II. The 30th Infantry Division lost another 64 killed, with 324 wounded and 60 more missing, probably blown to bits.[52] An additional 164 men were classified with 'combat fatigue'; nevertheless, the 30th was ordered to jump off as planned through the opening in the German lines.

Dazed men staggered forward and tanks rode over the dead. Infuriation at the airmen diffused into unmitigated fury for the enemy. Utter destruction was the norm as the bombardment also buried German tanks, knocked out enemy communications and strongpoints, and cratered the fields and roadways. For the next two days, 100,000 men poured forward as the Allied forces smashed out of Normandy and the hedgerow country. After 49 days of combat, the men of the 30th Infantry Division and the 743rd Tank Battalion were finally pulled off the line, with the

---

[52] *60 more missing, probably blown to bits-* Veteran Frank Towers recalled, 'Those who were missing were later recovered with bulldozers... and many of them are still buried in the American Military Cemetery overlooking Omaha Beach, where they first landed only a month earlier. Towers, Frank W. *Operation Cobra,* http://www.30thinfantry.org.

opportunity to take their first showers, replace more equipment and men, and maybe even catch a USO show or a few hours of much needed shut-eye. Soon enough, they would be back in the thick of it.

*

Summertime in France. At four o'clock, the birds began to sing, and the morning glow intensified as the tankers stirred from their half-sleep. Eighteen hours later, dusk would give way to dark, but the men on many of these days would still be on alert and on the go. German planes and artillery would take advantage of less than six hours of darkness to harass the weary men. Everyone was on edge but there was little time for settling in; they were on their way to relieve the 1st Division holding the line at a sleepy little town called Mortain. On the 45-mile trek to Mortain, the roads were lined with the young and old, welcoming the soldiers and tankers as their liberators, 'cheering and throwing bouquets, and offering drinks at every halt. One could easily feel that the Germans would not stop [retreating] short of the Rhine River,' one officer remembered.[46] It was a much needed boost to their morale, but little did the men know that Mortain was the very place that the Germans would launch a major counterattack with four panzer divisions, conceived by the Führer himself.[53]

The breakthrough in Normandy had telegraphed to the German High Command the unwelcome possibility that the Germans might have to withdraw from France or risk being encircled and trapped. Neither option was acceptable, so Hitler himself drew up the plans with the expectation of punching through the American lines and driving to the coast at Avranches, forcing a wedge into the advancing armies and stopping the hemorrhaging, perhaps even pushing the invader back all the way to the sea. Having survived the July 20 assassination attempt, he was in no mood to listen to objections; and so it was that the 30th Infantry Division, 743rd Tank Battalion, and the 823rd Tank Destroyer Battalion came to one of the crossroads of the entire Normandy campaign.

The soldiers and tankers took their positions in and around the small town of 1,300, but had had

---

[53] *panzer*-German armor, generally tanks.

little time to reconnoiter the surrounding territory. Roadblocks were set up, and on the high ground of Hill 314, with its commanding views of the countryside, 700 men tried to settle in. Control of the hill meant control of the roads. Five days later, only half were able to stagger off the hill under their own power.[47]

Shortly after midnight on August 7, 26,000 Germans and the first of 400 tanks, including the lead elements of the black-uniformed crews of the 1st SS Panzer Division *Leibstandarte SS Adolf Hitler*, began to attack. With a barrage of rockets, artillery fire, and mortar rounds, they enveloped most of the American positions on the roads surrounding the town in short order. The afternoon would bring counter attacks by the rockets of RAF Typhoon fighter bombers targeting the panzers, but also taking out some of the 743rd's Sherman tanks. As dark fell on the evening of the 7th, the men on Hill 314 were surrounded by the 2nd SS Panzer Division.[54] The 743rd's assault gun platoons fired

---

[54] *2nd SS Panzer Division* – The 'Das Reich' SS Division had already distinguished itself in keeping with the standards of barbarity the SS has been noted for. In a reprisal raid on June 10 in the quaint Norman town of Oradour-sur-Glane, members systematically murdered 642 French civilians and razed the town. Men were herded into garages and barns and shot; women

shells packed with morphine and medical supplies, which burst on impact.

As the Germans repeatedly tried to scale the hill, an artillery spotter called down round after round through his fading radio set, delivering death on his doorstep from five miles distant.[48] The hill held. Watching the battle closely, Hitler called for a renewed effort to take Mortain and this troublesome obstacle. Under a white flag of truce, the SS officer expressed his admiration for the stand and demanded surrender. The senior officer refused, releasing a pent-up, colorful reply and calling in an artillery barrage on his own position as the Germans attacked it.[49] The hill held, and on August 11 the Germans began their withdrawal amid constant shelling and harassment from the air. While the 30th had lost over 2,000 men, the Germans had had their attack blunted and nearly 100 tanks knocked out or abandoned.[50] It was the start of the German movement to the Siegfried Line and their westward defenses on the border of the Reich

---

and children were forced into a stone church and burned to death. The town was never rebuilt and stands today as a silent memorial to wartime atrocity. See Atkinson, Rick. *The Guns at Last Light: The War in Western Europe, 1944-1945.* New York: Henry Holt & Co., 2013. 94.

itself; by the end of August, some 10,000 Germans had been killed in the pocket and 50,000 captured. The German commander, relieved of his command and summoned back to Germany by Hitler, chose to commit suicide by cyanide instead. The Battle of Normandy was nearly over, and the Germans had lost the equivalent of 40 divisions— nearly a half million men, killed, wounded, or captured.[51] The Allies sustained over 209,000 killed and wounded, sixty percent of them being US ground troops.[52]

As the tankers and soldiers sped northward in pursuit, Paris was liberated on August 25, but they only caught glimpses of the top of the Eiffel Tower from a distance.[53] With the coming of autumn, the tankers and infantrymen pushed into the Low Countries, and the 30th Division was the first Allied division to enter Belgium and the Netherlands. In just three months they had fought from the Normandy coastline and were now knocking at the gates of the Reich itself.

Carrol 'Red' Walsh

Now let me tell you, that was the way to fight a war! We just ripped up through France, into Belgium, and into Holland. We were the first troops in those areas, and boy they were glad to see us, I tell you! We would have rations in the tank—cigarettes, chocolate, 10-in-1 rations, and K-rations.[55] We were throwing them out, these people didn't have much to eat, so they were so glad, and we were glad to be giving them these things. And then we ran out of cigarettes, and we almost died! Cigarettes, you know, who wants them today? But back then that was a big thing for us—we lived on cigarettes! God, we were taking coffee, ground coffee seeds, and wrapping them up in newspaper and smoking them! Honest to Pete, we gave our cigarettes away until supply caught up with us, but we were getting all the wine, the cognac bottles they were giving us, and we were running out of room. So we would take them in the tank. The shells were in these racks on the side. We got so we were throwing some shells out and putting the

---

[55] *10-in-1 rations-* one day of meals in a small case for 10 soldiers: breakfast, midday snack, evening meal. *K-ration-* individual daily combat food ration

wine bottles in. [*Laughs*] We knew we could get more shells, but we wanted that wine and the cognac.

We were in this place called Cambrai, and the Germans were running one way and we were going the other way. Anyway, we were on the line, and there was a nice Belgian lady coming down and offering a drink to all of us. I think that might have been calvados, which was the worst stuff that ever was, it burnt real bad.[56] There was this new kid [replacement soldier] from New York City, he didn't drink. He was a student at Columbia, so he was no dummy. We said to him, 'We know what [the drink] is, and what it would do to you if you just took a good shot?' [*Laughs*] We told him, 'Gee, it would be against proper diplomatic policy to refuse a drink—it would be ill-mannered! It certainly wouldn't hurt you just to take one sip offered by this woman, so that she would know that you were grateful,' and so on. So he agreed, [*laughs again*] and he was standing on the deck of the tank and he took it in hand. We told him, 'Now whatever you do, throw it down fast.' That was the worst thing

---

[56] *calvados*-an apple brandy produced within the French region of Normandy

you could do! [*Laughs harder*] He leaped right off the back of that tank, yelling!

When that happened, I was 23. Now actually I was kind of an old guy for the time. I was old, and I was looked upon as old. A lot of the infantry guys were eighteen, nineteen years old. [*Takes more serious, reflective tone*] Oh yeah, I was considered an old guy. Now let me tell you about the combat I was in. Like I said before, you couldn't remember what your mother looked like; you thought you had been there forever. I was in combat ten months straight. You have to realize that was a long time to be in combat and still be alive or not wounded. You just give up; you know there is no use to hoping that maybe you will get out tomorrow, you just are going to go on. You have that feeling and you just trot along; that's why we did that crazy stuff to the poor kid with the calvados. It was great through Belgium and Holland because Germans were not even fighting you. Oh, you would run into a firefight once in a while, but then they would just scatter. Once we got to the Siegfried Line, then they would tighten up. From October into December, it was bad. We were in

Germany, the 743rd and 30th Division. We were north of Aachen, we even fought at Aachen. That was tough going.

*

On September 14, Maastricht was liberated by the soldiers of the 30th, the first Dutch city to be liberated by the Allies. The path to the Fatherland from here across the Meuse River was only about twenty miles; German artillery opened up on the Americans as the push to the 'Dragon's Teeth' began. Here at the Siegfried Line, or 'Westwall' as Hitler called it, a three-mile-deep complex network of bunkers and reinforced concrete pyramid-like projections were designed to slow down advancing armor into a killing zone right at the German border. Every village along the line was part of the fortress system; pillboxes built by the hundreds were heavily concealed, interconnected, and houses were loaded with snipers.[54] Airstrikes from England and artillery barrages inspired terror and awe, but in the end it fell to the common foot soldier and the tanks to root out the defenders. The tankers began attempting to blow open the fortified positions with high explosive rounds, then hitting the opening with flame-throwing tanks, or burying the tenacious defenders alive with bulldozing tanks. The 743rd claimed 18 German tank kills but lost 22 of their own.[55] Heavier engagements were now the norm, and the men of the 30th found that if they did not swiftly move forward after subduing a German pillbox, a counterattack was likely to materialize.[56]

Sol Lazinger, from Brooklyn, New York, joined the army at age 17, and at age 18 found himself on the front lines with the 117th Regiment of the 30th Infantry Division.

Sol Lazinger

I was a rifleman. I was young. We [look back, and] try to compare ourselves after sixteen weeks of basic training—and we went into combat fighting German soldiers who had a minimum of five years' worth of army experience. It was not the easiest thing in the world, but we did the best we could.

I fought my way through France. I was very lucky because I was in combat for most of the time. I went through many battles all through France,

Belgium, and Holland; and when the big officers came around, they used to tap me and say, 'Oh, you're still here?'

When we broke through the Siegfried Line and attacked, many of my friends were killed. One fellow by the name of Ben Shelsky was a replacement soldier [like me]; he went over the Siegfried Line, too. He got a telegram from the Red Cross that said his wife gave birth to his child. The next morning a sniper killed him; the telegram telling him that he became a father was sticking out of his pocket.

So we went across the Siegfried Line and went to a town by the name of Lubeck, Germany. After the first day there, I was wounded in street fighting; I spent on and off almost two years in the hospital—I had most of my left ankle blown out by machine gun bullets.

When someone lost a friend, we sort of tried to stick together even though we were all from different parts of the country. And you get sort of down with everything, but as I say, you know, we did the best we could, but it was an uphill battle fighting against the soldiers who were trained for longer periods of time. But I think the American boys did very well.

Just six miles into Germany lay the first enemy city to be assaulted. Aachen's significance was also symbolic, for here was the old capital of the First Reich, and the tomb of the first Holy Roman Emperor, Charlemagne.[57] With the 1st and 30th Infantry Divisions committed, the battle raged for nearly three weeks at a cost of about 5,000 casualties on both sides. By the time of the battle for Aachen, Red had graduated from bow gunner to being the driver of a light tank in Dog Company. Months of combat seemed like one hundred years; survival was the name of the game. 'Just keep going' was his mantra.

Unshaven, dirty, and tired, the tankers moved north with the infantry to push through towns on the way to the Roer River, coordinating their attacks by leapfrogging objectives by which a group

---

[57] *the First Reich*- the First Reich refers to the Holy Roman Empire, 962–1806, the Second Reich to the German Empire, 1871–1918, and the so-called Third Reich was the Nazi Party characterization for their 1933-1945 regime.

of tanks and infantry would secure a location, and another group would then rush past towards the second objective, and once secured, a third would continue to bump the line forward, while the other units in the rear regrouped. They slept in bombed-out basements and the weather had been turning for a while, the first snow arriving on November 9. Days were much shorter now, and maintenance crews began tuning up the tanks for the cold. Winter gear was still in short supply for the men, though. They bided their time for the next offensive.

Shortly before Thanksgiving, the time had come to advance towards the Roer, although with it came more rain and cold, a 'constant cold drizzle that fogged tank periscopes'… 'a man got wet, and stayed wet,' said one tanker. 'At least we don't have to walk through it like the doughs.'[58][57] Tanks bogged down and several struck mines.

The day before Thanksgiving, resistance stiffened. Three of the tanks in Red's battalion were caught in the middle of a muddy orchard outside of the village of Erberlich, Germany, and

---

[58] *doughs*-infantrymen, from the World War I slang, 'doughboys'.

destroyed with an enemy self-propelled 75-mm gun. Two others were knocked out in the same orchard by direct hits from a German tank and burned; Red knew all of the men who were killed.

And now it was Red's turn to accept the inevitable. On this same day they were ordered to break a cardinal rule, because of what somebody above must have insisted was out of necessity. The jump-off time to take the tiny German hamlet of Fronhoven was delayed, another typical Army goof-up. The tanks and infantrymen were ready to go, waiting for the order. Soldiers would typically either ride on the tank or walk beside it, but not today; *'All right, c'mon, let's move out! Let's go! Just the tanks!* As daylight was fading, his tank and the four other light tanks of 2nd Platoon, Dog Company, were ordered to speed to the objective without their scouts, their eyes and ears. The tankers knew better—what looked like an ordinary dirt road was most likely zeroed-in by German artillery guns, and it made the anxious crews gulp. Common sense told them not to go to a place where it was wide open during combat. But with their orders to proceed down it immediately, the tankers' best bet to come through it unscathed would be to race down the road, leaving the supporting infantry behind to catch up later, and pray it was not mined. And so it began.

Carrol 'Red' Walsh

They made us move down that road and we left the infantry far behind. So, we are racing down the road and I have not been a driver for very long. We also had a new bow gunner. On the bow gunner's left side of the tank are the levers for driving the tank. If you could not drive from the left side then you would have to pull the levers down to the right side. So I asked the bow gunner, 'Do you know about moving the levers?' and he replied, 'Yes.'

In a tank you can pull down the hatch. Inside the hatch is the periscope. If you think I could have seen much out of that periscope, you are crazy! I never could see anything, so when I drove I always had the hatch open! I could let the seat down, and just stick my eyes out so I could see without putting myself in too much danger. I could most certainly use the levers too! So there I was, and I said to the bow gunner, 'If I get hit you are going to have to pull the levers down so you can keep the tank going.'

Racing along at speeds of up to forty miles an hour with the hatch open, peering just over the turret top to see where he was going, Red grimaced as the dreaded German artillery fire opened up right on cue, his knuckles white as he gripped the hatchway and the shells landed nearby and the enemy gunners found their range. Rocks, dirt, and shrapnel rained down as the shelling crept closer and closer to the tank column flying to outrun the barrage. An explosion just ahead poured debris down the hatch into the tank, and Red glanced down to gauge the reaction of the crew inside, only to see his bow gunner reaching for the steering levers that Red was operating with his feet. Over the din he screamed and kicked the gunner's hands away—'*No, no, I am not hit yet!*

Miraculously, all five light tanks made it to the town. His commander ordered that they swing around a three-story building, and Red pulled the tank around. He put the tank between the buildings and where new machine gun fire was coming from, stopped the tank, and closed the hatch. Now, they were all buttoned up and pinned down, stranded and isolated in the tiny German village. He knew he and his men in the tank had no infantry, he knew that they were caught, and they all knew that they could not get out due to the volume of fire. Their time as 'fugitives from the law of averages' was rapidly winding down, as shrapnel, timber, bricks, and rubble rained down on top of the tank and all around them with each methodical round of artillery fire.

Hours passed. Sometime during the night, Red realized that they were not going to escape with their lives. Most of the others came to this conclusion as well; his tank commander was troubled, muttering and sighing deeply. He had reached his breaking point. The commander rocked back and forth, the stress of combat taking its toll, and it was disturbing Red to the point that he assigned himself guilt for the predicament that they were in.

Carrol 'Red' Walsh

During the night I realized that I was going to die. When I accepted this I felt peaceful; there was nothing that I could do. I cannot explain it but to say that I was not troubled or panic-stricken. In fact, I was quiet—everyone in the tank was quiet. We all just sat in the tank.

During the night, I heard poor Schultsie, who was up in the turret behind me, say, '*What did a man ever do to deserve this?*' Well, I got to thinking about some of the things that I had regretted doing in my life. I thought, 'Jeez, I hope all these guys never find out all the bad things that I have done that I am getting paid back for now, and that they have to suffer for too!' 'I hope these poor guys never find out that this was all my fault!' or 'Man, I wish I had never done that!' Honest to God, that is all I thought about.

*

Somehow the November dawn broke, gray, rainy, and cold, Thanksgiving Day, 1944, in that miserable little town just over the border in Germany. The men dared not move. Red knew it was just a matter of time before the Germans moved in to finish the kill, if not with a direct artillery hit, then with an anti-tank grenade, a round from an enemy tank, or simple infantry grenades. And the shelling continued.

Carrol 'Red' Walsh

We were shelled all day long the next day. We don't move, we can't move. We were shelled all the next night. If you had to go to the bathroom you could use your helmet to pee in, try to get that hatch open and throw it out. That's all you could do. I think we had, you know, those K-rations. They were packages you'd have canned with like meatloaf or something, cheese, bad stuff—you could hardly chew it. Anyway, we were shelled all that day and all the next night. And then the following day, I can't remember now if it let up a little bit... but we moved from where we were. You know, that rubble was all around. And we went to a great big building and I think all the tanks went in with me, like a big airplane hangar of some kind. I don't know what it was, but we got in there under cover. And you know, planes would come over and they couldn't see you. I think we got so shelled those two days after we moved in, that it was over. But you were a little shaky after that because they were so methodical you could time it. They were famous for that…you're probably aware of that, aren't you, that they were famous for being methodical in what they did… here's this little dump of a hamlet—why did they keep shelling? What did they think was there? Maybe they thought that there was a plan by our units there to have a big push from this place, so they were going to break up or stop the attack of several divisions or something.

Red and his crew returned to their quarters, weary but alive.

Carrol 'Red' Walsh

I loved Schultsie, but he had just had it. And you know, when you're in combat, a week is a long time, and a month is a long time. You're there for months until you almost forget what life was like before. He'd been there for a while, and of course by that time, we all had a lot of experience so we could handle things, despite the fact that Schultsie was doing nothing; he couldn't do anything. Schultsie got so he couldn't eat, he was vomiting. And I remember we finally went to the captain and said, 'Gee, it's going to kill this guy. Give him a break, take him out.' So they did, but he stayed with the outfit; he stayed there for the rest of the war, so we continued to see him. I really loved that man and he was no coward, don't get me wrong, it just was too much for him, just absolutely enough.

As November turned into December, 1944, the Germans had shown that they were not about to roll over. Thanksgiving packages and letters arrived for the men from home. The parcels addressed to the tankers recently killed went unopened.[59] And a new offensive by the Germans

---

[59] *The parcels addressed to the tankers recently killed went unopened*- In 2012, the author was alerted to the existence of an unopened World War II-era letter in a memorial museum in Belgium. The envelope was postmarked Nov. 27, 1944, and addressed from the USA to PFC Marvin K. Boller, D Co., 743rd Tank Battalion. It was also stamped 'DECEASED.' I wrote to Carrol, and he wrote back: *'Hi Matt, I was stunned when I read your message. I remember Boller very well and remember when he got killed. I believe it was just before Thanksgiving 1944 when a big German tank wiped out four tanks of the first platoon of Co. D of the 743rd. Every member of every crew of every one of the four tanks was killed. I seem to remember packages arriving for some of these guys after they had been killed. I used to tease Boller, who was an older man, because he wanted to vote for Tom Dewey and I was big*

was about to usher in the costliest battle in the history of American winter warfare.

The Battle of the Bulge was about to break.

---

for my pal, FDR. Boy what a memory you stirred up. I knew all the guys that got killed in that engagement.'

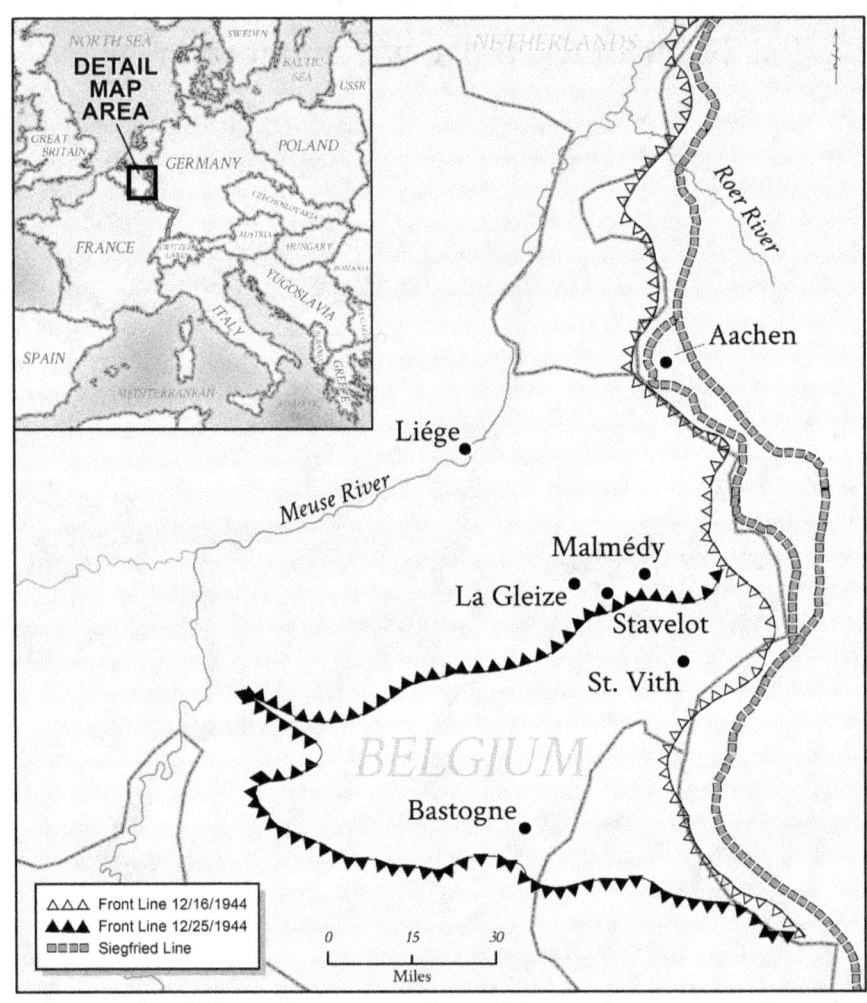

The Battle of the Bulge, December 1944, and areas mentioned in Chapter 11.
Credit: Susan Winchell.

CHAPTER ELEVEN

The Bulge and Beyond

On that beautiful day in July 2001, I left the Connolly house after having interviewed Judge Walsh armed with George Gross's contact information. A now-retired professor of English Literature at San Diego State University, Dr. Gross was delighted to learn of my interview with his old friend.

George Gross had enlisted in the Army in September 1943, after watching his friends and family go off to the war, giving up his deferment and his job in a California parachute factory. George joined up for many of the same reasons as Walsh, though it was clear from their first meetings that they were as different in deference to Army life as night and day. Where Red disdained Army rules and regulations, George seemed to thrive in it, earning a reputation for seriousness and respect among his fellow soldiers, even if Red would sometimes tease and tell jokes at his expense.

Carrol 'Red' Walsh

When I became the tank commander of that crew, and I tell you, when we were engaged in something, they were serious and followed things and would do what had to be done. But otherwise, they wouldn't pay any more attention than you guys [*speaks to students in author's classroom*] would pay attention to me. I became the tank commander and Gross stayed as the gunner, and that's when my friend Bruce 'Ace' Leyda became the driver and Peter 'Hot-Lips' Haverlock became the bow gunner. And Hot-Lips got mad at me… he'd been at headquarters company and he wanted to see more combat.

I said, 'You want to see more combat, Hot-Lips?'
'Yes.'

'Okay. So, we've got an opening for you. We'll put you in on Tank number 13, 2nd Platoon, Company D, 743rd Tank Battalion.'

So now he was the bow gunner and had a .30-caliber machine gun that goes out through the front of the tank. You see, there are hatches for the driver and the bow gunner, as well as a turret, but through the portal we had the .30-caliber machine gun. And we were called one time to help get some wounded guys who had been pinned down and fortunately there wasn't any major [enemy] armor in the area. So, anyway, we were called upon to go up to rescue these wounded, get them out of there, we could get some on the back of the tank and whatever. So, we start across this open area, and now we all got to fire a little bit, you see, so old Hot-Lips, in his first experience he's firing that .30-caliber. There was an opening between the tank commander where he stood on this basket and turret, and the bow gunner; he could give signals by kicking the guy in the head or something.

'Fire that gun there, Hot-Lips!'

So he starts firing the .30 caliber. Well, if you're not careful, that gun's going to rise, you see… and anybody who's handled guns knows that it's going to kick up. And you can watch it go, because every fifth bullet is a tracer round and you can follow how you're doing.⁶⁰ So anyway, there goes Hot-Lips and he's firing it, and boy, it's going right up in the air, and I said, 'Nice going, Hot-Lips, you shot down two ducks. We're lucky! We'll eat good tonight!'

And Hot-Lips got so mad at me and refused to fire anymore—he sat down and he wouldn't fire anymore! [*Laughs heartily*] Oh, man! That's some good stuff! Oh, he was so mad at me! So angry! But that was a great crew. That was a great crew, but they were fun.

Now George, our gunner, he was quite serious. Ace Leyda was our driver, Ace was quite the character and Ace and I would have fun; George was a good boxer back home and [within his earshot] we would say, 'Say, did you hear about Gross?'

'No, what about him?'

'Well, I hear he is a boxer, a champion boxer.'

'You don't say?'

---

⁶⁰ *tracer*-incendiary round making the trajectory visible to the naked eye during daylight, to correct aim

'Yeah, he could box more oranges in California than anybody else!' [*Laughs*]

But George was a good companion, fine, but he was a little more serious, and we called him 'GI George'…well, you know, he came from a military family. His father I think was a career Navy man, as I recall. So he was 'by the book,' and he didn't always approve of some of the behavior of the tank commander because I was really a—I was a civilian in an army uniform. I chafed a little bit on some of the discipline of things.

We were delayed one time, and I was very annoyed because we were supposed to help some infantry out, and we weren't moving. Something was holding it up, and I remember being quite annoyed thinking about these poor guys waiting for help. So anyway, here comes some brass. You know what I mean by 'brass.' Brass means like generals, or colonels, higher officer guys. They were very 'in charge,' I can tell you. And I didn't have the same feeling as George about the brass. So, as it so happened, one of the guys that was coming along to investigate what was going on, I don't know whether it was General Hobbs or not, who was you know, the head of the 30th Division, but it was a general, and I guess he saw that I was so annoyed. I think he came along, he said something, and I said, 'I'll tell you what, I wish they'd find out what the hell was going on up there because we want to get out of here, we want to help them out, and you better come back and tell us what's going on.'

Matthew Rozell: Did you know he was a general?

I guess—but in combat, Matt, you've got to remember, who cares in combat? But there was a gasp beside me from 'GI George,' and he never forgot that. You ask him about that encounter with the general sometime. He still gasps over that! [*laughs*] He couldn't believe that nothing happened! But that general was a regular guy. And he knew that there was no time for that nonsense, you know, that 'GI' stuff, really. I remember that, yeah. So there were moments… you had to do some things to kind of make yourself laugh a little bit.

George C. Gross

Carrol kept me sane through nine months of combat.

Recently married to his high school sweetheart Marlo, George left California to ship out to Fort Knox in Kentucky for armored training. He arrived in Normandy shortly after Red, and after the battle for Aachen, they found themselves sharing the same tank. Initially they clashed; bottled up in the same tank, sometimes they would lay out shells between them to delineate boundaries on occasions when they could not leave the confines of the tank during periods of rest. But the stress of combat also forged the bonds of battle. Cramped inside the tank during the two-day shelling at Fronhoven, the men both realized that their tank commander had reached his limits. Shortly thereafter, both Carrol and George received battlefield commissions to second lieutenant and command of their own tanks.

Unbeknownst to them, or anyone in the Allied ranks, Hitler's last gamble to counterattack between the advancing American and British forces in northern France and the Low Countries was in the staging phase of execution. The incredible magnitude of American industrial capacity dictated to Hitler that somehow the supply lines had to be cut, and he chose the Ardennes Forest for the avenue of attack in the hopes of reaching the port of Antwerp, combining the elements of surprise, rough ground, and bad weather for a quarter-million man offensive. On December 16, six hundred tanks broke through the thinly manned American lines after a tremendous artillery barrage, creating a bulge or pocket they hoped to exploit to the sea, and sowing desperation, panic, and confusion. The 30th Infantry Division and the 743rd Tank Battalion hurried south and found themselves in a desperate struggle for survival as temperatures plunged to the coldest in European memory during the winter of 1944–45.

Carrol 'Red' Walsh

It was muddy and cold, but we were doing okay. Then the Bulge came. We were doing just great, and then December 16 came.

We came back out, waiting to cross the Roer River. The Germans had the dams up there and we were hoping to get across the Roer before they burst the dams. While we were waiting to do that, we were getting everything together, and we were poised [to attack] when the Bulge hit. They were trying to get to the coast, to take Antwerp, to split the British and American forces to the north with the American forces to the south. We were in the Ninth Army then. We had been the First Army until September, I think, and then we joined the Ninth Army. We were in the north, and they were going to cut us off and annihilate us, they were going to let us have it. We were at Malmédy, Stavelot, St. Vith, and La Gleize. That is when we fought in the snow and cold. It was cold, and we had no winter uniforms. We didn't have any overshoes, and of course we couldn't wear any overcoat on a tank anyway.

Matthew Rozell, interviewer: So you slept in the tank?

Oh yeah, in the Bulge we slept in the tank.

*

430 | A TRAIN NEAR MAGDEBURG

Aftermath of Malmédy massacre. Credit: US Army.

On the northern front of the German offensive, on just the second day of the attack, the spearhead of the ruthless Joachim Peiper's 1st SS Panzer Division captured 150 Americans. Herded into a snowy field, the unarmed prisoners were mowed down by the SS with their machine guns, their Tiger tanks blocking any escape. More than eighty men were killed, the Germans moving through the field, kicking and delivering coup-degrâce pistol shots to the wounded. News of the Malmédy massacre steeled an unwritten American response: take no SS troops prisoners.[61] The barbarity extended to the civilian population as well. In the nearby hamlet of Stavelot, where more than 20 men, women, and children had been murdered, Joseph Couri of the 743rd Tank Battalion recalled:

> I observed an elderly man with a little covered wagon. He was pulling it and going into a garage directly across from my tank. He had made several trips down the street and when he came back he stopped at my tank. Since I could not speak Belgian, he pulled the cover from the wagon. I have never forgotten the sight of the two children's bodies. There they were, frozen with the older child's arms around the other as they were shot by the SS

---

[61] *Malmédy massacre- 'It was not until 13 January 1945 that American forces recovered the bodies. A total of 84 bodies (72 initially and 12 after the snow melted) were found. Because many of the dead were ravaged by animals or mutilated by artillery fire during the fighting to recapture the area, the exact number of prisoners that were shot during the shootings of 17 December 1944 will never be known. Autopsies, conducted in Malmédy, found that 41 of the prisoners were shot in the head and 10 had severe head injuries probably received from a rifle butt.'* –Frank Towers, www.30thinfantry.org/malmedy.

troops—they were still frozen in that position.[58]

Only days after this incident, the 30th Infantry and the 743rd Tank Battalion would repeatedly tangle with Peiper and their old SS nemesis from the battle of Mortain, regrouping and counterpunching as the tide of battle slowly turned. Peiper was denied his immediate target of Liège, on the way to Antwerp, having failed to breach the American line past Stavelot and Malmédy.

*

The German offensive collapsed by Christmas 1944 as the skies cleared and Supreme Allied Commander General Eisenhower brought to bear a quarter-million troops of his own at lightning speed. Although the Americans were now on the offensive, the US Army would suffer most of its battle casualties in pushing the Germans back through the sub-zero cold and waist-deep snow, artillery attacks, and enemy mines. Tanks ground slowly in low gear along snow-covered roads in the mine-free ruts of previous vehicles, any uneven surfaces liable to send the tank skating sideways without traction.⁵⁹

Carrol 'Red' Walsh

Of course, it wasn't very comfortable being in the tank in that cold, on cold steel. You were not very warm. We would take our boots off sometimes to rub our feet so they wouldn't freeze. It was so cold, but we had no winter clothes. They hadn't figured on that, you see; winter clothes were not a priority when they got the ports because the army was moving so well that the attitude was, 'The hell with that, we're going to get through with this [the war] by Christmas.' And they put the priority on food and shells and ammunition and things like that, and so we had no overshoes.

I was lucky; I had an undershirt like a sweatshirt and I had OD pants, you know, wool uniform pants.⁶² I had a pair of coveralls and I had a sweater, and my combat jacket. And I found a scarf. We had gloves but they weren't warm. The funny thing was, my father was a leather sorter in a glove shop in Johnstown and he sent me a

---

⁶² *OD*- army issue 'olive-drab'

beautiful pair of heavy mittens and that was great. I wrote to him and I said, 'Gee, Dad, that was great. They're nice and warm… the only problem, no trigger finger!' [*Laughs*] But the gloves they issued us were not warm enough in that climate.

Now some guys that came in later as replacement troops, they had more heavy clothes and they gave them overcoats. Of course they couldn't wear overcoats with the tank! You could not maneuver; you couldn't get in and out of the turret or out of the bow gunner's side door with a heavy overcoat! Oh, so cold… oh, man alive! I was never so cold ever in my life—ever! And it just stayed cold day and night. I mean, how are you going to get warm? The infantry guys were digging their holes—that was tough because the ground was frozen. Boy, they had to chop. That's where they lived. They lived in their holes and we lived in the tank.

George C. Gross

The tanks were so cold, our breath would freeze into little icicles about an inch and a half long on the roof of the turret, and our hands and our feet would be cold all the time. Once in a while we would come across some infantrymen who had built a fire. We would get out and warm one side of ourselves on the fire and then turn around to warm the other side and get back into the tank and freeze again. Occasionally we would be able to go into a house and stay in a house for a day or two and be warm but that would be it.

Carrol 'Red' Walsh

While we were in Malmédy, things had quieted in the latter stages of the Bulge. We would go out during the day—it was like going to work. About eight o'clock in the morning we'd be called and we'd have to go someplace, like to relieve troops.

I remember one day there was some infantry who had run into a firefight with some Germans. All infantry and, I guess, no armor, because they didn't want to send our light tanks against German tanks, because 37-millimeter guns were all we had on the light tanks, 75-millimeter on the mediums. Those Germans had the 88. That gun was the greatest gun that ever was, the 88. They used it for anti-aircraft, they used it for artillery, and they used it on the tanks, anti-tank gun, everything!

They could fire an 88 and I guess it could go two miles and still go through a tank! I think so; it was a long way.

Anyway, there was a group of Americans wounded and they were pinned down somehow. So we were told, 'You have to go up and clean out that nest of Germans and get those wounded back.' So we'd go up and we'd have our armored firepower and infantry, and then we'd give help. But then we'd pull back at night, and it got to some point we were able to pull back into Malmédy, and they said, 'Look, if you can find a place to sleep or stay, go ahead.'

We went to this house, three stories and everything. We went there and I can remember I could speak a little French from high school. We had our bow gunner at the time, 'Hot Lips' Havelock—he could speak some German, so we were in good shape. So I said, 'Avez-vous un lit pour quatre hommes?' (Have you got a bed for four men?) This woman was very nice and we stayed in her home. We hadn't had a bed in months! My God, she had those big comfortable featherbeds or whatever. [*Laughs*] When they could get rations to us, for the tankers...we could have 10-in-1 rations in a big box and they'd have things like bacon in one and some kind of meat or something in another. They weren't bad rations, [but sometimes] we could hardly eat some of that crap! Well, she was in bad shape because they didn't have much to eat in those areas and everything. So she would take that stuff and fix it up—she would fix it and cook for us, and we'd stay there. I think I can remember that she had two sons, and they were in the German army! Of course, that's where Malmédy was, that is, sort of on the border between Germany and Belgium. And I think that the two sons were on the Russian front, so you can imagine what that was like... But anyway, that woman was so nice to us, and we were nice to her too. And you know, we gave her as much food as we could get. We were there about maybe three or four days, I guess. Wasn't that something? There she was, taking care of us, with two boys in the German Army!

*

By the 25th of January, the Germans finally withdrew behind the West Wall once more and the lines moved back to the fighting at the

Siegfried Line and beyond. As anticipated, in February 1945 the Germans slowly released the dammed Roer River's waters. Once they began to recede, the Allies delivered a furious artillery barrage all along the front, and crossed onto the Cologne Plain. Heavy fighting continued, but as the end of March came into view, so did the banks of the Rhine River. In late March, Gross and Walsh and the rest of their outfit finally crossed the Rhine.

George C. Gross

I remember we crossed the Rhine River on March 24. I remember that because shortly thereafter, my first son was born back home.

We crossed the river on a bridge that the engineers had put together, a little rail bridge. We had to get our tank treads matched to the rail, and if we weren't careful, the tank would go off the side and fall into the river and we probably would have drowned, but we got across all right. The first tanks that went across were dual-drive tanks, like the ones they had on [Omaha Beach on D-Day]. They could float and had propellers in the back

THE BULGE AND BEYOND | 439

that would move them along in the water. They were very untrustworthy, but they got through all right. A couple platoons went across that way and then the others went across on rafts, and we were able to wait until the engineers got the first bridge built. We got across and established a beachhead on the other side and broke out from there.

It was a strange [part of the] war; we were going very fast and the order was to 'burn the bogies,' which meant to burn the bogie wheels off. Bogie wheels were supporting wheels on the tank, and if you went too fast, the rubber would burn on them. The order was to go ahead and burn the bogies. This was the end, so we went as fast as we could. We would leapfrog with the 2nd Armored Division and they would take the spearhead and we would clean up around them; they would go past the strong points, clean up those areas, and then we would trade with them for a while—we would take the spearhead and then they would clean up the strong points. One of the strong points we cleaned up was the town of Hamelin, where the Pied Piper of Hamelin piped the rats out of town with all the little children; Robert Browning's poem "The Pied

Piper," and they assumed the story of the children was an echo of the Children's Crusade where all the children marched out and they never came back because they all died on their way to the Holy Land. We were so cold and had been going so long without sleep that we stopped for two hours on the other side of the Weser River in Hamelin town, slept for two hours. We were so cold and though we never drank before we went into combat, we had two bottles of gin that had been liberated by the infantry, so we thought we would just have a drink or two. So we had a drink or two, got in our tanks, and there I was in the turret of the tank running across a cobblestone road, rocking back and forth, and pretty soon, the building started rocking back and forth! So I yelled at the driver to stop because the buildings were closing in, and he had a drink or two so it didn't seem strange to him at all, so he stopped. Everyone behind us had to stop because we were near the head of the column, and the buildings started to go back to where they were. No one ever said anything about it because everyone had a couple drinks, so no one cared.[63] It was very foolish thinking because later I found out I went through three firefights and I don't remember them at all. That was the only time I had drunk before combat. It taught me never to drink before fighting.

Spring had finally arrived amid the endless days of fighting. The days grew longer and the swiftness of the advance towards Berlin was stunning, the Ninth Army having been assigned the route through Central Germany as the British drove in through the north, and other American armies to the south of the Ninth. After the first few hundred miles, the GIs got used to encountering groups of unarmed German soldiers walking towards the oncoming Americans to surrender, and waved them on towards the huge 'PW cages,' the hastily wired prisoner-of-war camps to the rear. German civilians hung out white sheets of surrender from their windows, and in one instance, the

---

[63] *so no one cared*- the soldiers had overrun a Nazi supply depot with hundreds of cases of 'Jenever Juice,' a Dutch gin brew that the GIs labeled 'buzz bomb,' 'white lightning,' and 'denatured dynamite.' Each soldier was allotted 2 bottles. This incident certainly added to Gross's characterization of this part of the war as 'strange.' *Move Out, Verify: The Combat Story of the 743rd Tank Battalion.* 1945. 161.

tankers encountered a burgermeister who pedaled out slowly toward them on a bicycle with a white flag of surrender. It was apparent that many were incredulous that this could be happening to their Germany, and many stared at the Americans with sullen eyes or hid in their homes. On the other hand, some townspeople even smiled and waved at the tank crews passing by. No one waved back.[60]

At the city of Brunswick on April 11, General Hobbs demanded the unconditional surrender of the German garrison. It was rejected and a day-long battle ensued, and the German general was captured fleeing the town toward the east. Block-to-block mop-up operations quashed the resistance, and the 30th Division brass set up a command center. Meanwhile, the 2nd Armored Division was racing for the Elbe River. While the fighting was nothing like what the GIs had encountered through France, Belgium, the Netherlands, and up to the Rhine, pockets of resistance were a constant reminder that the war was far from over. Sniper fire killed men in areas where the spearhead had already raced through. On the 12th, a German plane tried to take to the air; a tanker shot it down with his .50-caliber turret-mounted machine gun just as the plane rose off the airstrip. At the town of Cremlingen, 100 more Germans surrendered, but Sgt. Gross in Dog Company's Tank 12 pursued an enemy command car and knocked it out before it could make its escape.[61]

On April 13, lead elements of the 743rd Tank Battalion and 30th Infantry Division reached the banks of Elbe River. The military objective was the ancient city of Magdeburg, which showed no signs of surrendering without a fight. Still, spirits were generally high as the tankers of 2nd Platoon, Dog Company mounted up to move out in the early morning sun; the soldiers could not know that their confrontation with pure evil would come well before the sun would set that day. And though they were just hours away from witnessing the horrors of the greatest crime in history, their personal worlds were about to be shaken to the core.

At midmorning, the column halted. A soldier went from tank to tank to pass the word. The joking stopped, the small talk ceased as a new kind of numbness crept over the column. That immortal father figure, the man who had led their families through the Great Depression, and now four years of the most brutal conflict in the history of mankind, was suddenly gone.

The president of the United States was dead. It was Friday the 13th, April 1945.

BOOK THREE

LIBERATION

'We Keep the Faith'
— Motto of the 743rd Tank Battalion

For the first time after going through sheer hell, I felt that there was such a thing as simple love coming from good people—young men who had left their families far behind, who wrapped us in warmth and love and cared for our well-being.

— Sara Atzmon, Holocaust Survivor

"At Eleven Fifty-five"

The train stopped under the hill
huffing and puffing
As though it reached the end of the road.
An old locomotive pulling deteriorating train cars
Not even fit for carrying horses.

To an approaching visitor
The experience was of a factory of awful smell
Two thousand five hundred stinking cattle
Heading for slaughter
Shoved to the train cars.
The butterflies into the surrounding air
Were blinded by the poisonous stench.

The train moved for five days back and forth
Between Bergen-Belsen and nowhere.

On the sixth day, a new morning came
To shine over our heads.
Suddenly the heavy car doors were opened
Living and dead overflowed

Into the surrounding green meadow.

Was it a dream?
Or a delayed awakening of God?

When we identified
The symbols of the American army
We ran to the top of the hill
As though bitten by an army of scorpions
To kiss the treads of the tanks
And to hug the soldiers with overflowing love.

Somebody cried—
Don't believe it, it is a dream
When we pinched ourselves; we felt the pain
It was real.

Mama climbed to the top of the hill.
She stood in the middle of the field of flowers
And prayed an almost silent prayer
From the heart.

Only a few words escaped to the blowing wind

Soon... Now...

From the chimneys of death
I give new life
To my children...
And this day
My grandchildren were born
To a good life.

Amen and Amen.

— Yaakov Barzilai, Israeli poet and Train Survivor, *written for his liberators on the occasion of the 70th anniversary of the train liberation and read aloud to them at the last gathering of soldiers and survivors, Nashville, Tennessee, April 13, 2015*

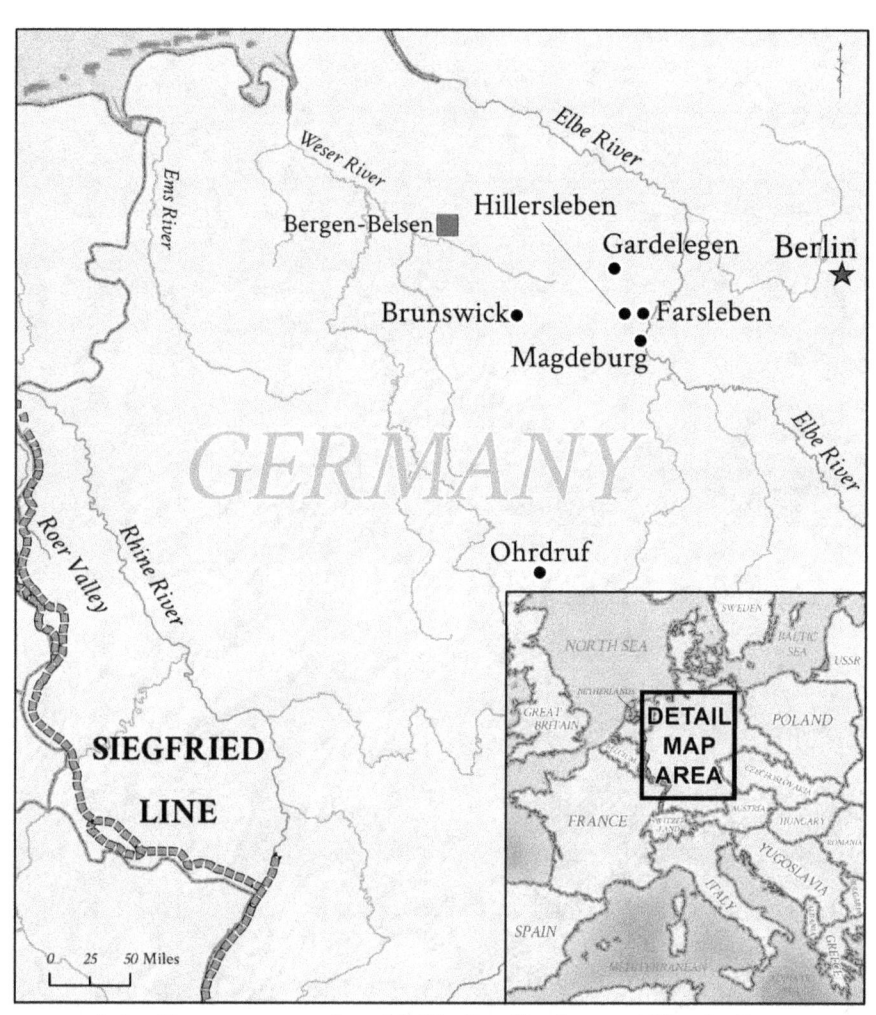

Into Germany, spring 1945. Credit: Susan Winchell.

CHAPTER TWELVE

What the Soldiers Saw

April 13, 1945/Central Germany

On April 13, 1945, World War II was in its sixth year. Allied troops were closing in on the crumbling Reich from all directions, and the war continued everywhere. On this day in the Pacific, Tokyo would burn—again—after 327 Boeing B-29 Superfortresses dropped their payloads. The brutal battles for Okinawa and the Philippines were raging with no end in sight. On this day, the US Eighth Army Air Force was heading out on its 945th mission over enemy territory, and Allied troops continued to slog it out against the retreating Germans in the north of Italy. Advance units of the 30th and 83rd Infantry Divisions reached the Elbe River and were preparing to cross it, although Eisenhower was now dictating that Berlin was a political prize which he would leave to the Russians, seeing no purpose in putting more American lives at risk when faced with the enormous tasks already at hand. Vienna fell to the Red Army and Soviet troops were also moving onto the Elbe River and closing in for the kill on Berlin even as Hitler celebrated the death of Roosevelt, his own death by his own hand only a few weeks off. The Red Army launched its final assault on Berlin on April 16. In the two weeks that followed, it suffered over 350,000 casualties.

The American Ninth Army, to which the 30th Infantry Division was attached, had now nearly cut Germany in two, spearheading towards the Elbe River. The First and Third Army closed in on Austria and Czechoslovakia. Resistance in the industrial Ruhr Valley was rapidly collapsing, and Allied supply lines were stretched to the limit, compounded by the German forces now surrendering literally in the hundreds of thousands, all of whom had to be fed in the hastily erected compounds. Thousands more Russian, American, and British POWs shuffled along on forced marches where many dropped from exhaustion, starvation, dysentery, and outright murder at the hands of their captors. And all over the Reich, inmates of hundreds of concentration camps were also on the move as the Germans tried haphazardly to shift and destroy the evidence of their crimes. In the northwest, the British Second Army closed in on major ports and the town of Celle, where a nearby camp called Bergen-Belsen was putting out feelers for the peaceful transfer of power to the Allies.

Into this churning cauldron of suffering we now pour the nearly incomprehensible element that was thrust onto the shoulders of the young American soldiers—the overrunning of the hundreds of concentration camps and subcamps, euthanasia centers and prisons—an overall tapestry of horror that unfolded on an hourly basis throughout the collapsing Reich from the first part of April 1945 forward.

On April 12, General Eisenhower reached Ohrdruf, one of the more than 80 subcamps of Buchenwald, joined by Generals Bradley, Patton, and other top brass. It was the first Nazi camp liberated by US troops, and here, for the first time, the commanders themselves came face-to-face with the horrors of the Holocaust; 'Blood and Guts' Patton got sick behind a shack. When aides pressed Ike to move on, he told them he was not to be rushed. He then ordered, *'I want every American unit not actually in the front lines to see this place. We are told that the American soldier does not know what he is fighting for. Not at least, he will know what he is fighting against.'*

Later, he would cable Washington:
The things I saw beggar description. While I was touring the camp I encountered three men who had been inmates and by one ruse or another had made their escape. I interviewed them through an interpreter. The visual evidence and the verbal testimony of

starvation, cruelty, and bestiality were so overpowering as to leave me a bit sick. In one room, where they were piled up twenty or thirty naked men, killed by starvation, George Patton would not even enter. He said that he would get sick if he did so. I made the visit deliberately, in order to be in a position to give first-hand evidence of these things if ever, in the future, there develops a tendency to charge these allegations merely to 'propaganda.'[62]

*

On the 13th, just 40 kilometers to the north of where the men of the 743rd Tank Battalion and 30th Infantry Division were now setting out towards their final battle, over one thousand Jewish slave laborers were herded into a large barn by SS guards and locals. The doors were closed and the guards stationed themselves on the perimeter. Gasoline-soaked straw was then lit, and as the conflagration spread, nearly all of the prisoners burned alive and others were shot to death as they tried to burrow under the barn walls to escape the flames. Two days later, the Gardelegen Massacre was discovered as US troops reached the still smoldering barn.

*

Now, it was the tankers' turn. Shortly after the war ended, Pfc. Wayne Robinson, the author of the 743rd Tank Battalion's official history, composed the soldiers' dramatic introduction to the Holocaust, even before it had a name.

> There was another sidelight to the death of fascism in Europe. Only a few of the battalion saw it. Those who did will never forget it.
> A few miles northwest of Magdeburg there was a railroad siding in wooded ravine not far from the Elbe River. Major Clarence Benjamin in a jeep was leading a small task force of two light tanks from Dog Company on a routine job of patrolling. The unit came upon some 200 shabby looking civilians by the side of the road. There was something immediately apparent about each one of these people, men and women, which arrested the attention. Each one of them was skeleton-thin with starvation, a sickness in their faces and the

way in which they stood—and there was something else. At the sight of Americans, they began laughing in joy—if it could be called laughing. It was an outpouring of pure, near-hysterical relief.

The tankers soon found out why. The reason was found at the railroad siding.

There they came upon a long string of grimy, ancient boxcars standing silent on the tracks. In the banks by the tracks, as if to get some pitiful comfort from the thin April sun, a multitude of people of all shades of misery spread themselves in a sorry, despairing tableau. As the American uniforms were sighted, a great stir went through this strange camp. Many rushed toward the Major's jeep and the two light tanks.

Bit by bit, as the Major found some who spoke English, the story came out.

This had been—and was—a horror train. In these freight cars had been shipped 2,500 people, jam-packed in like sardines, and they were people that had two things in common, one with the other: They were prisoners of the German state, and they were Jews.

Henry Birnbrey was part of an advance party that was one of the first to reach the train. As a German Jew, Henry had the good fortune to be sponsored for immigration to the United States before the war broke out; he applied to join the U.S. Army and was sent over with the 30th Division as a forward artillery spotter scouting positions in the lead-up to the final battle at Magdeburg; it was the advance parties which had probably radioed back to the command post the information about the existence of the train just ahead of the rest of the 30th Infantry Division.

Henry Birnbrey

I was a forward observer from the 531st Anti-Aircraft; we were searching for gun positions. We moved on to the Braunschweig (Brunswick) area. Here, along the highway, we encountered ditches full of dead concentration camp prisoners who had been marched from one camp to another and were shot before they had a chance to be liberated.

All of a sudden, I was attracted by this terrible odor and we could not figure out where it was coming from. I told my jeep driver to head 'over there.' Suddenly, I see these freight cars with people coming out of them. When I got out of the jeep, I realized what it was all about, and actually spoke with some of the people. Most of them, the first word out of their mouth was in Yiddish, '*Ikh bin a Yid,*' which means, '*I am a Jew.*' That was about the extent of our conversation—they only spoke Yiddish, and my Yiddish was very limited because German Jews hated the Yiddish language; my father would not allow it in our house. I communicated with a few people as best I could.

The sub-human conditions which these people were subjected to had reduced them to a very sorry state. We did not know how long they had been in those cars; they looked like walking skeletons and could barely speak. Unfortunately, we had no food to share with them, which gave us a very helpless feeling; headquarters was notified... I was very frustrated because I saw these people were starving, and I had nothing to share with them; all I had was my canteen with water. I had no K-rations; I had nothing to give them. I had an awful helpless feeling. I stayed about an hour and then I had to do my job that I was supposed to be doing.

I was in a state of shock; I had never seen people look that bad in my whole life. I was terrified. My biggest frustration was that I had nothing to help them with. I was reminded of the words of the prophet Ezekiel—

'He took me down in the spirit of G-d and set me down in the valley. It was full of bones.'

The train, Friday, April 13, 1945. Credit: George Gross.

George C. Gross

Major Benjamin led our two tanks, each carrying several infantrymen from the 30th Infantry

Division on its deck, down a narrow road until we came to a valley with a small train station at its head and a motley assemblage of passenger compartment cars and boxcars pulled onto a siding. There was a mass of people sitting or lying listlessly about, unaware as yet of our presence. There must have been guards, but they evidently ran away before or as we arrived, for I remember no firefight. Our taking of the train, therefore, was no great heroic action but a small police operation. The heroism that day was all with the prisoners on the train.

Carrol 'Red' Walsh

We were coming down this dirt roadway, as I remember. I had no idea what we were approaching or where we were going or what was going on. I can remember just approaching this area, and all of a sudden, ahead of me I saw this train. It was stopped. In my mind I can still see it, and I could see how long that train was, that long, long string of boxcars and the engine in the front. There were no SS guards around it at the time that we came upon it. I can remember swinging my tank to the right and proceeding alongside of the train. I didn't know what was really on that train until that tank stopped. Then I saw what the train held.

Interviewer: Did you see the doors of those boxcars open at that time?

Yes, I believe they were. I believe that they were open; some of the people were up. But I still remember peering into those boxcars and seeing those people just huddled and mashed together inside those boxcars.

Did you know at the time that these were prisoners, or had been prisoners, or that they had been held? Did you have any idea what they were doing there?

No, I had no idea. I had no idea who they were, where they had come from, where they were going—nothing. No idea. All I knew was, here's a train with these boxcars, and people jammed in those boxcars. No, I had no idea. And as I look back and I contemplate that thought, I suppose we were too busy in combat to think of anything except what we were doing at the time. And of course, you know, we were not privileged to hear any news. We did not know really what was going on. We did not know whether we were successful in our own endeavors or not! So, no. I was not aware of the extent of the horror that was perpetrated on the Jewish people. No, I had no idea at the time of the extent of the concentration camps.

*The train, April 14, 1945. Photographer unknown, probably U.S. Army.
Credit: USHMM, courtesy of Flora Carasso Mihael.*

George C. Gross

Major Benjamin took a powerful picture just as a few of the people became aware that they had been rescued. It shows people in the background still lying about, trying to soak up a bit of energy from the sun, while in the foreground a woman has her arms flung wide and a great look of surprise and joy on her face as she rushes toward us.

The original photograph inserted into the official After-Action Report.
Credit: Major Clarence L. Benjamin. Source: After Action Report, April 1945, 743rd Tank Battalion S-3 Journal History, p. 118.

In a moment, that woman found a pack left by a fleeing German soldier, rummaged through it, and held up triumphantly a tin of rations.[64] She was immediately attacked by a swarm of skeletal figures, each one intent upon capturing that prize. My yelling did no good, so that I finally had to leap from my tank and wade through weak and emaciated bodies to pull the attackers off the woman, who ran quickly away with her prize. I felt like a bully, pushing around such weak and starving fellow humans, but it was necessary to save the woman from great harm. The incident drove home to me the terrible plight of the newly freed inhabitants of the train.

I pulled my tank up beside the small station house at the head of the train and kept it there as a sign that the train was under American protection now. Carrol Walsh's tank was soon sent back to the battalion, and I do not remember how long the infantrymen stayed with us, though it was a comfort to have them for a while. My recollection is

---

[64] *that woman found a pack left by a fleeing German soldier-* The woman in the Benjamin photograph has been *possibly* identified as Sara Spitzer-Rubinstein of Havasmező, Hungary. She died in Brooklyn, NY, at the age of 97, but others have made claims regarding the identity of the woman, and the little girl clutching her hand, as well.

that my tank was alone for the afternoon and night of the 13th.

Carrol 'Red' Walsh

What are we going to do with these people? How can we handle this situation? Fortunately, there was another attached unit with the 30th Division. They were in the area. The 823rd Tank Destroyer Battalion immediately went around the neighborhood there, getting food from the local farmers and bringing it to the people. And then overnight or the next day, there were other units that arrived to assist these people and find shelter for them. That first night they stayed around the train.

George C. Gross

A number of things happened fairly quickly. We were told that the commander of the 823rd Tank Destroyer Battalion had ordered all the burgermeisters of nearby towns to prepare food and get it to the train promptly, and were assured that Military Government would take care of the refugees the following day. So we were left to hunker down and protect the starving people, commiserating with, if not relieving, their dire condition.

*

Colonel Dettmer of the 823rd Tank Destroyer Battalion, also attached to the 30th Infantry Division, set up his command post in Farsleben, a small German hamlet of 500, now suddenly invaded by several hundred more desperate skeletal figures. The swarm of refugees, many of whom had broken into the town's two bakeries, reported to him that they had had nothing to eat for days. Dettmer immediately summoned the mayor, and ordered the bakeries to bake throughout the night, for cattle and sheep to be slaughtered, and for families to open their homes to the survivors. When the burgermeister began to protest and made a display of reluctance, the battalion commander drew his sidearm, put it to the mayor's head, and calmly asked him to recite his instructions.[63] The following day, the 823rd's surgeon, Captain Baranov, spent the entire day setting up a makeshift hospital to try to contain a typhus epidemic that was rapidly escalating among those rescued. The Military Government was arranging to transfer the survivors to a Luftwaffe base and proving grounds recently captured; Dettmer's command post moved out, and shortly thereafter the burgermeister unceremoniously murdered his wife and committed suicide.[64]

The logbook for the 105th Medical Battalion of the 30th Infantry Division was kept by T/4 Sgt. Wilson Rice, who interjected colorful personal commentaries when typing up his reports.

Wilson Rice

April 13, 1945

Farther on down the road, when the convoy was halted again, Major Marsh from the Military Government drove up to Col. Treherne's jeep. He told him about a train of civilians that were prisoners of the Germans. Our jeep pulled out from the convoy and went to Farsleben, Germany, where the train was located.

Also in this town was the command post of the 823rd Tank Destroyer

Battalion, and we stopped there to pick up Capt. Baranov, the 823rd Battalion surgeon. He took us down there, and it was something that you've read about, but couldn't believe. They were people that looked of being very refined and cultured; it is said that among them was the French Consul to Germany.

Some great minds were among these people. There were two doctors that were members of the train, and they were caring for the people the best they could without any equipment. Capt. Baranov's men came up with a few drugs, bandages, etc. to use until they could get more. It was about the same as nothing, but it was to go to the women and children first. About 75% of the members of this train were Jews, so the drugs were given to the two doctors and the rabbi for distribution.[65] Major Lowell and Major Huff told them to get all of the contagious and seriously sick to be segregated into cars by themselves. These cars that they were traveling in were boxcars. Sanitation was terrible and the people had been traveling in them for eight days and nights, without food or water. Most of the sickness was due to malnutrition. There were only two typhus cases.

As all of the business was being transacted, a beautiful little girl, about eight years of age, came up to my side. She was very sweet and her complexion was very clear. I looked at her, smiled, and patted her on the head, and she smiled back. As Tommy and I were standing there, I soon felt a little hand slip through my arm. As

---

[65] *About 75% of the members of this train were Jews-* This statement, along with the one about the rumor of the French Consul to Germany being among the prisoners, were some of the speculations circulating among the soldiers that day. Probably all of the passengers were the Jews from the exchange camp, and no trace of a French consul has been substantiated.

I looked down, a big lump came in my throat.

As we were leaving, a man came up to our jeep. He was one of the American citizens and was from Detroit, Michigan. He was taken prisoner two years ago in Warsaw, and his family is still now in Detroit. He was a sick man, but there was nothing we could do for him, as we were not prepared for such things. The Military Government is taking care of things as fast as they can.

This is what I mean when I say that warfare such as this was not planned for by the Army. Things are going too fast. This man told us about the 33 American citizens.[66] He went on to say that he knew our circumstances, knew we had to take care of the troops first, knew that everything possible will be done for them as fast as

---

[66] *33 American citizens-* The doctor probably refers to Jews with American papers, real or assumed identities.

possible, and went on to say, '*We know how busy you guys are, what you will do for us, maybe one week, maybe two weeks, but even if nothing else is done, there is one thing we truly and dearly thank you for, and that is for our liberty.*'

There was a break in this man's voice, and I knew how he felt. There was a lump in my throat.

Victory, 1945. By Ervin Abadi. Hillersleben, Germany, May 1945. Credit: USHMM, courtesy of the family of American soldier Donald W Rust.

CHAPTER THIRTEEN

'The Americans Are Here'

Germany. Poland. The Netherlands. Hungary. Greece. From all across war-torn Europe, time was running out for the families on the train transport from Bergen-Belsen. What was about to unfold that April 13th is told here by the victims for the first time, the miracles that later in life many came to regard as the day they were re-born.

Hilde Huppert, a Polish woman who had survived with her eight-year-old son, noted one of the first encounters with the American soldiers.

Hilde Huppert

The first American jeep passed by at about ten in the morning, an iron bar across its front bumper searching for booby-traps and a radio mast waving madly in its rear. It was manned by four GIs with steel helmets coated in dust. They pulled up and approached us warily: a motley crowd of women and children together with a couple of men here and there, all clad in rags and tatters. We must have been a pitiful sight.

'Who are you?' they demanded.

'Hello, friends!' we shouted back in a chorus. 'We love you! We are Jews!'

They slipped off their helmets and mopped their brows; one of them pointed to the Star of David he wore on a chain around his neck.

'So am I!'

The reconnaissance jeep had to go on its way, but before it did, the GI called up his battalion headquarters and reported finding a large group of Jewish survivors.[67]

---

[67] *The reconnaissance jeep... had to go on its way-* this was most likely the 30th Division's 117th Regimental Reconnaissance and Intelligence Platoon consisting at the time of only 18 men, with 6 jeeps. Smith, Daniel D, *Memoirs of World War II in Europe*, 2013.

Later in life, Hilde Huppert added, 'Tell the American people I shall never forget those four American GIs who liberated us from the Germans. One of them was black; another wore the Star of David on a chain around his neck. I can still recall their amazed faces in that dusty jeep, and the U.S. Army symbol. I remember kissing one of them, and I want the American people to know that I am grateful to them.'

Shortly thereafter, the tankers arrived with another jeep carrying Major Benjamin. Peter Lantos of Hungary was now six and was with his mother.

Peter Lantos

I remember the first few hours of freedom. At the beginning, no one knew what was happening; that the train had been stationary for such a long time was not surprising—endless stops on the open track were common. But this stop was different. More and more people were leaving the wagons, and the German guards, who had previously ordered us back to the trains, were nowhere to be

---

Hilde Huppert's *Hand in Hand with Tommy* was one of the first survivor memoirs, written immediately after her arrival in Palestine with her son Tommy and hundreds of orphans, including 96 from Bergen-Belsen.

seen. The train had come to a stop at a siding—there was a clearing with a few trees and bushes, and an embankment that ran parallel with the track. We saw two tanks on the horizon, and those ahead of us started to shout: 'The Americans, the Americans!'

As the news spread, more and more left the train, still not believing that it was all over and that we were free. Soon it was all but deserted, although some were too weak to move, and a few had not survived the journey. We made our way towards the tanks, but we were so weak that the gentle slope of the embankment nearly defeated us. We managed to climb it slowly, and then we saw the first American soldiers. They were so different from us, and from anybody else we had seen during the last few months. They were very tall, or so it seemed to me, well-fed, and clean. They displayed a facial expression we had all but forgotten existed; they smiled at us. They explained, while someone translated from English into German and Hungarian, that they were going to get food and accommodations for us, but this might take some time.

Fred Spiegel of Germany was now almost 13.

Fred 'Fritz' Spiegel

Very soon, slowly coming over the hill, the first American soldiers appeared. We had never seen these uniforms before and were not sure who they were. The soldiers also were not sure who we were, but I suspect for a different reason. We must have looked terrifying, like nightmare figures, monsters from something out of science fiction, apparitions arisen from the grave. They obviously had never seen inmates from concentration camps.

Irene Bleier of Hungary had just turned 18.

Irene Bleier Muskal

The SS officers fled, leaving us to be liberated shortly by the US Army. Our leaders told us how to behave, letting us know that we could leave the cattle cars, but must stay close by. We were also told that we were in close range of an ongoing heavy battle. At long last, the enfeebled crowd began crawling out of its prison, although many were too faint to enjoy the very first steps of freedom. Many of us spent the night on the grassy hill just in front of us, beneath the open, starry blue sky. A nearby gun battle illuminated the area through the night. Sounds of cannons kept us awake and we prayed fervently now more than ever for our liberators' swift victory.

We soon spotted a small pond, and together with my sister Jolan, I took my first steps in its direction in order to take a real bath in real water. As we walked there, a band of SS German officers were running away. One of them aimed at us with his small gun and fired some bullets with an accompanying last farewell to us—'Swine Jew!' Luckily for my sister and I, we were far enough not to get hurt.

In front of the cattle car, we could see German civilians from the two nearby towns running in opposite directions on the main road, trying to escape from the approaching US forces. With dulled sense, we glimpsed towards them. Several SS guards stayed with us. Some of them asked for—and received—civilian clothes from our people.

The next morning we dug up recently planted potatoes we found, made a fire, and cooked them. They tasted delicious. I again started walking towards the small pond, but then Jolan excitedly hollered to me: 'Hey you, come back fast, the US Army has arrived!'

As much as my faint condition would allow me, I hurried to the scene of the miracle to welcome them, this being the big moment we so yearned for. Two angel-like American soldiers stood there beside their magic jeep. My sister and I looked on enchanted as they took captive the several SS cowards who stayed in their shameful and disgraceful uniforms. The SS henchmen held up their hands while one of the Americans stood opposite them with a pointed weapon. Then, the second US soldier searched their pockets.

Standing there and looking up at our liberators, I waited to sense some kind of emotion on this miraculous occasion—but no. Reality did not penetrate my consciousness. My senses were incapable of experiencing any signs of emotion; I had no tears of joy that appeared, nor even the slightest smile. My senses were left stiff, in the aftermath of extended suffering. We are liberated, but only outwardly. Our mind still remained under great pressure, as heavy, dark clouds obscured our world of comprehension. It will take a good many years to be free completely. When that time comes, if ever, we will be able to feel wholly liberated and shake off the shackles of bondage and imperceptible suffering.

The majority of our group was so feeble that they stayed inside the crowded cattle cars. Some ventured to the nearby small towns for provisions. The following day, early in the afternoon, the US Army arrived with a big army truck. They brought us a delicious hot meal, potato goulash with veal meat. Never before in my life, or after, did I eat as tasty a meal as this. I just looked on as those US soldiers of valor took care of our group of two thousand, going from cattle car to cattle car so patiently. After suffering so long from inhuman treatment, I felt a great distinction to be treated with human kindness by those American soldiers. It was like being born again.

With their kind devotion toward us they sowed back into our souls the sparks and seeds of human hopes and feelings. By Sunday morning, my sister Jolan and I plucked up some courage and crawled out of the cattle cars to look around at the nearby town of Farsleben. We were pleasantly surprised to discover that US soldiers were already patrolling the locality. Some of our fellow Jews were also around and about. The local population either locked themselves in their homes or escaped. None of them ventured to welcome the new liberators.

Aliza Melamed of Warsaw was 17.

Aliza Melamed Vitis-Shomron

What will happen now, to us? We were alone. Slowly, people started leaving the carriages; the train was standing in the middle of a field. I also got off, with my faithful friend Tusia. We saw a small pond not far away, and our people were catching little fish there. Those among them with initiative found a tin, made a fire, and cooked the fish. We joined in, glad to share the job.

We breathe fresh air, the sky is clear, it is spring. Although we are weak, exhausted by hunger, hope is reflected in all the faces. Of course, there are also some 'ravens,' prophesying that the Germans will not give up as long as they can harm us, but who listens to them? Mother is also pessimistic.

My sister Mirka and I join the stream of people going to the nearby village of Farsleben. The village houses are pretty, clean, surrounded by gardens with fruit trees. We entered a garden in full bloom; I knocked on the door of the house. A woman wearing a big apron came out. Her face expressed amazement at the two figures facing her. Evidently we looked like ghosts.

'Kartofel, kartofel, bitte,' (potatoes, potatoes, please) I whispered. At that moment, the woman started to scream. I didn't understand a word. She pushed us out. I ran to the trees and began to shake them, so the blossoms fell off the branches. A large stone flew at me. We ran away. That was the first and last time I asked for food. I felt ashamed. Mirka and I decided not to tell Mother about it.

That night we were right in the frontline. We spent the night lying under the carriages. We did not dare flee from there, there was nowhere to go. To hide in the German village? They'll chase us away like dogs and hand us over to the authorities. We had no choice but to remain in the carriages and underneath them. Whatever happens to the others will also happen to us. Cannon shells flew above us with a terrifying noise.

Before dawn the locomotive returned with our escort.[68] People who got out of the carriages in the morning were amazed to see lots of pieces of paper floating on the small pond. They looked strange, and they had not been there on the previous day. When they went to look at them, they were devastated—these were our certificates and other papers protecting us! So we did have such papers—it wasn't just a deception by the Germans! Now, at the end of the war, the Germans found them useless.

But the Germans escorting us had a different plan for getting rid of us. They didn't want to let the birds in their hands escape, even though the Allies had already encircled them on all sides. Someone ran from carriage to carriage, screaming in terror: 'The Germans want to drown the train in the River Elbe. Save yourselves!'

---

[68] *the locomotive returned with our escort*-The engine of the train had apparently uncoupled and for a time left the train carriages, probably during the aerial bombardment.

At the height of the [rumor], when we heard shots in the distance, we ran outside. People burst out of the carriages. Suddenly someone shouted, 'The Americans are coming!'

To our great surprise, a tank came slowly down the hill opposite, followed by another one. I ran towards the tank, laughing hysterically. It stopped. I embraced the wheels, kissed the iron plates.

The amazed soldier who came out called his friends and they immediately started throwing chocolate to us. They smiled in embarrassment and didn't know what to do.

Arie Selinger was from Poland, and had just turned eight years old.

Arie Selinger

Suddenly the trees behind the hill start to fall and I think, how come these trees are falling? You are a child, every hill looks like a mountain, the proportions are different, and as I see the trees falling down, I see tanks following them. The Americans came…

Arie picked up some of the chocolate tossed by the soldiers.

Mother was a nurse, so she knew; she kept saying, 'You don't eat anything, except for what I give you.' American jeeps passed there and threw chocolate. I took the chocolate and I ate it. I had marks on my face. My mother said: 'You ate, I can tell you did!' And she slapped me on the face: 'I told you not to touch anything!' It was the only time my mother ever hit me.

Lajos Reti of Hungary was twenty-four years old.

Lajos Reti

The day of April 13, 1945, was a Friday, a sunny and windy day. In the morning, the SS opened the doors of the freight cars, after they had argued with each other whether they should kill us with their submachine guns.[69] But the US troops were too close.

---

[69] *kill us with their submachine guns-* in corroborating with other statements, this may have actually been the previous day.

Several hundred people wrapped in rags streamed through the open doors, if they could be called people at all. We were all mere skeletons.

The train was idling in a deepening, so I climbed uphill, across a road and to a field. I was pulling out potatoes planted on the field, when a motorcycle approached. It was a motorcycle with a sidecar. There was an elegant SS or Nazi leader in the front—I could not decide which, since he was wearing a mixture of uniform and civilian clothes; it must have been his wife sitting behind him and his child in the sidecar. He pulled over and offered me a cigarette. I told him I did not smoke, so he closed his silver cigarette case and started the engine. He seemed to hesitate about the direction he should take.

Then two small American tanks arrived. I was standing in the middle of the road, and noticed that the American soldier leaning out of the turret of one of the tanks was aiming his gun at me.

The tank came closer and closer, and the soldier lowered his submachine gun. I must have looked terrible, so he did not take me for an enemy. I was lucky he had not shot me from the distance, since my small coat and boots vaguely resembled a military uniform. Lice were crawling all over my clothes and skin.

The few hundred former inhabitants of the concentration camp surrounded the tanks right away. Suddenly somebody remembered that [some of] the SS guarding us were still in the carriages. The SS were caught quickly, and lined up. The intrepid SS were trembling so heavily that their pants were flapping.[70]

My attention was drawn to something else; in the rear of the tank there was a box of canned food. I climbed under the tank, emerged at its end, and pulled out a can. It turned out that I stole a can of oranges. This was my luck. I ate the potatoes charred in the can with the oranges, and probably this combination saved my life. Everyone who ate meat or anything greasy died within hours or within one or two days at the latest.

I felt fever in my body, undressed completely naked in front of staring women, and went into the ice-cold water of the lake next to the railroad.

---

[70] *The SS were caught quickly*-12 prisoners were taken at the train and an additional 28 enlisted men and 2 officers surrendered by the end of the day on April 13. Source: 743rd Tank Battalion After Action Report, 13 April, 1945

People warned me not to do this, but I went into the water, felt good, felt that I got rid of the lice and the burning heat of the fever. When I put on my rags again, I felt the fever ever stronger.

In the evening, there was news that we should flee, because the Germans pushed back the Americans. The Germans would massacre us for sure; the women had pulled out material for parachutes from a carriage in order to make clothes.

I was already so weak that I did not care whether the returning Germans would kill me. I stayed in one of the carriages, and fell asleep.

On Saturday, April 14, German peasant horse-drawn carts came for us by some order, so I was carried to Hillersleben. I dragged myself to the first floor of the first building. It looked like an office building, so I lay down under the sink of the bathroom, and fell asleep.

I am sure the American soldiers had no idea who we were and what we went through.

Leslie Meisels of Hungary had turned 18 by the time of the liberation.

Leslie Meisels

After a while the guards opened all the doors and the commandant ordered all males above the age of twelve to get out of the wagons and go over to a little embankment across from the train. Then, while we were facing our respective cattle wagons that contained our family members, a machine gun was set up in front of each wagon, although not every machine gun was manned by an SS guard. We stood there facing the machine guns—and death—for a couple of hours; then, inexplicably, the guns were removed and we were ordered to return to our wagons. Even now, I do not know for sure what happened, but I think that it being so close to the end of the war, the guards couldn't be forced to carry out executions—they had to volunteer. Very fortunately for us, only eight SS guards volunteered, and I guess the commandant wouldn't dare try to carry out his plan with so few men. It is a very sad fact that all those volunteers were vehement antisemites from Hungary, our own native land.

That night, a fierce air battle developed around and above our train. The guns were blazing, bombs were falling, and explosions were shaking our wagons, but again, none of them fell on us. In the morning, the first thing we noticed was there were no SS guards—they had fled during the night, leaving us to our fate, which turned out to be our

salvation. These are things that I cannot explain, that no one can explain, but to me it looks like God was looking after us and creating these miracles.

People were milling around outside of the wagons, talking about what had happened. Sometime around midday, I had made a fire from some twigs and I was starting to boil some of the remaining red beets in a pot when suddenly a huge cry went up. When I looked over to the top of that little embankment, I saw some dirty, sweating American soldiers—the most beautiful human beings imaginable—appear with their guns ready. Instead of the enemy, they found us and heard our screams and our cries of 'Oh God, we are free! We are going to be human beings again!'*

I remember going back and forth between that pot of beets and the door of the wagon, telling my mother and brothers that we were free, crying at the same time. That feeling was not, and still is not, possible to express in words—after more than sixty years, whenever I think about that moment, my skin still shivers! Those soldiers from the United States Army not only liberated us, they gave us back our lives.

Steve Barry of Hungary, now 20, also remembered mounted SS troops appearing and ordering the men and boys out of the train. Barry and his friends remained where they were.

---

* Watercolor painting by Hungarian survivor Ervin Abadi, who was liberated from this train. During his convalescence, he created dozens of works of Holocaust art. Credit: USHMM.

Steve Barry

I was still in the passenger car, and no way would I have gotten out of there. In other words, if they wanted to kill me, they had to come into the car and shoot me…They could see me in there, of course. But, see, it's a huge, I don't know how many railroad cars were needed to contain twenty-five hundred people, but, you know, it's a long line of railroad cars. I mean, the only thing they could have done at that point was probably just keep shooting, but it just didn't make much sense, even to them. So when they saw that nobody was getting out of the car, they just packed up and rode away.[71]

A very short while later, they came back again in the opposite direction. My friends and I say, 'Uh-oh, we know what's going on. We are surrounded!' These guys can't get out because they went from left to right and they just disappeared…

---

[71] *they just packed up and rode away-* Several survivors mention the SS ordering the male occupants out of the train for execution, though there has been some confusion as to the exact morning. Based on my research, I believe it was the morning of April 12, not the 13th. Steve Barry confirms this in an unpublished manuscript written for his family.

It was April and it was close to the Baltic Sea, so the nights were chilly. I took one of these German overcoats [I had found] and I put it on because I was very cold. I wrapped it around myself and we spent that night sitting on the embankment next to the train and watched the most unbelievable carpet bombing of Magdeburg.

Interviewer: Were you afraid at that time that the bombs might fall on the train as well?

We couldn't care less if they fell on us, as long as they was falling. [*Chuckles*] And I'm not kidding; I'm dead serious. As long as they were killing Germans, we didn't care if we went with them…

It's an unbelievable sight and sound, because the roar of hundreds and hundreds of planes coming in waves over you is a gut-wrenching experience. And the sound of the bomb and the sight of the explosions, it was something to watch. We did see a couple of German planes, fighter planes, take off, and they were shot down almost instantly.

The next morning, Barry encountered his first American soldiers.

Interviewer: Were they in trucks or tanks? What did you see?

Well, actually there were two tanks. I still get tears in my eyes; that's what it was. Right now, I have tears in my eyes and I always will when I think about it. That [was the moment that] we knew we were safe.

1945 Ink drawing by Hungarian survivor Ervin Abadi, Credit: USHMM, courtesy of George Bozoki.

We found some matches in those German soldiers' [rail]cars. We had this tiny little fire going and we were sitting next to it, and I was sitting there with this great big SS overcoat on. One GI walked down the embankment, came over to the fire, sat next to me, took out his pen knife, and he cut off the SS insignia from my coat, and slowly dropped it into the fire. [*Gets emotional*] If my voice breaks up right now, it always does when I say that, because it's a moment that just can never be forgotten. I don't know who the GI was, but it just signaled something to me that maybe I'm safe and maybe the war ended and the Germans, or the Nazis, were defeated. It was an unbelievable symbol to me. And all I can tell you is, it still touches me very deeply, and probably always will.

Martin Spett of Tarnow, Poland, was seventeen years old at the time of his family's liberation. In a letter to his liberators in 2009, he wrote the following.

Martin Spett

The German commandant, who was in charge of the train, not knowing what to do with us, went to a nearby village to call Berlin for instructions. When he returned, we found out that he had orders to kill everyone aboard the train. You have to visualize this situation. Here we were in the middle of a forest with seventy German guards that set up heavy machine guns for our execution, waiting for orders from their commandant. But he apparently had a change of heart and did not wish to follow Berlin's instructions because the American army was closing in on all sides.

During the night, we saw the German army retreating near our train and we saw the American artillery fire that was aimed in our direction. We huddled together in fear, not knowing what our fate was.

The morning found us still on the train with only a small number of guards and a commandant who was waving to us from a bicycle as he was riding away. It was a beautiful sunny morning in the forest. All was calm and quiet.

Later that morning, we heard a loud metallic rumbling sound. A few minutes later, an American army tank came into view. As the tank stopped, an American soldier came from behind the tank and he started walking down the hill towards the train. He could only go a few steps when our people, in their great excitement, fell before his feet, kissing him.[72] At that time, the German guards surrendered and we then realized that we were liberated.

The soldier stood there with tears in his eyes, telling us that President Franklin Delano Roosevelt had died the day before.

Agnes Fleischer of Hungary was now ten years old.

Agnes Fleischer Baker

The first sight I had of the Americans from inside the train was of a vehicle such as we had never seen before—it had a great white star on it, and someone familiar with that star said, 'Oh my God, the Americans are here!'

Now I know that it was a jeep—and it must have been on a reconnaissance mission, and it was empty maybe, because the soldiers took cover, seeing the train. I will forever see the white star and that amazing jeep in my heart!

---

[72] *fell before his feet, kissing him*- A remarkable number of survivors remember a single American soldier crying in Yiddish, 'I am a Jew!' with tears streaming down his face. His name is believed to be Abraham Cohen, and it is thought that he may have been from Philadelphia. However, we have not been able to track down him or his family.

Soon, the soldiers came and told us sadly that Franklin Delano Roosevelt had died the day before on April 12. They told us that it was Friday, April 13, 1945—we did not know the months and the days anymore, we had lost count of time in Bergen-Belsen long before. The soldiers came, and were gentle, and gave us food.

As I was a child I fantasized that the soldiers were angels, with their wings hidden under their uniform shirts. Today I know that this was no fantasy. In that place and at that time the American soldiers were angels indeed.

Kurt Bronner, who had lost his parents in Bergen-Belsen, recounted the moment of liberation for his liberators in 2013.

Kurt Bronner

What I remember is that suddenly the doors of the cattle car were opened, and we were out there, hearing the machine guns, and the gunfire, very close by. We didn't have any food, we didn't have any water—but we were alive! We saw the German guards running; and we saw them taking their clothes off and changing into civilian clothes... and we were waiting. And suddenly we saw some convertibles, and some tanks on the road above, and looking up from the small valley, and seeing the white stars on the jeeps—we thought they were Russians, you know— 'stars.' Then one soldier came and started to speak in English. Very few of us spoke English, and he said in Yiddish, 'I am a Jew, too.' Excuse me [*puts hand over heart, gets emotional*]—memories coming back [*pauses*]... we were given our lives back. We were taken to the Hillersleben village, and I remember one of the American soldiers came by, and pointed us to a room. And twenty, twenty-five of us went into the room—and the first English expression I learned was, 'One only!' [*Laughter*] And it was a room for one person!

I go to schools and talk to the students, and one of them asked me, 'When did you know that you were free?' And I tell them, when I went to the bathroom, and closed the door, by myself, alone, in privacy, that is when I knew I was free; [I had my dignity]. And after the DDT, the new clothes, the white sheets on a bed—we felt free.[73]

At age 15, George Somjen was from Budapest, Hungary, and imprisoned into Bergen-Belsen, like Kurt Bronner, with his father. And like Kurt Bronner, Dr. Somjen's father did not survive.

George Somjen

I remember the liberation; I remember that the tanks were surrounded and mobbed by our people, who did not want to leave them alone. It was a rather intense and joyous moment. They took us to Hillersleben. In Hillersleben today there is a cemetery where 143 people are buried, who died after the liberation; one of them is my father.

Hungarian-born Robert Spitz also found himself all alone at age 15; his father, who had been with him at Bergen-Belsen, was suddenly shipped to Mauthausen slave labor camp in Austria, where he died. Bob would become an interpreter for the occupation US forces and go on to join the division that liberated him, as an

---

[73] *DDT-* insecticide used later in WWII to control malaria and typhus among civilians and troops. A white powder was generally sprayed on the subject; it was banned for agricultural use in the USA in 1972 as a threat to wildlife.

American soldier. *In a gathering with his liberators and fellow survivors in 2009, he related the following.*

Robert Spitz

I was sitting inside of that cattle car, where I would estimate that there were few inmates in the cattle car that had fewer than a million lice each [crawling on them]; naturally starved to death, skin and bones, very, very bad condition. We heard, I heard, that somebody was fiddling with the lock of our sliding door, from outside. Obviously that sliding door lock was open, and first thing I know is that the sliding door is sliding toward an open position. I saw a young man who wore an olive drab uniform, and he had a wide armband with a red cross in it. Behind him there were two or three younger men without the armbands, they were talking a language that I understood. I assume that I was the only one in my car that understood and spoke English; I had had English in school with other languages. I was the only one with these guys that was able to strike up a conversation! They were, I think, more delighted than I was. I didn't realize just how many advantages I just gained because I [had] successfully established a line of communication with these guys from another part of the world—they were delighted that they could start finding out information that was never available to them.

At this time I think I want to stop for a minute to try to convey to you the impression that I gained at that time from these three guys. It's hard for me to describe it accurately because

A) I was sick, terribly sick;

B) my perception did not function at all—I had a high fever, I'm trying to remember to the best of my ability.

The degree of shock, their shock, surprise, questioning on their faces: Where did these people come from? How did this happen? Within a few minutes this combination of emotions got transferred into the demonstration of concern, of care, of interest; a demonstration of wish and good intentions that was conspicuously demonstrated to each and every one of us.

Before I realized just what was happening, the strong arms of that young man with the white armband grabbed me, I don't know why; he probably didn't know how many lice I had on my skull. [*Laughter from audience*]

He pulled me out of that car and then the other soldiers started pulling people out of it.

I forgot to tell you. When the first soldier opened that sliding door, some bodies—our bodies—fell on him from the railroad car. They were dead. Naturally that came as a surprise to them—to us, you know, it was a matter of an everyday event.

He pulled me out and I didn't know what was going on. I was out of it—the first thing I knew, I am riding on a truck. The next thing I knew I was standing in front of a gun which was run by a gasoline-fed engine. They were spraying me with white powder, lots of it. Later on I found out that was the procedure of DDT, delousing. Believe me, they had to waste an awful lot of powder on me.

After this, they pulled me and took me into a room. By then the village of Hillersleben had all of a sudden gained 2,500 newcomers from that train, and many of them needed hospitalization—I assume the majority needed hospitalization. I was placed in a semi-private room, two people to the room. Well, later I found out that the second and third floors consisted of wards with 70 bunks and 70 beds, and here I have a semi-private room, because they could talk to me, and I could talk to them [in English].

After God knows how many medical examinations and everything else, the drastic change in my diet was really very, very easy. Going from no diet to a diet is a drastic turnabout, but it's an easy process. Again my food had to be supervised very carefully because many people, liberated people, got extremely sick and many died because of their food intake not being planned or controlled. A good Army [officer] with a cocked .45 pistol in his hand expressing his desire that the German peasant, the German farmer, the German citizen starts cooking for these people, the survivors—many of these people weren't ready for that food. It played havoc. But as time went on, I got better and better and I got rid of my typhus and my fever dropped.

Now I assumed a new duty. Often, as the day went on, one medic after another [would come and say], 'Hey, Bob. Will you please come with me to the 3rd floor? We have a problem with 'Tommy,' 'Billy,' etc. There's a problem, he can't talk to us, and we can't talk to them.' I found myself acting as a translator. Little did I know that was going to be the beginning of something big.

My recovery was very nice and satisfactory. They called this 'normalcy.' I have a problem with this word, 'normalcy'—what is normal? What's normal to you doesn't have to be normal to me. I think it's only a setting on a washing machine.

John Fransman was born in Amsterdam just three weeks before the start of World War II to a large Anglo-Dutch Jewish family.

John Fransman

The American soldiers took us in trucks to a small German town called Hillersleben and housed us in an apartment block which, we were told, had been [German] army officers' quarters. They had been emptied of their families to house us, the survivors of the train. We felt very honored. One of the first things the Americans did was to put us through showers, then to dust us thoroughly with a white powder (DDT) to disinfect us, and they gave us new clean clothes. In our new apartment,

I found my first toy; it was a wooden model airplane, but it had the German Luftwaffe symbols on it and I was not happy with it; I soon broke it.

Uri Orlev, a young teen from Warsaw, also remembered the first days of freedom in a German home.

Uri Orlev

On the wall there was a picture of Hitler and another one of a German soldier. My aunt took the glass off Hitler's picture and put it as a mat in front of the toilet bowl so that each time we peed, we would step on it.

In 2011, a survivor who actually lived just 100 miles south of our high school in upstate New York attended the last school reunion and addressed our students, and her fellow survivors, and her liberators.

Bruria Bodek Falik

The Germans with the machine guns were standing opposite us. We stood there for I remember several hours, or maybe for two hours, but you know for a thirteen-year-old, being in a world so unimaginable and honestly incomprehensible, it felt like a very long time. And there were rumors among us that somebody was negotiating with the Nazis to let us live, instead of being shot. And suddenly [they] were sent off; we were just left alone, and they disappeared.

We went into the village of Farsleben to look for food. I remember coming to one of the [German] families and one big, tall, blonde woman. When she came out she was really scary, we were little and skinny and hungry, and she was very scary, but it looked like she was more scared of us! Then she asked us in German, 'Who are you, who are you?' And I spoke some German from school and home; I said, 'We are Jewish, juden,' and she put her hands on my head and she felt for something. I didn't know what she was fully looking for, but when I came back, and I told my grandparents and my mother, she said, 'Oh, she was looking for your horns!' This was a stereotype [they had] of Jews in primitive areas, that Jews have horns! So these were my childhood experiences when I was about your age. Not a long time after that, maybe just a day, all of a sudden we see a row of people—they looked like shadows on the hill. Then we realized they were really people in uniforms, they were the American soldiers who liberated us! They were on the hill; they didn't want to come down because they didn't know, and rightfully so, whether we had diseases that they would not want to be exposed to. But they were rolling food down for us in cans—being from a small town in Hungary, not too many people outside of the big cities knew that food came in cans also—so they were rolling down cans, with bread in it, and beans, and chewing gum, and you name it, everything was in cans, and that was again, such a strange thing! Beans in cans, can you imagine? So this was so joyful for us that we were actually dancing with the cans, because some of them were big enough that my little brothers put them on their heads!

After that, we were taken to Hillersleben. My grandfather, may he rest in peace, passed away in the hospital. He was seventy-eight years old. He was a rabbi, he was the rabbi in our town, and he always prayed every morning that he would die a free man. And God really granted it to him—he died where he rested, a free man! Every year, [some of] my family go and visit his grave [in the cemetery at Hillersleben].

I grew up, I saw the world, and I question the reason for what we had to go through and what six million people have been killed for. I don't have an answer. If I can suggest something to you, look for the answer.

Catharina Soep was twenty-two years old, from Amsterdam. She and her family had been sent to Bergen-Belsen in 1944.

Catharina Soep Polak

All of a sudden I see these big, burly, tan guys, coming over the hill, in uniforms; they had no idea who we were! They were totally flabbergasted, they had no idea what a concentration camp was; they never heard of them. And then they smiled; they all had these fabulous, white, straight teeth— and some crazy thought came in my mind: *they must have all seen the same orthodontist!* And right away they took over.

A widow at age 21, Lisette Lamon was from the Netherlands; she had married Catherina's brother Benno, who was killed at Mauthausen. She was nearing her 25th birthday.

Lisette Lamon Soep

It was a beautiful, balmy morning in April 1945, when I entered Major Adams' makeshift office in Farsleben to offer my services as an interpreter. It made me feel good that I could show, in a small way, the gratitude I felt for the Ninth American Army, which had liberated us as we were being transported from Bergen-Belsen concentration camp.

Orders found by the Americans in the German officers' [rail]car directed that the train was to be stopped on the bridge crossing the Elbe River at Magdeburg, then the bridge was to be blown up, also destroying the train and its cargo all at once. The deadline was noon, Friday the 13th, and at 11 a.m. we were liberated![74]

---

[74] *at 11 a.m. we were liberated*-most survivor accounts place the time of the liberation between midmorning and noon. The after-action reports do not indicate the time of day, but the shadows cast in the Benjamin photograph appear to corroborate this time frame.

With the liberation had come the disquieting news that President Roosevelt had died, and while I was airing concern that the new President, Harry Truman—a man unknown to us—could continue the war, a sergeant suddenly said, 'Hey, you speak pretty good English. I am sure the major would like to have you serve as his interpreter.'

Major Adams had not been told of my coming so he was startled when he saw me. No wonder! There stood a young woman as thin as a skeleton, dressed in a two-piece suit full of holes. The suit had been in the bottom of my rucksack for 20 months, saved for the day we might be liberated, but the rats in Bergen-Belsen must have been as hungry as we were and had found an earlier use for my suit. For [seven] days we had been on the train and this was the only clean clothing I owned.

Major Adams quickly recovered from his initial shock and seemed delighted after I explained why I had come. He asked how his men had treated us, and I heaped glowing praise on the American soldiers who had shared their food so generously with the starving prisoners. Then he took me outside to meet the 'notables' of the German population, and with glee I translated orders given to them by the American commander. The irony of the reversal of roles was not lost on me or the recipients; I was now delivering orders to those who had been ordering me around for so long! The Germans were obsequious, profusely claiming they never wanted Hitler or agreed with his policies and hoped the war would soon be over.

When asked to come back the next day, I was delighted but hesitated, wondering if it would be appropriate to ask a favor. Major Adams picked up on my hesitation, so I asked him to help me contact my family in America. We had immigrated to the U.S. in 1939, but after six months I returned to Holland to join my fiancé, who was in the Dutch army. My parents knew that eight months after we were married my husband was taken as a hostage and sent to Mauthausen concentration camp, where he was killed in 1941, but they did not know if I was alive, not having heard from me in more than two years.

Major Adams gave me a kind glance and said, 'Give me a few lines in your handwriting, written in English, and I will ask my parents to forward it to them.' When he saw the address on the note he looked at me, his mouth open in total amazement, and then he started to laugh—his parents and my parents lived in the same apartment building in New York City!

And so it was on Mother's Day that his mother brought to my mother my message:

'I am alive!'

Sara Gottdiener of Hungary was 12.

Sara Gottdiener Atzmon

It is impossible to describe the liberation. The heart and the mind were frozen and could not awaken and rejoice so all of a sudden. Maybe the defensive system of our body protects us, so the heart and the mind will not leap too high from joy. Also, we were afraid that the murderers might come back.

It is hard to describe the warm smiles and the empathy these soldiers showed us in our terrible condition. We felt that love and compassion flowed from these combat-fatigued soldiers; they bestowed on us so much kindness and sympathy.

For the first time after going through sheer hell, I felt that there was such a thing as simple love coming from good people—young men who had left their families far behind, who wrapped us in warmth and love and cared for our well-being. Even today, as I am writing these words, I feel that I want to kneel before them, embrace and thank these angels, who have given us life.

Sgt. Gross and his tank and crew had been left with the train for a period of about 24 hours.

The train, Friday, April 13, 1945. Credit: George Gross.

George C. Gross

I believe that the ranking officer of the Finnish prisoners introduced himself to me and offered to set up a perimeter guard.[75] I think I approved and asked him to organize a guard, set out pickets, and handle the maintenance and relief of the outposts. However it happened, the guard was set up swiftly and efficiently. It was moving and inspiring to see how smartly those emaciated soldiers returned to their military duties, almost joyful at the thought of taking orders and protecting others again. They were armed only with sticks and a few weapons discarded by the fleeing German guards, but they made a formidable force, and they obviously knew

---

[75] *Finnish prisoners*-Gross's account of the liberation, written in 2001, mentions Finnish POWs. It is unlikely that Finnish POWs were occupants of the Bergen–Belsen train transport, so it is assumed that they had encountered the Americans in the area on their own, perhaps as escapees of another camp or transport. Masses of humanity were on the German roads during this chaotic period. Additionally, the After-Action Report for the day mentions, 'After scouting the area, the squad leader of the doughs, the tank commander of Tank 12 (SGT. GROSS), and the camp leader of the internees, got together to set up a guard. The civilians were very cooperative, and an efficient guard system was set up around the train and the tank positions. The civilians were posted in vital points, unarmed, to warn the troops of any trouble. A strong and alert guard was set up on the tank.' Regardless of the makeup of the improvised guard, a perimeter warning system was thus established, as the threat of German counterattack was still very real.

their duties, so that I could relax and talk to the people.

A young woman named Gina Rappaport came up and offered to be my interpreter. She spoke English very well and was evidently conversant with several other languages besides her native Polish. We stood in front of the tank as a long line of men, women, and little children formed itself spontaneously, with great dignity and no confusion, to greet us. It is a time I cannot forget, for it was terribly moving to see the courtesy with which they treated each other, and the importance they seemed to place on reasserting their individuality in some seemingly official way.

Liberation at Farsleben, April 13, 1945. Credit: George Gross.

Each would stand at a position of rigid attention, held with some difficulty, and introduce himself or herself by what grew to be a sort of formula: the full name, followed by 'a Polish Jew from Hungary'–or a similar phrase which gave both the origin and the home from which the person had been seized. Then each would shake hands in a solemn and dignified assertion of individual worth. Battle-hardened veterans learn to contain their emotions, but it was difficult then, and I cry now to think about it. What stamina and regenerative spirit those brave people showed!

Liberation at Farsleben, April 13, 1945. Credit: George Gross.

Also tremendously moving were their smiles. I have one picture of several girls, specter-thin, hollow-cheeked, with enormous eyes that had seen much evil and terror, and yet with smiles to break one's heart.

Little children came around with shy smiles, and mothers with proud smiles happily pushed them forward to get their pictures taken. I walked up and down the train, seeing some lying in pain or lack of energy, and some sitting and making hopeful plans for a future that suddenly seemed possible again. Others followed everywhere I went, not intruding but just wanting to be close to a representative of the forces that had freed them. How sad it was that we had no food to give immediately, and no medical help, for during my short stay with the train sixteen or more bodies were carried up the hillside to await burial, brave hearts having lost the fight against starvation before we could help them.

Liberation at Farsleben, April 13, 1945. Credit: George Gross.

The boxcars were generally in very bad condition from having been the living quarters of far too many people, and the passenger compartments showed the same signs of overcrowding and unsanitary conditions. But the people were not dirty. Their clothes were old and often ragged, but they were generally clean, and the people themselves had obviously taken great pains to look their best as they presented themselves to us. I was told that many had taken advantage of the cold stream that flowed through the lower part of the valley to wash themselves and their clothing. Once again I was impressed by the indomitable spirits of these courageous people.

Gina Rappaport stands before Tank 12, April 13, 1945. Credit: George Gross.

I spent part of the afternoon listening to [Gina's story], who had served so well as interpreter. She was in the Warsaw Ghetto for several years as the Nazis gradually emptied the ghetto to fill the death camps, until her turn finally came.[76] Since the

---

[76] *Warsaw Ghetto*- Gina was actually from Kraków, but deported to the Tarnow Ghetto in 1941. Interestingly, in 2008, a 5-page unsigned typewritten narrative of a young Polish woman's Holocaust experiences, written on the letterhead of the Commandant of Hillersleben (the former German military base where the prisoners recuperated), turned up on EBay several years after I published Dr. Gross's narrative about Gina on our website. A collector, Ron Chaulet, purchased the document and tracked information in it to my website; we worked together to contact her family, who gratefully verified its authenticity. A copy now resides at the USHMM and Yad Vashem.

prisoners had little food, many died on the purposeless journey, and they had felt no cause for hope when they were shunted into this little unimportant valley siding.

Gina told her story well, but I have never been able to write it. I received a letter from her months later, when I was home in San Diego. I answered it but did not hear from her again. Her brief letter came from Paris, and she had great hopes for the future. I trust her dreams were realized.

We were relieved the next morning, started up the tank, waved goodbye to our new friends, and followed a guiding jeep down the road to rejoin our battalion. I looked back and saw a lonely Gina Rappaport standing in front of a line of people waving us good fortune. On an impulse I cannot explain, I stopped the tank, ran back, hugged Gina, and kissed her on the forehead in a gesture I intended as one asking forgiveness for man's terrible cruelty and wishing her and all the people a healthy and happy future. I pray they have had it.

Gina composed the following words about her liberation shortly thereafter, while recuperating at Hillersleben.

Gina Rappaport Leitersdorf

We were liberated by the American Army on the 13th of April. It was the luckiest day of my life. At that moment I was bathing in the river when I saw the first American soldier from afar, what a joy! I couldn't believe my eyes.[77] I was sure it was a dream, but still it was true.

A few minutes before the American soldiers arrived we were told that we should have to go on foot over the Elbe River. But the American Army saved us from a sure death, which we will never forget. I was also sad this day because I remembered how many people of value had died and couldn't see the liberation... I shall never forget what I owe to the American Army. I hope I will be able to estimate its right value, what the Americans have done for us. Now, after five years of suffering, I shall know to appreciate the more my liberty.

---

[77] *Bathing in the river*-Gina probably refers to the pond, mentioned here by others.

Gina Rappaport Leitersdorf sees her 1945 liberation photograph and George Gross's narrative about her from the author's website for the first time,
September 2007. Credit: Leitersdorf family, Israel.

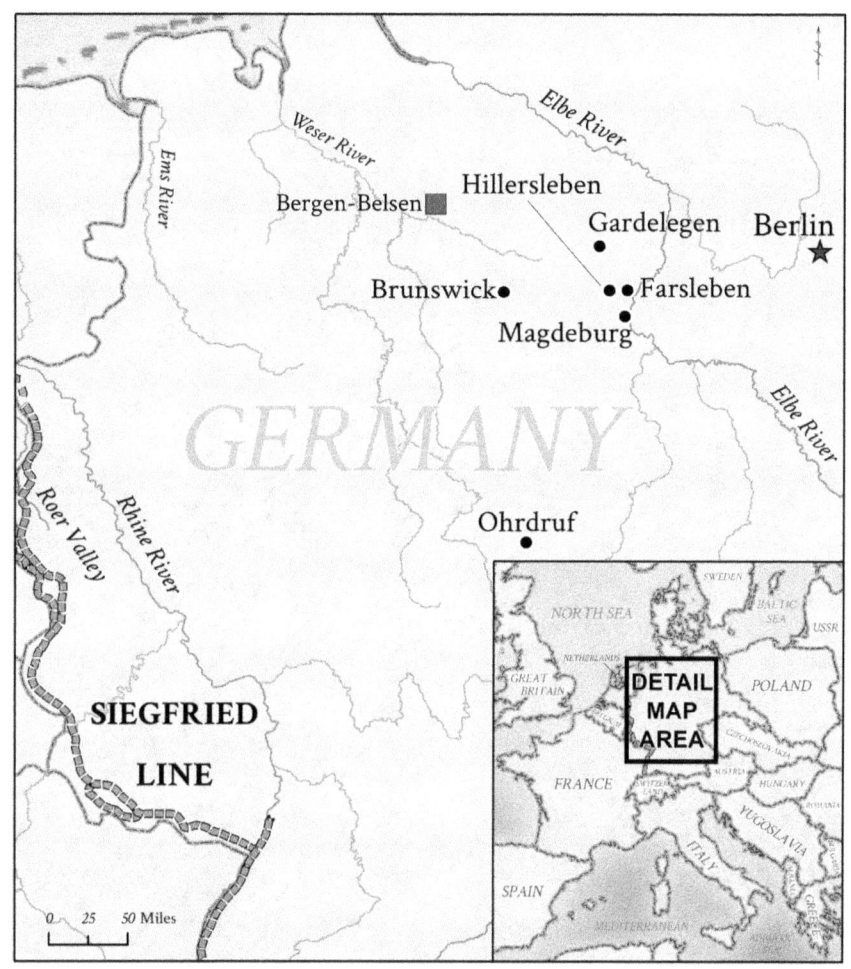

Into Germany, spring 1945. Credit: Susan Winchell.

CHAPTER FOURTEEN

'I'll never forget today.'

On Saturday, April 14, the sun rose as the newly liberated tended small fires to warm themselves and whatever food they had managed to scavenge from the countryside or the nearby town of Farsleben. Back at the train that Saturday morning, the 30th Division's liaison officer, Lt. Frank W. Towers, was charged with evacuating the refugees to a more appropriate and secure location, out of harm's way. Accordingly, the twenty-seven-year-old Towers organized a convoy to travel the ten kilometers to the just captured town of

Hillersleben, where a former German Luftwaffe base and proving ground was located, complete with barracks and a small hospital.

Frank W. Towers

As we were proceeding eastward from Brunswick, for days preceding [the liberation of the train], the roads were clogged with refugees fleeing from the east, to get out of the reach of the Russians. They were a tragic looking bunch of people, but happy to be escaping the clutches of the Russians, and to be greeting the Americans. They were carrying all of their worldly possessions in back packs, dragging carts of every variety. Through them, we gained a lot of intelligence on the disposition of German emplacements; they let us know where we might encounter enemy action, where artillery guns were located. [From them we learned of the existence of this train] and that [the Germans] were setting up an ambush for us when we approached the area. Thus, we sent the tanks of the 743rd Tank Battalion to reconnoiter the area prior to our foot troops. Upon their arrival at Farsleben, they did not encounter any enemy ambush, but were confronted with the train in the ravine.

As the 30th Division's liaison officer, I was told about the train initially by my counterpart, Lt. Floyd Mitchell, who was the liaison officer from the 743rd Tank Battalion, and as he was going back to his headquarters, he asked me if I would like to go with him to see [it]. I agreed to accompany him, and this was my first encounter with 'The Holocaust,' to witness all that we had heard about through the 'propaganda' [we had been told] in previous months—to see it with my own eyes, that our own Allied 'propaganda' was in fact true.

[The main roads in some places were impassable, so] the trip from Farsleben to Hillersleben was mostly over narrow back roads and dirt farm roads, in order to get to the destination in the shortest time. Due to artillery shelling and too much recent rain they were full of muddy pot holes, and the vehicles had to travel very slowly, or cause breakdowns of the vehicles. The drivers were very well aware of the hazards of driving over this type of road, as they had done so many times before. Fortunately, during these days it did not rain any more. As I acquired the vehicles for the convoy, some were covered, and some were not, but to these people, it did not matter. Rain or shine, they were on the way to freedom, and although hungry, dehydrated, and in frail health, they felt that they were going to a better place than they had seen in many months. They were happy in knowing that they were going to a place where they could get food, sleeping space, and health assistance.

As best I recall, we started moving these people in the afternoon, and we continued until dark, which at that time was not until after 10:00 p.m., so we halted operations until daylight the next morning, and continued on into the day until all were removed from Farsleben. I am not sure just who was involved in assisting the loading of the people at Farsleben, perhaps by some of the troops from our Engineer Battalion and some of the men of the American Military Government and Red Cross personnel, who also helped in unloading the people, orienting them as to where they were to go to get showers and new clothing, then feeding them and assigning them to appropriate quarters.

Then their processing began as to who they were, where they had come from, their birthplace, and their hoped for destination. All of this of course took several weeks before they were all processed and shipped to their destinations.[65]

Tech Sgt. Rice continued his written reports.

Wilson Rice

```
Saturday
14 April 1945
```

```
Around   noon   today   the   Germans
shelled us from the other side of the
Elbe River. Two of Company D's men
were hit, one in the knee and the other
in the shoulder. A German colonel was
captured yesterday, that pulled up the
artillery of their general headquar-
ters to the Elbe, and I guess that is
what was firing on us. Our artillery
soon found them and laid the ammuni-
tion to them.
```

Today they brought in a wounded German who was nicked in the arm. One of the recaptured British soldiers looked up and recognized him as being one of the guards on their long march. The Britisher said that he would make the men stand naked in the snow, and that he marched at the rear of the column, and as the men would drop out, he would probe and hit them with the butt of his rifle. The German confessed that it was true, but said that he was carrying out orders. The Tommy said that he saw this Jerry kill two American soldiers on the march. He was well enough to be taken to the PW cage, and the Britishers wanted to take him. They were going to let them, but the officers changed the idea and wouldn't let them do it. They kept him around here, and during the day, they gave him a good working over. 'Slim,' the Negro driver, was in charge. He had him out covering up a latrine with his hands.

Casualties to date:
Division   24,686
Civilian   957
Enemy   2,091
Other Units 3,588
31,322

*

Sunday
15 April 1945

This morning we were awakened, not by the man on duty, but by Jerries strafing and our ack-ack letting go at them.[78] I wish they wouldn't begin their warfare so early in the morning. It is so annoying!

---

[78] *ack-ack-* anti-aircraft artillery guns

The 2nd Armored Division and our [30th Division] 119th Infantry Regiment has been pushed back on this side of the river. Major Young was in the office today. It has been a long time since we have seen him, as the 119th has been with the 2nd Armored since crossing the Rhine. He said that the 3rd Battalion of the 119th really had it rough on the other side of the Elbe River; for example, out of one company, there were only five men left!

The town, Farsleben, which is located with the extermination train, was evacuated of the German civilians and turned over to the members of the train.[79] Capt. Fleming, of our 105th Engineers, found a warehouse filled with drugs, chocolate milk powder, baby food, bandages, and other medical equipment. Another warehouse was

---

[79] *turned over to the members of the train*-By this time, survivors were actually being moved to the more appropriate setting of the captured Luftwaffe base at nearby Hillersleben.

found. Major Huff went down to look into this one, and it contained about the same things. Trucks were sent to these warehouses, loaded and taken to the doctors in charge of these people. It was just like manna from heaven for them. Fifteen cases of typhus had developed, and three other doctors were discovered among the group of prisoners-making a total number of five or six. Dr. Schwieter was put in charge, medically, by Col. Treherne.[80] He was born in Poland, but is a citizen of Chile. He received his degree in Poland, probably University of Warsaw. He studied in Paris, Berlin, and Vienna. He specialized in Surgery, Obstetrics, Gynecology, and Pediatrics. Col. Treherne said that he was a very smart man and very cultured. The

---

[80] *Dr. Schwieter*-T/4 Rice was not certain about the spelling of the doctor's name; probably it was Schwieger, as he alludes later. Indeed, in 2019, the author was contacted by his great-granddaughter, and confirmed this.

doctor said that we were saviors from heaven.

Casualties to date:
Division   24,718
Civilian   962
Enemy   2,099
Other Units 3,606
31,385

*

Monday
16 April 1945

Dr. Julius Schwieger, the doctor that Col. Treherne put in charge of the concentration camp train, was in the office this morning. He came in for some vital medical supplies, and rode in on the back of a motorcycle. He showed us two pictures of himself before he was taken prisoner by the Nazis six years ago. He was a very fleshy man. This morning he stripped down to the waist. He was nothing but skin and bones. He would pull his skin and it would stretch out some three to four inches. He has his wife and two children with him. We gave him some white medical gowns, a stethoscope, medical supplies, and for himself, we gave him some soap, candy and chocolate for the children, sugar, coffee, soap, razor and blades, and other toilet articles. We also gave him some cigarettes and pipe tobacco. Concerning the medical supplies, when the Col. would ask him if he had enough, and he told him he could take it all, he would say, *'It is too much. All that I want is just enough.'*

He was very considerate. The thing that he seemed to get the most enjoyment from was the American Medical Journal that Major Lowell gave him. He subscribed to the Journal for fifteen years and hadn't seen an issue for the past six years. Dr. Schwieger was very interested that we write to a doctor friend of his in Detroit, as the friend believed him to be dead.

*

Wolfgang Groppe was a German boy living at Farsleben. The author contacted him in March 2016 after reading a comment he made on a video that was posted of an interview with soldier Frank W. Towers. He gave the following statement.

Wolfgang Groppe

I was a ten-year-old boy living on a farm in the village of Farsleben when the US forces with their tanks, trucks, and jeeps rolled into the marketplace. I have with my own eyes seen the suffering of the prisoners from that train in April 1945. After the US Army liberated the captive people, they wandered all over the village. The Army commandeered the bakery for the prisoners, and they gulped fresh bread and the food they were given from the Army, resulting in terrible retching as their bodies were totally unfamiliar with real food. There were carts of the unfortunate bodies that did not make it, and they died while still on the train. These were 'gueterwagen,' cattle cars. Yes, Frank Towers is 100% right, this happened and was just unbelievable suffering and tragedy for the 2,500 Jewish prisoners on that train. The US Army commanded the able German women to assist washing their laundry; my mother was one of these women! One more detail I can remember is the MP detail visiting the burgermeister's office and arresting several Nazis and driving away. Just a few weeks prior to the American arrival, Farsleben was a standpoint for one of the last [German] cavalry regiments, and we, as most boys are apt to do, admired their horses and we filled our pockets with their dried sugar beets feed. [The horses were] boarding inside some large barns in the village, and just a few days before the US arrival, they hitched up their gears, mounted the horses, and that was the end, for me, of the glorious 1,000-year German Reich. Can you believe the army on horseback with the US military at their doorstep?

I had a real tough time with the discovery of the death train at that siding just a few minutes from my home at that time in 1945. Somehow in my ten-year-old reasoning, it had a deep impact on me, and the pictures of all that suffering and the living skeletons walking all over the village, the carts full of dead bodies. The strange-looking military all over the place, the first contact with the US soldiers, and the unbelievable noise of the light infantry's rolling equipment—this whole scenario imprinted itself on my conscience. That was a dark day for everyone, but for the prisoners of that train, God and the United States Army got there in time. It took me some time to live with all that, but my 81st birthday is next week so I will just be thankful to have made it so far.

*

On April 17, four days after the liberation, the 30th Infantry Division's G-2 officer wrote up his report.

A PW stated that the camp Bergen-Belsen was run by two officers of the Totenkopf Verbande, SS/HauptsturmFührer (Capt.) Kramer and

SS/UntersturmFührer (Lt.) Klipp.[81] The prisoner's own attitude was one of hand-washing apathy. He was not responsible for what went on, was just a pawn-and if he was bothered by some of the things that went on, no one knows about it.

This is one of the many stories of the Nazis' organized cruelty of the German model of total warfare. Two other suspects of the case, which certainly will affect the task of Military Government, which will face many of the units now devoted to fighting, were developed at Farsleben. The first in the report by many of the prisoners, that the inhabitants of the town were very friendly when the train first stopped there-because they expected the hourly arrival of the US troops. Later, when our failure to

---

[81] *PW*-German prisoner of war. *Totenkopfverbände*-Death's Head Units, the SS organization responsible for administering the Nazi concentration camps for the Third Reich, among other duties.

arrive aroused some doubts, the populace reverted to hostility and contempt. Our troops, when they did arrive, however, found the citizenry of Farsleben most eager to be of help to the prisoners. The second observation was made by Military Government Officers, after the prisoners had been fed and deloused, and after beds and clean bedclothes had been set up for them in barns and other buildings. The setup looked beautiful, but only for a short time. The personal standards of cleanliness of many members of the group were bad, and some even went so far as to defecate on the floor of their living quarters. This rehabilitation for many of the victims of Hitler's Europe must mean far more than mere relocation and provision of adequate food and quarters, which itself is no great problem. True rehabilitation must provide for even so fundamental a thing as a sense of physical decency, for a large number of those who have been treated and have lived for years as animals.

```
Casualties to date:
Division        24,778
Civilian           974
Enemy            2,100
Other Units      3,628
                31,480
```

*

Nineteen-year-old 1st Lt. Charles M. Kincaid was a liaison officer with the 30th Division Artillery. As a young soldier, Kincaid rarely wrote home, but he did write to his minister about this event that evidently really caused him to stop and think. He was horrified by what he witnessed at the liberation of the train and was so distressed that he could not even tell his mother about what he had seen. His shock, trauma, and outrage are symbolic of the feelings felt by all the liberators of the victims of the Nazi regime.

Charles M. Kincaid

April 17, 1945
Dear Chaplain,

Haven't written you in many months now, it's funny how a few moments are so hard to find in which to write a letter way past due; it's much easier to keep putting it off the way I've done. I'll try to make up for it in this letter.

Today I saw a sight that's impossible to describe, however I'll try. Between 2,400 and 3,000 German refugees were overran by my division during our last operation; most of them were, or had been, inmates of concentration camps, their crimes the usual ones—Jewish parentage, political differences with der Führer, lack of sympathy for the SS, or just plain bad luck. Not one of these hundreds could walk one mile and survive; they had been packed on a train whose normal capacity was perhaps four or five hundred, and had been left there days without food.

Our division military government unit took charge of them, and immediately saw what a huge job it was going to be, so they sent out a call for help. Several of our officers went out to help them organize the camp they were setting up for them. The situation was extremely ticklish we soon learned; no one could smoke as it started a riot when the refugees saw the cigarette, and we couldn't give the kiddies anything or they would have been trampled to death in the rush that would result when anything resembling food was displayed. The only nourishment they were capable of eating was soup; now the army doesn't issue any of the Heinz 57 varieties, so we watered down C-rations and it served quite well. It was necessary to use force to make the people stay in line in order to serve them. They had no will power left, only the characteristics of beasts.

A few weeks of decent food will change them into a semblance of normal human beings; with God willing, the plague of disease that was already underway will be diverted; but I'm wondering what the effect of their ordeal they have been through will be on their minds; most will carry scars for the rest of their days for the beatings that they were given. No other single thing had convinced me as this experience has that Germany isn't fit to survive as a nation. I'll never forget today.

I was going to write Mother tonight but thought better of it. I'll be in a better frame of mind tomorrow. I'm only a few dozen miles from Berlin right now, and it's hard to realize the end is in sight. I'm always glad to receive your scandal sheet. You perhaps missed your calling, as your editorial abilities are quite plain.

As ever,
Charles.

BOOK FOUR

REUNION:

THE RIPPLES RETURN

I survived because of many miracles. But for me to actually meet, shake hands, hug, and cry together with my liberators—the 'angels of life' who literally gave me back my life—was just beyond imagination.

— Leslie Meisels, Holocaust Survivor

CHAPTER FIFTEEN

'The Indomitable Spirit'

I happened to come of age, as a young history teacher in training in 1984, just as the American president made his way to the bluffs overlooking the sands of Omaha Beach. Forty years after the war, he addressed the survivors of D-Day and the battle for Normandy, where nearly 9400 Americans lay at rest on over 170 acres of sanctified ground, watched over by the 22-foot-tall bronze statue, 'Spirit of American Youth Rising from the Waves.' Thirty-eight sets of brothers lie there, and on the Walls of the Missing, over 1500 names are inscribed, including soldiers of the 743rd Tank Battalion lost that day. Something inside me stirred; I nodded silently at the black-and-white television screen in my college bedroom, the American president asking a question that I would go on to ask, over and over again:

'Why? Why did you do it?'

Like the soldier Charles Kincaid, I began by writing letters to express my feelings, first to the newspaper. Veterans noticed my essays of recognition and appreciation. I began to interview D-Day veterans and others, and I began to collect stories—not relics, prizes, or artifacts. I really had little interest in captured Nazi flags or samurai swords.

I wanted to talk to the men (and women) who were there.

I had a lot of gaps to fill. In talking with one of my own history teachers later on, a Navy veteran of the Pacific and a survivor of a kamikaze attack on his ship, he reminded me that in high school, he did not go into his World War II experiences because it was 'all Hitler-this and Hitler-that'. In other words, a fascination that really clouded a more objective look at the World War II experience, perhaps a study in villainy that let the rest of humanity off the hook for the greatest crime in the history of the world. And I can't say I remember too much Holocaust education in my days in high school, or that I became a master teacher on the topic in college. I can't say I began my World War II Living History Project to 'rectify' that, but by being open, going down new paths, being proactive to new leads, and above all being receptive to the currents of the universe, more miracles were about to unfold.

*

March 2006/ Hudson Falls, New York

Four years had passed since I put the soldiers' narratives and photographs on our World War II oral history project website. Two days before my 45th birthday, I was sitting at the computer a few minutes after getting my students settled in with an exam. My email inbox quietly chimed. The kids all seemed to be properly on task.

I took a look.

From: Lexie Keston
Sent: Wednesday, March 29, 2006 1:38 AM
To: Rozell Matt
Subject: Your website

Dear Mr. Rozell,

I was directed to your Living History Project website by the people at the Bergen-Belsen Memorial in Germany.

I am what is now called a 'child survivor' of Bergen-Belsen. I was on the train in the story 'A Train Near Magdeburg' as recorded by Professor George C. Gross. I have had now the good fortune to speak to George Gross by telephone and also have had a number of email communications with him. On April 13, 1945, I was six years old. I had been on the train with my parents. I now live in Sydney, Australia.

I would very much like to make for myself a DVD copy of the 12 photographs in this story.

I hope you do not mind this request and that you will be able to help me.

Thanking you in anticipation.
Sincerely,
Alexandra (Lexie) Keston

I just sat there; I could not move.

Had I just been contacted by a person who lived through that nightmare, and found the photos of her liberation day?

Do I bear some responsibility for this?

*

In March 2002, exactly four years earlier, I had uploaded George Gross's narrative of the liberation, along with the photographs that he and Major Benjamin had taken that day, onto my website, with his most appreciative blessing for my endeavor. At that time the website had about 20 World War II veteran interviews posted that the kids and I had done over the years; on a good day, the website might have brought in 25 or 30 visitors. But unbeknownst to me, the staff at the Bergen-Belsen Memorial had taken note of it and was now directing survivors and their descendants to what was turning out to be our unique archive of Holocaust liberation photos and interviews, offered up by the liberators themselves.

Stunned, I read Lexie's words, over and over. The kids were still taking the test as I stared at the screen with my eyes welling up. I wiped my eyes, looking up to see if any of them were watching me.

No, not this time, but there will be many more such moments in my future. Over 10,000 miles away from me, reaching out across space and time, a six-year-old girl who was now a sixty-seven-year-old grandmother signaled to me that on some level, past and present just became one.

*

And so it began. In my first interview with Judge Walsh in July 2001, he had mentioned that a doctor in London had recently placed a notice in the 30th Infantry Division newsletter about this train, wanting to contact any of his liberators, if they were still alive. Walsh read the notice and responded, and only two months before my initial interview with Walsh, Dr. Peter Lantos became the first of the survivors of that train to contact his liberator George Gross. I was in contact with Dr. Gross by that time, and he told me about it, and also that Dr. Lantos was working on his memoir. And shortly after I heard from Lexie, he described his experiences.

From: Dr. George C. Gross
Sent: Wednesday, May 10, 2006 7:02 PM

To: Rozell Matt
Subject: Re: The Train story...

Dear Matt,

It was good to hear from you and to learn of your plans to write a book. You certainly have my permission to use any pictures and text of mine that you have, both for the interview and for the book.

I think the stories of Peter Lantos and Lexie are important for the world to hear. Both show the indomitable resilience of the human psyche, for both have led productive—and evidently happy—lives despite the terrors and tragedies of their childhood.

Peter has spent a career of service to mankind as an expert in clinical neuroscience and undoubtedly saved many lives and pushed back the limits of our understanding of the brain and how it works. Think how close we came to losing that great mind to the stupidity of the Holocaust, and think how many talents like his were lost to the world in that madness!

Lexie, with her charming family of daughters and granddaughters, shows another face of the triumph of the human will in building a rich family life despite the traumatic events of her childhood.

Their stories both carry stern warnings against antisemitism, racism, intolerance of other religions, fascism, and foolish prejudices of all kinds but also carry the hopeful message of the strength of humanity. I am happy that you, with all the demands you have upon your time as a teacher, have been willing to spend so much time with your students building and maintaining the web site and are planning to devote more time in writing a book. I thank you for that dedication.

I don't know if Lexie told you of our first telephone conversation. I was sitting in my LazyBoy, swearing at the newspaper's [distressing headlines], when the telephone interrupted my colorful monologue.[82]

'Hello!' I barked into the intruding instrument, forgetting that the innocent person on the other end of the line had had no part in the irritating news events.

'Hello?' a tremulous and tentative voice replied. 'Is this George C. Gross?'

'Yes,' I answered, in a gentler tone because I realized that the person calling was in a wrought-up state.

Almost crying, the voice continued, 'Did you have anything to do with a death train near Magdeburg in April 1945?'

When I said yes, with great interest at last, she started to cry, and then pulled herself together to tell me her story.

After years of searching for information about the train, she had discovered your site, read the story there, found my name and home city, and immediately decided to call. She told me she was ready to keep calling every Gross in Spring Valley until she found me. Luckily for her pocketbook, I was the first call she tried; the cost of one phone call from Australia must have put quite a dent in her budget. At any rate, we had a good, emotionally charged conversation, exchanged E-mail addresses, and have corresponded

---

[82] *LazyBoy*-[sic] La-Z-Boy, brand name for a popular upholstered reclining chair.

regularly since then. I put her in touch with Peter, and the two have corresponded.

I am still amazed to have gotten, out of the blue, a call from so far away about an event that occurred so long ago. That call was a direct result of the work you and your students have put into your site, and I thank you for it. The event remains lively in my memory, but such contact with people who were on the train makes the event even more vivid as I contemplate the day and its ramifications.

Gratefully yours,
George

---

*

The following November, another ripple arrived in my inbox.

From: Micha Tomkiewicz
Sent: Wednesday, November 01, 2006 10:44 AM
To: Rozell Matt
Subject: A Train Near Magdeburg

Dear Mr. Rozell. I am also a 'child survivor' that was riding on this train from Bergen-Belsen to an unknown destination. Yesterday I got the link through a historian in the camp.

My wife claims that she can identify me through one of the photographs, but since there is probably nobody alive that can confirm or refute this claim, I will let it stand. The larger issue for me is that we have suddenly the opportunity to thank these guys.

Since through your initiative you sort of deserve to become an honorary president of the 'graduates' of the 'Train Near Magdeburg'—it might be a good idea to try to organize a meeting of the survivors and the soldiers to give us a collective opportunity to say thank you.

Thanks again,
Prof. Micha (Marcin) Tomkiewicz
Environmental Studies Program, Department of Physics
Brooklyn College of CUNY, Brooklyn, NY

Dr. Tomkiewicz, or Micha as I would come to know him, called me about a month later and we had a good conversation. Micha was a young boy about the same age as Peter Lantos imprisoned in Bergen-Belsen, and like Peter, was later liberated with only his mother, his father having been killed trying to escape from one of the last deportation trains to Treblinka out of the Warsaw Ghetto. He helped to plant the seed of my efforts to have a reunion of sorts with the liberators and survivors, and the next catalyst was going to find me the following April.

From: Fred Spiegel
Sent: Wednesday, April 04, 2007 3:29 PM
To: Rozell Matt
Subject: Magdeburg 1945

Dear Matthew Rozell:

I will be 75 years old on April 21. I was liberated by American troops on April 13, 1945, near Farsleben and Magdeburg. It was one week before my 13th birthday.

I actually visit many schools here in Central and Southern New Jersey, to speak about my experiences during the Holocaust. I came across your web site through a teacher who is doing a project about my experiences and she found your website about George Gross and Carrol Walsh.

I have actually written a book, about my experiences, which was published in September 2004.

Anyway, it was very interesting to read the website. It is quite amazing what those soldiers remember.

Very best regards,
Fred Spiegel

This seemed to me to be almost beyond belief. With Fred, I had four survivors of whom I was now aware, and the seed which had been planted in my brain began to germinate. Judge Walsh, now retired, spent much of the year in Florida, but in the summer he would come to Hudson Falls as he had done that summer six years before when I sat down to interview him the first time. Why not organize an event to bring them all together? And since he would not be leaving until late September, *why not do it so that students might witness and hear the testimony, and learn?*

I immediately wrote to all of them, and over the summer of 2007, things began to fall into place. We set a date—Friday, September 14, 2007, at our high school in Hudson Falls. Micha and Fred lived only about a four-hour drive away, and Peter would be available to fly to New York City to drive up with Micha and his wife Louise. Fred and his wife Yael also would be driving up. They would all be driving right past the family homestead at 2 Main Street, Hudson Falls, straight up the road to our small-town American high school—a German survivor rounded up in Holland, a Hungarian survivor shunted by fate away from Auschwitz, and a Polish survivor of the Warsaw Ghetto, a microcosm of those persecuted during the Holocaust throughout Europe who shared at least one thing in common, besides their Jewish identity—they had the same liberators, and they had me. And now they were coming face-to-face with one of the men who saved them.

*

I started investigating the possibility of a reunion even before school let out in June of 2007. My school was very supportive and agreed that it would be a great learning opportunity for our students and community and went so far as to set aside a day in September so that all of the students at the high school could be in attendance. My fellow teachers were excited and planned many steps.

I also believed that this event would be of interest to a wider audience. I contacted several media outlets and a friend at the Associated Press, Chris Carola, who worked out of the Albany, New York, bureau and had come up to the region many times before to cover another project I was heavily involved with, the archeological digs in our region at military sites from the colonial wars and the American Revolution. Chris was very interested, interviewed Judge Walsh and some of the survivors, and sent a photographer up the day before the survivors arrived to be present as I had Judge Walsh in my classroom telling his story to my tenth graders. The camera shutter clicked as he and I and the students interacted. Chris wrote his story, then posted it on the Associated Press's New York State wires, and told me we could be getting calls from New York City-area television and radio stations. He also told me he sent it to the Washington, D.C., national operations, and he thought it was possible that it would be picked up internationally for newspapers overseas.

He closed with the caution, '*I just want to prepare you for a possible media onslaught on Hudson Falls High School.*'

*

On a crisp September morning in 2007, cars began arriving in the parking lot of a local restaurant where a small welcoming breakfast was planned for our guests. Judge Walsh's family was there, as were school administrators and several of the students and teachers who were involved in the project. Carrol finished up with an interview with a crew from the CBS Evening News, then greeted the three survivors who had come to meet him.

Carrol 'Red' Walsh

It was quite emotional. They had an early morning breakfast, and that was the first that I met three of the survivors. And you know what I said to them? 'Long time, no see!' [*Laughs*]

The three that I met were very young on the train. A couple of them were, I think, teenagers, but for the most part they were children.

*

So here we were at long last, survivors and the old soldier seated round a breakfast table, families, friends, students, and teachers witnessing the first miracle of our gatherings. Following breakfast, we headed to the high school for the day's testimony in front of the student body and staff. Students were excited, and some of the kids had worked on a short film introducing the liberators and what they encountered, juxtaposed with the photographs of the day of the liberation. Lexie Keston, the first survivor to contact me from Australia, had her greetings read to the assembled school.

Lexie Friedman Keston

I will never forget the day when I opened the website of the Hudson Falls High School World War II Living History Project, and before my unbelieving eyes I was looking back to 1945—more accurately to April 13, 1945—the day of my liberation by the Ninth US Army.

The eleven photographs before me were taken when I was six years old, younger than either of my two little granddaughters. The train had stopped at the siding of the small station at Farsleben, some 16 kilometers from Magdeburg. I had been on this train with my parents and some 2,500 people all from the Camp Bergen-Belsen. I had been incarcerated there from July 15, 1943 until April 7, 1945. In the camp we had the unusual classification of 'For Exchange to Palestine'; most were classified as 'Jew.' I think that this is the only reason that we were kept together and survived as a family for nearly two years in the most horrific of circumstances.

So now, some 61 years later in January 2006, in front of my computer at my home, I was confronted with photographs of the day of my liberation. I found this experience so raw and emotional that I screamed, and then burst into tears.

I studied the photographs looking and searching for myself. I thought that I could be one of the little girls, sitting in the group photo in January 2006, but I dismissed this for I assumed my mother would be somewhere nearby, and I did not see her.

I looked at the bleak, miserable geography of the site, the horrible train carriages, the skeletal human shapes—fortunately my memory is still a blank. I do not remember being in the train for 6 days; I do not remember being hungry or thirsty. All I remember is being out of the train, standing on the ground, and watching the German guards fleeing and dropping their guns. I picked up one of these guns, and before I could do anything, it was snatched from my hands. That is my only memory of that day.

'A Historical Miracle'

The events of the day are documented visually and that is incredible to believe. For no written words could describe so vividly the happenings of that day as do these eleven photographs. It is a historical miracle that Major Benjamin and tank commander George Gross had their small Kodak camera—and that on that day, there was film left to use and record the day.

With today's incredible technology anyone on our planet can see this photographic evidence of my liberation. It is the foresight of that other man of goodwill—your history teacher Matt Rozell—that these photographs were posted for all to access.

Following a series of events, I have developed a warm email relationship with Professor George Gross, with Judge Carrol Walsh, and Carrol's daughter Elizabeth. It is a great joy for me to hear about their lives today and of their family happenings. The fact that this connection was made some 61 years after the event is very difficult to believe possible.

But it is so.

The friendship I have developed with these two wonderful men has helped me to bring some sort of closure to that unfortunate time in my childhood. The interest they, as well as Matt, have shown in wanting to know my story has given me the encouragement I needed to write about some of my experiences. I did do so, and my story will be published in an anthology of some twenty stories of the members of my child survivors group here.

Thank you, Matt Rozell, for teaching your students about tolerance and the evils of prejudice. I applaud and compliment you on your good work. You have touched the lives of your students and a growing number of survivors. You have also, I think, affected the lives of the two liberators, George and Carrol.

Your history course on this Train at Magdeburg is teaching your students the evil that was perpetrated by the Nazis during the Holocaust, against innocent people, whose only sin was that they were Jews.

I hope one of the messages that your course has instilled into the psyche of your students is that 'Evil Happens When Good Men Do Nothing.'

Peter Lantos, who had just completed his memoir, Parallel Lines, spoke.

Peter Lantos

To get you accustomed to my accent, which hovers between British and Hungarian, I tell people of my American dream, which is not the traditional, classical American dream but a dream of a teenager, of myself, living in [postwar] Hungary, which at the time was a communist country, closed to the world. We had a relative in the United States, and Uncle Marcel left Hungary in the 1920s for a successful engineering career. And some of the things I really seem to remember were beautiful guide books of New York [City]. Living in a small Hungarian town in which the tallest building had only two stories, I could not believe that this building, buildings like this existed. So the dream was to see New York, and the States [someday]. And indeed I did see New York in the early 1970s. I visited many times for medical conferences, or visiting friends and relatives; I still have two cousins living here. However, as I was walking in Manhattan yesterday, it suddenly occurred to me that without Judge Walsh and Dr. Gross, [*with emotion*] I would have been dead.

Dr. Lantos described his book, and his life after surviving the Holocaust, and his initial contact with the liberators. He closed with the following.

And what I have wanted to do here [in my book] was not just [express] a morbid interest in the past. There is not self-pity; I just simply wanted to know what happened. Why it happened, that I don't know. So the end remains, and the only thing I have left to express is my gratitude to George and Carrol.

*

(L-R): Peter Lantos, Micha Tomkiewicz, Fred Spiegel, Carrol Walsh, author. September 14, 2007. Credit: Greg McDowell.

Judge Walsh was later interviewed and asked what this first meeting meant to him.

Carrol 'Red' Walsh

Interviewer: It may be a silly question to ask, but in the years after the war, did you ever think of that day when you came upon that train?

Not very much, no. No, it was… it was because… [*Hesitates*] it was just another day, you might say… I do not mean to put that down or minimize what was going on, but… it was just another incident, another day… and on you went! I had almost forgotten about [it] really, over the years. It was almost like another day in combat; nothing surprised me by then. No, I did not think much about it through the years, until I had this interview with Matt Rozell, the history teacher at Hudson Falls, New York, High School [*chuckles*]. My daughter said, 'Why don't you tell him about that train?' I had not even thought to mention the train to Matt Rozell, and I did, and as a result of that, that is how a lot of the programs and the connections with the survivors have come about.

You said it was emotional and I can understand why it was emotional for them [the survivors]. You guys, whether you knew it or not, were the saviors and the heroes but…

Well, let me stop you there. No, not heroes. It all came about, it just so happened, that Gross and I were the ones whose tanks were assigned to this particular scouting trip. Yes, those people look upon us as saviors. I do not, I don't know why [*chuckles*]… I do not feel like a 'hero'; I don't know if you can understand my feeling. Yes, the liberation came about, because we got there. Yes, at that particular time those SS guards took off, and it was the end of their ordeal; there is no question about that.

I mean, if you were not, you know, the 'sole hero' who saved them, certainly you and the other tank commander were the symbols of their liberation.

Exactly! That is a good expression. That is a good description, 'symbols.' Yes, indeed. Yes.

And so if it was, in a way, just 'another day in battle' for you, when you say that your reunions have been emotional, why—why are they emotional for you?

It's emotional for me when I think of where they were headed. They were headed for another concentration camp and extermination. And I get emotional now because I know what they went through, and what it meant to them, that we happened to intercept that train at that time. They are real people. When I look back, they were almost not like 'real people' when I first encountered them on the train on the cars! They were just a large group; 2,500 figures...now, all of a sudden, they have names. They had lives. They had families. They had stories. I guess that is why I find it emotional.

Sixty-two years ago, as those events happened, I never in my wildest imagination thought I would ever meet anyone from that train again.

Micha Tomkiewicz

All throughout my life, [my liberators] were always an abstract concept. Now suddenly they've got shape, voice, life. Suddenly, we have names. We can shake hands. We can put our own background into a context we couldn't put it in before. And now, [we] have an event that crystallizes that scenario. All of this to a large degree came out of a high school project. This to me is fascinating. When he started the project, he had no idea where it was going to lead. It is an excellent manifestation of what education can do.

*

George Gross, who was at the time not feeling well enough for the 3,000-mile journey from California across the United States, also had his statement read aloud to the assembled students and teachers.

George C. Gross

Sincere greetings to all of you gathered at this celebration of the indomitable spirit of mankind!

Greetings first to all the admirable survivors of the 'Train near Magdeburg,' and our thanks to you for proving Hitler wrong! You did not vanish from the face of the earth as he and his evil followers planned, but rather you survived, and grew, and became successful and contributing members of free countries, and you are adding your share of free offspring to those free societies. You have vowed that the world will never forget the horrors of the Holocaust, and you spread the message by giving interviews, visiting schools, writing memoirs, and publishing powerful books on the evil that infected Nazi Germany and threatens still to infect the world.

I have met and enjoyed the company of Dr. Peter Lantos and Drs. Micha and Louise Tomkiewicz, and I carry on a rewarding conversation with Lexie Keston, Fred Spiegel, and Micha Tomkiewicz's niece in France by email. I am enriched by the friendship of such courageous people who somehow have maintained a healthy sense of humor and a desire to serve through all the evils inflicted upon you. I am very sorry that I am unable to meet with you today.

Greetings also to the dedicated teacher whose efforts have brought us all together through the classes he has taught on World War II and the website he maintains at the cost of hours of time not easily found in his duty as a high school teacher. I know that several of you found your quest for knowledge of your past rewarded by the interviews and pictures Matthew Rozell and his classes have gathered and maintained. Selfishly, I am grateful to Mr. Rozell for leading several of you to me, bringing added joy to my retiring years.

And special greetings also to my old Army buddy, Judge Carrol Walsh, and his great family. Carrol fought many battles beside me, saved my life and sanity, and resuscitated my sense of humor often. We had just finished a grueling three weeks of fighting across Germany, moving twenty or more hours per day, rushing on to reach the Elbe River. Carrol and I were again side by side as we came up to the train with Major Benjamin, chased the remaining German guards away, and declared the train and its captives 'free members of society' under the protection of the United States Army, as represented by two light tanks. Unfortunately, Carrol was soon ordered back to the column on its way to Magdeburg while, luckily for me, I was assigned to stay overnight with the train, to let any stray German soldiers know that it was part of the free world and not to be bothered again.

Carrol missed much heartbreaking and heartwarming experience as I met the people of the train. I was shocked to see the half-starved bodies of young children and their mothers and old men—all sent by the Nazis on their way to extermination. I was honored to shake the hands of the large numbers who spontaneously lined up in orderly single file to introduce themselves and greet me in a ritual that seemed to satisfy their need to declare their return to honored membership in the free society of humanity. I was heartbroken that I could do nothing to satisfy their need for food that night, but I was assured that other units were taking care of that and the problem of housing so many free people. Sixty years later, I was pleased to hear that the Army did well in caring for their new colleagues in the battle for freedom. I saw many mothers protecting their little ones as best they could, and pushing them out, as proud mothers will, to be photographed. I was surprised and pleased by the smiles I saw on so many young faces. Some of you have found yourselves among those pictured children, and you have proved that you still have those smiles. I was terribly upset at the proof of man's inhumanity to man, but I was profoundly uplifted by the dignity and courage shown by you indomitable survivors. I have since been further rewarded to learn what successful, giving lives you have lived since April 13, 1945.

I wish I could be with you in person at this celebration, as I am with you in spirit. I hope you enjoy meeting each other and getting to know Matt Rozell and Carrol Walsh. I look forward to seeing again my friends whom I have met and to meeting the rest of you either in person or by email.

My experience at the train was rich and moving, and it has remained so, locked quietly in my heart until sixty years later, when the appearance of you survivors began to brighten up a sedate retirement. You have blessed me, friends, and I thank you deeply. May your lives, in turn, bring you the great blessings you so richly deserve.

Fondly yours,
George C. Gross
September 2007

Final reunion of the 30th Infantry Division Veterans of WWII Association, Nashville, TN, April 18, 2015. Credit: Larry S. Powell.

CHAPTER SIXTEEN

'Now I know what I fought for.'

The following morning, a Saturday, it was raining very hard. Our guests were making their way back to their homes after an electrifying Friday. The local newspaper had run a front-page story; after reading it over breakfast I set out according to my previous plan to go shopping for a new computer. I entered the big-box electronic retail store intent on making this a quick experience, but I also needed a new monitor, and asked the salesman to demonstrate the various models. As he fired up one of the larger screens, the Yahoo! News homepage came to life. And the lead story, complete with the Associated Press photograph of Judge Walsh talking to students in my classroom two days previously, flickered to life. I drew a deep breath and read the story, purchased the computer and monitor, and headed home in the driving rain.

At home, I checked my email. My brother Drew had sent me the screenshot of the Yahoo! News homepage with his prescient comment, *'Could be the start of something big'*. Rapidly multiplying by the minute on that Saturday morning were the congratulations and tributes, and thank-yous and kudos from all over the United States, Canada, and the world. As the day progressed, I checked the web counter on my school website. It also was growing by the hour, and by the end of the weekend it had been visited over twenty thousand times, straining the school's servers as people tried to view or download the photographs taken by George Gross and Major Benjamin on that April day 62 years earlier. Chris Carola's news article had been picked up by nearly every major news outlet in North America, and many overseas, including in Israel. Thanks to Chris, at least sixty more survivors or their children contacted me over the next few months.

> From: Steve Barry
> Sent: Tue 9/18/2007 5:31 PM
> To: Rozell Matt
> Subject: A Train Near Magdeburg
>
> Dear Mr. Rozell,
> Even before I proceed to tell you how I found you, I'm one survivor of that train nearly 63 years ago. Last Saturday the *South Florida Sun-Sentinel* published an article titled 'Vet unites with 3 death train survivors.' Needless to say, I was in a state of shock, and to some degree I still am, to find out after all the years, that the event burned in to my soul for all eternity, is shared with a lot of other people. I'm writing you all this since I'm planning to call you at the high school, and it will be a lot easier to have a conversation than writing down all this information.
> Sincerely,
> Stephen 'Berenyi' Barry
> Boca Raton, FL

Frank W. Towers, a retired administrator at the University of Florida and the head of the 30th

Infantry Division Veterans of World War II Association, also saw the article.

From: Frank W. Towers
Sent: Saturday, September 15, 2007 10:19 PM
To: Rozell Matt
Subject: Holocaust survivors

Dear Mr. Rozell:

Thank you for promoting the story of the Holocaust in your high school.

I am a veteran of the 30th Infantry Division, and we had the 743rd Tank Battalion attached to us. I believe that you are referring to a veteran of this unit that liberated this train of the Holocaust survivors at Farsleben, near Magdeburg.

I have more to tell you about this incident… I was involved in the displacing of these train survivors out of harm's way so that we could continue the battle without doing them more harm.

If interested, you can contact me.

Yours in 'Old Hickory' Friendship,
Frank W. Towers
President, Historian & Editor
30th Inf. Div. Veterans of WWII

I contacted Frank and we immediately began working together so that these additional survivors who had missed the first gathering could also meet the soldiers of the division who had liberated them. The 30th Division had been having annual reunions every single year since the end of World War II; back in the early days, their gatherings would fill more than one city hotel. I began working with Frank and his wife Mary to invite the survivors to meet their liberators, and in March 2008, several of them traveled to Fayetteville, North Carolina. I flew down with my ten-year-old son. Here I met for the first time many of the people who I would become close to over the next several years, besides Frank—Steve Barry; Elisabeth Seaman, a Dutch survivor who ran a conflict mediation service in California; Ern Kan, a survivor liberated not on the train but at the nearby Polte Ammunition Works slave labor complex on the same day. Micha Tomkiewicz and his wife Louise were also there, as was Peter Lantos from London.

This was the first of eight consecutive annual reunions held in the South between the soldiers and survivors of the train. The soldiers opened their hearts and turned the podium over to the survivors, who besides thanking the veterans, also had the opportunity to share their stories. The second and third generations of both the soldiers and the survivors bonded, and maintain relationships to this day.

At the close of one of these reunions, at the conclusion of my presentation, John, one of the soldiers, said to me, tears in his eyes, '*Yes. This is what I fought for. We didn't really understand why we were over there. This is what we fought for.*' Of course, it is more complex than a statement of emotion made 70 years after the war, but the fact was that John and the others were now feeling blessed that they could meet the actual people who they had saved from the continent which they came to liberate—and before these meetings, few of the soldiers had any idea of the now tangible magnitude of what they had really achieved.

But I struggled with my thoughts. *What did it all mean?*

Why was I in the middle of all these miracles?

CHAPTER SEVENTEEN

'For the Sake of Humanity'

September 2009/Hudson Falls, New York

As time passed after the very first reunion, and more and more survivors came into the picture, I began entertaining thoughts of holding a second reunion at Hudson Falls High School. This time, however, it would be a multi-day seminar, with the survivors and the soldiers and other guests addressing the students and staff in a more formal setting so that the lessons of history might be set forth for all. I designed it around the schedule of Judge Walsh and the beginning of the school year in September, and also so that students might take away high value lessons in ethics, responsibility, and morality early on in the academic setting. Frank Towers agreed to send me his list of World War II veterans of the 30th Infantry Division; over three hundred were on the list for the northeastern United States where we were located.

As anyone who has planned a conference or any event where strangers were being invited to come from out of town, this became a daunting task. Hotels have to be contacted. Speaker slots have to be carved out of the day. Programs need to be confirmed and printed. Teachers need to be notified that their regular lessons may be disrupted. Meals have to be planned. Transportation needs to be arranged. Politicians, VIPs, and the media all need to be invited. Compound that with the unknown— *how will the students, hundreds and hundreds of them, behave? Am I out of my mind to invite septuagenarians and octogenarians and people in their nineties to mingle with teenagers? And what if someone collapses?* Thoughts like these kept me up many a long summer night.

(L-R): Matthew Rozell, Ariela Rojek, Paul Arato, Fred Spiegel, Carrol Walsh, September 22, 2009. Credit: Twilight Studios.

Fortunately, the administration and staff at the school was very accommodating—everyone wanted to help. The principal's secretary became my secretary, fielding calls, relaying messages, co-ordinating welcoming gifts and packages with a core of other teachers who got involved in every aspect of planning and execution, right down to assigning seats in the auditorium for each of the six programs we would put on over the course of the next few days. Students from out of town were bussed in, as were some of the students from the other schools in our district. The United States Holocaust Memorial Museum, which had invited me to study intensively and become one of their Teacher Fellows the previous year, sent a representative to speak and also a film crew to document the event, and provided me a stipend with which to hire a professional photographer. The Bergen-Belsen Memorial in Germany also sent three representatives. And while I had contacted the major national news outlets, only one besides the Associated Press had indicated that it might be willing to send a team up to our small town. I began communicating with contacts at ABC World News back in late May. They were very interested, but would not commit until time grew closer. And then, just as school was starting and the final preparations for the grand reunion were being finalized, all communication ceased. An iconic U.S. statesman had passed away, and calling attention to our story did not appear to be in the cards.

*Frank Towers signs autographs for students,
Hudson Falls High School
September 2009. Credit: Twilight Studios.*

It didn't matter. And I needn't have worried. The entire community opened its arms in a wide embrace, and the love that burst forth, from soldiers to survivors, their children and grandchildren, all of the young people who became the new witnesses, was literally palpable. The elders became the new bonafide rock stars giving autographs and even dancing the night away on a steamboat dinner cruise on Lake George. Tears of happiness and joy flowed freely as the wires of the cosmos tripped once more.

*Second Reunion at Hudson Falls High School, September 2009. (L-R) Front row, survivors- Fred Spiegel, Ariela Rojek, Sara Atzmon, Micha Tomkiewicz, Leslie Meisels, Elisabeth Seaman, Paul Arato. Missing: Steve Barry.
Rear, soldiers: Frank Towers, Daniel Petriccione, Irving Shernock, Carrol Walsh, Bill Gast, Buster Simmons, Francis Currey (MOH); author.
Credit: Twilight Studios.*

And once I wrote off big network coverage of the event, the phone rang in my room just as our guests began arriving. ABC World News did indeed make the time to come up to our small town, making us their 'Persons of the Week' in the Friday evening broadcast with anchor Diane Sawyer narrating our story, which we were able to all watch together at our goodbye banquet at a local restaurant. The following spring, I was invited to the U.S. National Days of Remembrance ceremony in the Capitol Rotunda honoring the 65th anniversary of the end of World War II and the liberators. By this time, the United States Holocaust Memorial Museum's short film was ready, and at the breakfast honoring the liberators, survivor Steve Barry and I were recognized by the USHMM's director Sara Bloomfield, and the ABC News video was replayed for the over 100 U.S. liberators in attendance.

April 15, 2010/Washington, D.C.

We board the buses for the Capitol. Washington, D.C. traffic grinds to a dead halt in all directions as our convoy of three buses passes through intersections and sails down boulevards with a full Capitol police escort, every single crossroads blocked by police cars. Pulsing red and blue lights ricochet off the subterranean tunnel walls from which our buses are emerging, announcing to the citizens of our nation's capital that a convoy of VIPs is arriving, like conquering heroes of old, returning home after a great victory. And in a real sense, that is what they are. Here, now, nearly sixty-five years after the last battle was fought, the American liberators of the concentration camps are returning, many for the first time since World War II ended. We are on our way to the national ceremony at the United States Capitol Rotunda, and it won't do for us to be late.

The motorcade slows as it approaches Capitol Hill, and the three buses slowly maneuver and dock like lumbering giants at the sidewalk entrance. The pistons blast and the buses drop gently. The engines are cut. The doors open.

We have arrived.

The author and survivor Steve Barry, Washington, D.C., USHMM Days of Remembrance ceremony breakfast, April 15, 2010. Credit: USHMM.

It is a beautiful morning, and the Capitol Police dismount from their escort motorcycles and walk over, motioning and instructing for us to disembark and follow the guides. Emerging slowly into the warm April sunlight are the guests of honor, many of whom step down gingerly, clutching canes or holding the arm of a relative or friendly USHMM escort; nearly all sport caps festooned with pins and patches. One hundred twenty-one old soldiers, eyes sparkling as they pose for photographs, are escorted slowly through the entryway of the grand building. A single teacher follows the veterans on this beautiful spring day.

Me.

Passing through security and now inside the Rotunda, I am amazed at its beauty but also at the intimacy that emanates from under the hallowed dome as the veterans and survivors, the politicians and officials, process in. Scaffolding with TV crews and narrow towers with klieg lights illuminate the area, and as the ceremony begins, I am one hundred feet from General David Petraeus, who is about to address these old soldiers. The haunting sound of the Marine Corps violinist serenades the gathering with the 'Theme from Schindler's List', carrying our thoughts to the victims of the

Holocaust skyward in a silent prayer. The names of the liberating Army units are called out from the dais as each division is formally recognized, their unit colors hoisted aloft on cue and paraded in.[83] Sixty-five years was a lifetime ago. But really, it was just yesterday.

My cellphone buzzes as the ceremony ends. My congressman is here somewhere, and his staff would like me to come to his office. He was powerfully moved, but I have to dash for the airport to return to school.

But I'm walking on air.

---

[83] *names of the liberating Army units are called out*-The 30th Infantry Division was not formally recognized as a liberating unit until after heavy lobbying by Frank W. Towers. As author Michael Hirsh (*The Liberators*, 2010) has pointed out, the recognition agreement between the USHMM and the US Army Center for Military History is well-intentioned but poorly drawn. Soldiers who fell liberating Europe are not formally credited, and neither were the soldiers of the 30th Infantry Div. or 743rd Tank Btn., because they had not been found to liberate a 'recognized camp.' <u>The train did not count!</u> Further research revealed that the 30th had also liberated two subcamps near Magdeburg on April 12. Since 2013, thanks to Frank, the 30th's flag is now displayed in the Museum lobby and is part of the official Days of Remembrance ceremonies.

Frank Towers, Sr. and Frank Towers, Jr. with Ariela Rojek, September 2011.
Credit: Jason McKibben, Glens Falls Post-Star.

UNITED STATES HOLOCAUST MEMORIAL MUSEUM— 'HONORING LIBERATION' FILM, 2010

NARRATOR: They were men and women who came together from all across the United States, from Canada, and from as far away as Israel. For several, it was their first face-to-face meeting with each other in more than sixty years.

CARROL 'RED' WALSH, TANK COMMANDER, U.S. ARMY 743RD TANK BATTALION: How could a young guy like me be eighty-eight years old! I'm not sure how many more reunions I'm going to go to. I never thought I would see anybody on that train again. It's amazing! Just amazing.

NARRATOR: The occasion was to commemorate an event that occurred on April 13, 1945, as American armies rolled across Europe, liberating millions from the dominion of the Third Reich. On that day, the Army's 743rd Tank Division came upon a sight near Magdeburg, Germany, they never expected to see. Freight train cars alone on a track and filled wall to wall with over two thousand men, women, and children, all of them Jews.

CARROL 'RED' WALSH: I remembered seeing this long freight train, long string of boxcars, and I can remember pulling the tank to the right and driving along the side of the train and seeing all these people that were on these boxcars. It was totally unexpected and when I saw their condition I was overwhelmed, I can remember thinking, 'What are we going to do with all these people and for all these people?'

NARRATOR: This fateful wartime incident might have remained known only to those who were directly part of it, had it not been for a Web site created and managed by Matthew Rozell. A high school history teacher in Hudson Falls, New York, and a teacher fellow with the United States Holocaust Memorial Museum, Rozell conducted several interviews with men and women whose lives were directly caught up in the events of the Holocaust. It was during an interview with Carrol 'Red' Walsh, a tank commander with the 743rd, that the story of the train car outside Magdeburg came to light.

MATTHEW ROZELL, HISTORY TEACHER, HUDSON FALLS HIGH SCHOOL: ... And at the tail end of a two-hour discussion, a taped conversation I had with him in his daughter's living room, his daughter chimed in and said, 'Dad, did you tell Mr. Rozell about that train that stopped, that you had to go and investigate?' He said, 'Oh, that's right, that train.' And he launched into about how it was a beautiful April day. He and another tank commander went down and investigated this train stopped by the side of the tracks. They found it full of Jewish refugees. The other tank commander, he told me, was still alive in California, and actually had photographs that he took of the liberation. And this Dr. Gross allowed me to place the photographs on the Internet. We put those on our school Web site, and they sat there, not a lot of Web traffic. But all of a sudden, I got an e-mail from a grandmother in Australia who had been a six-year-old girl on that train. And she said that she clicked on the Web link, the photographs opened, and this was the day of her liberation in 1945. She said she fell out of her chair.

It was very organic the way it all unfolded. I would open up my e-mail inbox and there would be another message from a new survivor, somebody that I wasn't aware of before. These people are coming to me individually. They're not aware of each other for the most part before finding my Web site on the Internet, for example. So, it's just kind of unfolding.

RENE ROBERGE, MASTER OF CEREMONIES, HUDSON FALLS HIGH SCHOOL: [*Auditorium speech*] At this time, I would like to call to the stage the rest of our soldiers and survivors, beginning with Mr. Francis Currey. [*Applause*][84]

NARRATOR: The surviving veterans are modest about their accomplishments, but this did

---

[84] Francis Currey, MOH, was the vice president of the 30th Infantry Division Veterans of World War II at the time he came to the high school with the rest of the soldiers. At the time, he was the only surviving World War II Medal of Honor recipient in New York and New England, having received the nation's highest award for his actions as a nineteen-year-old during the Battle of the Bulge. Frank died at the age of 94 in October 2019.

not prevent the audience of students, teachers, town residents, and Holocaust survivors from honoring them at a special reunion event held at Hudson Falls High School in September 2009.

WILLIAM GAST, U.S. ARMY 743RD TANK BATTALION: [*Auditorium speech*] It's a gratifying and emotional experience to reunite with some of the survivors, to meet them face-to-face, and to call them my friends.

LESLIE MEISELS, SURVIVOR, TRAIN AT MAGDEBURG: [*Auditorium speech*] Those brave American soldiers, they were saying that they didn't do anything heroic, they just did their job. But with that job, they gave us back our life, and for that I thank you from the bottom of my heart. [*Applause*]

NARRATOR: [*Dancing and music*] It was a heady four days for the guests of honor and their families, a time to reminisce and reconnect, a time to enjoy each other's company, and reflect upon what brought them together.

BUSTER SIMMONS, COMBAT MEDIC, 30TH INFANTRY DIVISION: We were there. But it's still tough to wrap your mind around the situation that presented itself when those people were liberated on that train.

ELIZABETH SEAMAN, SURVIVOR, TRAIN AT MAGDEBURG: None of them put themselves up as being something special, and they have a great sense of humility, and also a great sense of love. I feel that love just emanating from them to me and the others, and I think the sense of love that they have I think is also what has kept them going and giving all their lives.

NARRATOR: Matt Rozell's spotlight as ABC News Person of the Week was a fitting conclusion to this special event. At the farewell banquet following the broadcast, Rene Roberge, the Hudson Falls High School teacher who served as the program's master of ceremonies, told liberators and survivors alike what he had learned from them.

RENE ROBERGE: The moral responsibility you had as a liberator to free a people from harm at a moment's notice, and, as a survivor, to save a generation from becoming complacent. [*Voice breaking*] You were heroes then; you are our heroes now.

MATTHEW ROZELL: I think we were in the right place at the right time, in the sense that we had people who are now at the stage in their life where they really wanted to send a message before they leave this earth. To see how it touched these students so deeply, that is where the real gratification is for me, and that's what this whole week was all about. You can't forget the past. You have to remember what happened. You can't just be a bystander.

FRANK TOWERS, PRESIDENT, 30TH INFANTRY DIVISION VETERANS OF WWII: You know, I bid those people goodbye and thought I'd never see them again. So now here we are, 65 years later, we're coming together, and it's a rewarding experience. [*Embraces survivor*][85]

*

We did another, final reunion at the high school in 2011. Just after it concluded, Steve Barry was seriously hurt in a car accident and passed away in January 2012. He had fulfilled a life's quest of meeting his liberators; his daughters honored me by packing up his library of Holocaust books and shipping them to me (many of which I referenced in constructing this book). His children and grandchildren honored his memory by creating a fellowship for scholars at the United States Holocaust Memorial Museum, and his inscription carved into the Donors' Wall simply reads:

---

[85] You can view this and the ABC World News video at the links in 'List of Reunions.'

STEPHEN B. BARRY
-FOR THE SAKE OF HUMANITY-

*Combat medic Walter Gantz, March 14, 2016.
Credit: Mike Edwards, 5 Stones Group.*

CHAPTER EIGHTEEN

The Medics

[After I got home] I cried a lot. My parents couldn't understand why I couldn't sleep at times.

— WALTER 'BABE' GANTZ, US ARMY MEDIC

The telephone in my classroom rang during a free period a few weeks following the last high school soldier-survivor reunion in 2011. The district had installed a direct line to the outside after fielding phone calls asking for me from all over the world, from survivors and others, but after four years of not hearing from any other American soldier who had something to do with this 'Train near

Magdeburg,' I had come to the conclusion that it was now all over.

'*Matt Rozell, God bless you!*, an elderly male voice piped jovially in my ear. Walter Gantz of Scranton, Pennsylvania, proved me wrong, and not only did he play an important role, he knew of several other former soldiers who were also still alive to share their experiences at the convalescent base/camp at Hillersleben.

Walter was part of the 95th Medical Gas Treatment Battalion, trained extensively to treat chemical warfare casualties. When no poison gas was deployed by the enemy in combat, Walter and his outfit stepped right into the role of treating other casualties of the battlefield. He recalled surveying the train at Farsleben, and the memories of treating the victims over the next seven weeks haunted him right up until his contact with me. I spoke with Walter several times on the phone, and we exchanged letters; I also put him in contact with at least four of the survivors of the train, two of whom would go on to meet him in Scranton to speak at a Holocaust symposium. At my suggestion, Walter was interviewed by a film crew in 2016.

Walter 'Babe' Gantz

Basically, there were four medical battalions—the 92nd, 93rd, 94th, and 95th. We were the 'baby battalion.' We were extensively trained in chemical warfare. In fact, that was our top priority, in case they used chemical agents and that was it. We were a sophisticated outfit. In fact, Colonel Bill Hurteau, our commander, he said we were the cream of the crop [*chuckles*]. Maybe he was right, I don't know.

Robert 'Bob' Schatz was one of Walter's fellow medics, and from Company C of the 95th.

Robert Schatz

We had tremendous equipment. We had our own showers, we had our own mechanics, we had our own telephones, and we had our own cooks. We were a completely mobile outfit. And we were always prepared, just in case the Germans used gas [on our troops]. But meanwhile, we operated as a medical battalion. We would always set up the tents, and then we would move out and go to the next place.

Walter 'Babe' Gantz

We were trained in the medical field also, and treating 'normal' casualties, both physical and mental. In fact, we treated hundreds of [cases of] what we called 'combat fatigue.' Today, it would be the post-traumatic stress disorder. That was quite a challenge, to take care of those people.

Robert Schatz

From the Battle of the Bulge, we had [casualties with] the trench foot, frozen toes, the battle exhaustion—it was terrible. The toes turned blue and a lot of [soldiers] had to have their toes cut off. We also had kids who were sick, who were crying, [soldiers] who we had to just calm down. We kept them for a couple days, and then we sent them back. We had a lot of nervous kids, a lot of kids from the 106th Division. They were really [just out of] basic training, they were going to college, and when [the Army] needed infantry replacements, they took all these kids out of the colleges, and I don't think they were properly trained.

Walter 'Babe' Gantz

I was a surgical technician. As the name implies, I worked on a surgical team, which was very interesting to say the least. The most difficult thing that I just couldn't accept was the amputations. That was very difficult, really.

Robert Schatz

I worked in the operating room most of the time. And we cut off some legs, some arms; we also had a lot of automobile accidents. You know, the roads were very slippery [in the winter]. You'd be surprised at how many automobile accidents we had.

The Advance Party at Farsleben

Walter 'Babe' Gantz

I was part of a so-called 'advance party.' There were about 10 or 12 of us from the 95th and, as you know, the train was discovered on the 13th of April of '45. Our advance party was at Farsleben on the 14th, or the next day—the situation was beyond description. These people were emaciated and like they say, 'living skeletons'; most of them could hardly walk. [*Shakes head*] It was a horrible sight. Some people say there were sixteen that passed away on the train. Other reports say thirty, so I would say thirty. They were buried down the knoll adjacent to the train.[86]

I must admit I shed a lot of tears and I prayed. I prayed that they would pass on, that they would find peace, and for those who survived, that their health would be restored—and dignity. Dignity is so important in life—dignity, that was the main thing. It was difficult. We spent just one night there and then we were ordered to go to

---

[86] *buried down the knoll adjacent to the train*-A friend touring the site in August 2016 noted, 'Near [the liberation site] was the local Farsleben cemetery and there are 36 Jews buried, four known and 32 unknown.' He added, '[At Hillersleben] There are 138 Jews buried in the park, all the names are on a fence marker, however, there were only 5 graves marked individually...and they do have a map where everyone is buried. The 5 grave markers were bought by their families, the rest of the graves have no individual marker although they all have their own spots in the park.' Ron Chaulet, email communication, 8-14-2016.

Hillersleben and to take over the hospital—there was actually a 100-bed hospital at the time there.

The 30th Division already had taken that area of Hillersleben, and it was chaotic. I mean, that's the only way to describe it. In the nearby area, there was a German air force base and also, they actually had an ordnance unit there! There were about 150 engineers and physicists, some of the top brains of Germany, and they were working on sophisticated weaponry, really. These barracks, they had deep underground bunkers. They had sleeping facilities or quarters, and food, and everything like that. [As far as] the barracks at Hillersleben go, when you talk about barracks, usually you talk about cots and beds all around. A lot of these barracks actually had apartments! We did our utmost to keep families together.

Frank Tower's group transported these people from Farsleben to Hillersleben, which is probably maybe four or five miles. Some of the survivors were in such a condition that they were set up into private homes in Farsleben, and then, later on when they transported the majority of people, a lot of them were put in private homes at Hillersleben.

It was difficult. It's hard to describe, I lived through it, but transporting these people was a difficult situation for the 30th Division. I have to tip my hat to the 105th Medical Battalion, which was a part of the 30th Division. I mean, they did a tremendous job trying to help these people. Of course, they had to move on because the war was still being fought!

We set up the hospitals, and it was tough on these people because they spent so much time at the Bergen-Belsen concentration camp and they were horrified at the thought that they were being treated by German personnel. I can understand that. This hospital was basically operated by Germans really, three or four doctors and 35 or 40 nurses, but a lot of them could speak English, so it would help a lot as far as we were concerned, and we did our best to comfort these people. A few days later, 'C' Company of the 95th, they came down to Hillersleben and there were about 127 enlisted men and about eleven or twelve doctors. Before we left, we were almost close to 500 beds between two hospitals [set up there].[87]

---

[87] Mr. Gantz wrote to the author on Nov. 3, 2011-'*On May 8, 1945, our unit began to re-staff our hospitals and clinic with German [POW] personnel. Twenty German medical officers headed by 2 Colonels, 86 German nurses,*

Robert Schatz

There were German doctors, yeah. In fact, one of us tackled one of them because we didn't like the way he talked. [One of our guys] tackled him and banged his head on the concrete, because he didn't like the way the German spoke to him, or something like that. I remember that. He just knocked him on the ground; he smashed his head on the ground, so we all cheered. And that was the only incident we had like that, but most of the time everybody listened and did what they had to do. We did supervision of the German nurses; we had to make sure they were doing the right things.

Grier Taylor was also a member of the 95th Medical Battalion, Company C, and did a range of jobs.

Grier Taylor

We were acting as a first aid station across the Siegfried Line going into Germany. We took [our

---

and 55 German enlisted men were brought to our camp from the prisoner-of-war compound controlled by our 95th Medical Bn. They were gradually filtered into the key spots until finally Co. C personnel acted in a supervisory capacity only. As you can surmise, Matt, after more than 65 years I myself could only present a very fragmented story. Thanks to the battalion's history, it was possible for me to provide for an otherwise lapsed memory.'

wounded] into the first aid station and sent some of them to field hospitals much further behind from where we were. Then, [in late April 1945] our next move was to a beautiful hospital [at Hillersleben] and we were told to set up. And when I say beautiful, it was the most [beautifully] equipped at that time. The yards were kept; Hitler didn't ever think that America or any other foreign country would have soldiers on this side of Germany. When we went into this hospital, we were told then what we would be doing is taking care of survivors from the train. Then, a few days after we got set up, well, probably the first day, we eliminated all these German soldiers that were there, except these two doctors, medical doctors.[88] They preferred to stay for a short time, which was about two weeks.

We were only there probably six weeks, eight weeks at the most. But we did an awful lot of cleaning up, so to speak, while we were there. Now, the first time I saw any Holocaust [patients], they came into our hospital in truck beds. Some of them were almost 'walking dead'; some of them were

---

[88] *eliminated all these German soldiers*-They were most certainly sent to the PW [prisoner of war] cages to the rear.

completely deceased, but there were others that seemed to have a little more strength.

Actually, when I went in there, I was a litter bearer; are you aware of what that is? Well, let me explain. The word 'litter' was an Army word, but it's kind of like a stretcher or whatever, you know, they transport the wounded on those things. Does that kind of ring a bell?

The American hospital at Hillersleben. Ervin Abadi. Completed at Hillersleben DP camp, May 1945. Soldier Monroe Williams collection.

I guess the most prominent job I had while we were in the hospital was bringing those starved-to-death people from the truck to the hospital, and getting them set up. We had many of them taken off of those trucks who were already deceased, and we kept them on the litter and carried them out to a tent that had been set up for the deceased people who were on the train. Now, while I was [at the hospital], I did some blood pressure taking, took temperatures and that [sort of thing]. I saw what was going on. Our job was to get these people cleaned up, and then to bed them down, and start seeing what they needed—which you knew right off, they were all suffering from malnutrition. Many of them had really lost their mind, their way of thinking, being so hungry. But our doctors went right in and did the thing that all good doctors are supposed to do—they started giving them the type of nutrition they could have. And in a few days, a lot of them, they were just different people! They could think [again]. Now, after they had suffered this malnutrition, they were so weak, they got to the point where they could talk. I didn't understand their language, and they didn't understand my language, but we had a way of sign language. I had this one man in particular, who I remember, and after he got over his weakness and could sit up in the bed, he and I talked for quite a while—by sign language! And he showed me a picture that he had in his pocket—it was ragged, [but this] picture showed him as a man of stature, about 6 feet tall, probably 250 pounds, and when he came into our hospital, he weighed 87 pounds. So that was really an accomplishment, to see him come around and be able to talk to people like that.

Walter 'Babe' Gantz

Interviewer: When you first saw the train, how did you feel?

When we left the 95th on detached service [to investigate the train, we went with] Captain Deutsch, who was one of the surgeons... He was numb. He didn't say anything, just that we were 'on a special assignment.' That was the extent of it, until we got to Farsleben and we went down to the train itself. That was a nightmare... God Almighty! [*Shakes head*] Boy... [*Pauses*]... Unbelievable. That's the only word I can think of, unbelievable... You know, you're seeing these people in person, and yet you just couldn't comprehend that these things happened in this world, that people would be so inhuman to other human beings. It was tough. You felt helpless, really.

[The initial scene] was chaotic. Most of the survivors were just wandering around, and you have to remember, these people, they were treated worse than animals. They were starved, and like I said, it was very chaotic. They were looting the homes and I can understand. They were getting fur coats and dresses. In fact, I remember there was one woman, I think she had three different dresses on. It was tough but ... A lot of them were lice-infested. God, I've seen so many lice, unbelievable. You could grab quite a handful, really. A lot of these people we had to clip their hair. There were so many unsanitary conditions. These people were in rags. In most cases, we had to burn their clothes. Fortunately, we had a means of setting up showers. There was a nearby pond and we had generators because we were a sophisticated unit, as I said. We would give these people showers or wash them down.

How do you settle all these people? We're talking like 2,400 people, and how do you feed them?

That was one of the biggest problems we had, but fortunately, we found several 'food dumps,' as we called them, and we were fortunate in getting a lot. Actually, we took over a dairy farm, and we were provided with beef, and pork, and milk for those who could sustain milk. You have to remember a lot of these people couldn't eat whole food, because if they did, if they were to gorge themselves, they would die. We had to feed them intravenously and that was one of my jobs. I have to say, I was a sharpshooter when it came to injections. It was difficult. We had so many.

Luca Furnari was a young New Yorker who served as the personal jeep driver for the company commander, Captain Hollander, a medical doctor.

Luca Furnari

We were only eleven miles away from the Elbe River, [so] it was a possibility that we would cross the river and go towards Berlin. We would not have been surprised if we got the order to 'close the umbrella' and follow the infantry forces right into Berlin. [Then] we were told that there was a train down by the Elbe River, and that we were going to jump in, and take care of the occupants. [The war] had taken on a whole new meaning; here was a trainload of Holocaust victims, right in our own 'backyard,' and they needed our help.

There were lots and lots of people; it was pandemonium, people looking to take care of themselves, for survival. It was overwhelming, it was difficult, and so we looked up to our commanding officers.

Walter 'Babe' Gantz

There were so many children! There must have been four or five hundred children. Infants! In fact, in doing research, there were several babies—one was like three months old. For some unknown reason, they would address us Americans as 'sir.' They were so polite—it was so embarrassing. Even the small kids, like, two, three, four years old! A lot of them were orphans. You have to remember they were orphans, really. We had some chocolate bars and things like that. The clothes were hanging on their bodies, really hanging on their bodies. They had smiles. I would imagine it was difficult for them to comprehend as to what was taking place, that they were free once again. A lot of orphans.

Grier Taylor

There were some very young children there. And some of them were really, really weak, but there was one little girl I remember; she was almost like a sun shining through a dark cloud. It was like I was in a dark mood; no one in the outfit could be smiling. Well, I know she was just so jolly and she was just a breath of fresh air in a dark moment. And that's all I can remember about her.

Luca Furnari

There were a couple young children that came to our building. They were looking in the window watching us eat, and we decided to help them. So we went back to the chow line after the crews were fed for those leftovers, which were brought back, and we helped feed them. There was this girl named 'Irene,' she was a victim naturally. I [had been] taking care of her for about a week and decided to notify my wife that maybe we can adopt her, and my wife wrote back right away, she said,

'Sure, do what you can,' you know? We took care of her for four weeks, every day we fed her with the extra food from the chow line. She enjoyed the food that we gave; to see her eat the food was a blessing because we knew that she needed it badly.

Her mother came to visit me, so we tried to find a way to get her into a position where [my wife and I] could adopt her, but we had to get her out of there. So we emptied out my duffel bag one morning [near the time to ship out]; one of my buddies took care of all my personal possessions, and we tried to put her in the bag, but she was too tall! Her head was sticking out, and her mother was there, pushing her head in. I tried and tried again, but it was not working.

I have no recollection about what would have happened to me if I did bring her on the ship; I wonder what would have happened to me if I succeeded. I'm very sorry that I didn't. [I was drawn to her because] she was an innocent young child, a victim of this horrible philosophy that was rampant in Germany, and as an American-born [citizen] I couldn't believe that they were scheduled for cremation, for genocide! I could not believe it; that disturbed me. I live with that memory every day.

May 1945. Caption on back reads: 'Hillersleben- Irene is in the flowered dress' Credit: Luca Furnari

Grier Taylor

There were one or two people that I can remember so well, who could have a meal, and then go out to the garbage can and start eating out of the garbage can. We had to assign guards at the garbage cans; we had to keep the two or three [survivors] from digging in to get food scraps! Now, my only reason for telling you that is, because of the lack of food and the high malnutrition, I guess it had affected their minds. They didn't realize they just had a meal, and then they try to go out and get more food.

Walter 'Babe' Gantz

Besides being malnourished, they had dysentery, diarrhea, so many different diseases, tuberculosis, typhus, typhoid, pneumonia, unbelievable. It was difficult. It's amazing how I lived through all that. In fact, we were fortunate. We had an epidemiologist by the name of Captain William Porter. I remember him so well. I got to be friends with him. He detected quite a number of typhus people, individuals. In fact, if my memory serves me, 294 cases of typhus. We had to quarantine these people, and the end result was 45 passed away and about 70% of these people were already [over the] age of 50, really. Typhus is a so-called louse-borne disease from lice and things like that, rodents. These people, they would get a high fever, as high as 105 degrees. That's really high.

I have to tell the story about Ariela. Ariela was only eleven years old and she came down with typhus. She told me she was in a semiconscious state of mind for about 10 days—these people could become delirious, and she told me that she attempted to jump out of the second-story window. Her aunt actually saved her life, but for those with typhus, that was difficult.

We had received different immunization shots. The uniform of the day would actually be a mask and gloves, and in many cases rubber aprons, and you'd ask yourself, why would you wear a rubber apron, but you have to remember, it became very messy.

Ariela Rojek

Those soldiers, they gave me my life, because I was very sick. He's one of the angels. I'm really grateful. Whenever I get a name and phone number [of a soldier from Matt Rozell], I always call them. They gave me a second life.

Interviewer: Is there any particular event or any particular thing that happened when you were at Hillersleben that really sticks in your mind?

Walter 'Babe' Gantz

We talk about nightmares and flashbacks. I never had any nightmares where I would scream, but there are two so-called flashbacks I remember and they stayed with me for many, many years. [In the first] I could see myself climbing these stairs, and all of a sudden, I'm inserting a needle into this elderly gentleman's arm. Of course, you have to remember, they were skin and bones. The veins would roll and he was screaming, really screaming. That had to be very painful, because they were skin and bones—to try to find a vein; it was easy to overshoot a vein. It was heart-wrenching to hear those people sobbing and actually screaming because a lot of them thought they were still at Bergen-Belsen, really.

May 1945. Caption on back reads: 'Hillersleben-some disorderly DPs getting a shower bath' Credit: Luca Furnari

[In the second] incident, I used to work a twelve-hour shift, from eight in the evening to eight in the morning. In the wee hours of the morning, this young girl died. For some reason, I wrapped her up in a blanket and I carried her down the stairs and I was crying.

We had a war tent that was used as a makeshift morgue. I placed her in there. I wonder why I would do that; I must have liked her for some reason. I didn't have to do that, because we had a team that took care of those who died, and placed them in the morgue.

I spent seven weeks with these people. Most of us spent seven weeks, and during our so-called watch, 106 people died… God, it was tough. [This girl] was actually fifteen years old. Her name was Eva, and you might say, 'How was it possible that he could carry her?' She probably weighed 60 pounds, maybe. I thought about that many times, and I must have been attracted to her for some reason. That haunted me, really. It really haunted me.

The 'casino' at Hillersleben. Ervin Abadi. Completed at Hillersleben DP camp, May 1945. Soldier Monroe Williams collection. Note Red Cross tents in foreground. May have served as temporary morgue station.

Grier Taylor

I do remember very vividly in my mind, when I get to thinking about it—the condition of those people and how they had been treated, for many,

many years—well, I just tried to get it out of my mind, but all of a sudden I would start talking and crying. I would [go back] those 67 years and it's still there, and I can still remember it.

Luca Furnari

I was able to help these little children, and I feel good about that. But we all had the same basic reaction—we couldn't believe that these people were destined [to be killed]. You know, what kind of a government would condone this? [Where was the] common sense? People condemn people—children, the parents, thousands of people! What the hell's going on here? It was crazy, we just couldn't fathom it, that there was no rationality. This is not normal, this is abnormal! [People say it] cannot happen here in this country; yes, it can happen here. I was twenty-one years old. I was there to see it happen.*

Walter 'Babe' Gantz

After 70 years, I still get emotional. I try to control my emotions, but it's impossible. I know I keep repeating the word, 'helpless.' It's a good way to describe this situation, really. Yet as medics we did everything humanly possible to help; I would say without a question we saved a lot of lives. We really did save a lot of lives. [But being called a 'hero'], that's another thing. That's very embarrassing. When you hear them saying 'heroes,' we medics weren't considered heroes, but I guess we were the unsung heroes. It's a long time ago, over 70 years [*pauses*]. It's a lifetime. Sadly, in time, your memories become dimmed. But you just can't [*shakes head, pauses*]—but there are certain events that will stay with a person all of their lifetime.

*

---

* Photo caption, 1945-*'Two of the children that lived in the D.P. center we were taking care of. Cute, eh, hon?'* Credit: Luca Furnari. The children appear to be playing with a DDT spray gun and abandoned German military garb, obviously after weeks of recovery.

Walter told a reporter what the experience of being contacted by those he tried to help so many years ago meant to him.

['The whole experience] has made me feel ten feet tall, and I have to use the word 'mind-boggling'—I guess you'd have to put it in the category of a dream... all they keep saying is, 'Thank you, thank you, thank you.'[89]

He wrote to me several times over the years. He closed one letter with the following:

Some of the boys couldn't take this type of duty and had to be sent back to our headquarters... My parents never knew of Hillersleben; the 95th held more than 40 reunions and barely a word was mentioned concerning Hillersleben.

Matt, I wish you well in all your endeavors. God's blessings to you and yours.

*As ever,
Walter (Babe) Gantz*

---

[89] *all they keep saying is, 'Thank you, thank you, thank you.'* - The author was familiar with the survivor Ariela Rojek and knew she would like to contact Walter. She called him, and later both gave their accounts to Walter's hometown newspaper. McAuliffe, Josh. 'Bergen–Belsen concentration camp survivors make contact with WWII medic Walter Gantz.' *The Scranton Times-Tribune*, March 4, 2012.

Member, 95th Medical Bn.

CHAPTER NINETEEN

The Orphan

Hello, Matthew,

My name is Lily Cohen and I was a little girl who was on that train coming from Bergen-Belsen. I was an orphan, probably about five or six years old at that time. I don't know my birthday, or year I was born. For so many years I didn't talk about my childhood even with my children; deep, deep, down I had the feeling that something was probably very wrong with me, something I should be ashamed of.

I am so moved to find this research, as most of my early life appeared to be 'erased' somehow by the Holocaust, and only now am I able to take small steps into what was my past to piece together fragments of memories. I remember the train. I remember the hill, I remember a German soldier running away, and I remember a woman who was trying to take care of me, dying at my side.

Tonight, I made dinner for 10 people in my home in Tel Aviv – six of whom came from me! My life has turned into a really wonderful victory over Hitler's attempt to obliterate the Jewish people.

You are really doing a holy work and I do hope to meet you some day. Amazing how things can come together when there are people dedicated to finding out 'the rest of the story.' Thank you for your dedication.

Still youthful and vivacious, Lily Cohen defies any mental stereotype of 'Holocaust survivor' with her presence, grace, and humor. Lily and I did meet, on several occasions; she came over to the United States to have dinner with my wife and me. Later, I arranged an interview for her at the United States Holocaust Memorial Museum, and they had done their homework, having researched her actual date of birth. I visited Lily in Israel in 2011, and again in 2016.

Like many of the survivors I know who were liberated on the train, Lily speaks to students. We had lunch, and she told me of her latest encounter with at-risk teens at a teen center in Jaffa outside of Tel Aviv. Before her presentation, they had self-segregated by group—Israeli-Ethiopian teens, Israeli-Russian teens, Jewish and Arab teens. And here she was, a survivor of the Holocaust, and a survivor of the War for Independence as a preteen in 1948-49, when the kibbutz that adopted her came under attack.[90]

She measured the kids up quickly, and spoke directly to their own experiences with alienation from larger society:

Maybe you are feeling like an outsider in a world that seems hostile, but you do not have to be a victim. I did not look like the rest of the children—I was blonde and blue-eyed. I did not want to play piano as a youngster; I wanted to dance. I did not know my parents; I did not know my past. But I made my way,

---

[90] *Kibbutz*-Hebrew; a collective community in Israel, traditionally a farm.

became a professional dancer, and built a strong family. Maybe you can make your way, too.

Matthew Rozell and Lily Cohen, Lake George, NY, 2010.

A forty-five-minute talk turned into over two hours from the heart of Lily Cohen, World War II orphan, Holocaust survivor, stage dancer and choreographer, therapist, and Tai Chi master. From out of the ashes, new life begins; the kids hung on her every word as they accompanied Lily out to her car in the parking lot. Maybe here by the sea in the ancient port of Jaffa, a cool night breeze also blew in a new outlook on life.

CHAPTER TWENTY

Denial

As the years go by, more and more see the famous Major Benjamin photo, featured on the cover of this book. Most people are astounded and emotionally affected. But some respond a different way. For me, it comes with the territory.

> *You're an emotional and propaganda-susceptible gullible fool.*
> *You're 'teaching history' and not going into the fraudulently alleged homicidal gas chambers? Or do you subconsciously already know it's bullshit?*
> *There were NO fake shower rooms disguised as gas chambers.*
> *That's a racist anti-German blood libel. Shame on you. The Bath and Disinfection 1 facility was just that!*

*

There were no 'gas chambers' other than delousing facilities to keep the prisoners healthy. Allied bombing caused disease and starvation because the camps could no longer be supplied by Germany.

*

The '6 million' number is a HUGE exaggeration. Jews use the Holocaust to garner sympathy and provide cover for their war crimes against the Palestinians. We studied this in college.

*

It comes with the territory, I suppose, that if you are passionate about teaching the Holocaust and attract high-profile attention, the trolls will begin their attempts to worm their way into the narrative. It began immediately after the very first reunion in 2007. I had received hundreds of emails from all over the world in support of my project, but I also got my first taste of this aberrant phenomenon known as Holocaust denial. Three emails, out of over three hundred, spewed forth their hate, with one containing in the subject line:

'SIX MILLION LIVES=SIX MILLION LIES'

My knee-jerk reaction was to delete them. But in the years that followed, as my blog built a following, more detailed attacks began; I began to archive them to create lessons for my students on Holocaust denial. One man, or woman—a hallmark of online Holocaust deniers is to hide behind false identities—even built a fictitious 'news' website attacking the first reunion, at a URL beginning with 'blockyourid.com':

> **Tank Commander Saves Fellow Jews From Gas Chambers'**
>
> *Who Actually Believes This Garbage?*
> *Izzie Gross, a tank commander, whose Sherman tank faced down a 'Death Train,' shows up at a local high school with three survivors. Oddly the dates are off, the camps were liberated four months earlier, but who are we to doubt?*
> *Maybe the Nazis were going to break through the Russia[sic] lines, crash in Auschwitz, and gas these poor survivors?*

The denier posted false photographs of the liberators and me, claiming that we were all Jewish co-conspirators, when the opposite was true. My students were horrified, though they got a kick out of the photograph of me, which obviously was <u>not</u> me. The website was so bad that it did have a comical element; even commenters in a notorious white supremacist chatroom wondered if the author 'Judicial Inc.' was losing his touch.

There were others who followed, like someone with the handle 'LittleGreyRabbit,' who took me to task for this and that at my blog. My policy is not to debate them directly, as there is no reasoning with these individuals, to be sure—rather, I have attempted to deal with their commentary by encouraging students to critically think and be aware. I no longer delete the lies, and depending on the nature of the ill-reasoned commentary, it is relatively easy to counterpoint the nonsense. A case in point that I wrote at my blog is below.

> *Hello, I came here after reading Dan Porat's* The Boy, *where some of the Hillersleben photos feature.*
>
> Hi, yes, I was consulted by the author, and helped him get some of the photos of the

liberation, which took place at Farsleben, not Hillersleben.

Maybe I am missing something here, but the people on this train don't look like walking skeletons to me. German civilian rations were 1600 calories 1944/1945, so the fact that the photos you present show individuals that look slim but hardly starved seems to undermine your central thesis – namely History Matters. Clearly, you don't think so or you would use your material more carefully.

Clearly, it was not I, but soldier eyewitnesses who referred to the prisoners as 'walking skeletons.' Also, these 'slim' individuals were so weak that many could hardly stand—again, more liberator testimony. Maybe the soldiers are lying, something that has been suggested by skeptics before. Several 'slim people' are lying dead on the hillside in the background—and the skeptic has missed the point, that the ones physically able to pose for a photograph have done so. Many more could not even get out of the cars without assistance—many were dead inside the cars, literally falling out on top of horrified soldiers as they slid open the doors—

something the skeptic would have learned had he been more thorough in his research of my work. Perhaps he would suggest that the boys in the photo below, in the book, taken by US forces the day after liberation, are the picture of health. And thanks for bringing in the plight of the unfortunate German civilians. Perhaps we should compare suffering here as well.

A woman and two children rest next to the train, April 14, 1945.
Credit: Harry E. Boll, US Army. USHMM.

Secondly, don't you think you are being rather disrespectful of the sacrifice shown by the American GI by continually reducing their experience down to the liberation of some detainees on a train. It verges on insulting to continually insist that people who repeatedly saw their buddies being blown away would privilege the experience of 2500 Jewish people on a train who don't look starved at all.

I think it is a little ironic that the skeptic ignores the many posts I have on the sacrifices of soldiers—and not the train liberation at all—a common thread throughout my work. And it is also stated there on my 'Welcome' page, that 'if you are a Holocaust denier/minimizer/revisionist, and/or run-of-the-mill hate-spewer, thank you in advance for sparing me your epistles… I've already heard it all.' Sadly, I'll also be adding the word 'skeptic' to my list. It can really get tiring, but thanks for writing to remind me that I have a better job to do.

*

Holocaust denial began with the perpetrators, their euphemisms, their secret orders, and their penchant for destroying and trying to hide evidence of their crimes. Even with the film footage of the liberators, or Eisenhower's admonition to future generations, and the importance of the evidence and testimony presented at the postwar trials, Holocaust denial increases as time passes. And let's not forget state sponsorship of Holocaust denial in certain quarters of the world.

I remember well one student's incredulous question, after witnessing survivor testimony, directed at the survivor who had just described his experience. The survivor replied, 'You see, it is easy for people to deny the Holocaust, because no one can truly grasp its magnitude and scope.' 'Unbelievable' is a word used by liberator and survivor alike. And it will take effort to not allow the memory of the original eyewitnesses to vanish in the rearview mirror of history.

CHAPTER TWENTY-ONE

The Mystery

'I often wonder what this world would be like, if those six million had never perished.'
— Frank Towers, 30th Infantry Division, Liberator

I watched the Perseid meteor showers last night. I could not sleep; I ventured outdoors on the hill, and looked up into the dark starry sky. The Earth we all share ventured again through the trail of cosmic debris left by the wake of an ancient comet, one that circles the sun every 133 years. Each trail of light I saw was the fantastic finale to a flyby that occurred millennia ago, each flash across the sky a culmination of a journey of a billion miles or more. Like the pieces of the cosmos, special people sometimes enter our lives in unforeseen and unexpected ways; they flash across our paths, and leave their marks seared upon our souls.

I never got to say goodbye to George Gross. It was George Gross who took the majority of the train liberation photos as a young man and composed the beautiful prose as an old one, which I then placed on our website and which then became the vehicle for leading the survivors to us. I chose the title for this book in a tribute to him, as that is what he titled his recollections. And it was he who cultivated a deep friendship with me via his wonderful email communications and telephone conversations. How amazed and happy he seemed to be to hear from all the survivors.

I was trying to figure out the logistics of a visit to California when I learned of his death on February 1, 2009. He had been ailing for a long time, and he died at home with his family around him. Though I never met him, he came into my life at a dark time dealing with the loss of my own parents; in many ways he was like a father figure and mentor to me. And perhaps not coincidentally, the survivors and I entered his life around the time that he was grieving for his wife, Marlo.

*George Gross and Micha Tomkiewicz, spring 2008.
Credit: Louise Hainline.*

Judge Walsh did not attend that last reunion in 2011 at our high school, either. He had not been feeling well, and just did not feel up to it, though before he headed back to Florida for the winter months, he went out to dinner with me, my family, his family, and two survivors and their families who were passing through town.

We had a small room to ourselves, and with many children—and profoundly, the corporeal fruition of the soldiers' actions those spring days of 1945—it was slightly noisy and very busy. I was seated across from Paul Arato, a child survivor from Hungary now living in Toronto who had contacted me, stunned, at the urging of his son a year after the very first reunion. The following spring, he met his liberators in Charleston, South Carolina, and briefly lost his composure telling his story for the first time, a young boy in the Bergen-Belsen camp with his younger brother and mother. As he told our students in the 2009 gathering a year later, *'I grew up and spent all my years being angry. This means I don't have to be angry anymore.'* After this reunion, he began developing a close relationship with Judge Walsh.

'Give me a hug, you saved my life!' Paul Arato and Carrol Walsh, September 22, 2009. Credit: Twilight Studios.

So here we were again, and I did not say much. I just wanted to watch and listen. Though Carrol was not feeling up to par, he roared with laughter as Paul told of getting on a plane to the United States at the tender age of 15, following his family's immigration to Canada—Paul felt he was destined to design cars in Detroit, you see—and being picked up by Detroit law enforcement at the airport and driven to the bridge to Canada and bid farewell by the seat of his teenage pants, as he had neglected the proper papers to immigrate. Carrol laughed so hard that his hands crashed down on the table.

Later, outside of the restaurant, he stopped and rested his hand on my forearm, and quietly thanked me for bringing these wonderful families into his life. I sensed there was something else there, something that I will never be able to share, or that our families will never be quite able to touch—the special bond between the liberating soldier and Holocaust survivor, the unspoken love and joy at having been reconnected after so many years.

Steve Barry knew this, too. At our 2009 school reunion, Frank Towers and Steve were sitting at a home economics table, doing a joint interview for a Florida TV station. During the course of their conversation in front of the camera, I noticed as Steve's hand unpretentiously crept over and rested atop Frank's hand while he was talking.

Is This a Beautiful Person?

In a 2009 radio interview, Carrol and Steve recounted the very first time that they were able to meet, face-to-face, in November 2007, and the close relationship they developed afterwards.

STEVE BARRY: We called [Carrol and Dorothy Walsh] on the cell phone. We called his home on a cell phone and said, 'We are almost around the corner from you,' so when we drove up, the five of us [the Barry family] drove up to the door, and Carrol was already outside.

INTERVIEWER: Was it an emotional moment for you?

Carrol Walsh and Steve Barry at Walsh's home, November 2007.
Credit: Barry family.

STEVE BARRY: Unbelievable; it still is. It just never went away! And I walked over to him and we just embraced each other, right in front of his house. I have all the pictures of that moment and then we went inside and we met his wife, Dorothy. She is a very lovely person. But for some strange coincidence, or maybe it was not, we connected immediately. It is like we became true friends in the matter of a half hour! And stayed that way! I call him on the phone, I exchange emails with him...

CARROL WALSH: I think in my mind it is such an amazing thing that our lives were joined in that moment on April 13, 1945; all the years that have gone by since. We have had lives, families, jobs, whatever. And here we are again, and now we meet face-to-face and recall together that moment when my tank reached the train.

STEVE BARRY: You know, I kept calling him my liberator. He says, 'I am really not your liberator. It was my job. I just happened to be there!' I said, 'I don't care what you tell me; you are my liberator!' [*Laughs*]

INTERVIEWER: I actually have here in my studio, Steve, a copy of a letter he wrote to you, and if you do not mind, I'll just read a couple of sentences. This is Carrol, writing to you, and he says, 'You are always expressing gratitude to me, the 743rd Tank Battalion, and the 30th Infantry Division. But I do not believe gratitude is deserved, because we were doing what we, and the whole world, should have been doing—rescuing and protecting innocent people from being killed and murdered by vicious criminals. *You do not owe us. We owe you. We can never repay you and the Jewish people of Europe for what was stolen from you—your homes, your possessions, your businesses, your money, your art, your family life, your families, your childhood, your dreams, and all your lives.'*

STEVE BARRY: Is this a beautiful person?

You know, when I got the letter, Carrol likes to write longhand. He is not a believer in typing. He likes to write longhand, and when I got the letter, I said, you know, I just cannot possibly keep this letter to myself. I asked him if I have his permission to give this letter to some other people to read it, and he said it was okay.[91]

CARROL WALSH: That is right! I cannot believe today, as I look back on those years and on what was happening; I cannot believe that the world almost ignored those people and what was happening! I cannot believe it! How could we have all stood by and have let that happen? We owe those people a great deal. We owe those people everything. They do not owe us anything. We owe them for what we allowed to happen to them. That is how I feel.[66]

*

My wife and I spent some time with Carrol on a summer afternoon in 2011 at his daughter's house in Hudson Falls, where it had all started so many years before. He and his wife Dorothy, his daughter Elizabeth, and her children were having lunch

---

[91] *give this letter to some other people-* the author shared the contents of this letter, with permission, at a meeting with top officers at the United States Holocaust Memorial Museum in the summer of 2009. The director was present and requested it for deposit in the Museum's repository, which the author facilitated.

with Agnes 'Agi' Fleischer Baker and her husband Ron, who were passing through Hudson Falls. Agi also became very close to Carrol and the family, and their little dog delighted Carrol's great-grandson.

After we bid them farewell, I sat with Carrol in his study in the house, discussing books of common interest in his library, listening to his tales of playing championship baseball as a high schooler, and watching him swoon with eyes closed and a smile, snapping his fingers to the swing of Benny Goodman's clarinet—*'Oh man, that's some good stuff!* He got up out of his seat to show me something, and fell short of breath, and gave a flash of frustration and anger that his body was slowing down. After quickly recovering, he and I also went through his 743rd Tank Battalion album at the kitchen table, where he pointed out his old friends and told more stories from a time in his life that he would not take a million dollars to repeat, but also one that he would not take a million dollars to never have experienced—perhaps even more so now.

On December 15, 2012, I called Carrol in Florida where he and Dorothy were now living full time. I did not want to admit it to myself, but my old friend was dying. We both knew it was our last conversation, but he was making jokes to the end. I fumbled a bit and told him that the weather had been extremely cold up here in the North—ever mindful that since the Battle of the Bulge, freezing in subzero temperatures in his tank, he had hated the cold. With fatigue in his voice, he chuckled and said, 'I hope that it is cold in the place where I am going!' He laughed, and his great-grandson made some noise in the background; I think I tried to laugh. Two days later, after bidding Dorothy and the rest of his family goodbye, he slipped away peacefully.

His memorial service was held on July 5, 2013. I could not attend, because as 'fate' would have it, I was at Bergen-Belsen on a study tour of authentic Holocaust sites. Paul Arato succumbed to a long illness a week later while I was still in Germany; near the day he passed, I saw his wife Rona's book about Paul's Holocaust experiences, and meeting his liberators, in the bookstore at the Sachsenhausen Camp Memorial site.[67]

*

In the years following Carrol's passing, Frank Towers continued to carry on with searching for more of the estimated 425 children who had been on that train. He would Skype frequently with friends in Israel and elsewhere, and work at his computer updating his databases of 'found' survivors, clacking away at his research with emails and updates, admonishing folks much younger than himself to 'get with the times' and get online. In hotels across the South, he would point to his crowing rooster wristwatch and herd survivors and old soldiers alike, their children and grandchildren, into the conference room as he stepped to the lectern to 'MC' the sometimes hours-long testimony sessions. In his words to me, *'No one in our organization has ever made any attempt in the past to look into a project such as yours, so we were not aware of the opportunities to bring about meetings with these survivors. It is time that they were recognized for the suffering that they endured for those years, and for them, like it is for us, time is running out!!'* Here was a man who felt his humanitarian obligation in 1945, and now felt a new urgency in getting out the word—'*At 90, I can only keep chugging along!!*', he wrote when we began in 2007.

Frank was also outraged that anyone would deny the Holocaust and became a passionate Holocaust educator, speaking to groups large and small. Just after a speech in Florida at a Memorial Day commemoration in 2016, Frank collapsed due to heart problems. The liberator who had presided over no less than eight major soldier-survivor reunions and a host of smaller one-day luncheon gatherings was now fighting for his life. Well wishes came in from all over the world. He had his 99th birthday on June 13 and seemed to rally; I left on a previously planned intensive Holocaust study program at Yad Vashem's International School for Holocaust Studies at the end of June.

*

July 5, 2016/Jerusalem

I'm in the City of God now, Jerusalem. It's the anniversary to the day of my visit to Bergen-

Belsen three years ago, when Carrol was being memorialized back in his hometown of Johnstown, New York.

I am studying at Yad Vashem, Israel's Holocaust Martyrs' and Heroes' Remembrance Authority, for much of the month with 29 other educators from all over the world. And although we just got started, one of the early takeaways is, think about what the world lost.

We talk about the story of human beings, of the 'choiceless choices' in the ghettos and the camps. About the will to live, about what it means to have nothing, from the perspective of the survivors. We discuss the 'survivors' guilt,' but also the victory over Hitler and Nazi ideology, as seen in the second and third generations of Holocaust survivors alive and flourishing today.

I am learning so much, and I am eager to learn more. But today I learned that Frank Towers, Sr., age 99, passed away peacefully with his family by his side in Florida yesterday, on July 4, 2016. Independence Day.

*

Today in class I was given the opportunity to speak in an open forum, ostensibly to comment on my thoughts about our collective, moving experience in being guided through the museum.

So I began. I told the group that I had been to Yad Vashem before, and that it was because of something very special in my life. In 2011, Frank and I met over 500 people who were alive because of the liberators' intervention and efforts at the 'Train Near Magdeburg' on April 13, 1945. Over 55 survivors were present, and later, Frank, Varda (the organizer and a train survivor's daughter), and I, along with three survivors of the train, had a personal tour of the museum and its complex atop the sacred mountain at Yad Vashem.[92]

---

[92] *In 2011, Frank and I met over 500 people who were alive*-Varda Weisskopf orchestrated this reunion in May 2011 at the Weizmann Institute in Rehovot, Israel. It was financed by the families of the survivors in attendance for Frank and his son. The author was able to attend because of the generosity of survivor friends, the 30th Infantry Division of WWII Association, and his own community.

Varda Weisskopf, Frank Towers, and author at Yad Vashem, May 2011. Credit: Ned Rozell

And as I closed my remarks with my new teacher friends, after a very long and emotionally charged day, I told them that a chapter in my life seems to have come to a close with the death of Frank W. Towers only 24 hours before.

July 8, 2016/Jerusalem

It's Friday, and I'm invited to the Great Synagogue here in Jerusalem as a guest for Shabbat services.[93] I have a guidebook with English, but I just

---

[93] *Shabbat*-the Jewish Sabbath, Saturday, commencing sundown Friday evening through sundown on Saturday.

follow the service in Hebrew, even though I don't understand any of it. Somehow this symbolizes my state of being right now. Almost half a world away, Frank is being bid goodbye by his family and friends, as the cantor begins to wail here. My eyes well up, and a single tear begins its run. I am powerless to push it away.

*

It has been an extraordinary day. It began with a tour of the Old City on foot with a very knowledgeable guide who is also an archeologist here in Israel. We walked near the ruins of the Second Temple destroyed by the Romans in 70 AD, and saw the remnants of the mikvah, the ritual purification baths a pilgrim would use before he could go near the Temple. We walked up the steps hewn into solid bedrock where a young rabbi named Jesus strode. At the Western Wall, I took it all in, and approached the site which for Jews is closest to the Holiest of the Holies. This has great significance; God dwells here. For the souls of Frank, and Carrol, and George, my friends, the liberators, and for my survivor friends who have passed, I placed a scrap of paper with my prayer for their souls into a crevice in the millennia-old stones. I did the same for my blessed mother and father, for though the loss is now tempered, it has never completely dissipated.

I moved on to the Church of the Holy Sepulcher, the church built over Christ's Crucifixion and Tomb. Incense blasted me as I moved into the doors. Jesus entered into Jerusalem the day after Shabbat, Palm Sunday, in a very tense political situation. We know how that turned out, and I am at the very place where a Jewish sect shortly after his execution would grow to become one of the world's largest religions—I'm free to walk about and drink it all in. And at this place I left the same petition, maybe hopeful that the questions that have perhaps distanced me from my own religious upbringing might be somehow answered.

Why are the guiltless and the good afflicted with suffering? Why are the innocent murdered, while perpetrators live out long lives? What about the role of my own church in the age-old persecution of the Jewish people? Where was God in Bergen-Belsen? Is it right to ask these questions?

*

At the Great Synagogue at sunset, I try to enter into a sanctified presence again in a more focused way, but I am finding it difficult. These thoughts come rushing forth, the same thoughts and questions I have entertained for years. But there is also another thought right now, and here it hits me like a steamroller: *The last liberator at the train has passed*, and here in the synagogue I am confronted with the enigma of the role I played in bringing the survivors and their descendants—certainly in the thousands of them now—together in person or in spirit with these old men in the sunset of their lives. But my centrality as the connector in this story does not become clearer to me in this attempt at deep communion with the Almighty; it remains hidden behind a fog that I cannot push away.

I recall again the experience of coming to the Holy Land for the first time, where Frank had met with over 500 people who would not have been alive today had it not been for the swift arrival of the soldiers of the 743rd Tank Battalion and 30th Infantry Division of the US Army. People are able to reach out and touch one of the actual soldiers who personally saved their families from annihilation; a woman was sobbing right behind me through much of the ceremony. Another woman, a granddaughter of one of those survivors whose name I cannot recall, stopped me. She thanked me and told me that my name meant something along the lines of 'mystery of God.' This struck me hard then, and it remains something that now roars forth in my turbulent state of mind.

The sun has set. The service is over.

*

Back at the hotel at the Friday evening Shabbat meal with the educators, we continue our meditation to enter into communal spirit to usher in an atmosphere of holiness and peace. We break bread, have the meal and conversation together, but I'm very quiet at the end of this long day. The mystery remains.

The hotel this evening in Jerusalem is jam-packed with Jewish families settling in for Shabbat—noisy, crowded, and together to bring in the Sabbath. Underlying the ebb and flow of activity all around is the disquieting undercurrent inside me about the fact that this day has arrived, the day that the last train liberator, the last soldier reunion organizer, is being buried. Tonight I am engulfed in a profound heavyheartedness, this loss, this questioning, and this wondering.

What does it all mean? What am I doing here, six thousand miles away from my home, my own family?

The giant dining room next door breaks out in rhythmic hand clapping and voices singing a song of happiness, symbolizing the togetherness and communal unity that closes out the Shabbat meal. I glance at the time; at this very moment back home, my old friend, the one who would lead me to the head table of every soldiers-survivors reunion banquet he hosted, is being lowered into the earth.

*

Later, I awake with a start in a bed that is not my own. A newborn is wailing somewhere nearby. The hotel here in Jerusalem is filled with these young Jewish families, full of young children. But though I have been jolted awake, nothing close to annoyance enters my being. Lying in the dark, I feel a warmth deep within my soul that is cutting through the sadness; in the crying of the baby and the laughter of the children outside of my door, I hear the song of the angels carrying Frank, and all the liberators I was privileged to know, onward and upward. And maybe I've finally solved that mystery…

These children are their legacy, and in this moment I know that while I will perhaps never understand God's will or why I was chosen to bring the soldiers together with the thousands of people alive on the earth today because of their deeds, the real epiphany is that it does not matter—

He wanted me here in Jerusalem for this moment, when the last liberator left me.

Train survivors and their families greet Frank Towers, Rehovot, Israel, May 2011. Source: Author.

CHAPTER TWENTY-TWO

'What do you want The world to be?'

I reached some of my final revelations in the summer of 2016 as the writing of this book drew to a close while I was studying in Jerusalem at Yad Vashem, Israel's Holocaust Martyrs' and Heroes'

Remembrance Authority. My fellow educators and I heard from dozens of excellent scholars and presenters in the field of the history of Judaism, Christianity, and Islam, of antisemitism through the ages, and learned from the nuanced dissections what we *thought* we knew about the Holocaust. One of our final lectures was from Dr. Yehuda Bauer, who at age 90 I consider to be the godfather of Holocaust historians. Sitting six feet away from me was a man who narrowly escaped the Holocaust himself, coming with his family in 1939 to the Palestine Mandate before the window closed. He became active in the resistance to British rule, and later fought in Israel's War for Independence. Early in his career he was challenged by Abba Kovner to study the Holocaust when few others were doing it. He mastered many languages, and it was he, after years of research, who concluded that the Holocaust was a watershed event in human history.

Today, sitting in his presence, and listening to him, I got the feeling that I was listening to a philosopher, one who also had been milking cows on a kibbutz for the past 41 years.

So the question came, as it always does—

What is the overarching lesson that we should take away from the study of the Holocaust?

To paraphrase his answer, he simply said, 'There is no lesson, except not to repeat it. The Shoah is used, all the time, for various agendas and causes…okay, fine. *But there is no lesson.*'

And I think I get it. When we talk about the Holocaust, its sheer magnitude and 'unprecedentedness' denies us the comfort of walking away with an overarching 'lesson.' 'Bullying gone wild' it was not. Instead, he continued, 'Maybe the real question to ask yourself, and ask your students, is this— *What do you want the world to be?* And then, maybe it is time to introduce them to the study of the Holocaust, because maybe the Shoah is the exact opposite of what they envision for their world, unprecedented in scope and sequence—but it happened, which means it can happen again.'

*

When we got back to the hotel to pack our bags and have a final evening to ourselves, we found out that for a few hours, we could not even cross the street to go back out—our hotel was now right on the route of one of the largest 'gay pride' parades in the world, right through Jerusalem. Security was tight; last year, a religious maniac stabbed six, and one teenage girl died here. But standing on the second-story hotel balcony, I could hear Dr. Bauer's words echoing in my ears, reminding us that democracy is not only very fragile, it is hardly even out of the cradle in the backdrop of world history. But what sets democracy apart from every other experiment in history, in its pure form and in theory, is its defense of minorities. It doesn't exist yet, but maybe this form of government needs to be protected, and nourished. And maybe this is what the soldiers were fighting for. The world does not have to be united, and, in fact, it never has been and never will be. We argue and we disagree all of the time. That is as it is, and as it should be. At the end of the day, we either kill each other, or we live, and let live.

We decide.

I had never seen a so-called 'gay pride' event before, so as I watched, there was another revelation.

For over an hour, my fellow educators and I witnessed miles and miles of this parade of young and old, of men and women, smiling and cheering and singing; I'm quite sure that many participants, and maybe even most, were, in fact, heterosexual. And for me, this experience became a metaphor for our common experience here in Jerusalem—from that hotel balcony, we were witnessing what simply was a massive celebration of life. In studying the Holocaust together, we have plumbed the depths of the abyss that humanity is capable of, but not because of a fascination with evil and death; rather, it is because of the opposite, because of our commitment to humanity. For me also there is this burgeoning sense of righteousness in promoting the men who made a difference with their sacrifices in slaying the Nazi beast. And these American soldiers who encountered the Holocaust were not some kind of super-action heroes who arrived on the scene to save the day, just in the nick of time. As you have read, there was no plan, and they had no idea. What matters more is what they did when they encountered this trauma deep in a war zone with people still shooting at them, and later committing themselves in their sunset years to reaching out to others, so that, in Dr. Bauer's words, the formally 'unprecedented' watershed event is not repeated. And maybe it's time for a good long look at the world we live in today.

I have been on a journey that has consumed half the career that I never even set out to have. I have been joined by many along the way, and I thank the reader for also sharing it with me; that afternoon in Jerusalem, I parted with my educator friends with a final word in our closing discussion:

We are the new witnesses. We bear an awesome responsibility when we become aware, when we teach, when we communicate with others; now, more than ever, what we do matters, especially in entering this world of the Holocaust—because there is no past, and it is never over.

We are shaping human beings. We are cultivating humanity. There are always the children, the young; there is hope amidst all the darkness in the world. The tunnel can lead to the light.

You decide.

M10 tank destroyers attached to the 30th Infantry Division move through the ruins of the city of Magdeburg after the final battle, April 1945. Credit: US Army.

Epilogue

A Letter To The Tankers

Kloster Kreuzberg, Germany
10 July 1945
Tankers of the 743:

You have accomplished your mission in Europe. You have accomplished it only as great soldiers could. Never, from the day you hit the Normandy Invasion Beach until this day, have I had any doubts as to your courage or your willingness to sacrifice your lives for those of your comrades.

'We Keep The Faith.' Yes, you have kept the faith of those who died in

Flanders Field in '17 and '18, of those who died in the water and on the sands of Omaha Beach, of those who died beside the hedgerows of Normandy, of those who fell in the orchards and farmlands of France, Belgium, and Holland, of those who threw their soft bodies against the steel and cement obstacles of the Siegfried Line, of those who pushed to the Roer, froze in the bitter winter campaign of the Ardennes, and of those whose bodies were strewn from the Roer River to the Rhine and from the Rhine to the Elbe River.

You have kept the faith your loved ones had in you, your country had in you, Colonel Upham had in you, and I had in you.

Never has a man had the opportunity of working with and associating with a finer group of officers and men than you of the 743rd. You have met and defeated the best the Germans had. Now, many of you will meet and defeat the best the Japanese have.

My prayers go with you.

WILLIAM D. DUNCAN
Lieutenant Colonel, Infantry
743rd Tank Battalion,
Commanding.

*

A schoolkid once asked a survivor I know if anything good came out of the Holocaust. The survivor thought a minute, because it was an important question, and replied, *'Yes. My rescuers.'*

And here is where the story of the 'Train Near Magdeburg' will end, for now. When we talk about the Holocaust, the sheer magnitude of it, there is no happy ending. For every single one of the approximately two-thousand five-hundred persons on the train who was set free, another two-thousand five-hundred persons perished in the Holocaust, most long before the Americans set foot upon the continent. And yet, at the end of the day, if we can say that somehow the soldiers and survivors in this book taught us something, perhaps the meaning is echoed in that three-word response.

I have found that in some educational circles the role of the American liberator is presented almost as an afterthought, and I would have to agree that when one is drawn into the unfathomable study of the Holocaust, liberation perhaps figures as a literal nano-episode. They were not rescuers, in the formal sense of the word—that title is reserved for those without weapons, who risked their lives and usually the lives of their families by hiding Jews or some such noble action—but the nobility of the would-be rescuers who had weapons, the ones still fighting and being killed, the ones wholly unprepared for the catastrophes that played out before them on an hourly basis in April 1945 deserves a larger place in our national examination of the essence of what, indeed, 'greatness' is all about. And here, I hope that the lesson is also one of humility; as they themselves stated in this book, it's not about hero worship, or glorifying the liberator as some kind of savior. Many of the liberating soldiers would resist this, to the point of rejecting the term 'liberator'— '*It all sounds so exalted, so glamorous,*' said one. But they will all accept the term 'eyewitness.' ⁶⁸ Eyewitnesses to the greatest crime in the history of the world; young men who 'kept the faith' of their fallen comrades, their country, and to humanity; witnesses who did something about what they saw.

***

Soldiers featured in this book

Frank Gartner (Introduction) was a technical sergeant with the 743rd Tank Battalion. Fluent in many languages, Gartner was the translator for the battalion's commander, Lt. Col. William D. Duncan. He was originally from Estonia, and resided in Los Angeles, California. He died in Alameda, California, in 1989.⁶⁹

Clarence L. Benjamin, the major who snapped the 'moment of liberation' photo, was highly regarded by his men. He was from Oakland, California, and died in 1989 at the age of 77.

Carrol S. Walsh established a law practice in Johnstown, NY, in 1946. He served as City Court Attorney, Assistant City Judge, and as a school board attorney. He continued his law practice until he was elected Fulton County Judge and Surrogate in 1969 and New York State Supreme Court Justice in 1977.

He retired after a distinguished career as a jurist in 1988. He passed away in 2012 at the age of 91.[70]

George C. Gross earned his bachelor's and master's degrees in English literature from San Diego State and received his doctorate from the University of Southern California in the early 1960s. Dr. Gross joined the San Diego State faculty in 1961. He was associate dean for faculty and dean of faculty affairs from 1970 to 1981 before returning to the classroom. He retired in 1985 but remained active on campus. He passed away in 2009. He was 86.[71]

Frank W. Towers served in Germany for postwar occupation duty. Returning to Florida with his family, Frank was self-employed and was later employed by the University of Florida, retiring in 1979. He was the President and Executive Secretary of the 30th Infantry Division Veterans of World War II Association, and co-founded Les Fleurs de la Mémoire, a foundation in France dedicated to caring for the graves of American soldiers who are interred in France and Belgium. He passed on in 2016 at the age of 99.[72]

Henry Birnbrey (Chapter 12) was one of a few who arrived in the United States as a German Jewish refugee on March 31, 1938, seven months before Kristallnacht, but later losing over forty family members to the Holocaust. He was given special permission from FDR to join the Army—he was previously classified 'enemy alien' due to his German birth—and came upon the train as an American GI in the 30th Infantry Division. Henry was active in speaking about his experiences in the Atlanta, Georgia, area, where he resided. He contacted the author in 2012 and later met Frank Towers, Henry passed in 2021 at the age of 97.[73]

Charles M. Kincaid (Chapter 14) was a liaison officer with the 30th Division Artillery. He was honored with an Air Medal in the battle of Mortain and a Bronze Medal in the battle of Saint-Lô. In the battle of Mortain he won his Air Medal by calling in artillery adjustments while flying in a Piper L-4 over four panzer divisions on August 9, 1944. After the war, he became a chemist in Ohio. He passed away in 2010 at the age of 92.[74]

William Gast (Chapter 17) landed on Omaha Beach on D-Day ten minutes before H-hour, driving a tank in Company A of the 743rd Tank Battalion. He was also a recipient of the Silver Star. Bill attended his first reunion in March 2008, where he met survivors; later he attended our Sept. 2009 reunion at the high school, where he addressed students and his new survivor friends. He passed in 2018 at the age of 94.

Buster Marion Simmonds (Chapter 17) was a combat medic in the 30th Infantry Division and served as the chaplain for their reunions. Buster attended the 2009 and 2011 reunions at our high school and became passionate about educating schoolchildren about the Holocaust. He died in 2013.

Walter Gantz (Chapter 18) worked at an American multinational telecommunications equipment company. He and his wife raised their family in

Scranton, PA, where he was a committed volunteer for the local chapter of the American Red Cross. Walter passed away a few weeks after his 95th birthday in November 2019.[75]

Robert Schatz (Chapter 18) lives in Long Island and was for years the driver for U.S. Senator Alfonse D'Amato. After the war, he was also a colonel in the New York State National Guard.[76]

Luca Furnari (Chapter 18) lives in the Bronx, New York City, where he ran a laundry/dry cleaning route. He was married in 1943, and he and his wife raised their family until her death 60 years later. He is still looking for the little girl 'Irene.'[77]

Grier Taylor (Chapter 18) lived near Columbia, South Carolina. Like many of the soldiers, he was contacted by survivors and their families after this project brought his contributions to light. He passed in 2016 at the age of 94.[78]

Sol Lazinger (Chapter 10) was the son of Polish Jewish immigrants. He was decorated with two Purple Hearts and the Silver Star. He was evacuated after being wounded in Belgium. He married **Jean Weinstock Lazinger** (Chapter 1) in 1950. Until they learned of the author's first reunion in 2007 through the news media, neither realized that it was Sol's division which had liberated Jean's train. Sol passed away in 2012 at the age of 87; Jean passed away in 2017.[79]

Survivors featured in this book who were on the 'Train Near Magdeburg'

Ervin Abadi was a survivor from Hungary who is the first name to appear on the train manifest list. During his convalescence at the hospital at Hillersleben, he created dozens of works of Holocaust art. In a book of his paintings published in 1946, he began by stating, *'Let these drawings serve as proof of my everlasting gratitude towards those to whom I owe my life… to the soldiers of the United States Army, particularly to our immediate liberators, those soldiers … [who] gave us bread, milk, chocolate, and cigarettes…'* He died in 1979.[80]

Paul Arato (Chapter 21) survived the Holocaust with his mother and brother Oscar. He was an industrial designer. He lived in Toronto with his family, and through a business meeting struck up a conversation with Leslie Meisels, and they both discovered they had been on the train. He got to address his liberators for the first time in 2009 in Charleston, SC, and came to the 2009 reunion at our high school. He passed away in 2013.

Sara Atzmon (Chapter 1) is a painter and artist who lives in Israel with her family and extended relatives. She attended the 2009 school reunion, and travels all over the world to educate the public and show her work.[81]

Stephen B. Barry went on to become a US Army ranger, serving in the 28th Infantry Division and referring to himself as the 'happiest Korean War draftee.' He served, in all places, occupation duty in post-war Germany. He attended many reunions, including the 2009 school reunion. He passed away in Boca Raton, Florida, in 2012; he was 87.[82]

Irene Bleier Muskal immigrated to Cleveland, Ohio, and later settled in Israel. Although she never met her liberators, she was always appreciative and even wrote a thank you letter to the Cleveland newspaper, which was published in 1970. Her lengthy memoir, penned for her family, was a testament to her commitment to telling the story of the Holocaust. She passed away at age 70 in 1997.[83]

Kurt Bronner (Chapter 1) spent a lengthy amount of time recuperating in Sweden following the war, and later came to the United States. He was a retired graphic designer who met his liberators at the emotional 2013 Louisville reunion. He passed away in February 2022 at the age of 96.

Uri Orlev (Chapter 1) was a well-known children's author living in Israel. Many of his themes dealt with his experiences in the Holocaust; he received the international Hans Christian Andersen Award in 1996 for his 'lasting contribution to children's literature.' He passed away in Jerusalem in July 2022 at the age of 91.[84]

Aliza Vitis-Shomron came to Palestine immediately after the war, settling on a kibbutz to rebuild her life and working on her manuscript to remember her promise to her friends who died in the Warsaw Ghetto Uprising. She accompanied many youth groups to Poland, and is committed to remembering the Holocaust; she is a national hero in Israel as the last survivor of the Warsaw Ghetto Uprising.[85]

'Agi' Fleischer Baker met her husband in Israel and came to the United States, where she raised her family. She became very close to her liberators and their families, especially in Florida. She found the author after the news of the very first reunion at our school in 2007. She passed away at the age of 85 in August 2020.[86]

Ariela Rojek wound up in the Bergen-Belsen Displaced Persons camp with her aunt after the liberation. She moved to Israel, where she met her husband, and later immigrated to Toronto, Canada, where they raised their family and where she still resides today. Ariela also attended several reunions, including our reunions at the high school in 2009 and 2011. She is the author's biggest fan on Facebook.[87]

Leslie Meisels returned to Hungary but eventually settled in Canada, where he and his brothers built a successful precision mold manufacturing plant. He retired in the late 1980s, and he and his wife Eva, a survivor of the Budapest Ghetto saved by Raoul Wallenberg, were very active in the Holocaust education community. Leslie was a sought-after speaker, and I had the pleasure of sharing the stage with him in Toronto in 2015. Leslie also attended several reunions, including our reunions at the high school in 2009 and 2011. His memoir was a valuable part of constructing the Holocaust as experienced in Hungary. Leslie would email all of his 'twins' each year on April 13th with a message of love and gratitude for their liberators; he passed away in 2018.[88]

Fred Spiegel was no stranger to Hudson Falls, attending all of the reunions at the school and several one-day visits with our students to talk about his book and his experiences in the Holocaust. Fred was the third survivor who contacted me. Immediately after the war, Fred and his sister Edith were reunited with their mother in England. Fred later immigrated to Israel, and then to Chile to be with his mother and sister, finally settling in New Jersey with his wife Yael, where he raised his family. Fred returned to visit the camp Westerbork in 2000. He passed at age 88 in July 2020.[89]

Dr. Peter Lantos was lucky to escape Hungary following the 1956 Revolution, and enjoyed a distinguished medical career in Great Britain, during which time he contributed to the understanding of diseases of the nervous system. He has become internationally known and was elected to the Academy of Medical Sciences. He penned his memoir *Parallel Lines* after his retirement, from which some of his testimony is drawn. He continues to write from his home in London. Peter attended several reunions, including the very first gathering at Hudson Falls in 2007.[90]

Yaakov Barzilai (poem, intro to Book 3) is an esteemed Israeli poet. Born in Hungary in 1933, he also survived Bergen-Belsen to be liberated on the train. His work speaks of the losses of the Holocaust, but also the eventual triumph over inhumanity.[91]

Hilde Huppert (Introduction) was an amazing woman. Her memoir *Hand in Hand with Tommy* was one of the first survivor memoirs, written immediately after her arrival in Palestine in July 1945. She escorted her son Tommy and hundreds of orphans, including 96 from Bergen-Belsen, on the first ship to arrive legally. She passed away in 2002. [92]

Arie Selinger (Chapter 13) is regarded as one of the greatest volleyball coaches of all time. Born in Poland in 1937, Arie and his mother survived Bergen-Belsen and were liberated on the train. He and his mother came to Palestine immediately after the war. Arie discovered his athleticism and went on to excel in sports; he led the USA Women's Volleyball Team to the Silver Medal in the 1984 Olympics, the first medal won by an American team in Olympic volleyball competition.[93]

Lajos Reti (Chapter 13) was a Hungarian survivor who returned to Hungary after the war; his wife was also a survivor of the Budapest Ghetto. He wrote his unpublished memoir, from which this account was drawn; he died in 1992.[94]

Martin Spett (Chapter 13) settled in New York after the war and became a designer of women's handbags. He also took up poetry and painting to convey his Holocaust experiences; some of his portfolio resides at Yad Vashem. He died in 2019 at the age of 90.[95]

Dr. George Somjen (Chapter 13) is Professor Emeritus of Physiology in Cell Biology at Duke

University in North Carolina. He attended several reunions of the 30th Infantry Division with his family.[96]

Robert Spitz (Chapter 13) was also from Budapest, Hungary, and spent 13 months in Bergen-Belsen as a teen before liberation. After the war, he settled in the United States. He also joined the US Army after liberation, serving in the 30th Infantry Division.[97]

John Fransman (Chapter 13) is a founder of The Child Survivors Association of Great Britain. He was born in Amsterdam, three weeks before World War II began. After the liberation, his family moved to Great Britain, where he was active in Holocaust and human rights education and activities. He lives in Israel.[98]

Dr. Bruria Bodek-Falik (Chapter 13) settled in New York State and founded the non-profit High Falls Center for the Developmentally Disabled to assist individuals in life-learning and residential programs. She has received numerous honors for pioneering work and commitment to people with developmental disabilities.[99]

Catharina (Ina) Soep Polak (Chapter 13) married fellow Dutch survivor Jack Polak, who was liberated on the 'Lost Transport' in 1946. Years later their love story was memorialized in the book and an award-winning documentary, *Steal a Pencil For Me*. The author corresponded with Ina but unfortunately never met her; she passed on in 2014 at the age of 91.[100]

Lisette Lamon (Chapter 13) became a psychotherapist at White Plains Hospital outside of New York City, pioneering in the treatment of trauma back in the days when the field was in its infancy. She was the sister-in-law of Ina Polak. Her first husband, Ina's brother, was killed in Mauthausen in 1941. She passed away in 1982.[101]

Gina Rappaport Leitersdorf (Chapter 13) immigrated to Palestine after the war. While in Bergen-Belsen, she was a teacher for children, including young Ariela Rojek and others. She married and began her family and was the only survivor to be conclusively identified by name by George C. Gross in his photographs. The worldwide publicity after the September 2007 reunion at Hudson Falls brought her in contact again with George Gross. She passed away in 2012.

Lexie Friedman Keston (Chapter 15) tasted her first ice cream in Belgium after the war and immigrated to Australia with her parents after the Holocaust, where she resides today with her family. Lexie was the first survivor to contact the author, back in 2006. Like many of the survivors, she enjoyed a meaningful relationship with her liberators, and the soldiers' families.[102]

Dr. Micha Tomkiewicz (Chapter 15) is a professor of physics and chemistry and is director of the Environmental Studies Program and the Electrochemistry Institute at Brooklyn College in New York. *'Welcome to the family!'* is the rejoinder from Micha every time a 'new' survivor or family member of someone who was on the train turns up. He was the second survivor to contact me, and the only survivor who has attended every single reunion ever held, on three continents, a promise he made to Frank Towers after the first reunions with him. He has also met with 'train' survivors in Australia.

Elisabeth Seaman (Chapter 17) is a conflict mediation specialist and author. She came to the 2009 reunion, and others, and speaks about her experiences in the Holocaust, including to a German audience at the Bergen-Belsen Memorial. She lives in California.[103]

Lily Cohen (Chapter 19) came to Palestine in 1945 as an orphan with Hilde Huppert, and was adopted by a family on a kibbutz, where she had a happy childhood. She became a renowned stage dancer and choreography instructor in England, and returned to Tel Aviv where, as a master, she ran her own Tai Chi and Qigong Academy. Lily was also a trainer and master practitioner of NLP Time Line Therapy. She passed away in June 2020.[104]

IF YOU LIKED THIS BOOK, you'll love hearing more from the World War II generation in my other books. On the following pages you can see some samples, and I can let you know as soon as the new books are out and offer you exclusive discounts on some material. Just sign up at my shop below. Some of my readers may like to know that all of my books are <u>directly available from the author, with collector's sets which can be autographed in paperback and hardcover.</u> They are popular gifts for that 'hard-to-buy-for' guy or gal on your list. Visit my shop at <u>matthewrozellbooks.com</u> for details.

The Things Our Fathers Saw ® Series:

VOICES OF THE PACIFIC THEATER

WAR IN THE AIR: GREAT DEPRESSION TO COMBAT

WAR IN THE AIR: COMBAT, CAPTIVITY, REUNION

UP THE BLOODY BOOT-THE WAR IN ITALY

D-DAY AND BEYOND

THE BULGE AND BEYOND

ACROSS THE RHINE

ON TO TOKYO

HOMEFRONT/WOMEN AT WAR

CHINA, BURMA, INDIA

Find them all at matthewrozellbooks.com.

ALSO FROM MATTHEW ROZELL

THE THINGS OUR FATHERS SAW, VOLUME I

THE UNTOLD STORIES OF THE WORLD WAR II GENERATION FROM HOMETOWN, USA
VOICES OF THE PACIFIC THEATER

DESCRIPTION

At the height of World War II, *LOOK Magazine* profiled a small American community for a series of articles portraying it as the wholesome, patriotic model of life on the home front. Decades later, author Matthew Rozell tracks down over thirty survivors who fought the war in the Pacific, from Pearl Harbor to the surrender at Tokyo Bay. The book resurrects firsthand accounts of combat and brotherhood, of captivity and redemption, and the aftermath of a war that left no American community unscathed. Here are the stories that the magazine could not tell, from a vanishing generation speaking to America today. It is up to us to remember—for our own sakes, as much as theirs.

How soon we forget. Or perhaps, we were never told. That is understandable, given what they saw. But, it happened.

From the book:

— 'I was talking to a shipmate of mine waiting for the motor launch, and all at once I saw a plane go over our ship. I did not know what it was, but the fellow with me said, 'That's a Jap plane, Jesus!'

It went down and dropped a torpedo. Then I saw the *Utah* turn over.' ~*U.S. Navy seaman, Pearl Harbor*

— 'Rage is instantaneous. He's looking at me from a crawling position. I didn't shoot him; I went and kicked him in the head. Rage does funny things. After I kicked him, I shot and killed him.' ~*Marine veteran, Battle of Guadalcanal*

— 'Marched to Camp I at Cabanatuan, a distance of six miles, which is the main prison camp here in the Philippines. Food is scarcer now than anytime so far. Fifty men to a bucket of rice!' ~*U.S. Army prisoner of war, Corregidor*

— 'They were firing pretty heavily at us... it's rather difficult to fly when you have a rosary in each hand. I took more fellas in with me than I brought home that day, unfortunately.' ~*U.S. Navy torpedo bomber pilot, Guadalcanal*

— 'I remember it rained like hell that night, and the water was running down the slope into our foxholes. I had to use my helmet to keep bailing out, you know. Lt. Gower called us together. He said, 'I think we're getting hit with a banzai. We're going to have to pull back.' Holy Jesus, there was howling and screaming! They had naked women, with spears, stark naked!' ~*U.S. Army veteran, Saipan*

— 'After 3½ years of starvation and brutal treatment, that beautiful symbol of freedom once more flies over our head! Our camp tailor worked all night and finished our first American flag! The blue came from a GI barracks bag, red from a Jap comforter, and the white from an Australian bed sheet. When I came out of the barracks and saw those beautiful colors for the first time, I felt like crying!' ~*U.S. Army prisoner of war, Japan, at war's end*

— 'There was a family that lost two sons in World War II. The family got a telegram on a Monday that one of the boys was killed, and that Thursday they got another telegram saying that his brother had been killed. There were about 35 young men from our town who were killed in World War II, and I knew every one of them; most were good friends of mine.' ~*U.S. Navy seaman, Tokyo Bay*

— 'I hope you'll never have to tell a story like this, when you get to be 87. I hope you'll never have to do it.' ~*Marine veteran, Iwo Jima*

Excerpt- THE THINGS OUR FATHERS SAW, Vol I

This conversation took place between the author, a married couple, and a group of teenagers about the age of the couple in the story at the time. Jim was a Marine in the Pacific battle of Okinawa, raging at the <u>exact same time</u> the 'Train near Magdeburg' was being liberated.

Jim Butterfield: I enlisted into the United States Marine Corps the seventh of December, 1943. I was seventeen years old then and I went because I wanted to help fight the good war. My mother didn't want me to go. Mary didn't want me to go. But I heard they threw a party after I left. [*Laughter*]

Mary Butterfield: Yes, we went to school together and Jimmy left six months before graduation. I told him, 'Don't go until after you graduate,' but he wanted to go. He was afraid the war would be over before he could get in. So he went in, in December, and I graduated in June.

Matthew Rozell: You were high school sweethearts?

Jim Butterfield: Mary and I have been palling around for over 60 years now.

Mary Butterfield: Well, we've been married 61 years.

Jim Butterfield: She couldn't wait to get married, but I think she's changed her mind a couple times since then… [*Laughter*]

It was an exciting time, it was an adventurous time, and it was a proud time. I lasted 61 or 62 days up to Okinawa before I got hit. When I got hit, we were going to take Shuri Castle because the 6th Division was already in there, and they were catching it real bad. So they decided to put us in there to pull some of the people away from them—to give them a hand.

***

I don't know where that guy, the shot, came from. I got it with a rifle [shot]. I lost part of the right side of my face. I don't know if it was a day, or two days later—I don't even know really what happened to me—the enemy laid a mortar barrage when I was on my way to the hospital at the beach, and I got hit again, in the face! That took care of the other side of my face. I was 14 months in the hospital having my face rebuilt, and that's why I am so good-looking today. [*Laughter*]

The corpsman came and said, 'How are you doing?' I said, 'How about loosening up these bandages, they're killing me.' He said, 'No can do.' So I sat up in the sack and started to unroll it myself. The next thing I know, I got a shot in the arm and I was knocked out again. The next time I woke up, I woke up in an aircraft. A C-54 transport. I never flew before. I had no idea where the hell I was! I put my hand out on the deck, and I just could not put it together—that I was in a plane! Someone must have had a word out to keep an eye on me, because the next time I reached out there, there was a patent leather shoe. I moved my hand a little bit, and there was a nice ankle with a silk stocking! [*Some laughter*] I thought, 'Jesus, I have died and have gone to heaven!' [*Much laughter from students*] I started running my hand up that leg, and she said, 'I think you've gone far enough.' [*More laughter*]

She said to me, 'Jimmy, would you like a turkey sandwich and a glass of milk?' I said, 'Real milk?' She said, 'Real milk.' I said, 'You bet your life!' She brought it down, and there had to be something in it, because I was out again. I woke up in Guam, in the hospital. I was there about three weeks, I guess.

I got an operation there. I didn't know they did it. But what was left of my left side of the eye and face, they took out. Now see, these people knew that I was not going to see again.

The doctor came up. I said, 'How am I doing, Doc? I have to go back up there. They're short of people.' He said, 'You're doing fine, my young boy.' That was all I would get, see?

I didn't know, until they told me there.

***

So here's the climax. Every morning there was inspection with the doctors. So the doctor came around that morning. He said, 'How are you, Jim?' I said, 'Fine.' He said, 'You need anything?' I said, 'Nope, I'm doing fine.' He says, 'Well, are you used to the idea?' I said, 'Used to what idea?' He said, 'That you're not going to see again.'

Well, you could hear a pin drop. I said, 'I don't think I heard you, Doc.' He said, 'You're not going to see again.' I said, 'What?' He said, 'Didn't they tell you in Guam?'

I said, 'No! But it's a good thing that [first] doctor isn't here, because I'd kill him!' I got so mad! I couldn't really grab the idea. I'm not going to see again? ... What the hell did I know about blindness? Nothing!

I said, 'How about operations?' He said, 'You've got nothing to work with, Jimmy.'

So a pat on the shoulder, and he just walks away. The nurse comes over and says, 'The doctor wants you to take this pill.' I said, 'You know what the doctor can do with that pill?'

Mary Butterfield: Don't say it.

Jim Butterfield: I'm not going to, Mary.

So I had a hard... two months, I guess. I kept mostly to myself. I wouldn't talk to people. I tried to figure out what the hell I was going to do when I got home. How was I going to tell my mother this? You know what I mean?

So they come around and said, 'You've got a phone call.' So I went in to where the phone was. They were calling me from home. They got the message, see... This one here was on the phone [*points to Mary*]. I said, 'Looks like things have changed, kiddo.' She said, 'No, we'll discuss this when you get home.' She was already bossing me around. [*Laughter*]

But that's how I found out, and that's how it happened. And after a while, I just started to live with it.

There are not days—even today—I go to bed and I wish I could see. So much I miss. I miss watching a nice girl walking down the street. I miss seeing my daughter, my wife. I even miss looking at Danny [fellow WWII Marine veteran present]. [*Laughter*]

Mary Butterfield: But you see, I'm only 17 to you now. That's a good thing.

Jim Butterfield: Since we got in the conversation, when I dream, and I do dream, everything is real. Everything I knew before, I see it as it was then, not today. My wife and daughter would never get old in my eyes. When I dream of Mary, she's still seventeen years old.

Mary Butterfield: But you never saw your daughter.

Jim Butterfield: I dream about my daughter. Mary's caught me doing this. We lost our daughter a year and a half ago. But I sit right up in bed and I'm trying to push away that little cloud of fog in front of her, but I can't quite make her out.

Mary says, 'What are you doing?' I say, 'Just dreaming'.*

Jim Butterfield was nineteen years old at the Battle of Okinawa.

In the final push at the Shuri Line that cost him his eyesight, the Marines lost over 3,000 men and the U. S. Army even more. When the island was declared secure near the end of June, in Lawler's K/3/5, only 26 Peleliu veterans who had landed with the company had survived Okinawa. It had been the bloodiest campaign of the Pacific, with over 12,500 Americans killed or missing and nearly three times that number wounded. For the Japanese, no accurate counts are possible, but perhaps 110,000 were killed.

---

*Mary and Jimmy Butterfield were married for 67 years. After the war, they were the proud owners and operators of Butterfield's Grocery Store in Glens Falls for 40 years. It was said that Mr. Butterfield could tell the denomination of the bill that was handed to him by its texture and touch. Mary passed in October 2012; Jim passed the following summer.

ABOUT THE AUTHOR

Photo Credit: Joan K. Lentini; May 2017.

Matthew Rozell is an award-winning history teacher, author, speaker, and blogger on the topic of the most cataclysmic events in the history of mankind—World War II and the Holocaust. Rozell has been featured as the 'ABC World News Person of the Week' and has had his work as a teacher filmed for the CBS Evening News, NBC Learn, the Israeli Broadcast Authority, the United States Holocaust Memorial Museum, and the New York State United Teachers. He writes on the power of teaching and the importance of the study of history at TeachingHistoryMatters.com, and you can 'Like' his Facebook author page at Author-MatthewRozell for updates.

Mr. Rozell is a sought-after speaker on World War II, the Holocaust, and history education, motivating and inspiring his audiences with the lessons of the past. Visit MatthewRozell.com for availability/details.

About this Book/ Acknowledgements

My wife Laura began beta reading the manuscript for this book just before publication and was peppering me with questions about the Holocaust, even before completing Chapter 1. I took this as a good sign, as I knew many of her questions would be answered as she read through it; however, questions about the people living under Nazi rule in Germany who did nothing were the most troubling to her, in the sense of, what if our places had been changed? What would we have done, as individuals? I hope questions raised in this work empower the reader to think about the power of choice.

A note on historiographical style and convention: to enhance accuracy, consistency, and readability, I corrected punctuation and spelling and sometimes even place names, but only after extensive research. I did take the liberty of occasionally condensing the speaker's voice, eliminating side tangents or incidental information not relevant to the matter at hand. In some cases, two or more interviews with the same person were combined for readability and narrative flow. All of the words of the subjects, however, are essentially their own, and sources are mentioned in the endnotes. My students helped identify troublesome words/phrases in the text, asking for clarification, and since they appreciated this, as well as the explanatory commentaries in the beta readings, it has been standardized throughout in the form of footnotes.

*

Over thirty years have passed now since I became a teacher. My early students went on, some to even become teachers themselves, while others today make many times my salary. Since the early days, I even had their kids in class (much better behaved, actually). We built a foundation and ventured forth to great things.

My parents laid that foundation. As educators themselves, they showed me the power of nurturing youth and being a role model by listening and advocating for the kids they cultivated. My father never came home from school angry or upset; my enduring afterschool memory of him as a teacher is of him humming or singing to himself.

Writing this book has been a catharsis of sorts for me, just as the reunions were for the survivor and liberator families. I knew I had to write it even before the reunions began, as evidenced in combing through nearly 15 years of email correspondence with the soldiers and survivors. Of course, I was gathering material along the way, and developments were really never-ending. The actual writing process began many years ago, I suppose, with the launching of my blog, TeachingHistoryMatters, soon after the very first reunion in 2007. Still, I did battle with the form for years, in hindsight because all of the pieces were not yet in place. As the twilight of my teaching career is at hand, it finally began to take shape in this form— even though as I write this, there are more developments; it will never end. Feel free to subscribe to the blog for updates.

I struggled with the framework for telling this story because my challenge was really three-fold. I wanted to do justice to the narrative of the Holocaust, as evidenced by this microcosmic event of the liberation of the train in the backdrop of the vastness of the macrocosm of the Holocaust. I tried to write it the way I teach my class. I start the narrative of the Holocaust at the end, with the discovery of the camps. And then we ask the hows, and the whys, and walk it backwards in time, to explore what happened, to try and search for context and meaning. For me, the most powerful way to do that was to utilize the voices of those who were there. I am indebted to those who submitted their testimony, and the authors who allowed me to use their previously published materials, which I edited for this purpose, especially the works of Aliza Vitis-Shomron, Leslie Meisels, Fred Spiegel, and

Peter Lantos. Irene Bleier Muskal's unpublished manuscript was graciously proffered by her family. Thank you all for allowing me to edit your works into the framework of the narrative here; to the reader, in the source notes you are directed to the full versions of their important narratives.

Secondly, I wanted to honor the experiences of the soldiers, both during the war and after the survivors began to appear. The only way to do that well was, again, to try to let them tell the story themselves.

Thirdly, as the curtain closes on this part of my life as a teacher, this book is also an attempt at personal self-exploration in the sense that I still cannot believe everything that has happened, or stop wondering how and why it all came about. Some readers have taken me to task for "inserting himself into the narrative", but as it clearly states in the title and the author's note, this was indeed a story where an ordinary teacher became part of the latter-day narrative. I hope that maybe it can also serve as an inspiration for any young teacher or young person struggling with the question of whether or not they are making a difference. The fact is, I have been lucky, but most often, a teacher may not really know until that letter, email, tweet, or post arrives in the most unexpected of ways. (And if you are one of those persons who was powerfully moved by a teacher in your life, what are you waiting for?)

Finally, lest I be taken to task for survivor/soldier narrative omissions, I apologize in advance. There are HUNDREDS of people affected by this story directly, most of whom I have never met. Unfortunately, there was no way to incorporate everyone's accounts in the book, so I tried to tell the story the way I knew best, the way that it unfolded for me. Each reunion could have a book written about it, and I go into much more detail at my blog. If you know more about this story, or spot an error or grave omission, I encourage you to visit and leave a comment. And if you enjoyed the book, please consider leaving a review/feedback at Amazon.com so that others might know more about it. This is especially crucial to keeping the story alive. You can also drop me a line via Matthew@ MatthewRozellBooks.com.

*

ACKNOWLEDGEMENTS

There are many people to acknowledge in the actualization of this work, and it is difficult to know where to start, so perhaps again, I should work backwards.

Alan Bush served as my wingman in reading the entire manuscript at several intervals and responding with pointed questions, excellent comments, and calling my attention to technical elements which needed addressing. Ashley Libben also sent me her commentary and encouragement, as did Donna Payne Hughes and Pauline Kolman Rosenberg. It is no surprise that all are passionate educators themselves, and all shared the experience of traveling to the authentic sites of the Holocaust with me in 2013 with Vladka Meed's Holocaust and Jewish Resistance Teachers Program, led by the incomparable Elaine Culbertson and Stephen Feinberg. The program is highly recommended and helped me to better understand the background of the many survivors I have been privileged to know. To learn more, or apply as a teacher or support the teachers who go on to change many lives because of it, search the internet for 'Holocaust and Jewish Resistance Teachers Program'.

Bernd Horstmann, the Custodian of the Book of Names at the Bergen-Belsen Memorial, took time to read my first two chapters and offer clarifications. Susan Winchell of the New York State Museum took time out of her busy schedule to put her remarkable talents to work to get the maps just the way I needed them. I have known Susan for over two decades, starting on archeological dig sites and beginning when she asked if she could feed my Labrador retriever a part of her peanut butter sandwich, which I denied; nevertheless, thereafter we became fast friends, and for this I am forever grateful. Mike Edwards, an Emmy Award-winning filmmaker at the 5 Stones Group, bounced ideas off of me, and I, him, as we brainstormed what a film would look like. He also supplied me with access to his interviews of the eyewitnesses I recommended to him. As our friendship grows, I hope that this element of my life's work comes to fruition, and I admire his tenacity in wanting to tell the story and getting it right; you can find more information on this major documentary series and view the trailer at teachinghistorymatters.com/a-train-near-magdeburg-holocaust-film-project.

My study at Yad Vashem's International School for Holocaust Studies near the completion of the manuscript also confirmed for me that I was on the right track with what I was trying to achieve with this work. To my fellow teachers, to our top-notch instructors and guides, and to the immediate parties who had a hand in my development, Ephraim Kaye and Stephanie McMahon-Kaye, my deepest thanks for an enriching experience.

My friend Varda Weisskopf in Israel offered encouragement and moral support. As noted in the book, Varda found many (90!) of the Israeli survivors and organized the great reunion in 2011, a major undertaking. I helped her get in contact with Frank Towers in 2010, and together, Frank, Varda, and I tracked down nearly 280 survivors of the train. She also looked out for my arrangements in Israel, getting me to the airport and back safely.

Again, working backward, I would also like to acknowledge Patricia Polan and her committee at the New York State Education Department for recommending me for an honor, The Louis E. Yavner Teaching Award for Distinguished Contributions to Teaching the Holocaust and Other

Violations of Human Rights. Thank you to NYSED for your faith in me in bestowing me with this highlight of my career, and to Chancellor Rosa for offering me her seat in the Chancellor's chair at the May 2016 Board of Regents meeting in Albany, and allowing me to express my support for Holocaust education. Thank you also for allowing me during the award presentation to recognize the support and accomplishments of my newly retired wife, Laura Vesey Rozell. Laura got an ovation, and while I know it does not make up for ignoring the 'honey-do' list at home while I was hammering out this book, I wanted people to recognize how important her work is, too. Laura spent 33 years in education, teaching on some days in the same school building as my mom, becoming my mom's confidante and road trip companion in that far away era 'BC'—before children. And later, she took my mother's hand on Mom's long, slow journey into twilight.

Another important nod is to the ladies of the Jane McCrea Chapter of the National Society for the Daughters of the American Revolution, especially Melinda Durrler and Sharon Jensen, who nominated me for state and national teaching awards, which I was blessed to receive, and to other organizations which have also honored my work. I have been humbled, and I hope that I have lived up to your expectations.

Naturally, I also wish to acknowledge the hundreds of students who passed through my life, especially my elective classes on World War II and the Holocaust, the kids who forged the bonds with the World War II generation and the Holocaust survivors. These students became time-traveling detectives as we pieced together fragments of the evidence of the Holocaust, listening to and recording original interviews, and now publishing them for the world to learn from. *'It's life-altering,'* said one teenager, *'and because we've heard these stories, it's our job to make sure it won't happen again.'* I promised you this book someday, and now that many of you are yourselves parents, you can tell your children this book is for them. As promised, a special shout-out to these beta readers of parts of the early manuscript, who provided important 'young adult' feedback, and in some cases, even hammered away with me at the interviews herein—Miki Carbona-

Cole, Taylor Carlisle, Casey Cicero, Abby Colvin, Caity Coutant, Kristina Delk, Nic Hall, Casey Heasley, Colin Kelsey, Tommy Kiernan, Leonard Kilmartin, Briannah Maloney, Christopher McKinney, Vincent Murphy, Antonio Nassivera, April Pelkey, Reanna Rainbow, Ned Rozell, Tom Salis, Destiny Sheldon, Megan Spirowski, Sean Valis, Rachael Weils, Cory Wilkins, Jacob Wojtowecz, and Connor Wood. Who says young people are indifferent to the past? Here is evidence to the contrary.

The Hudson Falls Central School District Board of Education and my teaching and support colleagues have my deep appreciation for supporting our reunions and recognizing their significance throughout the years. Former superintendent Mark Doody ardently supported the concept of the reunions from the start, as did my late principal C.J. Hebert. My current principal, James Bennefield, was equally supportive for the last school reunion in 2011. The entire administrative team recognized the value of providing these once-in-a-lifetime opportunities for our students, our community, and neighboring communities.

The district also promoted Holocaust education on a national and international level by allowing me the release time to travel to Washington, Toronto, Israel, and elsewhere for events I was invited to speak at. To Mary Murray, the secretary to the high school principal who also became the enthusiastic secretary for our multiple reunions, thank you for the invitations typed, the phone calls fielded, the messages cheerfully taken, the lists kept, the reservations made, the suggestions made that I never would have thought of, and on and on. But mostly, thank you for answering the phone in your cheerful 'Mary' voice—*'Mary Murray, High School'*—the mere hearing of which completely melted away my stress levels during the summer of 2009 when I was questioning my sanity for undertaking the largest reunion/symposium (Chapter 17). A huge appreciation also to master organizer and history teacher Tara Winchell Sano, and Lisa Hogan, for being a step ahead of me, every step of the way. Mr. René Roberge served as the master of ceremonies on all occasions, underscoring the magnitude of the importance of the event with characteristic dignity and delivery. Diane Havern,

Hudson Falls choral director, brought tears with her choraliers to the eyes of the veterans and the survivors with their rendition of our national anthem at the start of each day's testimony.[94] Our IT department was also instrumental in the background of our success. We really could not have pulled it off without all of you, and thank you to the rest of the high school staff who were so enthusiastic and supportive. It was all truly a miracle, and not just for the survivors and liberators in attendance.

Thank you also to the local businesses that generously supported the reunions, especially the Lake George Steamboat Company for two memorable evenings on the 'Queen of American Lakes,' and to the Havens family at Falls Farm and Garden in our town. Many, many local people also helped, so numerous to mention, but thank you especially to the John A. Leary family, who provided a generous contribution for reducing the expenses for our honored guests, made in honor of their father, a World War II torpedo bomber pilot who is

---

[94] *brought tears to the eyes of the veterans and the survivors with their rendition of our national anthem*-watch a clip of that emotional end of our reunions here: bit.ly/rtw2011.

profiled in my first book. Robert Dingman, my department chair for the first half of my career, introduced me to Judge Leary and other vets, and I suspect may have had a hand in bringing me on board at my alma mater so many years ago. Donald Bernhoft was the principal who gave me latitude in my darkest days (Chapter 8). My colleague Antoinette Sommo, the teacher who received 'the pink slip layoff notice' eventually returned to her job, and to this day thanks me for my knee-jerk suggestion that since she was suddenly out of work, she should 'start your family'; she is one of my biggest fans. I also want to acknowledge my very first principal, John Christopher at St. Mary's Academy in Glens Falls, for taking a chance on me as a new teacher and instilling some quality 'teacher life lessons' early on. My wife and I became close with John and his wife Anne in their later years.

As I prepared for the unprecedented scope of the 2009 school reunion in the weeks leading up to it, I had another person who helped me 'flip the switch' when I most needed it. My boyhood friend, Cold War submarine veteran Ted Chittenden, packed me up in his car and whisked me the four hours south to Yankee Stadium on a Friday after school to witness New York Yankee legend Derek Jeter beat fellow Yankee legend Lou Gehrig's All-Time Yankee hit record on September 11, 2009. Late that evening, as we dodged the puddles of Manhattan's thoroughfares, the memorial lights of the Twin Towers illuminated the clouds as we headed to my sister's apartment for the night, poignantly driving home the importance of 'never forgetting.' The following summer, Ted chauffeured my children and I down to a gig at the New York Mets' CitiField, where I was invited to speak on behalf of the United States Holocaust Memorial Museum's NYC Next Generation project initiative to an audience that included USHMM Council member and then part-owner of the Mets, Jeff Wilpon. That evening we raised 50K for the Museum's educational programming (although the Mets lost to the Cardinals in extra innings). After 50 years, it's comforting to know that just when you need it the most, your old buddy still has your back.

I wish also to thank the United States Holocaust Memorial Museum for their support over the years. While I do not represent the Museum in any official capacity, we have enjoyed a long relationship, beginning with Peter J. Fredlake, the former director of Teacher Education and Special Programs. It was Pete who saw the first Associated Press news accounts of the 2007 reunion, and who invited me to apply to their Museum Teacher Fellowship program. Here I developed other important contacts and resources. Christina Chavarria, the program coordinator for education initiatives and resources, was an early source of support in recognizing that my students and I were going beyond the classroom and actively 'collecting the evidence.' I also worked with others in acquiring resources for the USHMM, including Judy Cohen, the Chief Acquisitions Curator and Photo Archivist. That is why you can see the Benjamin photo and the Gross photo collection in Washington today, as well as many pieces of artwork created by train survivor Ervin Abadi. As researcher extraordinaire, Steven Vitto of the USHMM Holocaust Survivors and Victims Resource Center has proven himself time and again as a master detective when I needed obscure documents related to tracing a survivor's path. Josh Blinder, video producer at the USHMM, orchestrated the official filming of the 2009 reunion and executed the film, *Honoring Liberation*, in time for the 2010 USHMM National Days of Remembrance ceremonies in Washington. In the Division of Outreach Technology, David Klevan worked with me on his profile of our project in his chapter in the well-received textbook, *Essentials of Holocaust Education: Fundamental Issues and Approaches* (Totten and Feinberg, 2016). It's not inexpensive, but if you are a serious Holocaust education professional, you need it in your library. I also have a fond memory of the late Dan Napolitano, the former director of teacher education at the USHMM, encouraging me to go forth and tell this story. Finally, thank you, of course, to Museum Director Sara Bloomfield, who sat through my presentation for her development staff in the summer of 2009 and had the foresight to ask for Carrol Walsh's letter to Steve Barry for the USHMM collections (Chapter 21), and for recognizing me before the 2010 Capitol

ACKNOWLEDGEMENTS | 731

Rotunda ceremony honoring the liberators. It was hard for my feet to touch the ground after that experience.

Chris Carola, formerly of the Albany, New York bureau of the Associated Press (Chapter 15) also has my gratitude for moving this story along, and helping to bring more survivors into the fold. He interviewed Carrol Walsh on numerous occasions during this project, and to their mutual delight, they realized that Chris's dad was a highly regarded lawyer who Judge Walsh remembered from his time on the bench! Elizabeth Connolly, whose sons I had in class, welcomed me into her home to interview her dad and became a fast friend and supporter. Tim and John Gross, George C. Gross's sons, were instrumental in helping me to bring their father's photo collection to the light of day in the very beginning, when Dr. Gross wanted to share them with me, and later, the world. The rest of the families of Judge Walsh and Frank Towers were also very supportive and appreciative of this project; I hope that I did your fathers a measure of justice in this book.

To my younger siblings Mary, Ned, Nora, and Drew, all accomplished writers and authors, thank you for your encouragement as well, and especially to Drew, who first planted the seed of writing the book as a personal journey. We were lucky that we had such great parents and wonderful teachers at Hudson Falls when we were young.

Final and deepest appreciations go to my wife Laura and our children, Emma, Ned, and Mary. Ned accompanied me on many trips to the reunions as a young lad and was lucky to have had his old man as his history teacher in three out of four of his high school years. Mary is on track to suffer a similar fate while our oldest, Emma, continues to be one of my biggest supporters. Thank you for indulging your old man as he attempted to bring to life the stories he collected as a young one.

List of Reunions

OFFICIAL REUNIONS
OF THE
THE SOLDIERS AND SURVIVORS
OF THE
TRAIN NEAR MAGDEBURG

Hudson Falls High School—Hudson Falls, NY—Sept. 2007
30th Inf. Div. Vets of WWII—Fayetteville, NC—March 2008
30th Inf. Div. Vets of WWII—Charleston, SC—March 2009
Hudson Falls High School—Hudson Falls, NY—Sept. 2009
[ABC WORLD NEWS PERSON OF THE WEEK bit.ly/ABCWNPOW]
30th Inf. Div. Vets of WWII—Nashville, TN—March 2010
30th Inf. Div. Vets of WWII—Nashville, TN—March 2011
The Weizmann Institute—Rehovot, Israel—May 2011
Hudson Falls High School—Hudson Falls, NY—Sept. 2011
30th Inf. Div. Vets of WWII—Savannah, GA—March 2012

30th Inf. Div. Vets of WWII—Louisville, KY—April 2013
30th Inf. Div. Vets of WWII—Savannah, GA—Feb. 2014
FINAL: 30th Inf. Div. Vets of WWII—Nashville, TN—April 2015

NOTES

¹ Celinscak, Mark. *Distance from the Belsen Heap: Allied Forces and the Liberation of a Concentration Camp.* Toronto: University of Toronto Press. 2015. 42. Also, Shepard, Ben. *After Daybreak: The Liberation of Bergen–Belsen, 1945.* New York: Schocken Books, 2005. 4. And the figure of 60,000 is also given by the United States Holocaust Memorial Museum—see USHMM, Holocaust Encyclopedia. Bergen–Belsen. ushmm.org/wlc/en/article.php?ModuleId=10005224. However, the Bergen–Belsen Memorial currently puts the figure at 53,000. '53,000 prisoners were liberated at Bergen–Belsen by the British Army; 38,000 in the concentration camp and 15,000 in the satellite camp in the nearby army barracks.' See the Bergen Belsen catalogue pp. 258-59; also the web description at bergen-belsen.stiftung-ng.de/en/history/concentration-camp/liberation.
² Phillips, Raymond, Editor. *War Crimes Trials—Vol. II: The Belsen Trial–'The Trial of Josef Kramer and*

Forty Four Others' (with a foreword by Lord Jowitt). London: W. Hodge, 1949. This trial was held between September and November, 1945, at Luneburg, Germany, before a British military court for war crimes committed against Allied nationals in the concentration camps at Belsen and Auschwitz. A most excellent and complete online source of the testimony can be found below, and all the testimony found in Chapter 1 related to the trial was gathered here. www.bergenbelsen.co.uk/pages/Trial/TrialFront/TrialFront_01.

3 Bauer, Yehuda. *Jews For Sale? Nazi-Jewish Negotiations, 1933-1945.* New Haven, Conn. and London: Yale University Press, 1994. 168. There were numerous attempts to bribe officials in order to save Jews. Dr. Bauer's *Jews for Sale?* is the definitive source for research on this. Most efforts were unsuccessful, but two efforts in 1944 succeeded. More than 1,900 people, mainly Hungarian Jews (including a transport from Bergen-Belsen in early December), made it to safety in Switzerland. The principal negotiator for these two transports, Rudolph (Rezsö) Kasztner, remains a controversial individual, who was later assassinated for determining which Hungarian Jews to save during the Holocaust, while others perished. See also Anna Porter's *Kasztner's Train: The True Story of Rezsö Kasztner, Unknown Hero of the Holocaust* (2007).

4 Phillips, *The Belsen Trial.*

5 **Hadassah 'Ada' Bimko** lost her first husband and young son at Auschwitz. In 1946, she married

fellow survivor Josef Rosensaft, who was chairman of the Jewish Committee of Bergen–Belsen, which oversaw the day-to-day administration of the displaced-persons camp for Bergen–Belsen survivors from 1945 to 1950. Dr. Rosensaft also held high posts in the Bergen–Belsen displaced persons camp and the Central Jewish Committee in the British Zone. In 1980, President Jimmy Carter appointed her to the inaugural United States Holocaust Memorial Council. She passed away in 1997 at the age of 85. At her death, she had been the honorary president of the World Federation of Bergen–Belsen Survivors Associations for two decades. In 1981, she recalled, *'There was no ecstasy, no joy at our liberation. We had lost our families, our homes. We had no place to go, nobody to hug. Nobody was waiting for us anywhere. We had been liberated from the fear of death, but we were not free from the fear of life.'* Source Notes: Phillips, *The Belsen Trial;* Pace, Eric. 'Hadassah Rosensaft, 85, Dies, Saved Auschwitz Inmates.' *The New York Times,* October 8, 1997; Rosensaft, Menachem Z. 'Hadassah Rosensaft.' *Jewish Women: A Comprehensive Historical Encyclopedia.* March 1, 2009. Jewish Women's Archive.

[6] Shepard, Ben. *After Daybreak: The Liberation of Bergen–Belsen, 1945.* New York: Schocken Books, 2005. 14.

[7] Bauer, Yehuda. *Jews For Sale? Nazi-Jewish Negotiations, 1933-1945.* New Haven, Conn. and London: Yale University Press, 1994. 229.

[8] Celinscak, Mark. *Distance from the Belsen Heap: Allied Forces and the Liberation of a Concentration Camp*. Toronto: University of Toronto Press. 2015. 67.

[9] Phillips, *The Belsen Trial*.

[10] Stafford, David. *Endgame, 1945: The Missing Final Chapter of World War II*. New York: Little, Brown and Company. 2007. 88.

[11] The transports would be headed for the Theresienstadt concentration camp, which at the time was far enough from advancing Allied lines and indeed would prove to be the last camp liberated on the last day of the war. Only one train made it there. The other two were liberated, one by the Americans at Farsleben near Magdeburg, and the other by the Russians near Tröbitz. As conflicting information from various sources was found, the author contacted Bernd Horstmann of the Bergen–Belsen Memorial, who confirmed the following from his files:

'The following groups of the Exchange Camp left the Exchange Camp of Bergen-Belsen:
  a) 06 April 45 – around 2,500 Jewish people
  b) 07 April 45 – 179 Jewish people left Bergen-Belsen. This group was put into train wagons and those were attached to the first train a few kilometres after because the first train stopped for hours.
  This [first] train with nearly 2,700 people was liberated at Farsleben on 13 April 1945.

c) 09 April 45 – 1,712 Jewish people – train arrived at Theresienstadt on 20 April 45

d) 10 April 45 – 2,400 Jewish people – train was liberated at Tröbitz on 23 April 45

The date in the map of our catalogue should be corrected to 06 April 45. Probably it was written 07 April because the eye-witness of the route was in the group b) that left on 07 April. You are also right that after leaving Bergen-Belsen concentration camp it took hours and hours until the prisoners marched 7 kilometres to the ramp near the town Belsen (not Celle), and entered the wagons of the train. At the same time when the Jewish hostages of the Exchange Camp left Bergen-Belsen, thousands of other prisoners—slave workers—arrived at the ramp and marched in the opposite direction.' Horstmann, Bernd, email communication, May 24, 2013.

[12] Smitha, Frank. *Macrohistory and World Timeline: The Final Three Months.* www.fsmitha.com/h2/ch23-9.htm

[13] USHMM, *Common Questions about the Holocaust* www.ushmm.org/educators/teaching-about-the-holocaust/common-questions

[14] United States Holocaust Memorial Museum. Kristallnacht. www.ushmm.org/wlc/en/article.php?ModuleId=10005201

[15] USHMM, Holocaust Encyclopedia. *Kristallnacht.* www.ushmm.org/wlc/en/article.php?ModuleId=10005201

[16] Dart, John. *Scholars Seek Substitute for the Word 'Holocaust'.* Los Angeles Times, April 9, 1994.

articles.latimes.com/1994-04-09/local/me-44075_1_word-holocaust. See also Fleet, Josh, *History And Meaning Of The Word 'Holocaust': Are We Still Comfortable With This Term?* The Huffington Post, March 28, 2012. www.huffingtonpost.com/2012/01/27/the-word-holocaust-history-and-meaning_n_1229043.

[17] USHMM, Holocaust Encyclopedia. *Euthanasia Program.* www.ushmm.org/wlc/en/article.php?ModuleId=10005200

[18] Ginott, Haim G. *Teacher and Child: A Book for Parents and Teachers.* New York, NY: Macmillan. 1975.

[19] See Dubois, Patrick. *The Holocaust by Bullets: A Priest's Journey to Uncover the Truth Behind the Murder of 1.5 Million Jews.* New York: St. Martin's Griffin, 2009. This groundbreaking work by a French Catholic priest calls attention to the previously under-recorded chapter in Holocaust studies. See also the ongoing research and fieldwork at www.yahadinunum.org.

[20] Kaye, Ephraim. 'The Decision to Kill the Jews—The Final Solution and Its Implementation.' Lecture notes, International School for Holocaust Studies at Yad Vashem, Jerusalem, Israel. July 13, 2016.

[21] *some did ask to be relieved, and they were*- See Browning, Christopher R., *Ordinary Men: Reserve Police Battalion 101 and the Final Solution in Poland.* New York: Harper Collins, 1998.

22 Gleis 17 Memorial—Berlin Grunewald www.memorialmuseums.org/eng/staettens/view/338/Mahnmal-Gleis-17-E28093--Berlin-Grunewald

23 USHMM, Holocaust Encyclopedia. *The Rosenstrasse Demonstration.* www.ushmm.org/wlc/en/article.php?ModuleId=10008064

24 USHMM, Holocaust Encyclopedia. *Theresienstadt.* www.ushmm.org/wlc/en/article.php?ModuleId=10005424

25 USHMM, Holocaust Encyclopedia. *Belzec.* www.ushmm.org/wlc/en/article.php?ModuleId=10005191

26 Much of this section is excerpted from Aliza Vitis–Shomron's memoir, *Youth in Flames*. The author contacted her in 2016 and she graciously allowed him to use excerpts throughout this work; her writing powerfully conveys the spirit of the Warsaw Ghetto, and she notes that her book was 'partly composed of notes from an authentic diary; a larger part contains my memories, written in this country [Israel] at the age of seventeen, in Kibbutz Beit Alfa; and I also added another part later.' Aliza's full Holocaust narrative can be obtained at www.warsawghettobook.com.

[27] USHMM. Holocaust Encyclopedia. *Warsaw Ghetto.* www.ushmm.org/wlc/en/article.php?ModuleId=10005069

[28] USHMM, Holocaust Encyclopedia. *Warsaw.* www.ushmm.org/wlc/en/article.php?ModuleId=10005069

[29] From July 22 until September 12, 1942, German SS and police units, assisted by auxiliaries, carried out mass deportations from the Warsaw Ghetto to the Treblinka killing center. During this period, the Germans deported about 265,000 Jews from Warsaw to Treblinka; they killed approximately 35,000 Jews inside the ghetto during the operation. USHMM, Holocaust Encyclopedia. *Warsaw.* www.ushmm.org/wlc/en/article.php?ModuleId=10005069

[30] USHMM, Holocaust Encyclopedia. *'Lublin/Majdanek concentration camp: Administration.'* www.ushmm.org/wlc/en/article.php?ModuleId=10007300

[31] USHMM, Holocaust Encyclopedia. *'Lublin/Majdanek concentration camp: Administration.'*

[32] USHMM, Holocaust Encyclopedia. *Aktion 'Erntefest' (Operation 'Harvest Festival')* www.ushmm.org/wlc/en/article.php?ModuleId=10005222

[33] Chylak, Anna. *The 70th Anniversary of the Liquidation of Hotel Polski.* Jewish Historical Institute. July 13, 2013. www.jhi.pl/en/blog/2013-07-13-the-70th-anniversary-of-the-liquidation-of-hotel-polski.

34 Chylak, Anna. *The 70th Anniversary of the Liquidation of Hotel Polski.* Jewish Historical Institute.
35 Snow, Richard. *A Nation at War With Itself.* The Wall Street Journal. April 19, 2016. www.wsj.com/articles/a-nation-at-war-with-itself-1461104812
36 Porter, Anna, as relayed in Meisels, Leslie. *Suddenly The Shadow Fell* (The Azrieli Series of Holocaust Survivor Memoirs) The Azrieli Foundation. 2014. xvi.
37 Author notations from Ghetto Fighters' House Museum panels, Lohamei HaGeta'ot, Israel, July 18, 2016.
38 USHMM, Holocaust Encyclopedia. *Hungary after the German occupation.* www.ushmm.org/wlc/en/article.php?ModuleId=10005458
39 Gabor Aron Study Group. 'Hungary in the Mirror of the Western World, 1938-1958'. www.hungarianhistory.com/lib/mirror
40 Levi, Primo. *Primo Levi's Heartbreaking, Heroic Answers to the Most Common Questions He Was Asked About 'Survival in Auschwitz'.* The New Republic, February 17, 1986. newrepublic.com/article/119959/interview-primo-levi-survival-auschwitz
41 Porter, Anna, as found in Meisels, Leslie. *Suddenly The Shadow Fell* (The Azrieli Series of Holocaust Survivor Memoirs) The Azrieli Foundation. 2014. xxiii.

[42] {*Please refer to Note 3 for more on Rudolph (Rezső) Kasztner*}– 'Eichmann offered Kasztner a chance to send 30,000 Jews to Austria instead of Auschwitz. In fact, only 18,000-20,000 Jews, mostly from Debrecen, Szeged, Baja, and Szolnok, were sent to the areas around Vienna to work. The Nazis could have sent the women, the elderly, and the children to Auschwitz. In this case **they did not do so***, perhaps because of the Kasztner negotiations. By keeping these people alive temporarily—Kaltenbrunner [leader of the Austrian SS] pointed out... that the labor was indeed temporary—essential labor needs could be satisfied, and the prospect of further negotiations could be kept open. In the end, some of the 18,000-20,000 were shipped to Bergen–Belsen, some to Theresienstadt, and the rest stayed on near Vienna. About 12,000 survived.' Bauer, Yehuda. *Jews For Sale? Nazi-Jewish Negotiations, 1933-1945.* New Haven, Conn. and London: Yale University Press, 1994. 201. **they did not do so***-*My emphasis. It would appear that the testimony of Meisels and Bleier-Muskal, as recorded later in Chapter 7, contradicts this part of the above*

statement, regarding at least some of the elderly, women, and children.

[43] Atkinson, Rick. *The Guns at Last Light: The War in Western Europe, 1944-1945.* New York: Henry Holt & Co., 2013. 57.

[44] Folkestad, William B. *The View from the Turret: The 743rd Tank Battalion during World War II.* Shippensburg, Pa.: Burd Street Press, 1996. ix, 33,51.

[45] United States Army; Robinson, Wayne; and Hamilton, Norman E., *Move Out, Verify: The Combat Story of the 743rd Tank Battalion.* 1945. World War Regimental Histories.

[46] Kerley, Ralph A., *Operations of the 2nd Battalion, 120th Infantry*
(30th Infantry Division) at Mortain, France 6–12 August 1944
(Northern France Campaign)Personal Experiences of a Company Commander: An Isolated Infantry Battalion Defending a Key Terrain Feature Monograph written for the Advanced Infantry Officer's Class #1 1949- 1950, Major Ralph A. Kerley. Located at link below.

[47] The 30th Infantry Division Veterans of WWII. *Mortain.* www.30thinfantry.org/unit_history_mortain. This website was maintained by Frank W. Towers before his passing.

[48] Weiss, Robert. *Fire Mission!: The Siege at Mortain, Normandy, August 1944.* Shippensburg, Pa.: Burd Street Press, 2002.

49 Atkinson, Rick. *The Guns at Last Light: The War in Western Europe, 1944-1945*. New York: Henry Holt & Co., 2013. 157.

50 The 30th Infantry Division Veterans of WWII. *Mortain*.

51 Miller, Donald. *The Story of World War II*. New York: Simon & Schuster, 2001. 325.

52 The D-Day Museum [UK].*D-Day and the Battle of Normandy* www.ddaymuseum.co.uk/d-day/d-day-and-the-battle-of-normandy

53 Folkestad, *View from the Turret*. 60

54 Robinson & Hamilton. *Move Out, Verify*.98.

55 Folkestad, *View from the Turret*. 64.

56 Ambrose, Stephen E. *Citizen Soldiers: The U.S. Army From the Normandy Beaches to the Bulge to the Surrender of Germany*. New York: Simon & Schuster. 1997. 400-404.

57 Robinson & Hamilton. *Move Out, Verify*.112. Also, United States Army, After Action Report. *S3 Journal history for the 743rd Tank Battalion.1 Oct –31 Dec 1944*. World War II Operational Documents, Combined Arms Research Library. Fort Leavenworth, Kansas.167-169.

58 Folkestad, *View from the Turret*. 84.

59 Folkestad, *View from the Turret*. 85.

60 Robinson & Hamilton. *Move Out, Verify*.160-161.

61 United States Army, After Action Report, 743rd Tank Battalion, April 12-14, 1945.

62 Hirsch, Michael. *The Liberators: America's Witnesses to the Holocaust*. New York: Bantam Books. 2010. 99-102.

[63] '*the battalion commander drew his sidearm, put it to the mayor's head, and calmly asked him to recite his instructions* - 'Towers interview with author, 2008; Jacob Singer interview with author, 2008. Singer was a four-year-old child but remembered this event and relayed it to the author. He also noted that he remembered the liberation because this was the first time in his life that he remembered 'seeing adults smile.' In an email communication to interviewer Jerri Donohue, Towers wrote, *'Yes, the German civilians, as well as their Nazi Burgomaster, were very reluctant to offer any assistance to these 'Jew pigs'!!! I actually did not witness any of this unwillingness, but only heard it from another liaison officer from the 823rd Tank Battalion, Lt. Floyd Mitchell, who was a close friend, and he saw this firsthand. It was his C.O., Lt. Col. Dettmer, who held a pistol to the head of the Burgomaster, and ordered him to get his civilians of the town to cooperate. Reluctantly they acted accordingly.'* A similar incident is recounted in Cornelius Ryan's classic book, *The Last Battle*: 'The psychological effect of the camps on officers and men was beyond assessment. On the Ninth Army front in a village near Magdeburg, Major Julius Rock, a medical officer with the 30th Infantry, came up to inspect a freight train which the 30th had stopped. It was loaded with concentration camp inmates. Rock, horrified, immediately unloaded the train. Over the local burgomaster's vehement protests, Rock billeted the inmates in German homes–but not until his battalion commander had

given a crisp command to the complaining burgomaster. 'If you refuse,' he said simply, 'I'll take hostages and shoot them.' As an additional sidenote, in 2009 Major Rock's daughter contacted the author; you can see more here: bit.ly/MajorRock.

64 United States Army, After Action Report, 823rd Tank Destroyer Battalion, April 14, 1945.

65 Much of the oral testimony of Frank Towers in Chapter 12 was from an email communication between Towers and interviewer/author Jerri Donohue on December 31, 2011.

66 *That is how I feel*- the link to this 50-minute radio broadcast is archived here: www.thestory.org/stories/2009-05/memorial-day-special-reunion. See note below.

67 *his wife Rona's book about Paul's Holocaust experiences*- Paul Arato's wife Rona has written a popular young adult book on his Holocaust experiences and then meeting his liberators as a result of the author's work. Arato, Rona. *The Last Train-A Holocaust Story*. Toronto: Owlkid Books. 2013.

68 Quote from liberator Leonard Lubin, St Petersburg, Florida, in Hirsch, Michael. *The Liberators: America's Witnesses to the Holocaust*. New York: Bantam Books. 2010. 229.

69 Source Notes: **Frank Gartner.** The letter in the beginning of the book that Gartner composed for Hilde Huppert is in the possession of Mimi Huppert of Israel, wife of the late Tommy Huppert

mentioned in the letter. Gartner is frequently mentioned in the battalion's official regimental history. (United States Army; Robinson, Wayne; and Hamilton, Norman E., *Move Out, Verify: The Combat Story of the 743rd Tank Battalion.* 1945. World War Regimental Histories.)

[70] Source Notes: **Carrol S. Walsh.** The author formally interviewed Carrol Walsh on two main occasions, July 26, 2001, and September 13, 2007, from which most of his oral history narrative was taken. Carrol was also interviewed numerous times by the news media, most significantly by Dick Gordon for his radio show, *The Story With Dick Gordon*. In 2009, the author contacted 'The Story' with the idea of doing a program on his discoveries. They set up a dual interview between Carrol Walsh and survivor Steve Barry. In instances in the book where Walsh's testimony has another party besides this author posing questions, it was from this broadcast: *For Memorial Day-A Special Reunion*. The Story With Dick Gordon, North Carolina Public Radio, Chapel Hill, North Carolina, May 25, 2009. Radio Program. It is archived here online and well worth a listen. www.thestory.org/stories/2009-05/memorial-day-special-reunion.

[71] Source Notes: **George C. Gross.** The author formally interviewed George Gross by telephone on January 18, 2007, from which most of his oral history narrative was taken for this book. Additionally, his personal essay, 'A Train Near Magdeburg,' written in June 2001, which was published first on my

website, is reposted here: http://bit.ly/REUNITED. He also kept up a recurring email correspondence with the author, some of which is also noted in this book.

72 Source Notes: **Frank W. Towers.** The author formally interviewed Frank Towers by telephone in November of 2008. His testimony was also recorded at every reunion, and especially useful for this book were those recorded at our school in 2009 and 2011, which can be seen on the author's YouTube channel. Frank was also interviewed by many others, and he was in the news media quite frequently (a Google search will return many results). Frank and the author also kept up a nearly nine-year email correspondence, most of which is archived by the author.

73 Source Notes: **Henry Birnbrey.** The author conducted an informal telephone interview with Henry Birnbrey after being contacted by him through email in March 2012. His account of stumbling upon the train is taken partially from his testimony as given to the Breman Museum in Atlanta, Georgia, interspersed with his memories as privately published in his war memoirs, but mostly from a videotaped interview with him on January 7, 2016, conducted in Bradenton, Florida, by Mike Edwards of the 5 Stones Group, Columbus, Ohio.

74 Source Notes: **Charles M. Kincaid.** The author was contacted by email on March 11, 2009, and presented with his letter to his pastor from April 1945 describing the train: *'Dear Mr. Rozell: My father-in-law*

was 1st Lt. Charles M. Kincaid... He rarely wrote home. He did write home to his minister about one event that evidently really caused him to stop and think. Attached is a copy of that letter that his sister transcribed—making copies for others to read. The letter describes the Farsleben train and his experience there. I need to thank you for your website and work. You and your students' work enabled me to connect the letter with the actual historical event. It further enabled me to show my children the pictures and to make their grandfather's experience real, not just an old letter—that this event so affected him that he needed to tell his minister before he told his mother. Sincerely, Mark Anderson.'

[75] Source Notes: **Walter Gantz**. The author formally interviewed Walter Gantz by telephone on November 21, 2011, and subsequently exchanged letters over the years. Most of his interview in Chapter 17 is taken from a videotaped interview with Walter Gantz on March 14, 2016, conducted at Walter's home in Scranton, PA, by Mike Edwards of the 5 Stones Group, Columbus, Ohio. Walter was also interviewed at least twice about his WWII experiences for a local Scranton, PA, newspaper.

[76] Source Notes: **Robert Schatz.** The author formally interviewed Robert Schatz by telephone on December 8, 2011, and subsequently received letters from him.

[77] Source Notes: **Luca Furnari.** The author was initially contacted by Luca Furnari's granddaughter; his recollections in Chapter 18 were from a videotaped interview with him on August 8, 2016, conducted at his home in the Bronx, NYC, by Mike Edwards of the 5 Stones Group, Columbus, Ohio.

[78] Source Notes: **Grier Taylor.** The author formally interviewed Grier Taylor by telephone on January 6, 2012. Taylor was subsequently featured in a newspaper article in Columbia, South Carolina.

[79] Source Notes: **Sol Lazinger** and **Jean Weinstock Lazinger.** The author formally interviewed Sol Lazinger and Jean Weinstock Lazinger by telephone on December 4, 2007.

[80] Source Notes: **Ervin Abadi.** In another twist of fate, several of his original pieces of artwork were brought to the attention of the author by relatives of the members of the 95th Medical Gas Treatment Battalion. The author encouraged the families to donate the works for posterity to the USHMM. The soldiers that the artist gave his works to, or sketched at Hillersleben, were Donald W. Rust and Monroe Williams. You can read more here: bit.ly/EAbadi.

[81] Source Notes: **Sara Atzmon.** Sara Atzmon's testimony was written by her to be presented at 2009 reunion in Hudson Falls she attended from Israel with her husband. It is used in parts, with minor edits, with permission.

[82] Source Notes: **Stephen B. Barry.** The author formally interviewed Stephen B. Barry by telephone on November 29, 2007. Steve was also interviewed by Dick Gordon for his radio show, *The Story With Dick Gordon*. In 2009, the author contacted 'The Story'

with the idea of doing a program on his discoveries. They set up a dual interview between Carrol Walsh and survivor Steve Barry. In instances in the book where Walsh's testimony has another party besides this author posing questions, it was from this broadcast. *For Memorial Day-A Special Reunion*. The Story With Dick Gordon, North Carolina Public Radio, Chapel Hill, North Carolina, May 25, 2009.

[83] Source Notes: **Irene Bleier Muskal**. Muskal, Irene Bleier. *Bergen–Belsen and Beyond: Memoirs of a Holocaust Survivor.* Unpublished manuscript. 1989. Used with permission of Bleier Muskal family. *'Oh how I want now to reach through my writing to the soul and mind of mankind, have them change the whole world to a better one, more peaceful and meaningful for all. To create a different kind of human behavior, a brand new world where no one builds his life goals and happiness on the destruction of other human beings. A world that knows no hatred, neither jealousy nor cruel and heart-rending wars. I so wish for the existence of a world that erases the last flame of hatred from the human soul! All this may seem a childish dream, but because I so wish for a better world, I do believe it may come true—if only all mankind wants it. By each of us following the righteous path and just obeying human law! Then it would happen, my dream would become a reality.'* The original can be downloaded at https://bergenbelsendiary.org.

[84] Source Notes: **Uri Orlev**. Orlev was featured in the Israel Broadcast Authority's 2011 documentary,

The Train to Life, on the author's project, which was broadcast in Israel on Holocaust Remembrance Day in 2012, and from which this testimony is drawn.

[85] Source Notes: **Aliza Vitis-Shomron.** Vitis–Shomron, Aliza. *Youth in Flames.* 2015. The author contacted Vitis-Shomron in 2016 and she graciously granted permission to use excerpts throughout this work; her writing powerfully conveys the spirit of the Warsaw Ghetto, and she notes that her book was *'partly composed of notes from an authentic diary; a larger part contains my memories, written in this country [Israel] at the age of seventeen, in Kibbutz Beit Alfa; and I also added another part later.'* Get the full book at www.warsawghettobook.com.

[86] Source Notes: **'Agi' Fleischer Baker.** The author formally interviewed 'Agi' Baker by telephone on May 14, 2009. An additional source was a videotaped interview with her on January 7, 2016, conducted in Bradenton, Florida, by Mike Edwards of the 5 Stones Group, Columbus, Ohio.

[87] Source Notes: **Ariela Rojek**. The author formally interviewed Ariela Lowenthal Mayer Rojek by telephone on January 22, 2008. Ariela was also interviewed several times for newspapers across the United States, and appeared in the Israel Broadcast Authority's 2011 documentary, *The Train to Life*. Her family also provided the author with the videotaped interviews done with her in Toronto, Canada. Interviews: Paula Draper, interviewer, Shoah Foundation, February 19, 1992; Janis Raisen,

interviewer, Toronto Holocaust Centre, November 21, 1995.

[88] Source Notes: **Leslie Meisels.** Leslie Meisels attended the reunions in 2009 and 2011 at our high school, which can be seen on the author's YouTube channel. Especially important for this book was his memoir, which was used with his permission: Meisels, Leslie. *Suddenly The Shadow Fell* (The Azrieli Series of Holocaust Survivor Memoirs) The Azrieli Foundation. 2014. An additional source was a videotaped interview with him on January 7, 2016, conducted in Bradenton, Florida, by Mike Edwards of the 5 Stones Group, Columbus, Ohio.

[89] Source Notes: **Fred Spiegel.** Fred Spiegel gave his testimony several times over the years at our high school. Most important for this book was his memoir, used with permission. Spiegel, Fred. *Once the Acacias Bloomed-Memories of a Childhood Lost*. Margate, NJ: Comteq. 2011. Get the full book at your favorite retailer.

[90] Source Notes: **Peter Lantos.** Testimony from Dr. Peter Lantos's visit to Hudson Falls' first reunion in September 2007 is included in this book. Most of the testimony comes from his memoir, used with permission, and slightly altered stylistically to fit in with the rest of the book. Lantos, Peter. *Parallel Lines: A Journey from Childhood to Belsen*. London: Arcadia Press, 2006. Get the full book at your favorite retailer.

[91] Source Notes: **Yaakov Barzilai.** His poem was translated from Hebrew into English by Micha

Tomkiewicz, and slightly adjusted for style by the author to fit in with the book. The original poem in Hebrew can be seen here: bit.ly/at1155YB.

[92] Source Notes: **Hilde Huppert**. As mentioned several times in the book, her memoir is an important primary source of information. Huppert, Hilde. *Hand in Hand with Tommy*. Jerusalem, Israel: 2004.

[93] Source Notes: **Arie Selinger**. Selinger was featured in the Israel Broadcast Authority's 2011 documentary, *The Train to Life*, on the author's project, which was broadcast in Israel on Holocaust Remembrance Day in 2012, and from which this testimony is drawn.

[94] Source Notes: **Lajos Reti.** Lajos Reti's son, Zoltan Reti, contacted the author in December 2012 and translated the part of his late father's unpublished memoir dealing with the liberation of the train. It is used here with permission, slightly edited.

[95] Source Notes: **Martin Spett**. Martin Spett was formally interviewed by telephone on January 6, 2012. He sent the author the letter (included in this book) which was read aloud to his liberators at the final night of the 2009 reunion, September 25, 2009. Mr. Spett generously provided copies of his illustrated memoir, *Reflections of the Soul*, for student use at our high school.

[96] Source Notes: **George Somjen.** Dr. Somjen's comments for this book were recorded by Larry S. Powell at the 30th Inf. Div. Vets of WWII Reunion in Savannah, GA, in March of 2012.

⁹⁷ Source Notes: **Robert Spitz**. Robert Spitz's comments for this book were recorded by the author at the 30th Inf. Div. Vets of WWII reunion in Charleston, SC, in March of 2009.

⁹⁸ Source Notes: **John Fransman.** John Fransman also attended several of the 30th Inf. Div. Vets of WWII reunions; his testimony for this book was taken from an anthology of survivor narratives that he helped to publish: Child Survivors' Association of Great Britain *Zachor—We Remember: Child Survivors of the Holocaust Speak.* Leicester, UK: Matador, 2011. 51

⁹⁹ Source Notes: **Bruria Bodek-Falik**. Dr. Falik attended the 2011 reunion in Hudson Falls, from which her testimony here was taken. She also attended several reunions of the 30th Inf. Div. Vets of WWII.

¹⁰⁰ Source Notes: **Ina Soep Polak**. The author formally interviewed Ina Polak by telephone on February 15, 2008. Her testimony for this book about the liberation, as well as some of George Gross's photographs, can be seen in the 2007 film *Steal a Pencil for Me*, directed by Michele Ohayon.

¹⁰¹ Source Notes: **Lisette Lamon.** Lisette Lamon's account is taken from an op-ed she wrote for Mother's Day in 1979 for *The New York Times* on April 13, 1979.

¹⁰² Source Notes: **Lexie Keston.** Lexie Keston's accounts here were emailed to the author, as noted in the book. She has also had her story published in a child survivor anthology in Sydney, Australia.

[103] Source Notes: **Elisabeth Seaman.** Elisabeth Seaman came to the 2009 reunion; her comments here were recorded by the United States Holocaust Memorial Museum for the film about our project, *Honoring Liberation* (2010). She also attended several reunions of the 30th Inf. Div. Vets of WWII.

[104] Source Notes: **Lily Cohen.** Lily Cohen was interviewed at length for the author's college alumni magazine in 2010; she also emailed me, as noted in the book. Much of the conversation we had over lunch in Tel Aviv on July 2, 2016, formed the basis for the remarks and conclusions in Chapter 17. She, like many of the survivors mentioned here, met Frank W. Towers at the reunion sponsored by Varda Weisskopf in Rehovot, Israel, in May 2011.

*****

Special thanks again to the following:

ABC World News
Associated Press
North Carolina Public Radio–The Story with Dick Gordon
The families of 95th Medical Battalion soldiers Donald Rust and Monroe Williams (Ervin Abadi Hillersleben paintings)
The *Glens Falls Post-Star*
The *Glens Falls Chronicle*
The Israeli Broadcast Authority
The United States Holocaust Memorial Museum
Yad Vashem
Mike Edwards/The Five Stones Group

Please visit the author's blog at TeachingHistoryMatters.com for updates on this story and further reading recommendations—notables by Elie Wiesel, Primo Levi, Viktor Frankl, and others; if you are teaching about the Holocaust, I would heartily recommend Essentials of Holocaust Education: Fundamental Issues and Approaches *[Totten and Feinberg, 2016]. Though it has become a popular curricular choice, I* **would not** *recommend using* The Boy in the Striped Pajamas *in the classroom (see my post at bit.ly/TBITSPs).*

www.ingramcontent.com/pod-product-compliance
Lightning Source LLC
LaVergne TN
LVHW011925070526
838202LV00054B/4497